The Pursuit of
WEALTH

The Pursuit of
WEALTH

The Incredible Story of Money
Throughout the Ages

ROBERT SOBEL

McGraw-Hill

New York San Francisco Washington, D.C. Auckland Bogotá
Caracas Lisbon London Madrid Mexico City Milan
Montreal New Delhi San Juan Singapore
Sydney Tokyo Toronto

Library of Congress Cataloging-in-Publication Data

Sobel, Robert
    The pursuit of wealth : the incredible story of money throughout
the ages / Robert Sobel.
        p.   cm.
    Includes bibliographical references.
    ISBN 0-07-059613-1
    1. Money—History.   I. Title.
HG220.A2S63   1999
332.4'9—dc21   99-23274
                                                                CIP

McGraw-Hill

A Division of The **McGraw·Hill** Companies

1 2 3 4 5 6 7 8 9 0 DOC/DOC 9 0 9 8 7 6 5 4 3 2 1 0 9

ISBN 0-07-059613-1

*This book was set in Electra LH Regular by North Market Street Graphics.
Printed and bound by R. R. Donnelley & Sons Company.*

McGraw-Hill books are available at special quantity discounts to use as premiums and sales promotions, or for use in corporate training programs. For more
information, please write to the Director of Special Sales, McGraw-Hill, 2 Penn
Plaza, New York, NY 10121-2298. Or contact your local bookstore.

This book is printed on recycled, acid-free paper containing
a minimum of 50% recycled de-inked fiber.

Contents

Introduction

The objective of this book is to explore and discuss how people have attempted to attain wealth through the ages. The material naturally divides itself into three sections, each emphasizing a different aspect of the subject, although themes developed in the initial chapter reappear throughout. The first section, which takes the story from the ancient Middle East to the origins of the American and Industrial Revolutions in the late eighteenth century, is necessarily panoramic, in that it covers five millennia and begins at a time more often the province of archeologists than historians. During most of this period, wealth was predominantly generated through agriculture; raising crops and domesticated animals, the wealthy being those in control of large tracts of land or sizable herds. Trade—taking products from places where they were in abundance and inexpensive to those where they were scarce and expensive—was present, but in most ancient societies was secondary to agriculture in the creation of wealth. Yet labor specialization, the market workings of supply and demand, profit motivation, "money," and the activities associated with banking, such as lending at interest, all were present. While much of the trade in the first three millennia of this period was controlled by political or religious institutions, they often were less restrictive in their thinking and methods than are modern day multinationals.

In the beginning of the period, most people were poor peasants more concerned with survival than the accumulation of wealth. Much of this poverty was tied to the nature of premodern agriculture. In antiquity in particular, roughly 65 to 90 percent of the population of any state had to be directly involved in agriculture just to feed themselves and the minority of political and religious leaders, craftspeople, and merchants. Most of these farmers barely grew enough for their own needs. Today, in the United States, less than 2 percent of Americans engage directly in agriculture, and this small group feeds not only the American population but a significant number of others as well. Modern agricultural equipment, such as tractors and combines, pesticides, and hybrid seeds, have all made this revolution in agricultural productivity possible. For example, in the distant past, for a wheat farmer a 10-fold return on seed planted was considered exceptional, a 4 to 6-fold return normal. Today, an average return is 40 to 45-fold and often considerably more. Under premodern circumstances, then, only the largest landowners and a few others could hope to live above the subsistence level.

During the second period, which concluded in the late nineteenth century, commerce gained rapidly in importance and was upheld by governments and private interests in the form of infrastructure creation, which made trade easier and less expensive to conduct. Industry became increasingly consequential as the century wore on, but the American economy remained based on agriculture well into the 1890s. That classic confrontation between two divergent visions of wealth—Thomas Jefferson advocating an agrarian America on the one hand and Alexander Hamilton working toward an industrialized America on the other—was not as simple and clear-cut as many have imagined. In fact, both men were interested in wealth creation. No less than Hamilton, Jefferson was concerned with the establishment of a large class of wealthy Americans, which he thought possible through agriculture. During the nineteenth century, his vision seemed the more realistic, as cotton and wheat were the staples of the American economy, and as more and greater fortunes were accumulated by those who devised means of serving the agrarian sector, whether by providing implements to facilitate production, money to purchase the implements, transportation to take the goods to market, or outlets from which they might be purchased.

In the third period, which opens with the appearance of large-scale corporate creation and the emergence of a truly industrial America, the debate is embodied in the two representative figures of J. P. Morgan and A. P. Giannini, both major bankers who, not unlike Hamilton and Jefferson, advocated rival images of the American of wealth in the age of securities-based capitalism. Morgan and his fellow investment bankers were concerned with wealth creation in large corporate entities that could produce on a mass scale and send their products throughout the nation and even the world. Giannini was more involved with small business, believing that every employee was a potential capitalist.

From there, the narrative proceeds to the development of what at mid-century was called "people's capitalism," which turned out to embrace Giannini's ends with Morgan's means. The book concludes with a chapter entitled "The Democratization of Wealth," which discusses a period during which the realization of wealth lay within the aspirations of larger segments of the population than ever before. Thus, the book opens with a multitude of poor people and few wealthy individuals, and ends with a large number of wealthy Americans—1 million millionaires in a population of some 260 million—and far fewer poor people than is often assumed to exist. True, in the world as a whole, the poor are omnipresent, but this is less the case in the so-called developed countries.

Some readers, especially those whose knowledge of history is confined to the last two or three centuries, might be surprised that searchers for wealth in ancient times were motivated much the same way as modern day seekers although their methods differed and their opportunities were more limited. They will encounter slavery, one of the means by which wealth was created and accumulated. Later on, readers will see how planters and slave traders in antebellum America shared similar motivations. The second section, which starts with the Age of Exploration, they will see the honing of the capitalistic instinct and the search for more efficient means of obtaining and amassing wealth. The rise of a business nexus in the young United States that was essentially agricultural and agricultural service in nature will likely be more familiar and easily recognizable.

Today's readers will have little problem understanding the reasoning of Eli Whitney, Francis Cabot Lowell, Cyrus McCormick, and DeWitt Clinton, or the railroad, beef, and mining tycoons. They should also consider that if an ancient Mesopotamian, Egyptian, Greek, or Roman—or even a European during the Middle Ages and Renaissance—could have been given a glimpse of the way society functioned in the nineteenth century, what might have struck them most would be the wide variety of methods of obtaining wealth, the speed of the civilization, and the ephemeral nature of affluence. Except for a very small percentage who engaged in long distance trade, those ancient observers might also be surprised by the distances traveled to obtain wealth. Only a few merchants in the fertile crescent or in the Mediterranean cities of the Roman Empire knew of and had contact with counterparts in India and China. By the sixteenth century, however, the Portuguese, from a small base in Europe, constructed and administered a commercial empire that stretched from the Philippines to Brazil. Certainly by that time, talk of globalization would not surprise merchants and bankers who operated on such a scale.

Finally, this book is not intended to be encyclopedic. Some industries, even important ones, have been omitted, along with individuals who became fabulously wealthy. The goal throughout is to illustrate methods of achieving wealth, not to catalogue the tales of how some achieved enormous fortunes. The methods and techniques employed by one tycoon of the Gilded Age suffices; one need not recount them all.

Anthropologists and sociologists instruct us that three of the most powerful human motivations are the pursuits of wealth, status, and power. These appear in different mixes at different times in history. All of us know people who desire wealth in order to purchase status and power, and others who use their status to achieve wealth and power, and finally, those with great power who employ it in the acquisition of wealth and status. Also, individuals differ in the degree to which each motivation is a factor in their lives, and the mix changes as they age. The pages that follow trace the pursuit of wealth, but remember that this was not the only goal of the individuals and organizations discussed. Still, wealth more often than not was the spur, although we know of a few secular and clerical figures who rejected wealth, but then they also renounced status and power. The theory that informs this book is that in modern times, in the aggregate, wealth is the prime mover.

One need not look to western society alone to realize how wealth can motivate a people to labor and creation, and how its absence or removal can lead to stagnation. One of the more interesting examples of this is the Kwakiutl, a tribe that inhabited the northern part of Vancouver Island near the mainland of British Columbia at the turn of the twentieth century. The eminent anthropologist Franz Boas studied them and produced a report that foretold by a couple of generations what would come to be known as Keynesian economics. Boas' problem wasn't a lack of observational skills or analytical sophistication. Rather, he did not fully comprehend what he had witnessed.

The Kwakiutl were famous for the *potlatch*, in which competing clans met regularly to stage contests in which they demonstrated just how wealthy they were by destroying their most valued possessions: canoes, blankets, and fish grease. Boas noted that large copper plates were also thrown off cliffs, although he commented that the throwers would return later to gather the pieces. The blankets were the most important, for these were the common denominator against which all the other possessions were measured.

Boas understood why the Kwakiutl loved the potlatch, citing self-esteem and status as important elements. The Kwakiutl ranked themselves by just how much they destroyed.

Boas wrote of this in a report to the Smithsonian Institution in 1895. Four years later, economist Thorstein Veblen would produce his *Theory of the Leisure Class*, in which he gave us the term *conspicuous consumption*, which would seem to help explain the potlatch.

What Boas noted but did not comprehend was that the Kwakiutl were quite wealthy, far more than neighboring tribes. The reason was that they worked hard to accumulate those possessions destroyed at the potlatch. There was a strong element of competition present that encouraged productivity and excellence—and accumulation. The Kwakiutl developed a system of banking that featured rates that rose sharply according to the length of the loan and the creditworthiness of the borrower. In their search for greater and greater wealth, they even created a system of credit purchasing, with copper plates serving as "credit cards." This too encouraged hard and imaginative work. Moreover, the system exhibited many of the aspects of modern reserve banking. Boas noted that in a village of 150 people, there were only 400 blankets, but debts were owed amounting to 75,000 blankets. If the lenders had called in their loans, there would have been what Boas termed a "disastrous panic."

Distressed by what to them was the wasteful nature of the potlatch, Canadian authorities attacked the practice, suggesting it was deleterious to economic development. Despite some setbacks, the authorities succeeded. The potlatch fell into disfavor. The Kwakiutl turned to commercial fishing to fit into the larger economy. But without the economic spur of the potlatch, initiative declined. So did the Kwakiutl economy. With the best of intentions, the authorities caused grievous harm to the Kwakiutl.

Whether Boas knew of Bernard de Mandeville's *Fable of the Bees* (1705) is unknown. This work dealt with how a prosperous, hardworking community fell into distress when they abandoned their profligate ways in order to save. The pursuit of wealth is fundamental to western civilization. It was there at the dawn of recorded history, and probably even before.

Acknowledgments

As the last book completed by my late husband in his long and very prolific career, *The Pursuit of Wealth* holds special meaning for me. It is my privilege to thank, on behalf of Bob and myself, some of the many friends, colleagues, and associates who helped make this book a reality, especially those who generously gave their time, wisdom, and support following Bob's death in June of 1999.

An indispensable contribution to the book was made by Professor Edward Anson of The University of Arkansas at Little Rock who redrafted beginning portions of the text after Bob became too ill to do so, and did a splendid job of sustaining the tone of Bob's prose. In addition, Dr. Karl Bahm reviewed the book in its early form, and made several excellent suggestions.

Professor David Sicilia of the University of Maryland, a colleague and dear friend of Bob's worked very closely with me in the editing of the final version of *The Pursuit of Wealth*. David's keen eye and support helped me weather a trying time.

Several members of the Hofstra University faculty were most helpful in fact checking, especially Professors Michael D'Innocenzo and Susan Yohn.

In addition, Professor Linton Thorn, Bob's long-time associate at the university shared his insights about the Ancient World with Bob and read and astutely commented on the first portion of the book.

Bob has thanked the librarians at Hofstra University in scores of books, and I am pleased to do so again here. Of course, all of these acknowledgments can not repay decades of professionalism and good cheer.

And, finally, I would like to thank my close friend, Beryl Brummer, who, when asked, was always available to help. With patience and grace she did research for both facts and grammar as well as offer continuous encouragement.

As Bob's wife and editor for the past 41 years, I have met or heard about many individuals who helped, challenged, and inspired Bob in his work. I would like to use this occasion to collectively thank all of those good people. I think you know who you are. I sincerely hope so.

Carole Sobel

The Pursuit of
WEALTH

CHAPTER 1

The Ancient World

EALTH took many forms in the ancient world, primarily land ownership, but also precious metals, slaves, ships, and manufactures. It could be obtained in several ways, the most obvious being through agriculture, herding, mining, commerce, and finance. Wealth also could be amassed through the exercise of power, obliging others to act in ways that they might not find beneficial. The right to collect taxes, for example, was a form of wealth. Rulers granted such rights in return for other kinds of wealth or services. A good reputation for business, governance, or warfare also could be considered a form of wealth.

The creation of wealth through commerce is of special interest. In antiquity, although usually a distant third, behind growing crops and breeding livestock, today, the majority of the world's population is engaged in some aspect of the broad category of commerce. This simple wealth-building technique appeared quite early in the history of civilization and, of course, remains important to this day. It appears prominently, in different manifestations but always recognizable, in all of the chapters that follow.

How commerce originated is one of those mysteries that probably never will be solved. Theories abound. It may have arisen from simple gift-giving. A farmer with a surplus would help out a neighbor. Even some later trade took the form of modified gift-giving. Correspondence between the kings of Babylonia and Egypt in the fourteenth century B.C. not only indicates a wide range of items being given but also significant transferals of wealth. For example, one gift to the Babylonian king included more than 1000 pieces of clothing, over 100 bronze objects, plus jewelry, furniture, and chariots adorned with over a half ton of gold. On occasion, the royal gift-giver would hint at an acceptable return present. Perhaps the most famous example of a major exchange of goods as the result of gift-giving is that recorded between the Queen of Sheba and King Solomon:

> She gave the king a hundred and twenty talents [about 4½ tons] of gold and a very great quantity of spices and precious stones; . . . And King Solomon gave to the Queen of Sheba all that she desired, whatever she asked besides what was given her by the bounty of King Solomon. (1 Kings 10:10, 13)

Alternatively, commerce may have originated when farmers producing surpluses traded their excess for someone's overproduction of a commodity they lacked. Surviving records show clearly that, from the earliest times, most villages and towns had regular fairs for the exchange of goods. But how then might one explain the shift to merchants acquiring handcrafted items and then transporting them a distance to trade for goods in abundance someplace else? Then, when the merchant accumulated a surplus, how did he think to employ it? While many invested in land, some went into pawnbroking, money lending, or banking. Some engaged in all of these occupations simultaneously. Those with wealth could lend it and receive interest, or invest funds in projects, which, if successful, would bring them profits. As will be seen, the path from one occupation to another differed by time and place, but it was always a variation on this theme, the pursuit of wealth.

Wealth might be stolen, or it might be gathered by the state through taxation and tribute. It might be accumulated by priests accepting gifts for performing services or for granting absolution or access to paradise. Specialists in such professions as medicine, law, writing, or any of a dozen other areas could charge fees for services. There was some manufacturing, especially of textiles, pottery, armor, ships, and the like, but this was not a dominant occupation until after the advent of the Industrial Revolution. Later still, wealth could be obtained by creating and distributing information. This is not to suggest that information was not valuable much earlier, but rather that the modern phenomenon of rapidly expanding technology and knowledge proceeded at a far slower pace in the past.

While the craving for wealth may not be a prerequisite for civilization, it is found in all civilized societies. Anthropologists describe societies in which there is no desire for wealth, but these are preliterate cultures. (In fact, writing was invented to keep commercial and governmental records.) Such societies often lack any form of money as a medium of exchange. They are not noted for restlessness and a desire for change, and they even lack a clear idea of the passage of time. According to historians, the pursuit of wealth in one form or another appears to have been present for at least nine millennia, or from about the time when human beings began a settled life in villages and cities. During the long nomadic period that preceded sedentary life when humans lived primarily by hunting and gathering, most things were shared among the members of the group, and there was little competition for private wealth. But even then some social hierarchy developed, and in the sharing some were more equal than others. With villages—and later, cities—came private property and land ownership—in short, the pursuit of wealth. Civilization, those human cultures in which cities and complex levels of political, social, and economic development are commonly present, saw the pursuit of wealth become a central feature of human activity.

The Ancient Near East: Economies Dominated by Political and Religious Institutions

The Western world's first civilizations developed in northeastern Africa and western Asia, in the lands of Egypt and Mesopotamia, respectively. While much is unknown with respect to what led to these civilizations, one factor was constant: they all developed in river valleys. At a time when agricultural techniques were at their most primitive, river valleys supplied adequate moisture for irrigation and rich, easily worked alluvial soil for agriculture.

For the peoples who inhabited the Tigris-Euphrates River Valley in Mesopotamia and the Nile River Valley in Egypt, the rivers were essential for existence; neither area received more than 10 inches of rainfall a year. These two earliest Western civilizations, although having in common their dependence on river valley conditions, differed markedly, both with respect to other environmental circumstances and with regard to their basic patterns of civilization. Mesopotamia—geographically equivalent, roughly, to the modern state of Iraq—had limited natural resources and lacked physical barriers to invasion. As a result, on the one hand, Mesopotamians had to import a wide range of goods in large quantities, while on the other, they were subject to frequent disruptions caused by migrations and invasions of new peoples. By contrast, the Nile River Valley of Egypt exists in relative geographic isolation, with deserts to the south, east, and west, and an inhospitable coastline to the north. As a result, the Egyptians seldom were invaded successfully until long after their earliest civilization had disintegrated. Moreover, Egypt was a land replete with natural resources. Copper, turquoise, gold, limestone, and sandstone were found in the desert regions surrounding the valley. The only serious deficits in the Egyptian supply of necessary raw materials were wood and iron. So whereas Mesopotamian civilization literally could not exist without commerce, Egyptian civilization could survive on a minimum of trade.

Beside the environmental differences—or perhaps because of them—these civilizations also differed in some of their basic institutions. For approximately its first 1000 years (ca. 3500–2500 B.C.), Mesopotamia exhibited a basic pattern of civilization, but no political unity. The valley and, indeed, much of what is today Syria, Turkey, Lebanon, Jordan, and Israel contained hundreds of independent city-states, countries centered on a dominant city with its surrounding territory. The Syrian city-state of Ebla, which flourished in the third millennium B.C., included 800 towns and villages as well as the city of Ebla itself, with a population estimated at 30,000. Estimates of the overall population of the state of Ebla range from 250,000 to over 300,000 people. But even by the standards of the ancient Near East, Ebla was not a large state. The modern archaeological site (all that remains today is a mound) covers 140 acres. By comparison, the wall of the city of Uruk in southern Mesopotamia enclosed 1280 acres, and Babylon, the greatest city of Mesopotamia, grew to occupy 2500 acres and to control an empire that included all of southern Mesopotamia. Repeatedly, from around 2500 B.C. on, respective cities united large sections of the Near East under their dominion, creating empires that often encompassed both the valley of Mesopotamia and many of the other lands of southwestern Asia. In spite of these empires, the cities within them retained much of their individual character. One reason for the instability of the region has been the frequent revolt of these cities against imperial authority.

The key, for Mesopotamia then, was its cities. While empires came and went, the cities remained as the mainstays of Mesopotamian culture. Egypt developed a very different pattern. For Egypt, political unity was essential for its civilization. Indeed, for at least the first 1000 years of its history (from ca. 3100 B.C.), Egypt did not possess cities in the Mesopotamian sense. There were administrative centers, but the population was not concentrated in these locations. The people were spread out in villages all along the banks of the Nile. When Egyptian unity collapsed, so did Egyptian civilization.

Despite these environmental and political differences, the two civilizations exhibited a number of common economic features. The primary occupation of all these peoples was agriculture, with grain the principal item of trade. As one modern-day historian has remarked, "Grain was for the ancients what oil is to the modern world." However, wine, copper, tin, lead, bronze, iron, silver, gold, lapis lazuli, woolens, linen, timber, slaves, perfumes, and olive oil were all traded throughout the Near East. Olive oil, in particular, was a most important multipurpose product. It was used as the primary cooking oil, as a skin lubricant, and as fuel in lamps to provide light.

Like much of the economy of these early civilizations, trade was usually either directly or indirectly under the control of the state or various religious institutions. Rulers and priesthoods owned large tracts of land, extensive herds of livestock, storage facilities, large workshops, weaving mills, breweries, and trading companies. In short, the government and the priesthoods were to the ancient Near East what multinational corporations are to today's economy. But land, herds, and other capital assets also could be held by families, by companies, and by individuals. Likewise, trade and commerce could be conducted by individuals and private companies. An example of the latter comes from the records of the Mesopotamian city of Ur (second millennium B.C.). In one particular document, two individuals, Lu-Meslamtae and Nigsisanabsa, formed a partnership and received from an investor, Ur-Ninmar, silver, sesame oil, and clothing, which was to be taken to the city of Tilmun to be exchanged for copper. It was agreed that, after their return, they would repay the investor at a substantial profit, based entirely on that individual's initial investment, not a percentage of the profits. While it is unclear who would bear the burden of catastrophic loss from natural disaster or brigandage, it is certain that any risk arising from the vagaries of the market were to be borne entirely by the partners. All of these conditions were framed in a contract "sworn conjointly by the king," indicating that the document conformed to the laws of the city and would be enforced by the authority of the state. Another common pattern is seen in the trading practices of the merchants of the cities of Ashur, Babylon, and others in Mesopotamia. In these communities the merchants were typically organized into guilds (karums). The guilds were private firms, licensed by the state, that controlled various categories of trade and commerce, most often at state direction.

Indications of the extensive roles of the palace and temple in the economies of the ancient Near East abound in the surviving literature: the ruler of Egypt, Pharaoh, collected one-fifth of the harvest from nonpriestly cultivators; the Israelite king, David, conquered Jerusalem from the Jebusites and held it as his personal possession, as he did with many other conquered territories; one Egyptian temple in the second millennium B.C. controlled 2400 square kilometers and employed 86,486 people; the king of the Mesopotamian city of Ur, as noted in the surviving records of the late third millennium B.C., owned 347,394 sheep; and the ruler of Ebla possessed two million sheep and a half million cattle. In the *Bible* the prophet Samuel warns the Israelites of the changes a king will make in the everyday lives of his subjects.

These are the ways of the king who will reign over you: he will take your sons and appoint them to his chariots and to be his horsemen . . . and he will appoint . . . some to plow his ground and to reap his harvest, and to make his implements of war and the equipment of his chariots. He will take the best of your fields and vineyards and olive orchards and give them to his servants. He will take a tenth of your grain and of your vineyards and give it to his officers and his servants. He will take . . . the best of your cattle and your asses, and put them to his work. He will take a tenth of your flocks, and you shall be his slaves. (1 Samuel 8:1–17)

Much of our knowledge of these ancient economies has been derived from excavations conducted during the last two centuries. One of the most recent and spectacular (from excavations begun in 1964) has been the discovery of the ancient city of Ebla, from which 20,000 clay tablets and fragments dating back to 2500 B.C. have been taken. With the exception of the Egyptians, who wrote on a form of paper made from the papyrus plant, the basic writing material of the ancient Near East was clay. From these thousands of tablets, one can obtain a fairly clear picture of what constituted wealth and how it was accumulated in this particular city-state. We know from the tablets that there was a king in Ebla, elected for a term of seven years, apparently by a group of wealthy merchants who ruled with him as a council of "Elders." Elective kingship was not common in Mesopotamia, but may have been so elsewhere. Until further discoveries are made, just how typical the nature of the monarchy at Ebla was must remain an unanswered question. What is not debatable is that the rulers of Ebla, unlike those of many of the states of Mesopotamia, were more interested in creating a commercial empire than a political one. As one scholar has commented, "Ebla seems to have been a society grounded on the profit motive." The treaties the kings of Ebla made with other states dealt with freedom of movement, the establishment of trading colonies within each state's territory, and matters of taxation, but they most always confirmed the respective states' autonomy.

Beside facilitating trade with neighboring states, the government of Ebla was heavily involved in the production process. Cloth was made in state-owned mills, and the state employed its own smiths and metalworkers to fashion objects from copper, tin, gold, silver, bronze, lapis lazuli, and the like. This practice of government ownership of much of the means of production was common throughout the Near East. A single tablet from Ur lists in that government's textile mills 6400 tons of wool for processing and indicates that as many as 9000 slaves may have been employed in that state-owned industry. While it is clear that free enterprise also played a role in the economy, the dominance of the state is apparent. Through the Ebla state treasury moved tons of silver and gold. Indeed, although they did not possess money in the sense of paper or coins, the Eblaites did use as an accounting standard 11-pound gold and silver ingots. Moreover, gold and silver were used for the purchase of imported goods, including the metals that the Eblaites refined. If money is defined as a medium of exchange, a standard of accounting, and a means of payment, then the Ebla tablets demonstrate that throughout the third millennium B.C. in the Near East, there was monetary as well as barter exchange. And from the evidence of other sites and sources, it is clear that Ebla was not unique in this regard.

Not only were the people of Ebla interested and deeply involved in commerce, but it is very clear that the city-state's great wealth came from trade. It has been estimated that the farmers of Ebla harvested enough grain to feed 70 times their own population. Add to this the surpluses created in the textile and metal industries and the centrality of trade to Ebla's economy becomes unarguable. Trade, as with production and so much else in the Eblaite economy, was in the state's hands. Merchants were most often agents and representatives of the government, with a commissioner overseeing their activities. The state secured treaties guaranteeing the merchants' safety, confirming the conditions of exchange, and often establishing trading monopolies. In the absence of international agreements protecting trade and commerce, the involvement of the state in some fashion was essential. Only the government could secure from other governments the kinds of guarantees so crucial for the uninterrupted flow of commerce. Even though the government appears involved in virtually all aspects of commerce, there is no evidence in these documents that prices were established in any fashion other than by market forces.

This state control is found in many near eastern societies, including that of ancient Israel. Solomon built a merchant fleet and, in league with the king of Tyre, sent it to Ophir on the Red Sea coast of the Arabian Peninsula. His merchants returned with more than 15 tons of gold. Traders in his employ are also recorded buying horses in Egypt and elsewhere, and then selling them in Syria. Indeed, much of Solomon's reputed wealth was generated by acting as an intermediary in the trade between Egypt and western Asia. Israel also mined iron and copper and produced wine, olive oil, and textiles for export.

The pharaohs of ancient Egypt likewise dominated their economies. Around 2200 B.C. one of the pharaoh's traders made this report regarding his mission to Nubia, in what is today the Sudan:

> I descended with 300 asses laden with incense, ebony, . . . grain, . . . ivory, and every good product. Now when the chief of Irthet, Setu, and Wawat saw how strong and numerous was the troop of Yam, which descended with me to the court, and the soldiers who had been sent with me, then this chief brought and gave to me bulls and small cattle, and conducted me to the roads of the highlands and Irthut, because I was more excellent and vigorous than any count, companion, or caravan-conductor, who had been sent to Yam before. Now, when I was descending to the court, the king sent . . . the master of the bath, Khuni, upstream with a vessel laden with date-wine, cakes, bread, and beer.

Most of the wealth of Egypt was either in the hands of the pharaoh, the temples, or the pharaoh's regional governors, the nomarchs.

One very clear indication of the immense resources at the disposal of the Egyptian government was the construction of the pyramids. Built to house the bodies of the dead pharaohs, these structures represent some of the most impressive construction projects ever undertaken. The largest, the Great Pyramid, is 786 feet on a side and 481 feet high. The resources needed just in the materials of construction are staggering. This one structure contains approximately 2 million stone blocks weighing over 2 tons each. But even more impressive is the fact that this pyramid took two decades to complete, with an estimated work force of 100,000. These individuals had to be housed, clothed, fed, and in many cases, even paid. The workers were free Egyptian farmers who worked on the pyramid during the season of the Nile flood. The project, then, represented both income during the months when the land could not be worked and the religious devotion of a people who believed that their rulers, the pharaohs, were living gods whose earthly death was simply a transition, not an end. During the third millennium B.C., approximately 35 large pyramids were constructed in Egypt.

Merchants and traders in the ancient Near East faced one very formidable task in pursuing their careers: transportation. For those living along the banks of the Nile or the Tigris or the Euphrates, river transport was both efficient and relatively inexpensive. River barges could carry between 10 and 15 metric tons at a cost, calculated for grain shipments in the later Roman Empire, of 5.9 percent per 100 miles. Ships on the Mediterranean could carry 500 metric tons and add to the cost at a rate of only 1.4 percent per 100 miles. Land transportation, which was accomplished most often in this early period by the use of donkeys, was (for many products and distances) prohibitively expensive. While estimates vary considerably for land transport, the expense would be at a minimum 13 percent per 100 miles. In spite of these high costs, significant trade took place on land, as evidenced by the great wealth of Ebla, whose commerce was carried, at least at its outset, entirely by land.

One of the most extensive surviving records of long-distance overland commerce involves the northern Mesopotamian cities of Ashur and Kanesh, in what is today the nation of Turkey. Ashur's merchants shipped tin, originally obtained in Afghanistan, and woolen textiles the 700 miles to Kanesh, where these goods were exchanged for silver and gold. It is estimated that, over a 50-year period, 80 tons of tin and 300 tons of textiles traveled by donkey caravan from Ashur to Kanesh. Grain, too, apparently could be shipped overland for profit. In the early second millennium B.C., a caravan of 3000 donkeys set out from Mari in northern Syria seeking to acquire grain and wool, and in the late third millennium B.C., 72,000 bushels of grain were shipped by land between the two Mesopotamian cities of Ur and Isin. Apparently, so common was the overland transport of grain to the city of Ashur that grain came to be measured there in units called "donkey loads."

Although there is little mention in the Ebla tablets of any role for religion in the economy, the surviving texts from Egypt and Mesopotamia place religious institutions at the center of their respective economics. Priests were among the wealthiest individuals throughout the Near East, and temples became the centers of economic life in many of the cities in Mesopotamia. Temple archives disclose that they owned a great deal of land, some of which was rented, with the rest farmed by a large force of laborers. Among the records are receipts for animals, grain, perfumes, and precious metals brought to the temples as contributions.

The connection between the temple and the economy derives directly from the perceived relationship between the gods and the well-being of the community. In general, the gods were seen by the Mesopotamians as the true owners of the cities; it was, therefore, only natural that the gods' representatives would possess or control much of the community's wealth. During the earliest stages of Mesopotamian civilization it was not uncommon for the priests to hold political control of their respective cities. From a very secular, business perspective, the temples had other advantages as well. Temples and their holdings enjoyed tax exemptions, which could be considerable. The rulers of the city of Ur in the second millennium B.C. levied a 10 percent tax on all private commercial activity. To avoid taxation, many merchants would dedicate themselves to the gods, and by so doing receive "the protection of the gods," which included exempt status. Working for the temples entailed some loss of freedom, but most of these merchants, while doing the temple's business, also did much of their own.

Temples for the worship of a particular city's gods often were established as part of the creation of a trading colony in a foreign city. Such a foundation would offer sanctuary to foreign merchants, owing to its religious nature. Since these religions were polytheistic, there was a tendency to identify gods from different communities that shared common attributes. Such identification would further enhance the trading community's respectability and importance, making the relationship between the two societies that much closer. There is some evidence that certain temples and priesthoods were established by merchants purely for pursuit of profit. In a polytheistic religion, the addition of some hitherto unknown god to the pantheon was always possible. By creating such a religious establishment themselves, the merchants would be entirely in control.

In their gratitude and "to honor the god," the merchants often would give offerings to the god. Among the many contributions were vast quantities of gold and silver. This wealth would be in addition to what temples earned from their lands, flocks, factories, and fees for the use of large storage facilities. The latter initially were built to hold the produce from the temple's estates, but they later became commercial ventures, like modern grain storage companies. Moreover, since the temples were considered to be under their particular god's protection and had large secure doors and often guards, many private individuals would leave their valuables with the temple. It was probably in this manner that banking arose in the Near East.

Early on, only kings and priests had the necessary capital for banking services, in particular, giving out loans at interest. In time, private individuals as well as temples and palaces joined in the profession. Grain and specie were loaned, with the usual rate in the Near East for grain being 33⅓ percent and for silver, 20 percent. As noted earlier, temples often were associated with merchants and with trading colonies, and as a result regularly would serve as clearinghouses for trading accounts. A foreign merchant might have an account with a local temple. When it came time to pay for goods, instead of personally coming to the temple and retrieving the necessary funds, he would give the seller a written note ordering the temple to pay the bearer the amount owed from the account. By the sixth century B.C., in addition to temple banks, there were prominent private banking houses in Babylon—large even by modern standards—which made loans both to private individuals and even to governments. The evidence suggests, however, that these did not much predate the sixth century B.C.; for most of the history of the ancient Near East, it was the governments and temples that had the capital and made the loans.

While much of the commerce of the Near East was dominated by governments and temple corporations, private citizens often pooled their resources and formed partnerships to conduct trade. Many such arrangements appear in the tablets: "Itti-Marduk-Balatu and Shapik-zer pool a mina of silver as the capital of a partnership. The result of their operations belongs to them jointly." This document and similar ones are the equivalent of incorporation papers. This particular record tells us little about the operations of the firm. Itti-Marduk-Balatu's name appears on several tablets, suggesting he was a substantial businessman. There is another partnership with Marduk-Shapik-zer, likely the same person as in the previous contract, to pool five mina of silver and some spices, possibly trading goods. The existence of so many tablets like this indicates that such arrangements were quite common and that Mesopotamian merchants were both sophisticated and willing to take risks in the hope of wealth. On the traveler's return, the merchandise would be sold, and the money obtained would be divided according to shares. Some of the partnerships were ongoing, however, in one case for 31 years. But as with the early private banks, most of these concerns were not very large and did not involve great sums.

What is especially interesting in these various documents is the presence of women as lenders of capital. Certainly, women of independent means were not that unusual in the Near East. In the third millennium B.C., Baranamtara of Lagash sent textiles and silver to Tilmun and sold copper to the city of Umma and cattle in Elam. In the Book of *Judges*, Micah's mother possessed 1100 pieces of silver (Judges 17:2–5). This is true despite the fact that in most respects, the rights of Mesopotamian women within the family were circumscribed. In the Code of Hammurabi, the king of the Babylonian empire in the eighteenth century B.C., a man was free to use his wife and, indeed, even his children, as collateral for a loan. If he defaulted on the loan, his wife and/or children would be handed over to the creditor to work off the debt. A later Assyrian law code from the twelfth century B.C. states that a husband "may pull out the hair of his wife, mutilate and twist her ears." Yet the same law codes state that a woman, even if married, could own property out of the control of her husband. Aristocratic or royal women in particular were prominent in the production and sale of wool and textiles. Women in ancient Egypt bought and sold land and held important positions within state-run industries. In part, this apparent contradiction in the legal status of women was due to the importance of the family in agriculture and business. Women were part of a family, not outsiders whose loyalty would be to their own families. Also, many women were in charge of temples. Throughout the Near East, priestesses enjoyed a special legal status and frequently ran temples devoted to the worship of female deities.

Hellenic Greece: Seafaring Entrepreneurs

The geographic setting for Greek civilization was quite different from that of Mesopotamia or Egypt. Located in southeastern Europe, the Greek peninsula has no great rivers, is dominated by mountainous and rocky terrain, and while receiving more rainfall than either Mesopotamia or Egypt, still has a semiarid climate. The mountains of the Greek mainland made land travel difficult and expensive, but the long coastline of this peninsula meant that few Greeks were far from the sea. Such geographical circumstances influenced Greek political and societal development. The mountains tended to compartmentalize Greece, creating small, relatively isolated valleys. It is partially for this reason that the Greeks in antiquity never forged themselves into a united political state but like the earliest inhabitants of Mesopotamia, developed city-states, or in Greek, *poleis*. This was the political organization of Greece from approximately 1500 B.C. until the Roman conquest of the Greek world in the second century B.C. Moreover, these ecological circumstances meant that to be prosperous, the Greeks had to engage in trade and commerce. Here, the transport of products was most often by sea. In fact, to deal with economic and other problems in the peninsula, the Greeks, using knowledge of the Aegean and Mediterranean seas that they had gained through trade, often established colonies at desirable locales. By the end of the sixth century B.C., there were Greek cities along the shores of the Black Sea, the western coast of modern Turkey, eastern Sicily, all along the western and southern coasts of Italy, and elsewhere in the western Mediterranean. Syracuse, Naples, and Marseilles were all originally Greek colonies. Although they became independent states, severing all but religious and cultural ties with their mother cities, they were most often situated in rich agricultural areas. As a result, a flourishing trade sprang up between the new city-state and its founding city.

Whereas in the beginning of their civilization (about 1500 B.C.), the Greek *poleis* were ruled by kings and later by aristocratic councils, by the end of the sixth century B.C., the Greeks had created governing systems based on the concept of the citizen. In the ancient Near East, most of the people would correctly be classified as subjects, individuals owing their service and often their lives to their rulers and receiving protection in return. These subjects, however, did not participate directly in the decision-making process of running their government; Greek citizens did. The Greeks came to organize their states around voting citizen assemblies. These assemblies were sovereign; they made the laws that governed society. While the qualifications for citizenship varied from one Greek *polis* (singular of *poleis*) to another, the major distinction revolved around the ownership of property. Some *poleis* were known as oligarchies, because they limited the franchise to male citizens meeting a particular property qualification. Oligarchies could have very small bodies of voters, if there was a high property qualification, or large numbers of voters, if the property requirements were kept to a bare minimum. Certain Greek states eliminated the property qualification altogether, and created democracies. All male citizens above a certain age, usually 20, could then attend the assembly, debate, and vote. In neither oligarchies nor democracies was government representative, however. If you fulfilled the qualifications to be a voting citizen, you didn't elect others to vote your interests, you showed up and voted your own. Potentially, this meant that even an assembly meeting in a broad-based oligarchy could have as many as 9000 citizens in attendance, while a democracy might have as many as 20,000 to 40,000. This direct participation in government was only one feature that set Greek culture and civilization apart from that of the ancient Near East. The following excerpt is from a speech given by the Athenian leader Pericles at the conclusion of the first year of what would prove to be a long war with the rival state of Sparta. This excerpt, though meant to extol particular Athenian values, also exemplifies a confidence in the individual that permeates Greek civilization and that has become one of the cornerstones of Western civilization:

> If we look to the laws, they afford equal justice to all in their private differences; if to social standing, advancement in public life falls to reputation for capacity, class considerations not being allowed to interfere with merit; nor again does poverty bar the way, if a man is able to serve the state, he is not hindered by the obscurity of his condition. The freedom which we enjoy in our government extends also to our ordinary life.

While Greek governments certainly permitted far more participation by the people than did any previous political system, it must be pointed out that even in democracies, only male citizens reaped these benefits. Women were excluded from all direct political activity, and many inhabitants of these city-states were slaves, with very few rights of any kind. Moreover, there was no system that standardized the conferral of citizenship on aliens. In the case of a commercial state, such as that of the Athenians, where a sizable number of residents were not native, these individuals stood little chance of ever receiving full political rights. This was not the case, however, with respect to economic rights. Most commercial states, while often limiting the rights of noncitizens to own land, treated business activities very evenhandedly.

This emphasis on individual rights and responsibilities carried over fully into the economic sphere. Even though the government usually had large public holdings in lands, forests, and mines, these were not worked by state corporations, but rather were contracted out to independent companies or individuals. There were no requirements that state contracts be given to citizens. Many of these companies sold shares in their firms, for there were great fortunes to be made in such exploitation. During one three-year period, the silver mines of the Athenian state at Laurium produced for its contractors a profit of 300 talents (a unit of weight which for Greeks was equal to approximately 57 pounds) or about 8½ tons of silver. The state also leased public lands to individuals and even "farmed out" taxes. In the latter practice, companies would bid for the right to collect particular taxes for the state, saving the state the necessity of creating a large government bureaucracy.

Another difference between the Greeks and their counterparts in the Near East was that temples and priestly colleges usually were part of the state governmental structure, and with only the exception of certain national religious shrines, they exercised very limited independence. Indeed, one of the major state expenditures was for the maintenance of the state religion. While in Mesopotamia and Egypt religious institutions often operated as entities unto themselves, with little if any state interference, Greek religious bodies were almost always under the strict control of the state. As part of the government, the temples conducted their business operations in the same manner as the state. They leased their lands and contracted out major and minor projects. Surviving records illustrative of state practice are especially common with respect to the building of public structures, most often temples. The Erechtheum in Athens, built in 409–408 B.C., used 71 separate private contractors just in the final stages of construction.

The building accounts of the Asklepian sanctuary at Epidauros from the fourth century B.C., which are the most complete of all such surviving records, show that separate contracts were awarded for parts of a section of the temple, and that even very small jobs were separately contracted to private individuals. There was very little subcontracting. The largest contract involved the construction of the colonnade and entablature of the temple itself. This project involved a labor force of 50 men working for six months. Even the quarrying of the stone was divided among several companies, and the polishing of the finished project was given to yet another. Every contract specified conditions, time frame, and often the methods to be used. Individuals would then bid at public auction. Each contractor would have to supply guarantors who would be responsible for fines and the cost of completing the contract if the successful bidder defaulted. Without such backing, the bid would not be awarded. These guarantors were most often local individuals who took on the responsibility more from a sense of civic pride than from any hope of profit. The only state officials involved in the building process itself were the inspectors.

What is most striking about these accounts is the absence of involvement by large companies. This was true even though the auction for these contracts was advertised throughout the Greek world. And what is found here with respect to temple building was apparently true for other commercial activities as well. There seem to have been no big companies and few extravagantly wealthy businessmen in the ancient Greek world. The largest industrial concern during this period, a shield factory, had only 120 workers. This establishment was owned by Pasion, an Athenian banker noted for his great wealth, who at his death left an estate valued at 70 talents. Greeks worth 100 talents were the exception, and in these cases, their wealth most often derived from agriculture. Although it is impossible to equate ancient monetary values with modern ones, by any measure, these are not great fortunes by present-day standards, or even those of the ancient Near East. The possession of such sums might place an individual in the realm of the rich, but not in the ranks of the Vanderbilts, Rockefellers, Waltons, pharaohs, or Eblaite kings.

Given the typical Greek state's general lack of involvement in the exploitation of its own resources, or even in the collection of its own taxes, it is not surprising that trade and commerce were likewise in the hands of independent entrepreneurs. Although commerce was an essential part of Greek economic life and the Greeks were net importers of grain, it should not be forgotten that the large majority of Greeks were still subsistence farmers, like their counterparts in the Near East. However, since grain could be produced far cheaper elsewhere, beginning in the fifth century B.C., many farmers turned to cash crops, such as olives and grapes.

The importance of commerce to the Greek world was, nonetheless, apparent everywhere. The central feature of every Greek city was its marketplace, or *agora*. Almost every aspect of Greek life revolved around it. Often, it was the place of popular assembly meetings and judicial proceedings; the philosopher Socrates wandered through the Athenian *agora* talking to his students. The *agorai* of the *poleis* were not the sites of periodic fairs, but were continually occupied by merchants and townspeople doing business, exchanging information, and socializing.

Commercial activity in the local markets was enhanced by the introduction of coinage. First developed in Lydia (modern western Turkey) about 650 B.C., coins were quickly adopted by the Greek city-states. Although the issuing state guaranteed the weight and purity of the coins, they were not always trustworthy, for counterfeiting was practiced and shaving coins was prevalent. The smallest Athenian coins were made of copper, eight of which made an obol, which was of bronze, and six of these comprised a drachma, a silver coin. One hundred drachmas was a mina, and 60 minas a talent. There was no paper money. While trade and commerce, especially among city-states located near the sea, employed a sizable segment of the population and were responsible for the prosperity of many communities, most merchants and traders were small entrepreneurs.

The chief Greek exports were olive oil, fine pottery, and silver from Athens; textiles from Miletos and Samos; wine from Chios, Naxos, Lesbos, and Thasos; copper from Euboea and Cyprus; and iron from Sparta. The chief imports were grain and timber. The Athenians, in the fifth and fourth centuries B.C., imported three-quarters of the city's food supply from the northern shore of the Black Sea. In the sixth century B.C.,

Solon, the Athenian lawgiver, obtained an embargo on the export of grain from Athens that was never repealed, proscribing the severest penalties for its violation.

Where there are merchants there are people who will provide funds, for a price. The Greek moneylenders charged rates of 12 to 18 percent for what today would be considered personal loans secured by collateral, 10 to 12 percent for real estate loans secured by the property, and 12 to 33⅓ percent for noncollateralized commercial loans. Ten percent was considered an acceptable rate to charge friends; anything above 18 percent was considered usurious, but there were few laws regulating the rate of interest. Among the Athenians, the only set rate was with respect to the return of the dowry in a divorce (18 percent). In fact, there were no regulations prohibiting the commingling of personal and deposited funds, no requirement to pay interest on deposits, no rules compelling uniformity of practice, no restrictions on the bank's use of deposited money, and no cash reserve requirement. In short, Greek banks, *trapezai*, were very different from modern banks; they were unregulated.

Initially, banking had been the province of the temples. They loaned money chiefly to the state with which they were associated, while most private loans were handled by individuals. Greek bankers, *trapezitai*, performed three functions: they changed money, received money for safekeeping or investment, and lent money at interest. Money-changing was a necessary function because of the great number of city-states, literally hundreds, all of which produced their own coinage. Foreign merchants or travelers often would need to exchange their money either for the currency of the state they were visiting or for a generally recognized one. This practice probably represented the origin of banking in the Greek world, but it was considered a barely reputable profession in later times. Larger institutions usually abandoned money-changing altogether.

The larger banking concerns held money for their clients and dispersed funds to third parties. Banks offered a cash return on funds deposited with them, not in the modern sense of interest, but as if the banker had obtained a loan from the depositor. As a result, banking was often referred to as "owing funds to many." Owing to many then meant that the banker was doing very well. During the era of the *poleis*, Greek banks never were very large concerns, and most of their operations were conducted on a very personal level. As Demosthenes, the fourth century B.C. Athenian orator, records:

> It is the custom of all bankers, when a private person deposits money and directs that it be paid to a given person, to write down first the name of the person making the deposit and the amount deposited, and then to write on the margin "to be paid to so-and-so"; and if they know the face of the person to whom payment is to be made, they do merely this, write down whom they are to pay; but, if they do not know it, it is their custom to write on the margin the name also of him who is to introduce and point out the person who is to receive the money.

This way, merchants did not have to carry large sums from city to city. Theoretically, this rather cumbersome process protected the client from loss and the bank from lawsuits. It is interesting to note, though, that our knowledge of the practice comes from a lawsuit. Part of the business of banks was to circumvent the prying eyes of government, especially taxing authorities. The Athenian banking business was helped considerably by foreigners hiding assets, much in the way "offshore" banking has become synonymous with organized criminal activities these days.

While banks gave loans for a multitude of activities, from the purchase of businesses or property to ransoming captives, most of the surviving records refer to maritime loans. A merchant might borrow from bankers to purchase goods in foreign lands, the security being his reputation and the cargo. He would also sell a contract to deliver a cargo at a specified price, receiving payment in advance. Then, when the merchant returned with his cargo, he would sell it in the marketplace. If it brought more than the futures contract, he would pocket the difference. If not, he had to make up the difference. And of course, the loan would have to be repaid as well. There also were "bottomry loans," in which the lender advanced funds for a voyage that was secured by the hull and its cargo. However, if the ship failed to arrive safely at its destination because of shipwreck or piracy, the loss was borne by the lender. These were, consequently, very high-risk loans, but they were also high-yield loans if all went well. In any case, the rate of interest usually was high, ranging up to 30 percent.

Two moneylenders, Darius and Pamphilus, who had the misfortune to lend money to a defaulter, told a court before which their claims had been set what life was like in this part of the business:

> We whose business it is to finance shipping ventures and put our capital into the hands of other men know only too well that the borrower has the advantage of us at every point. He takes our good money, actual cash in hand, and leaves us with a bit of writing on a sheet of paper which costs a penny or so, his agreement to deal honestly with us. As for us, we don't merely promise to pay, but actually pay down the money to the borrower on the spot. What, then, is the security we receive when we make a loan, and what assurance have we of getting back our money? We trust in you, gentlemen of the court, and in the law, which provides that all contracts entered into voluntarily shall be valid. Yet, in my opinion, neither law nor contract offers any security whatsoever if the borrower is not a man of upright character and is either not afraid of the courts or ashamed to violate an agreement.

In another example of the dangers of moneylending, Demon, a second cousin to Demosthenes, was a *trapezita* who became the defendant in an action brought by Zenothemis. The latter had sailed on a trading mission to Syracuse on a ship owned and commanded by Hegestratus. These two were partners in a scheme to defraud not only Demon, who had loaned the money to purchase the cargo, but to other investors as well. When the ship arrived in Syracuse, Hegestratus and Zenothemis borrowed large sums of money, using as collateral the cargo just bought with Demon's loan, claiming it belonged to them free and clear. In accordance with customary practice, the agreement was that the cargo had to reach port safely for the loans to be collectible and for their crime to be discovered. Once on the high seas, the two conspirators planned to sink the ship, escape in a small boat, and declare to both sets of creditors that the cargo was lost and, therefore, that the collateral was gone. They would then pocket the money obtained from the Syracusans and owe nothing to Demon. But when Hegestratus started cutting a hole in the ship's hull, the noise led to his detection. Passengers, who would have gone down with the ship and its cargo, crowded around to see what was happening, and to escape them, Hegestratus leaped overboard, missed the boat, and drowned. Meanwhile, the ship was leaking and had to put in for repairs. While there, Zenothemis attempted to change the final destination from Athens to his home city of Marseilles, but failed. On arriving in Athens, Demon took possession of the cargo.

Zenothemis protested, outrageously claiming that the cargo was his, alleging it had been purchased by the now deceased Hegestratus from Protus, Demon's agent, who had sailed with the ship from Athens. The outcome of the trial is unknown, but this case offers an insight into the pitfalls of business in this period and place.

One unpleasant aspect of economic life in both the ancient Near East and in the Greek world was the presence of slavery. Slaves were acquired in war, through purchase or birth, and through debt. As noted earlier, Hammurabi's Code demonstrates that a man could secure a loan with himself, his wife, or even with his children as collateral. By the Code, such individuals had to work for the creditor for three years, but would be freed in the fourth. This form of contractual slavery is also found in the Bible (Exodus 21: 2–8; Deuteronomy 15: 12–18), where the contractual period is six years. Such debt slavery also could last for the duration of the debt, or forever. Debt slavery in Greece came to an end in the sixth century B.C. Most slaves, however, were captured in warfare, and warfare in antiquity never ceased. In the middle of the second millennium B.C., Pharaoh Tuthmosis III enslaved 89,600 people and brought them from what is today Israel to Egypt. In spite of the prevalence of slaves, they did not monopolize labor in the pre-Roman era. In many cases they worked alongside free individuals and often were paid for their services, although almost always at a lower rate than their free counterparts. Most slaves worked in the households of the wealthy and the upper middle class as domestic servants. But slaves were often employed in hazardous endeavors as well. This was especially true in mining, where the dangers were great and the work grueling. Free labor was reluctant to endure either. While the condition of slaves was not as harsh as in societies where slavery became racial in nature, these individuals were still property. They could be abused with little recourse to any authority other than the humanity of their owners, which often seems to have been in short supply.

Such was the nature of the western pursuit of wealth down to the latter half of the fourth century B.C. It was in this century that an area on the fringe of the Greek world rose to prominence and briefly united all of Greece and the entire Near East under its dominion. Culturally, Macedonia was Greek. Its people spoke a Greek dialect; its origin was linked mythologically to the Greek world; and its religion was Greek. But politically, Macedonia was primarily a tribal society ruled by kings. During most of its existence, this northern Greek land was divided, its king able to hold on to only a small part of the territory known as Macedonia. In 359 B.C., all of this began to change dramatically, when Philip II came to the throne. By 336 B.C., through clever diplomacy and military success, he had united Macedonia in its entirety under his leadership and had joined the Greek city-states to him in a federation. To cement his hold on the *poleis*, Philip planned an expedition against the Persian Empire. This was the last and greatest of the near eastern empires, stretching from the Nile and the Aegean Sea east to the Indus River. Philip never got to carry out his grand design. Shortly before his army was to march east, he was assassinated. Two years later, his 21-year-old son, Alexander, led his father's forces on what was to become perhaps the greatest adventure and conquest in all history. When Alexander "the Great" died in 323 B.C., the entire Western world had been altered for all time. Though political unity did not survive Alexander, the cultures of the Greeks, Egyptians, Mesopotamians, Jews, and many other peoples had been and would continue to be intertwined. And the results would be breathtaking.

CHAPTER *2*

The Imperial Age
of Alexander and Rome

LEXANDER died in Babylon in 323 B.C. at the age of 32. His unified empire did not long survive him. Although officially he was succeeded by a feebleminded half-brother, Arrhidaeus, and an infant son, Alexander, his actual heirs were his generals, who for the next two decades fought for the right to be the new Alexander. These wars were fueled by more than 180,000 talents of gold and silver "liberated" from Persian treasuries. Through warfare and other means, the fabulous wealth of the East was now put into circulation. Politically, by 301 B.C., the basic makeup of the Hellenistic world was defined. In place of one great empire, there were three kingdoms. Egypt, many of the Aegean islands, parts of Libya, and much of the eastern coast of the Mediterranean made up the kingdom of Egypt, ruled until its conquest by Rome by the Ptolemaic dynasty of kings, descended from Ptolemy, one of Alexander's Macedonian generals. Macedonia, the land of the great conqueror's birth, was ruled by the Antigonid dynasty, the descendants of the Macedonian general Antigonus. Making up most of Alexander's Asian conquests was Syria, or Seleucid Asia, ruled by the heirs of Alexander's general Seleucus. While these three kingdoms dominated this new world, the political and cultural milieu was far more complex. Most of the Greek city-states on the mainland, in the Aegean, and in Sicily and southern Italy remained independent, bit players in a now-wider world to be sure, but participants just the same. And encouraged by the rivalry between the three kingdoms, a number of independent states came into being in Asia on the borders of the great powers.

The Hellenistic Civilization

Alexander had spawned a new civilization described as Hellenistic, a fusion of Greek, Middle Eastern, and Oriental elements. However, most of the economic components of this new age, such as banking and the commercial web, predated Alexander. The greatest changes brought about by the conquest were a general breakdown of barriers to trade and the influx into circulation of vast sums of gold and silver previously hoarded in Persian treasuries, which stimulated trade and industry. In effect, there came into being a vast trading area that stretched from the Indus River to the British Isles, with strong governments in many places capable of maintaining order and preventing piracy from disrupting commerce. While there were wars and revolts, trade was promoted assiduously. Alexander did not live long enough to see this era of greater commercial and cultural interaction between the West and the East, but it was not long in coming. There was a quickening of contacts in the third century B.C. Trade increased substantially among lands bordering on the Red Sea, the Persian Gulf, and India, and in time it would extend as far as China.

The differences between the Hellenic and Hellenistic ages can be seen in the contrast between Athens at the height of its power and prestige and Alexandria, the greatest of the new Hellenistic cities. The comparison is somewhat akin to one between eighteenth-century London and twentieth-century New York. London was an important city, to be sure, with commercial tentacles that stretched throughout the world, but it was undoubtedly English. New York was more far-reaching, a global city with a varied population that included people from all quarters of the globe.

Similarly, Athens was decidedly Greek. Alexandria, in contrast, had a population of some 400,000 Greeks, Jews, Persians, Arabs, and Egyptians, among others, and the economy was far more complicated and diverse than that of any previous Greek city. People of varied backgrounds joined together to form trading companies; money changers dealt in coins from all parts of this complex world.

Alexandria was one of the chief grain markets of the world, and also a major manufacturing center, producing papyrus, flax, glass, cosmetics, and jewelry. Cities tended to specialize in specific products. Woolen goods were manufactured in Miletus, Ephesus, and Pergamum, in what is today western Turkey. The Aegean islands of Rhodes and Delos, by virtue of geography, became important transfer points. Antioch, on the Orontes River in Syria, was another major trading center, as was Seleucia on the Tigris.

Although the new rulers in Europe, Asia, and Africa did inaugurate certain economic innovations, they basically followed established economic patterns in their domains. For all three kingdoms the major source of revenue was, as before, agriculture. The state owned large tracts of land that were cultivated by peasants who paid an annual rent to the government. Other lands were taxed. All three kingdoms maintained control of certain natural resources, most often mines, forests, and quarries. Usually these were exploited through contracts with guilds of specialists or private contractors, except in Egypt, where government officials were in charge. As in the previous age of the Greek city-states, most taxes were collected by tax farmers. The auction of taxes in Egypt was held once a year in Alexandria. Those areas of the kingdom outside Egypt alone produced 8000 talents annually.

But there were differences from one kingdom to another. The Seleucids, in particular, followed a policy of limited state interference in trade and commerce. Their domains were both more geographically expansive and more culturally and ethnically diverse than those of either the Ptolemies or the Antigonids. Especially in the Greek areas along the eastern Aegean coast and in the newly formed Greek cities of Asia, these Seleucid rulers adopted the economic practices of the Greek city-states, thereby permitting much free enterprise. Egypt was a different case altogether. Here, the state monopolies so characteristic of ancient Egypt not only were maintained but expanded.

The Ptolemies held exclusive rights to the manufacture of various products. Papyrus, beer, honey, salt, and most vegetable oils were state monopolies. In these industries, state officials controlled every stage in the production process, from planting and gathering to retailing, with all wages and prices fixed. What is perhaps most striking, is that the control extended all the way to the village level. Nor could these goods be easily acquired from abroad. To import products for which the state claimed a monopoly required special permission. All such items then had to enter Egypt at fixed points, be registered, and be assessed a duty. Even the temples had to obtain royal permission to produce a product regarded as a state monopoly. With other industries, primarily textiles, there was a sizable state-controlled segment, but private weavers and companies were permitted to operate.

One of the great innovations of the Hellenistic Age was the creation of state banks. These appeared first in a number of city-states, but the most noteworthy of these government banking corporations was organized by the Ptolemies in Egypt. The main bank was in the capital, Alexandria, with branches throughout the country. These branches were, in fact, farmed out to individual contractors, and as a result, even villages often had their own state banks. These institutions collected the state's revenues from royal officials and tax farmers and sought to invest any funds that were not immediately spent on government activities. The bank also attracted private capital, primarily from government officials. Investment was most often in the form of loans to private individuals and to members of the government, but much of this money was used to finance trade. Private banks handled most of the needs of more common people. Elsewhere in the Hellenistic world, banking conformed to preexisting models. The independent bankers of Athens remained, as did the temple bankers of Asia and the large commercial banks of Mesopotamia.

This economic mix produced a startling increase in the number of financiers and traders, many of whom became quite wealthy. In addition, a new class of entrepreneurial bureaucrats was created to administer the government. This is not to say that the bureaucrats of the pre-Hellenistic Near East did not engage in personal business while conducting that of the state, but the Hellenistic bureaucrats intermingled public and private activities so thoroughly that it is often difficult to untangle them. We get a glimpse of some of these individuals in Egyptian papyri of the third century B.C., most notably those from the surviving archive of Zenon, the secretary-steward of Apollonius, the chief financial officer of King Ptolemy II. Apollonius had his hand in many ventures, and Zenon left a record of several of these projects.

Through his staff and directly, Apollonius engaged in trading ventures in wine, oil, papyrus, and cloth, with correspondents in what are today Turkey, Lebanon, Israel, Syria, and the countries of the Arabian peninsula. Many of these goods were carried by his own merchant fleet. In addition, he held an estate from the king comprising 6200 acres at Philadelphia in central Egypt, about 60 miles from Cairo. Apollonius worked with other politicians and bureaucrats, who were regularly in on his deals. Even Zenon acquired businesses of his own. Economically, then, the Hellenisitic world absorbed aspects of the state-dominated economies of the Near East as well as much of the free-wheeling, entrepreneurial spirit of the *poleis*. While in many respects the Hellenistic Age represented a blend of the best of the ancient Near East and the Greek city-states, one sinister legacy of the previous Hellenic *poleis* remained: political division and warfare. One reason for the adoption by the respective states of the near eastern practice of state monopoly was to maximize revenues to support large armies and fleets. And owing to these fratricidal conflicts, the Greek world failed to meet a challenge arising to the west in the Italian peninsula: the growing power of Rome.

The Roman Republic: Private Enterprise Unleashed

According to tradition, the city of Rome was founded April 21, 753 B.C., and for the next 250 years was ruled by kings. Throughout these roughly two and a half centuries, Rome was a small city-state in central Italy whose greatest opponent, the city-state of Veii, lay barely more than 10 miles up the road. By the end of the first century B.C., Rome ruled an empire that stretched from the Sahara in the south to the English Channel in the north, and from the Atlantic to the Rhine, Danube, and Euphrates rivers. The Romans accomplished what only one Greek, the great Alexander, could even imagine: they created one state that included virtually every center of Western civilization.

The government that engineered this accomplishment was the Roman Republic. In a revolution in 509 B.C., the last Roman king was driven from the city, and in his place was imposed the Republic, a government with popular assemblies, elected magistrates, and in which a council of powerful and wealthy Romans, the Senate, dominated the state. For much of the Republic's history, the Senate controlled, in particular, the public treasury. It authorized payments for services and construction projects and saw to the collection of taxes and tribute. While there is great debate over how the Romans conquered their vast empire, one thing is not in doubt: to meet the ever-growing financial needs of this expanding state, the Romans turned to private enterprise.

Like the civilizations discussed previously, the wealth of the Roman state ultimately depended on control of natural resources, especially land. As more peoples fell under the sway of Rome, more territory was added to the Roman polity. Much of this land was given out to Roman colonists, but the state kept far more and leased it to individuals. The Republic collected rent of 10 percent on grain; 5 percent on vines, orchards, etc.; and varying amounts for grazing land. These rents formed a sizable part of the early Republic's income. To these revenues over the years were added various taxes paid by subject peoples. Provinces paid either a tithe on their production or a fixed amount. These issues were typically settled by a senatorial commission after the conquest of an area. The government also collected harbor dues and customs duties. Moreover, particular natural resources, especially mines, which most often had been under the control of the previous government, were taken over by the Roman government. The mines of Macedonia alone produced for the Roman treasury 1 to 2 million *denarii* (between 166 and 330 talents) a year; and those in North Africa, 9 million *denarii* (1500 talents) annually. By the end of the Roman Republic, the income of the state surpassed that of any previous near eastern empire or Hellenistic kingdom. Indeed, as a direct result of the conquests, after 167 B.C., Roman citizens were free from direct taxation.

Although Roman officials were in charge of the treasury, they seldom collected any of the money themselves. During the Republic, Romans did not see these activities as part of the state's function. The government did not consider supplying police and fire protection as its responsibility. These two services were seen as strictly private affairs. The republican Senate left virtually all economic activities to private individuals and companies, known collectively as the *publicani*. Tax collection, supplying the army, providing for religious sacrifices and other ceremonies, building construction and repair, mining, and so on were all contracted out. There was even a contract for summoning the assembly into session and one for feeding the sacred geese. The latter probably calls for some explanation. These particular geese were sacred to the goddess Juno, and in 390 B.C. had saved the defenders of Rome from a nighttime assault by cackling and awakening the sleeping Roman soldiers in time to repel the attack.

By the end of the Republic, the *publicani* fulfilled virtually all of the state's economic requirements. Each year, Roman magistrates would auction off whatever had to be done or whatever tax or rent needed to be collected. Many of these items were actually let over a longer period than a single year, but there were always contracts to be put out for bid. In the case of taxes, the highest bid would win; in the case of supplies or construction, the lowest. Bidders were typically organized into companies. While some of these companies were small, many would rank with modern-day corporations. The company that obtained the mining contract in North Africa employed 40,000 people in these mines alone. Certain of the construction contracts were worth 45 to 50 million *denarii*. Tax collectors also served as wholesale traders. With taxes in kind, whatever the *publicani* collected over and above what they were contracted to deliver they sold for profit. Transport was also in the hands of private companies, and these firms would carry other goods in addition to those under government contract.

Even though certain companies came into existence for a particular contract, the partners separating after the fulfillment of the task, many businesses maintained themselves for long periods of time, and their capital was such that they could bid on many contracts simultaneously. The days of needing a few hundred contractors to build a temple were over. These larger companies often were registered as legal entities. As such, they could own property and transact business as corporations. However, the partners in a company did not have their liability limited to the company's assets; they were personally responsible. In any case, the company had to put up surety for the value of its entire contract. For taxes, the company was to pay half when the contract let and the remainder at the end of a designated time period. In addition, contractors were only indemnified in case of enemy action. All transportation risks were borne by the *publicani*.

In spite of the hazards, there were fabulous profits to be made. The richest Roman in the first century B.C., Marcus Licinius Crassus, was worth 48 million *denarii*, or 8000 talents. In this context it should be noted that a common infantryman made 225 *denarii* a year, and a day laborer earned 250. As was typical with the very wealthy, Crassus received income from diverse sources: from state and private building contracts, mining leases, large agricultural estates, and rental properties within the city of Rome. Many who were partners in firms contracting for state services also were involved in commercial and financial operations. Rabirius Postumus, who also lived during the first century

B.C., is described as having "whole peoples" as his debtors, and having lent vast sums to Ptolemy XI, the king of Egypt.

While many made legitimate fortunes, the system of employing the *publicani* for tax collection and state service was easily abused. In the provinces, Roman governors, in league with the *publicani*, could exploit the provincials literally to the point of impoverishing them. The most notorious example involved a governor of Sicily, one Gaius Verres. Often in the presence of others he boasted of his plans to rob the Sicilian people during his three-year term as governor. In the first year, he declared, he would take care of himself; in the second, his friends; and the third he would devote to securing the funds to bribe his jurors in case he was ever brought to trial. Extortion in the provinces was made possible by the wide latitude granted to a governor who was in charge of the courts, the administration, and law enforcement. Verres made a deal with the tax farmers to collect not the 10 percent tax on production allowed by law, but rather 50 percent, the additional revenue to be shared. Sicilians who protested were threatened with flogging or were simply beaten on the spot. At the conclusion of Verres's term, most of the cities of the province, acting collectively as plaintiff, sued him for the restitution of 100 million *denarii*. Fortunately for the Sicilians, they found a politically ambitious and very able advocate named Marcus Tullius Cicero, who, in spite of numerous legal obstacles put in his path by the many friends of Verres, prosecuted him in criminal court for extortion. So overwhelming was the evidence that Verres went into voluntary exile in Marseilles. This case is unusual in two respects. The level of corruption was extraordinary, and the wayward governor was successfully brought to trial, although he never made restitution, only paying a fine of 750,000 *denarii*.

The Republic, though, had far greater problems than political corruption in the provinces. This was a government that had arisen to administer a small city-state in central Italy. It now governed a vast empire. To a degree, the Republic was a victim of its own success. Its blend of popular sovereignty, powerful elected administrators, and an overarching council, the Senate, dominating the political scene through the prominence of its individual members and the prestige of the institution as a whole, came to be tested in the new, wider world of empire. The great wealth that accrued to the *publicani*, businessmen, bankers, and other entrepreneurs created a powerful economic class that came to challenge the power of the Senate, most of whose members represented landed wealth. Rather paradoxically, while the empire brought wealth to many, it brought poverty to an even greater number. Italian agriculture had been based on the small farmer, but with the expansion of Roman power came the importation of foreign grain. Grain produced in Sicily and Egypt could be imported into Italy and sold for less than what contemporary Italian farmers needed to break even. The result was a consolidation of land into fewer and fewer hands, and the migration of large segments of the rural population into the cities. On the new estates cash crops were cultivated most often, and instead of the free labor that had prevailed in early Italy, the new work force was increasingly slave.

During the late Roman Republic, slavery existed on a scale far greater than it had previously. Despite the absence of precise figures, the information that does survive is indicative. Aemilius Paullus sacked the Greek region of Epirus in 167 B.C. and carried off 150,000 people into slavery. It is estimated that during his campaigns in the first century B.C., Julius Caesar enslaved more than 1 million people. It was not unusual for private individuals to own thousands of slaves. In his will, Gaius Caecilius Isidorus left 4116 slaves to his heir, and Crassus employed 500 slaves in all but one construction crew. Estimates of the proportion of slaves to free range from one-fourth to one-third of the population of Italy. Complicating the issue is the ease with which urban slaves gained their freedom, with the result that the numbers of former slaves would also be large. Though these individuals were technically free, they were obliged to continue to serve the interests of their former owners.

While many urban slaves labored on construction gangs and in factories and shops, most were employed in the household. A wealthy Roman would have slave gardeners, cooks, hairdressers, house cleaners, secretaries, launderers, tailors, child-care providers, and so forth. What is truly remarkable is the apparently wide distribution of slave ownership. Even members of the lower middle class owned a slave or two. Although many slaves enjoyed good relations with their masters, Roman law was very clear that they were property, not persons. Slaves had no rights during the Republic. They could be flogged, branded, mutilated, or killed with impunity.

Beside being responsible for this explosion of slavery throughout Italy, foreign wars also gave rise to professional armies and unscrupulous commanders willing to use their troops to secure political advantage. The combination of the demands of the powerful business and merchant class, the great poverty and desperation of large numbers of the Roman free population, and professional armies more loyal to their generals than to the state gave rise to a series of civil wars. Emerging from these as the ultimate victor was Gaius Julius Caesar Octavianus, or Augustus, who defeated his last rival in 31 B.C. and sealed his supremacy and that of his family. This dynasty created a government known to history as the Roman Empire. In its earliest stages it was a hereditary military dictatorship with all the trappings of the old Republic. The Senate continued to meet, and so did the assemblies for a time. Magistrates were elected, but the emperor controlled a growing bureaucracy and, of course, the armies.

The Roman Empire

With the end of the civil wars and peace along the frontiers, Augustus presided over a prosperous and serene empire. With the Mediterranean serving as a great highway, trade moved freely throughout the Roman world. No pirates, no wars, just the Augustan peace. Gaul, today what is mostly France, produced and exported grain, pottery, and textiles; Spain: lead, iron, tin, gold, and silver; Asia: textiles, jewelry, iron, and various manufactured goods. Egypt, added to the Empire by Augustus, exported grain, papyrus, linen, and glass. From outside the Empire came slaves, hides, amber, spices, and silk. Pliny the Elder, writing in the first century A.D., states that each year the Empire experienced a 12½ million *denarii* deficit in its trade with India alone. While goods from beyond the Empire were a component of its trade, the vast majority of commerce was internal. Foreign commerce represented a very small percentage, and its effects on the overall economy were minimal.

Beginning with Augustus, there were changes in the relationship between the state and private contractors. The rapacity of many of the *publicani* had undermined confidence in this system. Soon, imperial financial officials, *procurators*, were handling taxation, the exploitation of natural resources, and the provision of supplies for the army and the civil service, without recourse to private manufacturers. Likewise, most mines came to be run by procurators and were staffed mostly by criminals and those with "hostile attitudes." In addition to their various official responsibilities, these agents of the emperor also served as his eyes and ears throughout the provinces.

Increasingly over time, under the direction of the imperial procurators, wealthy individuals in the cities of the Empire were made responsible for collecting the tribute and arranging for its transport. This practice of compulsory service of the wealthiest citizens—liturgies—was common in the Near East and with a number of Greek city-states as well, but during the Empire the Romans perfected it into an elaborate administrative system. Indeed, much of the work previously done by the *publicani* came to be performed by municipal and provincial officials who carried out these duties without compensation. At first, civic loyalty and competition between prominent citizens kept the various positions filled, but by the end of the first century A.D., it was becoming increasingly difficult to find individuals willing to take on the responsibilities and the costs. With respect to tax collection, in addition to performing the work without pay, if the quota was not reached in actual collections, then it was the duty of the official to make up the difference. Imperial administrators often had to intervene and draft candidates into service. In the words of a late imperial commentator, "The main object of the system was to get public work done at private expense; in effect, it was a heavy tax on the moneyed classes and eventually brought them to ruin."

Changes in the economic function of government from republic to empire were most notable in the grain trade. As it had been since the beginning of commerce in Mesopotamia, grain was the principle item of trade. During the Republic, private individuals and companies collected the grain and private shippers transported it to its destination. In the Empire, the shipping firms responsible for the transportation remained in private hands, but they were under government control and were usually organized into guilds. In time, membership in the guilds became hereditary. Typically, grain for the great cities of the Empire was raised on vast imperial estates worked by tenant farmers. The emperor was the largest landowner in the Empire. Property accrued to him from a variety of sources. Routinely, estates were willed to the emperor; or they were confiscated from those guilty of crimes or from those who died intestate with no legal heir. All property bequeathed to freedmen with the stipulation that it pass to descendants was confiscated by the state on the recipient's death, when there was no direct descendant. However, by far the largest and richest imperial estates were added to the government's holdings when Augustus acquired Egypt from Cleopatra, the last Ptolemaic ruler. These lands Augustus regarded as his personal possession, and he and his successors maintained them under basically the same system as the Ptolemies. Most of the Nile River valley, the richest land in the entire Mediterranean basin, was directly under the control of the emperor.

Although the state had become a major force in the Roman economy, private enterprise still existed. Especially with respect to textiles, there was a flourishing trade in all areas of manufacture. From the very poor to the immensely wealthy, everyone needed clothing. Also still in private hands were the creation and distribution of numerous luxury items. Jewelry, perfumes, wine, olive oil, glassware, and the like remained the provinces of independent entrepreneurs. The transportation of goods, whether the government's or those of private individuals and companies, rested chiefly in the hands of independent shippers. Here, the state was even helpful. The Empire expended large amounts of capital to improve harbor and storage facilities at its ports, with fees and internal customs duties remaining low. Banking was another area in which private enterprise flourished. Even in Egypt, where they had inherited the state banking system of the Ptolemies, the Romans abandoned the state monopoly. Into this void private municipal bankers expanded. These banks accepted deposits, paid interest, made loans, and even transferred funds from one city to another.

One major and beneficial change that came with the Empire was a decline in slavery. This was not the result of an abolition or civil rights initiative, but rather a direct consequence of the virtual cessation of territorial expansion that had characterized the Republic. The tapering off of foreign wars and the continuing practice of manumission led to a steady decline in the number of slaves. Slaves now had to be imported from outside or born to slaves within the Empire. In many occupations that in the late Republic had employed large numbers of slaves, free labor made a return. Agriculture, in particular, saw tenant farmers rapidly replace slave labor.

In the third century, the Empire began a steady decline that eventually led to a separation into western and eastern parts, divided at the Adriatic, and finally to the collapse of the western half. There were many causes for this decline. In the second century A.D., large numbers of Germanic peoples to the north and northeast of the Roman world began to migrate westward, putting increasing pressure all along the northern frontiers. This crisis called for more troops and more expenditures. Adding to these financial pressures, the Empire had never succeeded in creating a system by which imperial power could be transferred smoothly in the absence of a clear heir. Whenever there was a disputed succession, the result was civil war, with all the physical destruction and economic disruption associated with such conflict.

In many respects the Empire's decline was set in motion at its inception. Augustus installed the state bureaucracy that replaced the *publicani*, and in so doing created the expensive government bureaucracy the Republic had avoided. From a financial perspective, one of Augustus's innovations that most benefited the provincials proved to be a major economic drain on the system. Prior to Augustus and the succeeding emperors, the Roman government did not station troops in the provinces except in time of actual war. The Roman Republic would react to invasions, but it did little to forestall them. Augustus created a frontier system with approximately 200,000 soldiers stationed along the borders of the Empire to prevent incursions. These troops needed to be paid well, since in the final analysis, Augustus had gained power through their fighting abilities in the civil war and retained power in part because of their loyalty to him. Keeping such a large standing army even in times of peace represented a major drain on the resources of the Empire.

But probably what undermined the economy of the Empire most was that with the new imperial government, the territorial acquisition that had characterized the Republic ceased. And even though the Ancient World witnessed a number of technological innovations, none of them was applied in a way that transformed the economy. It is difficult nowadays to imagine a society where technology remains virtually unchanged for centuries and in many respects for millennia. Today's economy is driven by changing technology. Without such change, or the addition of outside resources, ancient economies were slow to grow. So in the Republic, wealth was generated by the conquest of additional territories and their assets. While the Empire added a few new areas, these additions were infrequent and were seldom suitable for economic exploitation. Much of the capital that had created the personal fortunes of so many during the Republic now evaporated. One indication of the change is that great wealth during the Empire was found almost exclusively among landowners. By the late Empire, it is estimated that as much as 95 percent of the Roman economy was agricultural. Although trade and commerce continued, without the lucrative government contracts, no longer were there immense fortunes to be made. In the fourth century A.D., the greatest recorded worth of a merchant was less than 20,000 *solidi* (275 pounds of gold). The annual incomes for great estate owners of the same period were between 100,000 and 300,000 *solidi*. Furthermore, these estates were increasingly becoming self-contained entities, producing most of what was needed for the estate locally and even employing its own merchants to purchase those items that could only be acquired elsewhere. Often this commerce was carried out in the form of gift-giving. Many of the great estates even established their own river ports to facilitate this trade.

The Empire in the west began to unravel in the fifth century. Revenues were insufficient to meet the growing needs and demands of the army. The conditions on the frontiers deteriorated, and large numbers of Germans migrated into the Empire, creating their own states. In A.D. 476, the German leader in Italy set aside the titular Roman emperor, fittingly named Romulus Augustulus. The original Romulus had been the founder of the city of Rome and Augustus, of course, the first emperor. The Empire in the west was no longer. The eastern empire, however, survived and would evolve over time into the Byzantine Empire, or Byzantium, with its capital in Constantinople. As the Byzantine Empire, this Roman legacy would persist into the fifteenth century. When the Empire fell in the west, it did so as a Christian empire. By the late fourth century A.D., Christianity had gone from a small and persecuted offshoot of Judaism to the official religion of the Roman world.

In many cases, the towns and cities of the Empire survived because of the activities of the Christian Church. By the fifth century, many communities were under the direct political authority of their resident bishop. Beside its political authority, much like the temples in the ancient Near East, the Church had acquired immense property holdings from believers and from large donations by the Christian emperors. By the end of the Empire in the west, the Church was one of the great landowners in Europe. Much of its surplus was used by the clergy to meet the needs of the ever-increasing ranks of the poor. Bishop John of Alexandria even possessed a large merchant fleet with which he transported grain from Egypt to Britain in order to relieve a famine there. As in the Near East, this religious establishment enjoyed immunities from imperial taxation. As a consequence, the Church attracted a number of merchants who sought its protection from the growing financial exactions of government tax collectors. By doing the Church's business, they could maintain their own businesses. And it was not only merchants who felt the increasing burden of taxation. By the end of the Western Empire, taxes had become so burdensome that whole communities fled to escape the ever-increasing demands of taxing authorities. Writing in the fifth century, the Christian priest Salvianus asked:

> What else can these wretched people wish for, they who suffer the incessant and even continuous destruction of public tax levies? To them there is always imminent a heavy and relentless proscription. They desert their homes, lest they be tortured in their very homes. They seek exile, lest they suffer torture. The enemy is more lenient to them than the tax collectors. This is proved by the very fact that they flee to the enemy in order to avoid the full force of the heavy tax levy. This very tax levying, although hard and inhuman, would nevertheless be less heavy and harsh if all would bear it equally and in common. Taxation is made more shameful and burdensome because all do not bear the burden of all. They extort tribute from the poor man for the taxes of the rich, and the weaker carry the burden for the stronger. There is no other reason that they cannot bear all the taxation except that the burden imposed on the wretched is greater than their resources.

The Church, despite its public activities, was also a drain on the economy. Roughly half of its income went to support the clergy, whose numbers surpassed even the imperial civil service. Also, in the Church's quest for doctrinal purity it enlisted government forces to combat paganism and heresy, thus further depleting the already drained coffers of the imperial treasury.

CHAPTER 3

The European Middle Ages: The Birth of a New Economic Age

 HE Roman Empire wasn't there one day, only to vanish the next. An entirely new scheme of things, usually designated as medieval, did not replace Rome in a twinkling, or even in a few generations. The Germanic invaders who succeeded the Romans admired the civilization they infiltrated and conquered, and their kings had accepted titles from the emperors in Rome and Constantinople. In addition, a good deal of the economic structure they inherited remained intact for centuries. But ultimately, the Germans and those they conquered would create a very different economic world from that of the Roman Empire, or, indeed, of any of the states of western antiquity.

Someone familiar with life in northern Italy or southern Spain in the first century B.C. would have noted changes there at the end of the third or fourth centuries A.D., but the processes of life still would have been comprehensible. But were it possible for a person alive in the fourth century to be transported to the eighth or ninth centuries, he or she would have realized that the old economic life had broken down and a new dispensation was in place.

Economies within the borders of the old Roman Empire continued along the path set in the late imperial period, that is, large, mostly self-sufficient agricultural estates. By the fifth century A.D., a small wealthy aristocracy monopolized landowning and thus the economic system of the Roman world. The distribution system, in particular, was inefficient, leaving the majority of the population near starvation. Germanic society, however, was little better. Most Germans had been herdsmen and farmers, and within their ranks there was also an hereditary nobility who owed their prominence to their positions within the clans that dominated Germanic society. Like their Roman counterparts, German magnates exercised control over large estates. Within the German villages, most of the population was subservient in some fashion to the magnate. These peasants differed only in the depth of their dependency, as reflected in their obligations to the noble. Many of them were outright slaves.

In all of this, there was little room for the merchant, the manufacturer, or the banker, all of whom had been present in substantial numbers in ancient Mesopotamia, Egypt, Greece, and Rome. In his *Commentaries*, Julius Caesar wrote of the Germans trading amber, furs, and slaves to the Celts for horses. And Roman merchants actively traded with the Germans, on a barter basis, from the first century B.C. onward. Several Roman towns near the frontier, such as Marbach and Augsburg, had become trading centers. While some of this trade survived the collapse of the Roman government, commerce in general remained at the low levels found in the late Empire. If by capitalism we mean the desire for wealth, the accumulation of capital, and the search for profit-making ventures, a form of capitalism had existed in those civilizations. The pursuit of wealth did not die during the early Middle Ages, but it was muted and tied almost exclusively to the acquisition of land.

To add to the confusion of this period, some of the invaders remained nomadic. Describing the Huns who appeared in Europe in 375, Ammianus Marcellinus commented on their filth and primitive lives, noting that they seldom cooked their food, and ate raw meat.

> They all have fine and firm limbs and graceful necks; they have strange and twisted bodies, such as you would think them to be beasts on two legs, or such as are inelegantly cut and carved as statues on the parapets of bridges. But though they have the form of men—albeit unpleasant—they appear to be so rude that they need neither fire or seasoning for their food, but feed on the roots of the grasses of the fields and on the half-raw flesh of any kind of animal whatsoever which, borne between their thighs and the backs of their horses, they submit to a kind of cooking. . . . On horseback every man of that nation lives day and night; on horseback he buys and sells; on horseback he takes his meat and drink. . . . Not one among them cultivates the ground or ever touches a plow handle. All wander abroad without fixed abodes, without home or law or settled customs, like perpetual fugitives, with their wagons their only habitations.

For their part, the Huns much preferred their way of life, scorning wealth and the softness they perceived in the Romans. The Byzantine historian Priscus wrote tellingly of this, describing a conversation with a once well-to-do merchant who had been captured and enslaved, whom he found quite cultured. How might such a person adjust to his new circumstances?

> I consider my present mode of life much preferable to my past. For when war is over, the people live a life of ease, enjoying themselves to the full and free from care of any kind. But the people in Rome are easily worsted in war because they place their hopes of safety on others rather than themselves. Their tyrants will not allow them the use of arms. . . . Then, too, think of all the cruelties practiced by the collectors of taxes, the infamy of informers, and the gross inequalities in the administration of justice. If a rich man offends, he can always manage to escape judgment; but a poor man who does not know how to fix matters has to undergo the full penalty, unless indeed he be dead before judgment is pronounced, which is not unlikely, considering the notoriousness of the law's delays. But what I call the most shameful thing of all is that you have to pay money in order to obtain your legal rights. For a man who is injured cannot even get a hearing from the court without first paying large fees to the judge and the officials.

This from a slave!

The Germanic tribes that inherited the Roman infrastructure permitted much of it to decay. For their part, the Franks in Gaul—modern France—the Angles and Saxons in England, and the Visigoths in Spain allowed trade with the Mediterranean world to decline sharply, as did the grain trade between Italy and Egypt. The Goths continued Roman metalworking and leather production, but the mines in their area of Germany were abandoned. The Vandals operated an economy based to a large extent on piracy. The Ostrogoths provided northern Italy with competent government, but there too the economy fell off.

The Manorial Age

With the entry of so many Germans into the Roman Empire, a blending of the two cultures occurred long before the Empire ceased to exist. As part of this amalgamation, by the seventh century, a basic form of land management evolved in many parts of Western Europe, one involving both dependent peasants and controlling magnates. In this system, called *manorialism* by historians, the relationship between the dependent peasants and their "lords," the individuals who controlled the large agricultural estates, or manors, was roughly standardized. Peasants would retain the use of strips of arable land for their maintenance, while owing labor service on lands held by the local noble or high-ranking churchman, such as a bishop or abbot. Among these labor services would be planting and harvesting the lord's land and building and maintaining property on the manor. Perhaps a majority of Europeans were serfs, peasants who were bound to the soil and under the thumbs of their respective lords. In fact, however, peasants in much of Europe had specific economic rights. Their homes, poor as they were, their tools, furniture, and perhaps some livestock were their own, though the lord could make demands that rendered this status theoretical at best. Peasants might own land, though this too was subject to conditions set down by the lord. The peasants were subject to manorial justice, in which the lord was their sole judge. While they might bring cases against fellow peasants and hope for a just verdict, against the lord they had no rights. And, of course, peasants had to pay taxes to both the lord and the Church.

In such a society, the capitalism that had marked part of life in the ancient world had no place. Indeed, as indicated, all conspired against it. Part of the reason for this was the Christian religion itself, which at the time considered this life the antechamber for the more important stage, the afterlife and the resurrection. In itself, this was not new; Egyptian religion was based on a similar concept. But unlike the Egyptians, who considered great wealth an accompaniment to the afterlife, the Christians considered private wealth a sign of vanity, hardly an imitation of the life of Jesus, who told the affluent of his time to give what they had to the poor. How might a person, argued the religious establishment, become wealthy except by taking from others? It was well and good for the Church to enrich itself for the purpose of spreading the gospel, but this wealth could only be acquired in acceptable ways. There is no dearth of theoretical works on the subject. Gratian, a twelfth century monk, put it this way:

> Whosoever buys a thing, not that he may sell it whole and unchanged, but that it may be material for fashioning something, he is no merchant. But the man who buys it in order that he may gain by selling it again unchanged and as he bought it, that man is of the buyers and sellers who are cast forth from God's temple.

As late as the fourteenth century, Henry of Langenstein, a philosopher, could write:

> He who has enough to satisfy his wants and nevertheless ceaselessly labors to acquire
> riches, either in order to obtain a higher social position or that subsequently he may have
> enough to live without labor, or that his sons may become men of wealth and impor-
> tance—all such are incited by a damnable avarice, sensuality, or pride.

This is not to say the medieval economy was without money. Funds were needed by nobles and knights to obtain armor, ransom relatives seized in battle, or provide a dowry. Artisans might borrow money to purchase tools or materials. The matter of interest arose in the cases of such loans. Usury was condemned by the Church, and lenders trod carefully when it came to such things. Also, the concept of investments in order to obtain profits and wealth was muted.

Piratical activity in the Mediterranean increased and commerce declined, and by the seventh century Moslem incursions made travel there perilous. This was the essence of the thesis promulgated by Belgian historian Henri Pirenne in the early twentieth century. Pirenne thought Roman economic institutions were maintained by the Germans until the Moslems effectively closed down the Mediterranean, which cut off Europe from the gold of Africa and compelled the continent to evolve an economy less reliant upon commerce and coinage. By the beginning of the eighth century, commerce had become deeply depressed, although it never disappeared completely. As early as the middle of the eighth century, Christians in Italian coastal towns and Moslems in North Africa competed with the Jewish merchants. While Jewish influence in commercial activities continued in time, others came to dominate European and Mediterranean trade.

Lacking safe access to much of the Mediterranean, the Europeans were obliged to resort to the continent's rivers and the roads. Land travel in Europe, despite the fabled Roman roads, always slow, expensive, and tortuous, was also more dangerous without the presence of Roman military might to maintain order. Never as wealthy as Asia Minor and North Africa, Europe now became more impoverished.

In any case, gold and silver were scarce, and the possibility for profit and wealth severely limited. It would not be going too far to state that from the fall of Rome to around the twelfth century, medieval Europe was not capitalistic in spirit or action. This is not to say that capitalism was dead in all of Europe; rather, it hardly existed in areas controlled by those people generally deemed to be European, and not all the continent was under their rule. To the east lay the surviving remnant of the Roman Empire, and its capital, Constantinople, flourished commercially, artistically, and culturally. Banking, insurance, and other occupations that had grown increasingly sophisticated during the Hellenistic Age continued apace.

The Next Invasions of Europe

After conquering North Africa, Islamic forces invaded Spain in 711, then went on to threaten France, and were finally stopped by the Franks under Charles Martel at Tours in 732. Moslems took the Balearic Islands, Corsica, Sardinia, and Sicily, and from bases there dominated the Tyrrhenian Sea, the body of water bounded by Italy and these islands. They ruled the eastern Mediterranean trade, forcing the remaining European and many Byzantine ships from the waters. To the east, Moslems had a lively trade with India and China.

Their ships plied the Red Sea and Persian Gulf, bringing rubies, emeralds, and other precious stones from Persia, ebony and sandalwood from India, and spices and musk from China. A Moslem colony, with diplomatic representation, was a permanent fixture in a number of Chinese ports. In addition, gold and slaves arrived from southern Africa.

While Moslems attacked from the south, others invaded Europe as well. From the north came the Vikings, who traded with Russia; established outposts in Iceland between 874 and 930, went on to Greenland; raided England, Scotland, and France; and came to America around 1000. The Slavs were arriving from the east. Magyars settled in the Danubian region and threatened Italy itself.

While it might appear that Europe was doomed, the myth of the "Dark Ages" is just that. In this period, there was much technological innovation and consolidation of power by kings, but European economic life did reach its nadir in the ninth and early tenth centuries. Even under these trying circumstances, however, some commerce continued. In the middle of the ninth century a Persian geographer, Ibn Kurdadbeh, wrote of the routes used by the Franks to engage in trade with China. Their ships would hug the shores, hoping to avoid the Moslems and pirates, until arriving in the Levant, and by combination of land and water travel, they would reach the Indian Ocean, and from there cross over to the trading cities. But such ventures were unusual in this time of distress.

Commercial activities, however, were largely the sphere of non-Europeans. Commerce with the East was almost completely controlled by Jewish, Greek, and Syrian traders. The Syrians concentrated on trade between their lands and the Orient. While some Byzantine colonies remained in Italy, there was little trade between them and the East. The Greek merchants dealt with the East through intermediaries. By then, Jewish merchants had become more visible. In the interior regions of Europe, they had virtually all of the trade. Not so in the developed coastal areas, where they had to compete with Italian Christians and Moslems. Thus, the Jewish merchants dominated trade between Europe and the eastern Mediterranean and points east. While Europeans learned of the inner life from the Church, they discovered the world beyond Europe from the Jewish merchants. The medieval Jews often were portrayed as moneylenders, but they were predominantly merchants.

The role of the Jews as traders was due to several factors. They were barred from military employment, and while Jews were not prohibited from owning or dealing in land and engaging in agriculture in some parts of Europe, in many others they were forbidden to do so. There was anti-Semitism in Europe during the early Middle Ages, and the sentiment intensified during the Crusades. Nor were Jews at ease in Moslem countries.

The operations of these merchants were described by an Arab contemporary, Ibn Khurradadhbah:

> These merchants speak Arabic, Persian, Roman, Frankish, Spanish, and Slavonic. They travel from the East to the West and from the West to the East by land as well as sea. They bring from the West eunuchs, slave girls, boys. Brocade, beaver skins, marten furs and other varieties of fur, and swords. They embark in the land of the Franks on the Western Sea [the Mediterranean], and they sail toward al-Farama [Egypt]. There they load their merchandise on the backs of camels and proceed by land to al-Qulzum, 25 parasangs distant. They embark on the Eastern [Red] Sea and proceed from al-Qulzum to al-Jar and to Jiddah [Arabia]; then they go to Sind [between Persia and India], Hind [India], and

China. On their return from China they load musk, aloe wood, camphor, cinnamon, and other products of the eastern countries, and they come back to al-Qulzum, then to al-Farama, and from there they embark again on the Western Sea. Some of them sail for Constantinople in order to sell their merchandise to the Romans. Others proceed to the residence of the king of the Franks to dispose of these articles.

Around the year 1000, an economic recovery began that was due in part to an increase in agricultural production, which, in turn, resulted from the introduction of redesigned tools, such as heavier plows, the more widespread use of three-field rotation techniques, and the more efficient use of draft animals. Windmills also came into extensive use. These devices, which had existed in Hellenistic times, were redesigned and appeared in great numbers. The lords obliged their peasants to use them to make them more productive. These changes and improvements made it possible to feed Europe with fewer peasants, freeing some for commerce and manufacturing while also providing the merchants with additional goods to trade. Europe was poised once again for expansion, driven in part by the pursuit of wealth.

The Economic Quickening and the Crusades

Europe started to meet the political and economic challenges posed by Islam and Byzantium in the eleventh century. In 1036 the Normans, from north central France, struck out against Byzantine strongholds in southern Italy, and by 1053, one of their leaders, Robert Guiscard, had established a kingdom there, while other Normans took Sicily. Christian nobles were on the march in Spain. Italian city-states, barred from commerce by the Moslems, were eager to retake the eastern Mediterranean. Finally, there was the matter of wealth, which the Moslems had and the Christians lacked, and which could be obtained through trade and conquest.

Amalfi, on the eastern coast of Italy, possessing a good port in an area poorly suited for agriculture, turned to the seas. Its fishing fleet was sent out to catch and then salt fish, which became an important trade item. As one of Italy's most southerly ports, Amalfi was well-positioned to trade with the Byzantines and Moslems, and it exchanged salted fish, wine, olive oil, fruit, grain, timber, and linen with Egypt and other lands to the south for wax, gold, and ivory. The city flourished. In 972, Ibn-Hawqal, a Baghdad merchant, wrote that Amalfi was "the most prosperous city of Lombardy, the noblest, the most illustrious for its conditions, the richest, and the most opulent." But the city was open to invasion and had strong competition from nearby Naples and Gaeta, as well as the more distant Salerno. Along with other Italian cities in the region, in 1073 Amalfi fell to the Normans.

While Amalfi chose the sea as its highway, others were willing to chance land transport. Historian Robert Reynolds wrote about the "caravan merchants," Flemings from Arras and Italians from Asti, two towns that produced large quantities of cloth, a major trade item. They would sell their cloth and use the funds obtained to purchase pepper, alum, and other products not available in their areas. As already noted, merchants from ancient times to the present have carried products from places where they are plentiful and inexpensive to sell in areas where they are scarce and expensive.

By the middle of the thirteenth century, bankers, who had far greater resources than the traveling merchants and remained sedentary, became more common. They dispatched networks of agents to fairs and other commercial meetings. In this period, the merchants, their agents, and bankers became more three-dimensional than they had been earlier. One who left papers was Symon de Gualterio of Genoa. His records indicate investments and loans in addition to purchases and sales of cloth, silk, and saffron. Wool was among his more important wares. His agents bartered for spices in the east, which de Gualterio sold throughout Europe. The purchases often were made on credit, with the provision to pay within a certain period of time. If all went well, de Gualterio made large profits without the risk of his capital. There is a record of his having purchased 30 pieces of English woolen cloth in March of 1253 for payment in mid-July, by which time he would have sold the cloth (at a fair in May). He acquired a three-quarter interest in a ship that March, which he used in the northern trade, and the same month, de Gualterio arranged for the procurement of a large quantity of silk and saffron for sale at one of the Champagne-area fairs.

Wool remained the key to de Gualterio's fortunes during his career, and it was one of the major trade goods throughout Europe. Parliament asserted in 1297 that wool represented half of England's wealth, and others called it the "jewel of the realm." Sacks of wool served as currency. In 1273, the value of wool exported from England came to more than $30 million in current prices and fetched $600,000 in taxes for King Edward I. When Richard the Lion Hearted was captured by the German emperor, his ransom was 50,000 sacks of wool, an enormous amount at the time. Edward I's foreign adventures were financed by wool, and taxes and loans on wool paid for much of the Hundred Years' War. Taxes on and sales of Spanish merino wool later would provide, among other things, the funding for the voyages of Columbus.

At about the same time de Gualterio was making his fortune from wool and other trade commodities, Orlando and Bonifazio Bounsignori, two Sienese bankers who began as merchants, graduated into moneylending and pawnbroking, and then branched out into other forms of banking, establishing themselves as bankers to the Church. The popes of this period had many sources of income, and required the services of professionals to collect funds, advance them when necessary, and provide investment advice. The Bounsignori made imprudent investments with their own funds in the early fourteenth century, and despite a bailout from Pope Boniface VIII, their bank failed. Several of their French agents fled the country, and King Philip the Fair seized their properties and those of other Sienese merchants. Pope Clement V did the same in Siena, and the city fell into an economic slump. Other monarchs, nobles, and churchmen followed this pattern. The practice of bankers providing the financial muscle for political leaders' wars and expeditions did not originate in the Middle Ages. As we have seen, it was present during ancient times. But the medieval configuration was closer to that of modern times than one might imagine.

In this period, scholars made distinctions between two different kinds of trade: regular and privileged. The former was subject to rules, regulations, and taxes levied by both the importing and exporting political authorities. These taxes constituted an important source of revenue for the monarchs and the nobles able to levy them. Privileged trade occurred when one city was given special concessions in a Moslem or Byzantine city in return for payment to a ruler. For example, Venice obtained such rights in Sidon in

1102 and in Tyre in 1123, with other cities following. Granting privileged trade rights usually occurred when the monarch needed funds immediately and could not wait for tax collections, or when he wanted to reward a favored banker or courtier.

By the early eleventh century, Europe was showing signs of economic life. Byzantine, Moslem, and pirate vessels were being routed from the Mediterranean. In 1087, Genoese and Pisan ships raided the Moslem port of Mahdia in northern Africa. The Normans recaptured Sicily from the Moslems in 1090. Corsica was taken the following year, which opened the Straits of Messina and the entire central Mediterranean to European shipping. The Seljuk Turks were being contained by the Byzantines. Castile was on the march in Spain. The mining of gold and silver was expanded in central Europe. And the population was increasing, the result, in part, of larger harvests and a generally higher standard of living.

Along with the growth of maritime commerce, there was a quickening of internal trade. This can be seen in the growth of the aforementioned merchant fairs, which were increasing in number, size, and duration. Markets had never disappeared, but the fairs were quite different from markets. The markets were regularly scheduled events, in which customers came to buy and merchants to trade and sell. The fairs were sponsored by political authorities and served a wider and broader population than did the markets. They were seasonal, rather than weekly, and were geared to wholesale rather than retail customers. These fairs were a feature of late medieval life.

Once a year, merchants and customers would gather at a specified locale—Paris, Geneva, London, Reims, Bruges, Frankfort, and other central places—to buy, sell, and exchange information and ideas. The most famous of these, held in Champagne to the southeast of Paris each January, lasted six weeks and attracted merchants and customers from all over Europe and beyond. Other towns in the area also had fairs, carefully timed so they didn't conflict with one another, and so that merchants could move from one to the other over a period of several months.

The management of the fairs would be quite familiar to those who organize conventions today. The merchants would gather prior to the opening to pay the required fees and set up their stalls. Then business would commence with the sale of cloth, textiles, leather, fur, and the like. Spices, dyes, and other smaller goods would then follow. After the fairs ended, those involved would have two or three weeks to settle accounts.

The local noble who organized the fair would dispatch his knights to the fairgrounds to help police the transactions and settle disputes through arbitration or mediation. If these techniques did not work, there would be recourse to commercial courts, also controlled by the noble. In the thirteenth century, Lambert of Ardres wrote of one such fair sponsored by Count Baldwin of Guise:

> The market also which in the days of his predecessors had been at Sutkerka, not for any
> special cause but because of change, he changed to Alderwicum, but following the
> advice of the Church did not change the day; where assembled and came to reside those
> living round about as for a virtuous deed, to all the people, as much merchants as other
> peoples, because of the abundance of merchandise which came there from all parts,
> ordered to be held each year in that place during the feast of the solemnity of Pentecost a
> public fair, and this decree he confirmed by oath. The villa he surrounded by a double
> ditch and rampart in the midst of which he built halls and necessary buildings, and was

fitting he built with diligence and reverence a chapel at the entrance of the first enclo-
sure, to the honor of St. Nicholas (the patron saint of merchants), where he placed a holy
man named Stephen as chaplain, with sufficient books and various ecclesiastical orna-
ments, to the glory of the town.

Potential purchasers would visit stalls tended by merchants exhibiting their wares
and enter into contracts. They also exchanged news, bandied ideas, and generally
became better informed on a wide variety of subjects besides business. After all, the
machinations of political and religious leaders, happenings abroad, and new technologies were important to merchants, bankers, and producers.

The fairs were bound by rules and regulations. At the time of the Paris fair, in honor
of St. Denis, local merchants had to close their shops and open stalls at the fairgrounds,
and for the priviledge paid a fee to the king, who used the money to defray expenses.
When the kings of France took over management of the fairs, they raised tents and
charged high sales taxes, which discouraged the wholesale merchants from attending.
Then too, as trade spread, there was less need for the fairs, and their popularity declined.

Concomitant with the popularity of fairs was the growth of town life. In towns, too,
trade was growing, but with a difference. Wholesale merchants would sell goods purchased at the fairs to retailers. In most jurisdictions, the wholesalers were forbidden to
sell at retail. Thus, in the charter of the city of London was found the following:

> And after he has entered the city, let the foreign merchant be lodged wherever it please
> him. But if he bring dyed cloth, let him see to it that he does not sell his merchandise at
> retail, but that he sell not less than a dozen pieces at a time. And if he bring pepper, or
> cumin, or ginger, or alum, or brasil wood, or resin, or incense, let him sell not less than
> fifteen pounds at a time. But if he bring cloths of silk, or wool, or linen, let him see that
> he cut them not, but sell them whole. But if he bring wax, let him sell not less than one
> *quartanum*. Also, a foreign merchant may not buy dyed cloth, nor make the dye in the
> city, nor do any work which belongs by right to the citizens. Also, no foreign merchant
> with his partner may set up any market within the city for reselling goods in the city, nor
> may he approach a citizen for making a bargain, nor may he stop longer in the city.

This charter was not unique. Nor were the terms limited to English cities. Similar limitations are to be found in the charters of virtually all of the medieval cities, meant of
course to protect local merchants, and placed in the charters at their insistence.
Nonetheless, the fact remains that the fairs and the towns were rival forms of commerce.
In time, the towns would develop shopping and business sections, some of which were
retail, others wholesale. In this respect they came to resemble permanent fairs, and were
perceived as such. In the late twelfth century, Chretien of Troyes wrote, "One might well
believe that in a city a fair is being held every day." And others noted that commerce
worked its way much more smoothly in shopping districts than at the fairs. In all of this,
a commercial nexus was becoming more important in the everyday lives of many people.
Most Europeans remained wedded to the land, as they would be until well into the nineteenth century. But beginning in the twelfth century, economic power shifted from landholding to commerce, though this would not appear evident for several centuries.

The proliferation of cathedral construction that began in the early eleventh century
and lasted for more than 300 years, was another sign of recovery, and this too enhanced
the power and prestige of the towns. In twelfth century France alone, more than 80

cathedrals, 500 abbeys, and 10,000 parish churches were built. Laborers might work on a cathedral for generations, even centuries, with the same ardor that the Egyptians displayed in constructing the pyramids, which is to say with devotion, and also out of a sense of security. They hardly would have started such long-term projects if they believed that new barbarian or Moslem conquests were imminent. It can be argued that such enterprises did not represent a part of the search for wealth and fortune, or lead Europeans to look beyond the horizon for challenges. Yet they were, and they did. These edifices might appear to the present-day secular mindset as simply the medieval counterpart of the pyramids, which is to say expensive, extravagant, and uneconomical. But they were far more than that. Towns vied with one another to erect the largest, most splendid edifice, with the finest interior and the highest spires—the height of the spire being considered a measure of a town's wealth. They were not only sources of self-respect and looked upon as part of the community's wealth, but also could be the focus of pilgrimages and thereby bring in the medieval equivalent of tourist trade.

Construction funds came from several sources. The contributions accumulated by the episcopal sees were important. A miracle occurring at or near the site often resulted in a surge of contributions. Workers often donated their labor. All involved took pride in having so magnificent an edifice to show off and in which to worship. For individuals such as these, cathedrals were a form of wealth.

While religion played an important role in the somnolent nature of economic life in the half millennium following the fall of Rome, it was also a major factor in bringing the early Middle Ages to a close. In 1070, as the European recovery quickened, the Turks seized Jerusalem. Europeans returning home from pilgrimages told stories of the desecration of holy places and persecutions. Tradition has it that one of them, Peter the Hermit, wrote a letter to Pope Urban II in 1088 detailing these horrors and asking for assistance. A corollary problem was the progressive weakening of the Byzantine Empire, which was also being threatened by the Turks. While the Roman Church and the Orthodox Church in Constantinople were not on particularly good terms, they were both Christian, and this threat from Islam bothered the Pope and other European leaders.

In 1095 the Pope issued a call for a crusade. After outlining the outrages visited upon Christians in the Middle East, he appealed to the desire for wealth harbored by his listeners, something the Church had taught was ungodly, but which persisted nonetheless. Moreover, at the end of his address the Pope indicated that those who went on the crusade not only would benefit economically but would also receive salvation:

> Let none of your possessions keep you back, nor anxiety for family affairs. For this land which you now inhabit, shut in on all sides by the sea and the mountain peaks, is too narrow for your large population; it scarcely furnishes food enough for its cultivators. Hence it is that you murder and devour one another, that you wage wars, and that many among you perish in civil strife. Let hatred, therefore, depart among you; let your quarrels end. Enter upon the road to the Holy Sepulcher; wrest that land from a wicked race, and subject it to yourselves. Jerusalem is a land fruitful above all others, a paradise of delights. That royal city, situated at the center of the earth, implores you to come to her aid. Undertake this journey eagerly for the remission of your sins, and be assured of the reward of imperishable glory in the Kingdom of Heaven.

There were eight crusades in all, the last of which ended in 1270 in a defeat for the Europeans. During the Crusades, the Italian and other Mediterranean ports engaged in a lively and highly profitable trade, and when they ended, it was through these cities that Europe imported those desired Oriental and Middle Eastern goods, paying for them in part with wealth seized and brought home from the Crusades. There was a steady flow of gold and silver back to Europe, some of which returned to Moslem lands in exchange for trade items. While the wealth seized in the Holy Land and from captured Moslem ships was sizable, still more was obtained through trade. As a result, by the mid-thirteenth century, Italian city-states were minting the first gold coins since the end of the Roman Empire.

The growing prosperity of the Italian city-states can be seen in the ways they invested their funds. Consider the growth in Mediterranean shipping. In the middle of the twelfth century, shipowners would offer their services to merchants, who in general did not invest their funds in such vessels. Toward the end of the century, merchants would band together, usually in units of four, to purchase quarter shares in ships, thereby reducing individual investments and risks. Later, as investment needs grew, so did the size of the groups, with each member having a smaller share. By the thirteenth century, the shares, called *loca*, were bought and sold like shares in companies, and there was a lively market in Genoa and Venice. *Loca* could be used as security for loans, and for a while they served as a form of currency. The practice soon faded, however, for as the merchants became still more prosperous, they desired to own ships outright, and so they did.

The Lenders

Bruges, Cahors, and Arras were thirteenth century French capital centers, described by one observer as "glutted with usurers," prepared to lend to any sound risk, even those engaged in warfare against France. Writing of the moneylenders and bankers of Cahors in 1235, an English bystander said:

> In those days the abominable plague of Cahorsians raged so fiercely that there was scarcely any man in all England, especially among the prelates, who was not entangled in their nets. The king was indebted to them for an incalculable amount. They circum-vented the indigent in their necessities, cloaking their usury under the pretense of trade.

Dante agreed, assigning the moneylenders of Cahors a special place in hell. But another medieval writer, commenting on *The Divine Comedy*, rebutted, "He who takes it [engages in usury] goes to hell; he who does not goes to the workhouse."

The rates were high, in line with the risks. Powerful rulers were the greatest risk, since they commanded armed forces and might default with impunity. Emperor Frederick II had paid 30 to 40 percent to his bankers in the thirteenth century. The rates could be lower, however, depending upon the collateral, which would be seized if the loan was not repaid. In this regard, the bankers resembled pawnbrokers. Byzantine Emperor Baldwin II borrowed a large sum from a Venetian merchant banker, Morosini, the collateral being what was purported to be Christ's crown of thorns. The loan was not repaid, whereupon France's King Louis IX redeemed the collateral. When King Ferdinand of Portugal was captured in war, his wife was able to borrow his ransom at the rate of 18 percent, indicating the collateral was quite attractive. All could be lost if a banker provided funds for a noble at war who was not the victor. Even victory could be dangerous, for monarchs found excuses to confiscate the wealth of successful bankers.

The strictures against usury, then, were honored in their breach. There was always some method of getting around them. A noble desiring funds might obtain them by trading the right to collect taxes or rents. Loans might be made at discounts, the full face amount paid on maturity. The noble might agree to make a purchase from the money-tender at a price higher than merited. Partnerships might be formed, and payouts of dividends instead of interest disguised the usury. So it went.

As has been noted, far too often — usually in popular histories and motion pictures — the Middle Ages is depicted as a period during which no important innovations appeared and progress of any kind was rare. Moreover, it has been characterized as a time of economic stagnation, during which the standard of living declined and the pursuit of wealth was subordinated to contemplation of the afterlife. As we have seen here, however, all of this has been overstated. Commerce continued, especially on the Mediterranean, and the medieval fairs were venues where business was conducted and information exchanged to a degree that exceeded that of the Roman meetings. Those who attended the fairs were concerned with the business at hand. They cannot have realized that they were creating a new form of business that would dominate, as a part of family capitalism, in centuries to come. Rather, they were improvising and adapting in a positive way. This was a period of growth, development, and adjustment to new realities. The medieval merchants and bankers, no less than their Alexandrian counterparts, were products of their age who adjusted their actions to the world in which they lived. Those who did so well often proved successful in their pursuit of wealth. The failures fell by the wayside.

The medieval merchants, bankers, and nobility in no way considered themselves inferior to their Roman predecessors. Nor did the churchmen hold this view. Merchants who purchased shares in ventures and in other ways pioneered in capitalist forms of business were opportunists, in the best sense of the term.

CHAPTER 4

The Italian Bankers and Their Clients

TALIAN cities became the major money centers for thirteenth and fourteenth century Europe. Those aforementioned family firms would remain the dominant form of business enterprise until the eighteenth century. The Pisani and Tiepoli families in Venice and the Bardi and Peruzzi in Florence were among the leaders. There were many more, however—more than a hundred families to which monarchs and businessmen could apply for loans. Their banks (from the Italian word *banco*) developed techniques and institutions that remain in force to this day. They accepted deposits and paid interest on them, made commercial as well as political loans, engaged in merchant banking activities, offered lines of credit to favored clients, and arranged letters of credit for those involved with international and national trade. Security often was required to back the loans, and so they would accept jewelry, land, and buildings—testimony to how some of the banks evolved from pawnbroking activities. From nobles they would take the right to collect taxes or commissions to conduct business in the realm. Merchants could buy and sell without transfers of coin or barter, instead drawing upon accounts at one or another Italian bank. The banks provided commercial insurance for voyages. From the Arabs, the Venetians learned bookkeeping and the Arabic numbering system, both of which rank among the basic building blocks of commercial society. All of this is not to suggest that "modern" business practice began in the late Middle Ages, but rather that the more worldly outlook of businessmen and bankers of the period was creating a new dispensation.

Banks often were organized as *societas*, in which the members contributed either labor or capital. The liabilities were unlimited, so that each member was liable personally for debts the society incurred. The benefits of this form to creditors are obvious, as are the drawbacks to the partners. Consequently, a new form came about, the *compagnia*, in which liabilities remained unlimited, but the partners' contributions were in the form of shares, with voting rights and distributions assigned by the number held. In addition, there were three forms of long-term liabilities: earnings retained in the business, additional funds contributed by partners, and investments in the form of deposits made by outsiders, each accruing interest according to earnings, generally between 5 and 10 percent.

The Results of the Crusades

The failure of the Crusades resulted in a loss of prestige and power for the papacy. Islamic states also were weakened, however, and the Byzantine Empire was destroyed. There was dislocation, to be sure, but an energizing sense of adventure emerged as well. The French monarchy was enriched; the German kingdom was enfeebled. Some knights suffered impoverishment, whereas a few reaped great wealth. In many cases, nobles had to sell land and manorial rights to townspeople who were enriched by profits from trade. Peasants, whose produce was fetching higher prices, were able to acquire sufficient earnings to pay for rights and liberties. All of this resulted in a liberation of labor and capital that provided major stimulation for capitalism, the kind that would be seen in the late twentieth century when communism imploded and market forces became predominant throughout eastern Europe.

Most important, thousands of Europeans had gone to the Holy Land, and this broadened their vistas. During the Roman Empire, Europeans had enjoyed eastern spices, such as pepper, which traded ounce for ounce with gold; many spices from southwest India; cloves that came from Indonesia; and cinnamon from what today is Sri Lanka. This commerce had ended during the early Middle Ages. Now the Crusaders rediscovered the joys of these and other condiments, along with eastern fruits, vegetables, and luxury items. From the Moslems, they learned of damasks, muslins, velvets, and satins. Of great importance was the knowledge of banking and the use of credit gained from Byzantium and the Moslems. Perhaps all of this would have occurred without the Crusades, since Europe was making progress along these lines before the First Crusade had begun. As it turned out, the Crusades seem to have accelerated the movement and quickened the pursuit of wealth, power, and status among nobles, kings, and the rising merchant and manufacturing classes.

The Venetian Way

Venice was best situated to capitalize on these new developments, and it was one of the principal beneficiaries of the Crusades. The city was surrounded by navigable waters, but was protected from attack by marshes. Looking at a map of Europe, one can see that Venice, in a significant way, stood at the center of things, while at the same time had good access to the East and to the great Christian cities. The Adriatic led southward to the Mediterranean and relatively easy reach of Africa's northern shores. And while Spain was further away, it too lay within the range of Venetian vessels. To the west, the Po and Adige rivers enabled Venice to trade with such cities as Padua, Milan, Ferrara, and Mantua. The cities of southern Germany could be reached through the passes of the eastern Alps and the western passages of Switzerland.

Venetian wealth came early. The doge Justinian Partecipazio, leader of the city when it still was considered a minor ally of Byzantium, wrote of 1200 silver pounds he invested in commercial activities. The city's merchants would buy or trade for northern European lumber, iron, naval stores, and slaves and exchange them for eastern spices, silks, and ivories. Venetians went to the Near East to learn its crafts and methods, among them Arab techniques for manufacturing glass and embroideries, which then were employed in Venice, making that city a center for the production of these two highly desirable products. In addition, salt extracted from its lagoons was sent both north and east.

Venice pioneered in creating banking techniques, making a virtue of a necessity. In the 1170s, Frederick Barbarossa, the German emperor, was trying to restore some aspects of the Roman Empire. Standing in his way were local rulers struggling to maintain their power, some of whom were organized into the Lombard League, which comprised 15 leading northern Italian cities. Venice, a founding member, at the same time was involved in a frustrating war against Byzantium. The doge financed these wars by borrowing heavily, pledging the government's revenues for the next decade. In addition, there was to be a forced loan, with each citizen assessed according to his means. The armies of the League defeated Frederick at Legano, just north of Milan, in 1176, and with this victory won complete independence.

Conditions worsened, however, for Venice. The other war went badly, and a plague struck. The doge was assassinated, and the commercial aristocracy took matters into their own hands, selecting another doge and transferring power to a new 480-member council. The new doge promptly refinanced the old loan, but in so doing instituted a change the merchants demanded. The new loans, they said, had to be transferable, since they intended to sell the paper to customers and so remove their exposure. This term was accepted, with a registrar appointed to keep track of who owned what. Before long, money changers were buying and selling loans on benches near the Rialto Bridge. Thus, elements of modern investment banking and securities markets were "invented" in twelfth and early thirteenth century Venice. All the while, Venice's wealth expanded. In political structure, Venice was coming to resemble a modern corporation more than a feudal state. The Great Council was dominated by a hereditary commercial oligarchy, as was the senate, and the doge (the executive) followed the will of this class, and usually was one of its members. What was true of Venice applied in other Italian city-states. They were governed by merchants and for merchants. If ever there was rule by those chiefly concerned with the pursuit of wealth, it was in Italy during this period.

Venice stayed neutral during the early Crusades, supplying the Moslems with iron, arms, timber, and naval stores. In addition, Venetians purchased Europeans captured by the Mongols in eastern Europe and sold them at a profit to the Moslems. They then went on to buy manufactured goods from the Moslems. Indeed, it is the view of several historians that the slave trade was Venice's largest source of revenue during the early Crusades. When the Pope forbade unauthorized commerce with the Moslems, Venetian merchants purchased letters of authorization and continued their trade.

With the announcement of the fourth Crusade, Venice abandoned its neutrality. The doge, Enrico Dandolo, assumed a leadership role, not out of a conversion of any kind, but rather to gain wealth and the assistance of the Crusaders in his military ambitions. Dandolo also had a personal score to settle. He had been partially blinded in an accident in Constantinople and wanted revenge.

The French Crusaders who arrived in Venice in 1201 asked for transport to the Holy Land for 4500 knights and horses, 9000 squires, and 20,000 foot soldiers, along with provisions for nine months. Dandolo set his price: 85,000 silver marks and half the booty taken in the expedition. In addition, the doge would provide 50 armed galleys.

Impoverished, and unable either to advance or return to their homes, the Crusaders rejected these terms, but they were obliged to consider another offer. The doge would accept as partial payment French assistance in the capture of rebels in the seaport town of Zara in Dalmatia (200 miles east of Venice), which had become part of the kingdom of Hungary. While some of the French refused to march against fellow Christians, others were willing to do so, and Zara fell.

When the nobles then insisted on being taken to Egypt, the doge demurred. The Egyptian sultan was an ally and had promised the doge an agreeable tariff in Alexandria if he would divert the Crusaders elsewhere. The doge proposed instead an attack on Constantinople, which, although Christian, was not Catholic and so might be considered an enemy of the Church. There would be much to plunder there, he noted, and afterwards the Crusaders could go on to the Holy Land.

Most of the Crusaders agreed to do so, and in 1204 they were transported to Constantinople, which they ravaged, with the Venetians obtaining more than half the booty. In addition, they received preferred trading rights, most of the Mediterranean islands that were part of Byzantium, and parts of Constantinople itself as well as posts in other cities, all of which enriched Venice's leading families. The Venetians then sold Byzantine prisoners as slaves to the Moslems. Byzantium was no more, and although it would be reconstituted, it was never again an important power in the region. At the time, however, it appeared the most wondrous of cities. Geoffrey of Villehardouin, one of the principal chroniclers of the Fourth Crusade, wrote of Constantinople:

> You should know that people who had never before set eyes on Constantinople were astounded, for never had they imagined that so rich a city could exist in the world, and as they gazed at the high walls and noble towers that ringed it around, and the splendid palaces and the towering churches—there were so many of them that one could not possibly believe it until they saw it with their own eyes—they were amazed by it, and especially by the heights and breadth of the city, which was sovereign above all other cities. You should know, too, that there was not a single man among us whose flesh did not tremble at the sight of it. It was no wonder, for never was so great an enterprise undertaken by any people since the creation of the world.

Much of the wealth of Constantinople was taken to the West and still can be seen in such places as Venice. Along with the obvious wealth—precious metals, artwork, tapestries, and the like—the invaders took a large number of relics, such as that aforementioned crown of thorns. These might be seen as wealth-producing items, since they attracted pilgrims, donations, and other forms of income. Indeed, after the influx of all of these relics, counterfeiters appeared with their own versions, obliging the papacy to start certifying them.

The Venetians were willing to act recklessly in their pursuit of wealth. In 1241, the Mongols, with an empire larger than continental Europe, defeated the Poles and Germans in the battle of Liegnitz, in part as a result of intelligence obtained from Venice, in return for which the Mongols agreed to oust the competing Genoese trading center in the Crimea.

Venice became the leading naval power of the time and grew into an imperial force during the early thirteenth century, seizing the Sporades Islands off the coast of Crete as well as cities on the Black Sea. Genoa was defeated in a struggle for supremacy in the Black Sea and the Levantine trade, but continued to control commerce on the Tyrrhenia Sea. Venetian merchants traded grain, lumber, and wine with their counterparts in Constantinople, receiving manufactured goods, which they subsequently sold to areas north of the city. Genoa did not go into decline as a result of the defeats. In 1293, its Mediterranean commerce was three times that of France, whose kings, along with those of other countries, sent their emissaries to Italy for loans. In fact, most of the Italian city-states prospered in this period of reviving commerce.

In the late thirteenth and early fourteenth centuries, Venetian naval architects developed new designs for merchant galleys. They were more than 120 feet in length, with crews of between 100 and 200 to provide the muscle power, and sails for use when the winds were right. Ships such as these enabled the Venetians to trade with England and Flanders, and even with the Scandinavians. To these places they would take spices, cloth, drapery, paper, and glass obtained from as far east as China and India, and then load for the return trip with wool, hides, leather, iron, lead, tin, pewter, and other products, some of which were obtained at the fairs.

A good deal of the trade was indirect. An Indochinese or Malaysian merchant might travel to China and make a purchase of silk, which he would bring home and sell to an Indian merchant, who might then use it in trade with an Egyptian merchant. That same silk, sold in Alexandria, might attract a Venetian merchant, who would then bring it home for further resale.

Some of the transactions were quite impressive and involved violence. In 1319, Nicoleta Basadona, who served a Venetian merchant as his agent, arrived in London to sell 10,000 pounds of sugar and 1000 pounds of sweets. He invested the money he received in wool, and then sailed for Flanders. Basadona either died or was murdered, and the crew sold the wool. Three years later, the crews of five Venetian galleys docked at Southampton and battled with some of the city's natives, resulting in deaths and property destruction. The following year, two Venetian ships were ravaged by the Southamptonites. These Venetian excursions did not elicit any objections from King Edward III, who had close ties with the Venetians and in any case did not want to forgo the taxes he was charging them, which constituted an important part of his income.

Naval power, shrewd investments, and capable political leaders enabled the Venetian Republic to remain independent until the arrival of Napoleon in Italy in the late eighteenth century. If there were superpowers in the Mediterranean world of the fourteenth century, certainly one of them was Venice.

Florence

Florence was one of the leading challengers of Venetian commercial supremacy. That Florence would rise to such eminence is somewhat surprising. It is landlocked and located a distance from major land routes as well. The Florentine landscape is rocky, unsuited to most farming and lacking in mineral wealth and forests. While Florence is located on the Arno River, that waterway is not navigable all the way to the Tyrrhenian

Sea, and in any case could not be used without the sufferance of Pisa and Lucca. But in 1406, Florence conquered Pisa and its port, Porto Pisano, and in this way gained access to the sea. By then, however, Florentine banking had become so important that commerce played only a secondary role in the city's fortunes.

Florence's major asset was its cloth industry, but since the wool in the area was second rate, the prices obtained for the product were low. Therefore, Florentine merchants purchased wool in northern markets, and by the 1330s the city had become an important source of cloth. The profits from cloth were used by manufacturers to enter into pawnbroking, moneylending, and eventually banking and other activities. Giovanni Villani, a visitor to Florence in 1336, described the scope of the cloth industry at that time:

> The workshops of the Arte della Lana (the gild of wool merchants) were 200 or more, and they made from 70,000 to 80,000 pieces of cloth, which were worth more than 1,200,000 gold florins. A good third of this sum remained in the land as the reward of labor, without counting the profit of the entrepreneurs. And more than 30,000 people lived by it. To be sure, we find that some 30 years earlier, there were 300 workshops or thereabouts, and they made more than 100,000 pieces of cloth yearly, but these cloths were coarser and one-half less valuable, because at that time English wool was not imported and they did not know, as they did later, how to work it.

Several families dominated the wool business. One of these, the Alberti, left fairly extensive records that indicate how they operated and became wealthy. The family arrived in Florence in the late thirteenth century from Catenaia, some 50 miles to the south, and soon were involved in the wool business. Three brothers, Alberto, Neri, and Lapo, started the firm, which began by purchasing wool wholesale at the Champagne fair. They then brought the wool to Florence to be dyed at an establishement managed by Lapo. The dyestuffs were purchased from merchants who obtained them from the east. An account book dated 1307 documents the shipment of 466 bolts of cloth, a sizable amount for the period, and an indication that the Alberti were doing well. A partnership contract from the following year provided for the partners to invest all of their funds in the company and receive a minimum dividend of 8 percent. There were minimum contributions, but the partners could add to this and receive the same return on the supplementary funds. At that time, the company had agents in Venice, Naples, Barletta, and Milan, and by 1348, there were offices in London, Majorca, Constantinople, and Flanders as well. By then the company had moved into spices, dyes, and banking.

During the first half of the fourteenth century, three powerful Florentine family companies, the Bardi, Peruzzi, and the Acciaiuoli, emerged to straddle the financial life of Europe. Giovanni Villani, one of the Peruzzi partners, called them "the pillars of Christian trade." These were large, complex organizations. Beginning in commerce, they extended into banking, shipping, insurance, manufacturing, land speculation, farming—literally any occupation that promised wealth. The Florentine banks bore a resemblance to modern conglomerates. Each had its own unique structure, but all were comprised of a series of satellite companies, control of which was in the hands of the senior partners, all family members.

The original formulation of the Peruzzi operation appeared in 1292, although there had been family activities prior to then. By 1335, the Peruzzis had evolved into the conglomerate form, with many partners. Those resident in Florence could vote on company affairs, but there were so many that, in practice, the chairman was absolute. It was to him that the banking, trading, manufacturing, and other domestic operations, each headed by a family member, reported directly. The foreign branches were controlled differently. Some were headed by partners, specifically those located in Naples, Sicily, Avignon, England, Bruges, and Paris. Others were directed by agents, and they were the businesses in Barletta, Cyprus, Rhodes, Sardinia, Tunis, Majorca, Venice, and Pisa.

The Peruzzi holdings were in the form of a joint stock company. Originally, family members owned most of the shares, although by 1335 outsiders held a majority. Dividends were paid annually according to the number of shares owned. The Bardis had a similar structure, but managed to retain a majority of shares for family members.

The Bardis' successful pursuit of wealth began in 1294, when they lent funds obtained through trade to the king of Naples to finance his wars. In return, the family was awarded control of the exports of grain, fruit, and dairy products from southern Italy and of the grain trade of Provence. By 1303, the Bardis were lending funds to the papacy, for which they were given commissions to collect Pope Peter's pence in England. The family used earnings from the collections to purchase raw wool, which was sent to Florence to be manufactured into cloth at their factory. By then, the 13 partners were scattered over northern Europe, each managing affairs from a different city.

Both families came to grief through the default of a major borrower. During the Hundred Years' War, France and England engaged in heavy borrowing to finance operations, since pillage and ransom would come only after the battle had begun. The English had paid for the early stages of the war through loans from the Bardi and Peruzzi banks, secured by anticipated revenues from taxes on wool. Bardi, perhaps to hedge its bets, also lent funds to the French. When the loans—600,000 Florentine florins from the Peruzzi and 900,000 from the Bardi—could not be repaid, both were in trouble. To complicate matters, in 1341 war broke out between Pisa and Florence, which ate further into bank reserves, and the King of Naples repudiated a large debt owed both banks. As a result, the Peruzzi failed in 1343, and the Bardi the following year. One of the more interesting lessons of the period was that loans to well-regarded private parties were more secure than those to monarchs. Bankers might seize collateral if the private party reneged. Doing so from monarchs who had armed forces at their disposal was another matter.

In time, parts of the loans were repaid, for deadbeats could not hope for further loans unless this was done. Until this was accomplished, the monarchs were obliged to borrow from bankers in their own lands, often with threats and promises that might more easily be acted upon.

One of these was Tiedemann of Limburg, a town in what now is the Netherlands. Tiedemann, however, was a banker who conducted extensive business operations in London. He arrived in London in 1346 and joined others among his countrymen who made their fortunes in trade and then went into moneylending to nobles, merchants, and even the Crown. In return for grants made to King Edward III, he received tax farming concessions and rights to the operation of the royal tin mines. Tiedemann was one of the many merchants and bankers who lent funds to King Edward III to help carry on the Hundred Years' War. He left London under unknown circumstances in 1360, relocated in Cologne, and there became a wine merchant, importing wine from the south. He also reentered banking, acting as a go-between for the Pope and bankers in Bruges. Tiedemann died in 1386, and in his will made large bequests to Limburg and Cologne.

Another merchant who operated from London while Tiedemann was there was Nicholas Bartholomew of Lucca, who imported silks and other luxury items into the city, sold them, and then used the funds to purchase raw wool for export. He, too, entered moneylending and was one of the small army of creditors accumulated by Edward III. Sir John Pultney counted himself in that company. The mayor of London from 1331 to 1337—a reward for making the loan—Pultney was permitted to export wool during a wartime embargo without paying duties.

Richard Whittington, who was mayor of London three times and the hero of the fairy tale *Dick Whittington and His Cat*, married Alice, the daughter of Sir Ivo Fitzwaryn, a wealthy Dorset knight. He used his gentry connections in his business affairs. Making large loans to Kings Henry IV and Henry V helped his career, as did the alleged banquet he threw for Henry V, at which he is said to have burned 60,000 pounds worth of the royal debt he owned. For this, he was employed by Henry to manage the construction of Westminster Abbey. However, the story about burning the debt may be a fabrication.

The Venice of the North

While merchants and mariners in southern Europe—the Italian city-states in particular—were profiting from the Crusades, their counterparts in northern Europe also were reviving trade and flourishing. By the late tenth century, nobles in Flanders had repelled the Vikings and reestablished order. Long a center of cloth production, the Flemish manufactories traded their products with Scandinavians for furs and other products. The merchants would bring their cloth to areas where sheep were being raised and trade for raw wool, which would be turned into more cloth in Flanders, and then the process would be repeated. The Flemish trade area ran from England to Germany, where water transport was possible. They did not reach Italy, though, since land transport remained quite poor, and parts of the western Mediterranean were still controlled by the Moslems.

Another commercial revival took place in northern Europe, centered around the Baltic Sea. In the middle of the twelfth century, German merchants established outposts on the Swedish island of Gotland, and in London in an area known as "the Steelyard." They led the way in rekindling trade in the towns along the Rhine River, such as Dortmund and Munster, while also expanding along the south Baltic coast. In the thirteenth century, the rising cities of Lubeck and Hamburg allied themselves to protect northern roads and the Baltic trade routes, and from this evolved what later came to be known as the Hanseatic League, which included Luneberg, Wismar, Rostock, Stralsund, and other towns concerned with commerce. The earliest membership list appeared in 1360, at which time there were 52 members.

The Hansa towns actively traded raw materials, such as timber, pitch, iron, and copper, as well as livestock, salted fish, leather, wool, grain, beer, and the like; and they prospered, with Lubeck coming to be known as "the Venice of the North." They traded in an area bounded by Russia to the east, England to the west, and Scandinavia to the north, setting up "factories," or branch offices, where trade was the most active. From the factories they would sally forth with their mercenaries and oblige providers of raw materials to accept their prices. When the Hansa towns attempted to spread their influence to the south, they were blocked by yet another commercial alliance, the Rhenish League, formed in 1254 by Cologne, Mainz, Speyer, Worms, Strasbourg, and Basel. Still further south, Augsburg, Ulm, and Nuremberg handled the trade coming north from Italy.

Thus, merchants led the way to European economic revival, and were the up and coming class on the continent. There were Hanseatic factories in the Italian city-states. Lubeck, in particular, did a lively business in carved wooden rosary beads, the first European manufactured product to be standardized. Through the "putting out" system, families would concentrate on their production of these beads, with even a measure of specialization of labor.

The Hanseatic League would engage in military action if its members considered it desirable. The first unified assault came in 1367, when the members attacked Denmark, captured Copenhagen, and forced King Waldemar IV to accept the Treaty of Stralsund three years later. By then, he had relinquished to the League four castles in Scania, which dominated the maritime approaches to Copenhagen, two-thirds of Scanian revenues for 15 years, and the right to veto the succession to the Danish throne. The treaty marked the apogee of Hanseatic power. Thereafter, the rise of Burgundy and the Netherlands, together with growing opposition to its strength from England, Scandinavia, and Russia, caused the League to decline. The lack of a cohesive internal structure also hurt, and although the League continued on until 1669, it no longer possessed a shadow of its fourteenth century power.

It might be useful at this point to sum up the larger trading picture in the Mediterranean in the fourteenth and fifteenth centuries. The major profits came from carrying large quantities of fairly mundane products or small quantities of high-priced items. The merchants went to the Orient or traded with Constantinople. Merchants who concentrated on the former did quite well for themselves. Chinese and Persian silks were prized items in Europe. Indian cotton cloth was more expensive than wool. Emeralds from India, Burmese rubies, and Ceylonese sapphires were all highly valued. In a fourteenth century merchant's handbook were listed 288 different kinds of spices, but this included such items as glue, gums, waxes, and several different varieties of sugar, which in this period sold in small quantities at high prices, and almost all of which came from Crete and Cyprus. Pepper was the most popular spice, much of which came from India. Cinnamon came from Ceylon, nutmegs from the Banda Islands off the southern coast of New Guinea, while cloves were obtained from the Moluccas, also near New Guinea, to the west. Except for products from the Americas, European merchants had created a global economy by the fifteenth century.

Most Mediterranean commerce, however, was of the "staple" variety, with grain the most important cargo—understandable when you consider that approximately 60 million people lived in the countries and city-states that surrounded the Mediterranean, many in places where the soil's productivity was poor. The Italian cities and others on the northern littoral and along the western Mediterranean coast were never self-sufficient in grains. They imported large quantities from the Nile Valley, Syria, and other parts of the Levant. In return, they sent wine and olive oil to the south, and in addition, Venice was a major supplier of salt. There was fishing throughout the region, but strikingly, the Mediterranean could not meet the demands for salted fish. Italian, Spanish, and especially Portuguese fishermen went into the Atlantic, bringing in hauls from as far away as the banks of Newfoundland. Just as the European reach to the east for trade occurred earlier than many appreciate, so the stretch across the Atlantic before Columbus often has not been recognized. Other foodstuffs that figured in trade included cheese, raisins, nuts, and fruit.

Woolen cloth, the universal product, was shipped overland from Flanders to the northern ports and then to the southern ports. Milanese armor was prized throughout Europe. Copper, lead, and iron mined and smelted in central Europe were shipped from there to all markets.

The Bankers

All this trade was largely financed by the merchants themselves and, when larger sums were required, by the aforementioned bankers, who by the fifteenth century had become even more powerful than they were in the thirteenth and fourteenth centuries. Jacques Coeur, a Frenchman, who was born in 1395, was one of the leading bankers of the first half of the fifteenth century. The son of a Bruges merchant in the cloth trade, Coeur began his career on a mission to the Levant in 1427, where he sold cloth, used the proceeds to purchase luxury goods to bring home for sale, and more important, established contacts with other merchants and bankers in the area. He earned a fortune by trading with the port cities of the eastern Mediterranean, taking a great deal of business from the Italian merchants.

Coeur started making loans to local rulers, and in 1436 was asked by French King Charles II to become master of the royal mint and was given the task of creating a new national currency. Coeur rose rapidly in the government, but always his eye was on the Mediterranean trade. He won major concessions for the French in this regard, and in 1440, he became the paymaster of the royal household. For the rest of his career Coeur combined commerce, banking, and politics. He had warehouses and agents in Tours, Marseilles, Paris, and other French cities, and he curried favor with the Vatican. In 1446, the Pope gave him permission to trade with the Saracens, and in the process, he won special concessions in Turkey for the French. At the same time, he gained permission to work silver, copper, and lead mines near Lyons. Coeur provided the funds that enabled Charles to fight his wars, and it was his wealth that enabled the French to expel the English from Normandy.

Coeur was now one of the wealthiest and most powerful men in France. It was said that there was no business transaction in France that excluded him from a share. In 1450, however, his enemies asserted that he had poisoned the King's mistress, had sent Christians as slaves to the Turks, and kidnapped free men for service in his galleys. The King ordered his arrest and the seizure of his fortune. Coeur was obliged to repent, to do public penance, and pay an enormous fine. In 1455, he managed to escape and go to Rome, where he was embraced by Pope Nicholas V, who was attempting to organize an expedition against the Turks and needed his help. Coeur obliged.

Meanwhile, the rise of indigenous bankers and merchants that followed the failures of the Bardi and Peruzzi banks in Florence did not mean that city was finished as a financial center. The greatest of the Florentine banks, the Medici, made its appearance in the late fourteenth and early fifteenth centuries, when Giovanni de Medici made his fortune in commerce and then originated the bank. Giovanni retired in 1420 and died in 1429, and leadership of the family business fell to Cosimo, whose inheritance included silk and woolen factories, farms, and trading outposts that ranged from Scotland to Syria, as well as the largest bank in Florence.

Learning from the mistakes of the Bardi and Peruzzi, the Medici prohibited branch managers from lending to princes and obliged them to concentrate on commercial transactions. Each bank was organized as a separate entity so that the failure of one would not affect the others. They would start new enterprises as limited partnerships, meaning that only the original capital was at risk. If all proceeded according to plan, the Medici would invite outside investors into the project. The Medici placed more reliance on junior partners than on agents, and tended to prefer local partners who would contribute services and expertise, while the family provided the needed capital. Cosimo managed all of this because he seemed to possess an extraordinary ability to locate precisely the right individuals for tasks he wanted done.

Cosimo became the dominant force in Florentine politics and a member of the *Dieci*, a war council of 10 members, but he usually acted behind the scenes. With all of this, Cosimo was a favorite banker for the papacy and an important patron of the arts during the Renaissance—but not for long. In 1433, he was arrested and banished to Venice, perhaps because he was planning a coup. In any case, he seemed to have been aware of the situation ahead of time, and liquidated some of his holdings to take into exile. However, he was recalled the following year, whereupon he took virtual control of the government. He banished those who opposed him and taxed other enemies until they collapsed financially. So great was his power that, in addition to being the wealthiest man of his period, he was the most influential individual in all of Italy, not just Florence.

Cosimo died in 1464 and was succeeded as head of the family business by his only surviving son, Piero, who himself died five years later. Then two of Cosimo's nephews, Lorenzo the Magnificent and Giuliano, took over. More concerned with church affairs, politics, and art than commerce, they entrusted the business to Francesco Sasseti, who was not a strong or sophisticated individual. The bank declined. France invaded Italy in 1494, and on November 17th, King Charles VIII entered Florence. He confiscated all Medici property. Virtually bankrupt, the bank was shuttered. The family businesses survived, however, and the Medici remained a significant force in politics and the Church into the eighteenth century.

The End of the Era

Despite all these developments, the fourteenth century was a period of turmoil during which many of the economic and financial gains of the thirteenth century evaporated. This was the time of the Hundred Years' War between France and England, among many other, smaller conflicts. The Black Death (the bubonic plague) appeared in Sicily in 1347, and then spread northward. It took more than a third of Europe's population in less than five years, and would recur sporadically thereafter, leading to labor shortages. Inflation, which accelerated in the thirteenth century, rose even more in the fourteenth century, driving up prices and causing distress among consumers. Even the climate conspired against the continent. Abnormally heavy rains hurt crops and caused grain prices to rise even more sharply in poor harvest years. At one point, as a result of two consecutive bad crop years, the price of grain in England shot up 800 percent. The so-called "little ice age," which lasted until the eighteenth century, caused the Baltic to freeze over and wiped out agriculture and settlements in northern Europe and Greenland.

The Church became factionalized and in 1305 moved to Avignon in what is today southern France (the so-called "Babylonian Captivity"). Corruption in the Church during this period reached scandalous levels, helping prepare the way for the Protestant Reformation. At Avignon, the pursuit of wealth was stronger than it had been in the Mediterranean during the previous century. The popes of this period sold offices, indulgences, remission of sin—anything that would bring in funds for the papal entourage. "I am living in the Babylon of the West," wrote Petrarch in the 1340s, when high church officials, seated in ornate rooms in splendid palaces, were served meals on gold plates. They rode on horses "decked in gold, fed on gold, soon to be shod in gold if the Lord does not check this slavish luxury." In 1378, conditions worsened when a disputed election resulted in the creation of two popes, one in Avignon and the other residing in Rome. This situation lasted until 1417, during which period the prestige of the papacy fell to a new low.

The fourteenth century also saw growing political power for the middle class. Rulers would ask their legislatures—relatively new to the scene but growing in power—to provide funds, usually through taxes, and the legislatures frequently responded by demanding more rights. In 1344, for example, King Edward III asked the English Parliament for funds. The response was legislation requiring landholders to serve in the army or provide substitutes or funds based on their wealth. But there was also insistence that the King grant Parliament further rights. In France, the Estates General provided funds on condition that it be given new powers. Thus, wars often prompted the granting of additional rights to the emerging middle class.

Three elements combined to empower the middle class: the revival of commerce, in which they participated; the reappearance of a money economy, which greatly lowered transaction costs; and the growth of urban centers, where merchants and artisans could specialize in their trades and crafts, engage in commerce, and purchase their food, clothing, and shelter with profits and earnings. As has been observed, the growth of towns made the fairs redundant. These "artificial towns" declined and then disappeared as permanent towns became ever more important. Artisans had existed throughout the Middle Ages, but most worked for their lords, to whom they had an obligation. We have seen how some of them were able to purchase their freedom, whereas others simply abandoned their posts, fled to the towns, and attempted to set themselves up as independent contractors. At first, the nobles were wary of such developments, but by the eleventh century, as they became aware of the possibility of taxing them, they actually tried to attract artisans to their towns.

Town charters spelled out the rights and obligations of the townspeople, such as taxes, rents, and other charges, as well as the limits of their freedom. Many charters permitted artisans to organize guilds, the precursors of craft unions. The guilds had specified rules, regulations, and rights—and leaders to enforce them. The guilds often achieved their status through grants from rulers, who would receive payment for the privilege. Imports into the town had to be sold to guild members or else bear a heavy tariff. Guilds provided protections and benefits for their members. How one progressed from apprentice to journeyman to master was determined by the guilds, which also ran schools to train the sons of members. Guilds also secured monopolies of their town's business.

Initially, many guilds had as members both merchants and artisans, but over time the differences in their interests caused them to separate. For example, merchants who imported goods wanted to sell them for high prices, while artisans, who were also consumers, favored lower prices. Thus, merchant and artisan guilds often were in conflict, especially since the merchants usually were town officials working hand in glove with the lords and the artisans were their subjects. More important, however, was what they had in common. Merchants and artisans literally were bourgeoisie (the very word means "men of the towns"), which were capitalistic outposts in the feudalistic world. Below them were the unskilled workers and above them, in theory at least, were the nobles, princes, and monarchs.

Unskilled workers had little hope of rising in a society in which wealthy merchants and united craft guilds (which barred them from entry) were gaining power. Some of the guilds were closed affairs, in which only relatives of members could hope to gain admission. Others, the less desirable trades, were more open. One of these was the barbers' guild in Marseilles and the outlying district of Sestri, in which the term of indenture was only two years, quite short by the standards of the time, which usually required from four to seven years. One of the apprenticeship contracts read:

> April the thirteen, in the year of the Lord 1248, I, William, barber of Sestri, in good faith and without equivocation, place myself in your service and engage myself to work for you, Armand the barber, making my home with you, for learning the art of craft of barbering for a period of two years, at the salary or wage of forty solidi in the money now current in Marseilles, promising to be faithful to you in all things, not to rob you, or take anything away from you, and not to leave you for a greater or less wage for any reason whatsoever, and to give you in good faith whatever money I am able to take, to tell you the truth, and to bear faith with you in all that I do. I also promise to reimburse you for all expenses you incur in my behalf; and I promise to do all the things by agreement, and under pledge of one hundred solidi in royal crowns, the pledge being forfeited when the agreement is broken. For greater security I swear upon the Holy Gospels, touching them with my hand. And I pledge all my goods, etc., and renounce the benefit of all laws, etc.

The barber's pledge or contract was much shorter.

> And I, the said Armand, admit all the foregoing, and promise by this agreement to give to you, the said William, forty solidi every year as your wage, and to provide for you, in sickness or in health, food and clothing for two complete years. Pledging all my goods, etc., and renouncing the benefit of all laws, etc.

The nobles were able to tax both of the rising classes, but their powers were waning. Increased commerce and the removal of barriers to trade enhanced the powers of the monarchs. While some nobles, such as the Count of Flanders, who drew large revenues from the fairs were wealthy, the decline of the fairs and the inability of the nobles to band together—on the continent, if not in England—caused their powers to diminish. This was a lengthy and uneven process, taking different courses in the different countries, and in some areas, most notably Italy, consolidation did not occur until much later than the rest of the continent. Moreover, none of this takes into account the powers of the Church, which remained a strong if somewhat diminished element in late medieval society.

It has been said that during the Middle Ages, life was a contemplation of the hereafter. While this is an exaggeration, it certainly contains more than a little truth. By the twelfth century, this situation had already changed markedly. Materialism was no longer frowned upon. Even the Church had to come to terms with it. In the past it had condemned usury; now it only censured those who charged unfair interest.

This century and the one that followed often have been designated the "High Middle Ages," a period in which the revival in commerce was making for a more worldly and less contemplative Europe. By the fourteenth century, inventions such as the compass prepared the way for oceanic navigation. The spinning wheel and the treadle loom made cloth production cheaper. Universities sprouted in all corners of the continent— at Oxford and Cambridge in England, Bologna and Padua in Italy, Salamanca and Valladolid in Spain, and Paris and Toulouse in France. Merchants entered the Red Sea route and the Persian Gulf, moved on to the Arabian Sea, and from there sailed to Indian and Chinese ports. Venturesome Italians and Jews traversed the Black Sea, and from Trepezond and Caffa on the Crimea traveled by caravan south to Delhi and east to Peking—a trip that could take a year to complete, was now deemed reasonably safe. Europe learned of the wealth of the region from travelers. John of Plano Carpini and William of Rubruquis visited China in the mid-thirteenth century and wrote of what they found there. Marco Polo, the scion of a Venetian trading family, went to China afterwards and served Kublai Khan as an official between 1275 and 1292. His book, *A Description of the World*, was published and translated into several European languages, and it also told of the wealth of China:

> The inhabitants of the city [Hangchow] are idolaters, and they use paper money as currency. The men as well as the women have fair complexions, and are handsome. The greater part of them are always clothed in silk, in consequence of the vast quantity of that material produced in the territory of Kij-sai, exclusive of that the merchants import from other provinces. Amongst the handicraft trades exercised in the place, there are twelve considered to be superior to the rest, as being more generally useful; for each of which there are a thousand workshops, and each shop furnished employment for ten, fifteen, or twenty workmen, and in a few instances as many as forty, under their respective masters.

The book was a sensation, but Europe's merchants knew of what Polo had written long before it became widely available. By then, the search for new avenues to the East was intensifying, and for reasons that would be understandable today: new forces in the area threatened to cut off existing routes.

Merchants have always searched for new sources of supply and new markets, and of course the two go together. In our time, this often takes the form of a quest for items to be acquired at low prices in one market and then taken to another where higher prices and willing customers are waiting. Prescient merchants know that the best places to obtain goods are those where the natives are not aware of their value to others and will sell them for the proverbial song. In like fashion, the best markets are in locales where the natives are wealthy, have strong demands which are not being met, and are prepared to pay high prices for what they want.

What it comes down to is that the successful merchant is the one who possesses the ability to fill the needs of wealthy customers whose demands for his goods or services are highly inelastic. The voyages of Marco Polo and others to the East, and their writings, helped stimulate demand, which in this case meant the search for other pathways to the East. And if merchants were blocked from one route, they would seek another. In this way, what is often called the "Age of Exploration" was initiated.

This age was not predicated upon love of adventure, curiosity about geography, science, or even the desire of rulers for new lands to dominate. Rather, it was founded on the pursuit of wealth—by merchants, rulers, and the two groups in league with each other.

CHAPTER 5

The Atlantic Age

HE opening of the Americas to western civilization is one of the most important benchmarks in human history, and certainly had major consequences for humankind's pursuit of wealth. In this regard, it had a greater impact than even the creation of Hellenistic Civilization. As has been seen, Alexander the Great's efforts brought the wealth and knowledge of the East to the Mediterranean world. Commercial contacts with the East predated Alexander, however, whereas such was not the case with the Americas before 1492. More wealth in the form of gold and silver was extracted from Central and South America in the sixteenth and seventeenth centuries than from Asia in the previous millennium. In addition, the period of discovery united the destinies of the Americas, Europe, Asia, and Africa as nothing else had since the dawn of history. The explorations, settlements, and related developments provided an impetus to wealth creation that continues to this day.

Before turning to an account of just how this happened, it is necessary to consider, if only briefly, a series of events that did *not* happen. In the period of discovery, the Chinese had the most advanced civilization in the world, as well as ships that were more seaworthy than those used by the Iberians and other Europeans. Admiral Cheng Ho went on journeys to Arabia and East Africa that were longer than those undertaken by Columbus and other Europeans of his time. Why did he and others not consider a voyage to the east, to the western coast of North and South America? They simply were not interested in such matters. As will be seen, the Europeans *were* interested.

The pursuit of wealth was the motivating force in the discovery and subsequent exploration of the Americas. Whereas in the 1960s, advocates of space exploration compared their proposed efforts to the discovery of the "New World," nothing could be farther from the case. During the debate on space, there was little mention of the economic benefits that might be realized. Indeed, one problem was that would-be explorers had to justify the enormous costs of their projects. Perhaps there would be military and technological payoffs, but nothing economic, at least not for the foreseeable future. If there are to be economic rewards from space exploration and settlement, these will not come from the desire to explore the cosmos but rather in the form of products developed for the mission that can be applied to general uses, such as electronic miniaturization and fuel cells. The larger benefits will not likely become evident for many generations, and when they do, they could take forms those living at the end of the twentieth century can hardly imagine.

Such matters did not interest those considering voyages to unknown areas (and known ones as well) during the fifteenth and sixteenth centuries. They were not primarily concerned with pure knowledge and the joy of discovery. Christopher Columbus and those who set the stage for his celebrated 1492 voyage and the many more who followed wanted to enrich themselves. Support from monarchs and others who bankrolled them was seen as an investment, not a contribution to the greater glory of God or the human race. Were the latter the major considerations, those voyages would not likely have been made.

The Drive to the East, the Way to the West

One reason for the search for new routes was the desire of western Europeans to expand their commerce, but there were other factors as well. The Netherlands, France, England and the Iberian nations, Portugal and Spain, hoped to enjoy the kinds of profits reaped by the Italian city-states, the Moslem and Jewish traders, and others who dominated the Mediterranean. Capital had accumulated, banking techniques were evolving, and it had become possible to raise substantial sums for profitable ventures and loans. During the early Middle Ages, monarchs concentrated on the division of wealth. By the fourteenth century, they were more concerned with its creation.

Finally, in Asia, powerful states appeared that threatened existing routes. The Ottoman Turks took Constantinople in 1453. This had been expected for several decades and so did not shock Christian Europeans, but the emergence of the Ottoman Empire that displaced the Byzantine was more consequential. Not only was that empire the new dominant force in the eastern Mediterranean, but it was more powerful militarily than any European nation or any possible combination of them. The Turks were willing to permit the Mediterranean trade to continue and did not challenge the Venetian monopoly, but they blocked other expansion and trade eastward.

Meanwhile, there were stirrings in the Atlantic that were barely noticed in the face of all these changes. They occurred at a time when the European habit was to look to the east for opportunities, and the Europeans continued doing so in the fifteenth century, despite some isolated precedents that had come earlier. Around 1270, Genoese sailors entered the Atlantic and reached the Canary Islands. In 1291 Ugolino and Vadino Vivaldi, two Genoese merchants, loaded two galleys with trade goods and sailed west through the Straits of Gibraltar and kept going into the Atlantic, hoping to discover a new route to the Orient. They never returned. We know little of their plans, but given the times and the knowledge of the world they would have had, it can be assumed they hoped to go south and seek another route to the Indies.

In this period, merchants would send their ships to eastern Mediterranean ports and from there organize caravans to travel across Asia Minor, eventually discharging their cargoes in Chinese and Indian towns. The overland routes were costly, but the rewards were great. Imported saffron sold for more than 3000 marks a ton, ginger 500 marks. Pepper, a leading trade commodity, was sold for more than 300 marks. By way of contrast, such necessities as rye, wheat, and barley, all of which were homegrown, sold for less than 4 marks a ton, while salt fetched 6 marks. European merchants would send out a dozen or more expeditions, and if even one returned with a full cargo, they would realize large profits. So they did: the Italians, the Moslems, the French, and the Aragonese who sent their vessels from Barcelona and the Balearic Islands—all went searching for new routes to lands where spices and finery were inexpensive.

The Portuguese Pioneers

Portugal, in the western corner of the continent, was not well situated to engage in Mediterranean commerce. It had become an independent country in 1385, ruled by the House of Avis. In 1386, King John I married Philippa, the daughter of the English noble, John of Gaunt, and the two countries signed the Treaty of Windsor, which began a long-standing relationship between them. The key figure in Portugal in this period was not the monarch, but a prince, namely Henry (the Navigator), John's third son, who was more interested in religion, knowledge, and business than politics. Like most educated people of the time, Henry had heard stories about Prester John, a legendary Christian king who supposedly ruled a wealthy empire in the area of present-day Ethiopia. Contact with Prester John could lead explorers to abundant wealth and enable Portugal to open a second front in the crusade against the Moslems.

Henry was one of the leaders of an expedition in 1415 that seized Cueta, a Moorish city on the north African coast, and he remained there as its governor, supervising trade and realizing immediate benefits for Portuguese fishermen, who now had the Mauritanian waters to exploit. Henry came into contact with merchants and others engaged in the Mediterranean commerce with the East and became intrigued with the idea of discovering a new route to the Orient by sailing south and then east. He also took note of the large quantities of gold in the region. Where had it come from? Henry and his compatriots learned of the hoards of gold in west Africa, and that Moroccan merchants had taken their wares there to exchange them for the precious metal. One of Henry's captains, Fernao Gomes, wrote in the accounts of his voyages of 1444 and 1463 that Henry wanted to locate those countries "in order to trade with them and so maintain the gentlemen of his household."

Henry encouraged merchants to sail southward. The going was slow because he had difficulties convincing them such voyages would be profitable, and he lacked funds to finance his own expeditions. He proceeded nevertheless. Portuguese ships reached the island of Porto Santo in 1418, and in 1434, Gil Eanes sailed past Cape Bojador. Eanes found nothing commercially valuable and no gold, so he returned home. In 1441, an expedition headed by Antam Gonsalves and Nuno Trista also failed to discover trade items or gold, but they did encounter the Africans in the area, and took 10 of them back to Portugal. The captives told the captains that if they were returned home, rewards would be forthcoming. Gonsalves shipped them back to Africa and was given in exchange "10 blacks, male and female, from various countries, and various goods, including a little gold dust." Several of the Africans were sent to Pope Eugene IV as a gift. The rest were sold in Lisbon, where they fetched high prices. Prince Henry asked Eugene to bless a campaign against the natives, and in the spirit of the Crusades, the Pope granted "to all those who shall be engaged in the said war, complete forgiveness."

Portugal and the Slave Trade

As we have seen, slavery was present from the dawn of history, and during the Middle Ages there was a thriving trade in slaves, most of them white individuals captured during war and invasions. Such slaves were important articles of commerce for the Italian city-states in their trade with North Africa in the Middle Ages and afterwards. Ironically, in a fit of pique, Pope Clement V excommunicated all of Venice in the early fourteenth century and authorized the enslavement of its citizens.

Of course, the slaves of this period had a different status than those of the nineteenth century United States. For one thing, they could be hired out for wages, part of which they might keep and use to purchase their freedom, and they did retain certain rights of freemen. In some cases, they were permitted to marry free people, and this would result in their liberation.

The modern slave trade did not begin with a rush to Africa's west coast. When the Portuguese established colonies, they first tried to induce their own citizens to settle there, and then nationals of other European countries. Since not many Europeans volunteered, they imported Africans.

In 1482, the Portuguese erected the fortress of Sao Jorge de Mina, better known as Elmina Castle in present-day Ghana, which served to defend the area's trade in gold, slaves, and pepper, for which the Portuguese paid with exports of cloth and hardware. Pepper was the most important product from the area in this period, but this created a problem. The Portuguese controlled the pepper trade from India, and so to protect this, export of the condiment from Elmina was prohibited, whereupon slaves became more important. From 1458 to 1460, between 700 and 800 Africans were exported from Africa to Europe, where they were seen as curiosities and employed for the most part as house servants. The African slave trade had begun.

The trade developed slowly, with the Portuguese purchasing 1000 or so annually in the latter years of the fifteenth century. This changed in the early sixteenth century. Around 1506, one observer, Duarte Periera, wrote of the trade in slaves and elephants' tusks. "When trade was good here, as many as 400 slaves could be had in this [Senegal] river . . . in exchange for horses and other merchandise." That number of slaves hardly put a dent in the Spanish and Portuguese need for labor.

While Spaniards were actively engaged in the "industry" during the sixteenth century, Portugal was the leading force, the only power of the time that maintained *barracoons* in West Africa, compounds in which the slaves were inventoried before being loaded on the ships. Portuguese slavers had the best relationships with the African chiefs who provided the slaves. Recognizing Portugal's supremacy in this area, the Spaniards granted them rights, or *asientos*, to deal directly in slaves with the Spanish colonies. How the Portuguese managed their relations with the African chiefs is a matter that has received little attention from historians. Only recently has interest turned to the other side of the equation, the machinations of the Africans and their complicity in the trade. What is known, however, is that without African cooperation, the slave trade would have been much smaller than it was.

Most of the slaves came from the Guinea coast of present-day Ghana, although the Portuguese slave trade with Brazil originated further south, in Angola. The area was quite varied. Its savannahs, forests, river valleys, deltas, deserts, and jungles supported hundreds of tribes and kingdoms, some of them large and wealthy. Ghana and Melle had risen to great heights, only to fall by the sixteenth century, and Songhi was in decline. Bornu, in the central Sudan, was a powerful state, and in the early period of discoveries, Idris II and Mohammed V ruled over an area as large as France and Germany combined. On the other hand, some of the tribes numbered little more than 100 members. These kingdoms and tribes had practically no direct relationship with Europe, or before then, with Greece or Rome.

The slavers became acquainted with the political, economic, and cultural status of the region. The arrival of the slave trade altered the structure of tribal life. Warfare became more prevalent, since the booty of war included the enemy people, who could be sold into slavery for good prices. Successful traders set themselves up as petty rulers, and some gained substantial power. The slavers soon learned there were scores of tribes and that they differed, often sharply, from one another. For example, the Mandingos, who were generally docile, were much favored, whereas the Coramantins were considered brutal, aggressive, and difficult to bring to bear, and so fetched lower prices. The ultimate purchasers in the Americas also learned the differences, and in this period, at least, they counted for much. There also were preferences with regard to gender: males sold for more than females. Premiums were paid for light-skinned Africans, and those with physical blemishes sold at discounts. Cripples and others with disabilities could be had for a fraction of the price of those sound of body.

Ghana was home to 36 of the 42 slave fortresses eventually erected in the region, and the vast majority of the Africans captured and dispatched to the New World would end up in South and Central America and the Caribbean, with less than 10 percent going directly to what is now the United States. However, these figures are somewhat deceiving. Some of the slaves taken to the West Indies were ultimately destined for the English mainland colonies. They would be "seasoned" for three months or so to take the rebelliousness from them, and then transshipped to the north.

The Spaniards had come to African slavery gradually. They first enslaved those natives who lived locally and forced them to work in the mines. The natives knew the area, however, and with the aid of those who remained free, escaped whenever they could. Another source of labor would be needed. Some Europeans were lured to the New World, and European slaves were dispatched as well. Indeed, the white slaves were preferred to the black ones, since the latter proved rebellious. In 1503, the governor of Hispaniola asked Queen Isabella to put an end to the exportation of Africans to his colony, but he changed his mind in 1510 due to the shortage of workers. Not only was there a need for slaves to work the mines, but sugar was becoming a big business, and slaves were required to work in the fields and refineries as well as on the docks.

Soon after, an economic debate ensued that continued for close to three centuries. In a letter to a colonial official, King Ferdinand professed an inability to "understand why so many Negroes die." This set off discussions on "tight" and "loose" shipments. Those favoring tight shipments, meaning the slaves were stacked as closely as possible, noted that while some might die in the passage, enough lived to make this method preferable to the loose shipments, in which fewer perished, but the total cargo was less on arrival than the tight shipments. The King had reason to be interested in this matter, since he collected a tax of two ducats for each slave sold, in addition to a stiff export tax. As a result of these revenues, an active business in slave smuggling developed.

Other European Ventures in the Slave Trade

Other European countries were concerned with the slave trade as well. There were French settlements in Canada, Guadeloupe, and Martinique, while the Danes took St. Thomas in 1671, and there was the demand for Africans in these islands as well as in the Portuguese settlements. They were not major players in this period, however. The French did become dominant in the Senegal area, and the Danish West Indies Company, formed in 1625, had settlements on the Gold Coast and was followed there by the Swedish African Company. The German Duchy of Courland had a presence in northwest Africa's slave trade, and other German states made their bids for the trade. These latter political entities had no need for slave labor, but rather entered the trade for profit. It was estimated that each African sold in the Caribbean in the eighteenth century returned a profit of 20 pounds to the investors. While comparisons can be deceiving, this would be approximately $1000 in today's purchasing power.

There are no reliable statistics on the slave trade, but the conclusion set forth by many historians is that more than 15 million Africans were taken to the Americas between the sixteenth and the nineteenth centuries, with the most—some 7 million— arriving in the eighteenth century. However, there is one historian who believes the figure to have been as low as 3.5 million and another who asserts it was 25 million. Philip Curtin, who has devoted more time and energy to this subject than any other recent historian, estimated that the total slave imports into Spanish America came to around 1.5 million, with Cuba accounting for more than 700,000 of the total. Curtin's estimate for Brazil is around 3.6 million; for the English holdings in the Caribbean, 1.9 million; the French, approximately 700,000, and the Danes, 28,000. His figure for the United States until 1807, when the trade was legally ended, was 345,000. What about the illegal trade afterwards? "Only a shot in the dark is possible," Curtin wrote. "A figure of perhaps 1000 a year is not unreasonable, including the slave trade to Texas before it joined the union." This would yield an estimate of 54,000 for the 1808–1861 period. Curtin's figures are as close to accuracy as we are likely to have; his total for the entire period of the slave trade is in the vicinity of 9 million. And, as previously mentioned, most of the Africans taken to English settlements went to the Caribbean, not the United States, although, of course, there is the matter of transshipment to the North American colonies later on to take into consideration. Curtin believed that close to twice as many Africans went to Jamaica alone than to all of North America.

The numbers question continues on, since ideology has taken on an important role in the debate. Some African-American scholars argue for a total of 20 million. Paul Lovejoy, writing in 1982, assented his belief that the total number coming ashore in the Americas was 9.8 million.

Curtin did not take into account those Africans who perished on the voyage. Although authoritative statistics for mortality are unavailable, from contemporary accounts the consensus view is that 5 percent or so of the slaves died in Africa after capture and on the way to the coast for shipment, another 13 percent in transit to the Amer-

icas, and close to a third of those in the West Indies died before being sent to their ultimate destinations working in the Southern tobacco fields and other occupations in
North America. These figures, too, are impossible to corroborate with any degree of
accuracy, but they bring Curtin's numbers somewhat closer to those of the earlier consensus. To indicate just how far apart scholars are, in 1969, Curtin wrote:

> Among the recent English language textbooks on African history, Robert Rotberg sets the
> loss of life during the maritime leg of the journey into slavery as 25 to 33 percent. J. D.
> Hargeaves says it was about one-sixth (or half the rate given by Rotberg) and J. D. Fage says
> it was "at least" one-sixth. Donald J. Weidner is still more precise: "Many of the trading
> records have been lost or destroyed, but enough has survived to permit at least an estimate
> of the percentage of slaves who died during the rigorous ocean voyage: about 12 percent in
> French ships, contrasted with 17 percent in Dutch and British ships; Portuguese losses in
> the early centuries ran about 15 percent, but when nineteenth century abolitionists forced
> the slave traders to take chances, the casualty rate rose to 25 to 30 percent."

Not surprisingly, the economics of American slavery has become a bloody battlefield
for proponents of political agendas as well as for scholars.

The Portuguese Empire

The Portuguese sailed on until they reached the mouth of the Congo River. They now
embarked on a three-pronged effort to reach the Indies: up the Congo, through the
Mediterranean along the established routes, and to the south. In 1487, Portugal sent
Bartholomew Diaz on an expedition to the south. Diaz rounded the Cape of Good
Hope and went up the east coast of Africa until his crew forced him to return to Portugal. Others followed. Pedro de Covilha was one of the most successful and colorful of
these explorers. He left Lisbon the same year Diaz started on his journey. Formerly in
the employ of Spain and Morocco, de Covilha posed as a Moslem merchant and set off
for Cairo and then to Aden, where he hired an Arab dhow to take him to Calcutta. From
there he traveled the entire Malabar coast of southwest India, and then on to Ormuz,
the major commercial city on the southern reaches of the Persian Gulf. Turning southward, he next went to Sofala on the southeastern coast of Africa, all the while collecting
information and making commercial contacts. Next back to Cairo, where he arrived in
late 1490. In 1493, he turned up in Abyssinia, where he remained for the next 13 years
as a servant of the emperor. By then, King John II had received the reports that de Covilha had dispatched from Cairo, which had valuable intelligence of what might be
found in the Indies and what might be expected in terms of trade and opposition. Apparently, one of de Covilha's messages was that Portuguese explorers had to expect opposition from the Venetians and other Italians and their clients in the area.

In 1497, King Manuel I sent Vasco da Gama on an expedition to the Indies around
the Cape of Good Hope. This was not a voyage of discovery, or even of commerce.
Rather, guided by de Covilha's information, Portugal opted to send to the Indies not a
mariner, but a soldier, merchant, and diplomat, who bore resemblance to the *conquistadores* who would plunder Central and South America for Spain soon after. Da Gama
did not sail with merchant ships, but rather with square riggers, each armed with 20
guns. Some of his 170 men had sailed with Diaz, and Diaz himself accompanied the
ships out of the harbor.

They made landfall at Mombasa on Africa's east coast, a port under Moslem influence, where da Gama's force met local opposition. They did better at Malindi, where they secured the services of a navigator who knew the waters, enabling the Portuguese to make landfall in Calcutta in May of 1498. There da Gama learned that the trade goods he had brought along, cloth and hardware, were not desired by the merchants, who in any case were closely allied with Moslem counterparts and reluctant to enter into commercial arrangements with da Gama. Even so, he managed to load up with pepper and cinnamon, retraced his path, and returned to Portugal in September 1499, two years after his departure. The profits reaped from the voyage were 60 times greater than the original investment. It was one of the most impressive maritime feats of the time in terms of knowledge and wealth obtained, for which da Gama and his men were well rewarded. Once again, a merchant had gone to an area where certain goods were inexpensive, made purchases and trades, and then had taken them to a place where they were prized.

In 1501, Portuguese spices showed up in Antwerp, which became an important entrepot for the shipments. The Portuguese, and later the Dutch, were taking business from the Venetians, who till then had a monopoly of the spice trade in that part of Europe. These setbacks for Venice were exacerbated by the Turkish conquest of Egypt, which cut off the route the Venetians had used to the Orient. After 1512, Venetian merchants were reduced to purchasing spices from the Portuguese in order to meet commitments. In time, Venice would come to terms with the Turks, but in the future would have to pay high tariffs on their imports. For the time being, the trade in silk, cotton, glass, and wines remained in Italian hands, but the impact of the new routes was being felt. In the sixteenth century, the Mediterranean remained the center of commercial life, but it now was being challenged.

Within months of da Gama's return, a larger fleet under the command of Pedro Cabral was sent to Calcutta, and in 1502, da Gama set out on a second voyage. This was more a military than a commercial expedition. Da Gama forced the Sultan of Kilwa, a kingdom not far from Mombasa, to pay tribute, bombarded Calcutta when the city's merchants continued to oppose trade with Portugal, and forced the Moslems out of the area by military means. There was no other way to do it, he believed. The Portuguese goods were inferior and higher priced than those of the Moslems.

Another Portuguese mariner, Afonzo d'Albuquerque, sailed to the area and wreaked havoc wherever he went, capturing the strategic city of Goa in 1510 and opening communications with Siam, Java, and China. Three years later, Portuguese vessels reached the Moluccas, south of the Philippines, one of the major sources for spices, cloves in particular. Portugal not only was the major power in Africa and an important presence in the Persian Gulf, the Indian Ocean, and the Asian mainland, but also was the master of a wide swath of wealthy islands in the south Pacific. By then, too, it had significant bases in the Atlantic: the Canary Islands, the Madeira group, the Azores, and the Cape Verde Islands. Portugal lost the Canaries to Spain in 1475, however, a change that would yield important consequences.

The Madeiras, which may have been known to the Phoenicians, the Greeks, and the Romans, were discovered by the Portuguese in 1418. Commercially, these islands became the most profitable of the four island groups. The early explorers found hard-woods there, which were harvested and sent to Portugal to be made into high-quality furniture. The Malvoise grapevines, native to Crete, were introduced, and from them came the famous Madeira wine, soon a favorite in the Iberian peninsula, England, and elsewhere. Most important, the climate and soil were right for sugar cultivation, and since the demand for sugar was high, the settlers grew cane, processed it, and the product was sent throughout Europe for sale.

The Europeans already were familiar with sugar cane, which was taken home by Alexander the Great's soldiers. The sweetening agent of choice in Mesopotamia and Egypt, however, had been honey. Sugar cultivation began in the Mediterranean in the sixth century, and the Crusaders who came across it called sugar "honey from the reeds." Small quantities were used in Spain and England. Now, this would change. Sugar from Madeira entered Spain in larger quantities, and its popularity spread.

The Azores, which apparently were known to the Greeks and Romans, were thought to be St. Brendan's Isles, a mythical place mentioned in medieval records. They were taken by Portugal in 1432 and were soon settled by Portuguese tradesmen and artisans who serviced ships bound to and from the Indies. Likewise, the Cape Verde Islands, discovered by one of Prince Henry's mariners in 1456, provided the same assistance to shipping.

Portuguese ships arriving in Lisbon from India and China were laden with spices and gems as well as ketchup (from a Chinese word meaning "brine of pickled fish") and fruits (most citrus originated in southern China and Malaysia), but the cargoes were mortgaged to German and some Genoese bankers. The King permitted foreign bankers to invest in one of the voyages that departed in 1505, and funds flowed into Portugal from Italian and German banks. The voyage was a success, with profits close to 200 percent. This was the first and last time the King utilized banking services. Next, he financed the voyages, but upon landing and unloading, the cargoes were sold to the bankers and then shipped to Antwerp. In time, the King would sell the cargoes in advance of landing or would borrow against future cargoes.

Portugal was not interested in creating a political empire; it was primarily concerned with commerce, extraction of precious metals, and, eventually, the slave trade. It was a small country, with a population of fewer than 2 million, insufficient to colonize effectively while maintaining a presence of any consequence at home. The enormous wealth that entered Lisbon corrupted the court and resulted in unwise expeditions. For example, in 1578, King Sebastian commanded a crusade against the Moors in North Africa in which he and 8000 troops were lost, whereupon Cardinal Henry became king. When Henry died in 1580, there were seven claimants to the crown, the most powerful of whom was King Philip II of Spain, who invaded Portugal and was named King Philip I of that country. Spanish kings would rule Portugal for 60 years, and by the time Portugal was once again independent, its empire was in decline. Subsequently, Portugal was hammered by new forces in the colonial race, the Netherlands and England, and to a lesser extent France. By the end of the eighteenth century, all that remained of the empire was Brazil, Macao, part of Timor, Goa, some posts in India, and some ports and colonies on the African coast.

Spain and the Race for Wealth

Of course, by the time the Portuguese were solidifying their grip on Indian Ocean commerce, Columbus had sailed for the Spanish monarchs, King Ferdinand and Queen Isabella, and discovered the Americas, and the Spaniards had started exploring the region. Allusion already has been made to Spanish experiences in the age of exploration. It is time now to go back to the beginning of the Spanish involvement, which was with Columbus in 1492. Then it seemed that the Portuguese discoveries were more important. Not only had that country's mariners found a new all-water route to the riches of China and India, but they were opening a continent whose southern reaches had been unknown to Europeans, which soon proved to be rich in gold and a source for slaves. So as the new century began, farsighted Europeans might have concluded that the focus of trade might be moving from the Mediterranean Sea to the Indian Ocean.

The outlines of the story of Columbus are familiar. We know that he, as well as most mariners of the time, believed the earth was round, the land mass of Eurasia larger than it actually proved to be, the earth itself smaller than it was, and that although there might be land between Europe and Asia in the "ocean sea," it was not the major goal for western voyagers. Columbus also had a great deal of experience sailing on the Atlantic. There may have been others who went to the Americas before him, including the Phoenicians, St. Brendan of Ireland, Lief Erickson, and Thorfinn Karlsefni, among them. Portuguese fishermen went far afield in the Atlantic. They knew of Iceland, perhaps Greenland, and some of them might have made landfall in North America. If one or more of them did arrive in America before Columbus, it counted for little. Unlike Columbus's voyages, theirs had no consequences.

After spending more than a dozen years trying to convince one of Europe's monarchs, including King John II of Portugal, to bankroll his plan to reach the Indies by sailing west, Columbus finally found a backer in Isabella. Columbus was not a romantic adventurer, but like those mariners who sailed under the Portugese flag, he was interested in wealth. He wanted to discover the new route, to be sure, but he wanted to become rich as well. "Gold is treasure," he wrote, "and he who possesses it does whatever he wishes in this life, and succeeds in helping souls into Paradise." In 1485, he had an audience with the Count of Medina Celi, who was willing to provide ships, and Columbus was prepared to go on the voyage for expenses and nothing more. The Count had second thoughts, however, and suggested that Isabella was the person to see for so ambitious an undertaking.

In 1491, when he presented himself at court, Columbus had reason to believe he might be successful in obtaining backing. The Spanish crusade to rid Spain of the Moors and Jews was nearing its conclusion, and Isabella's attention could turn elsewhere. Knowing this, Columbus asked for the title of admiral and 10 percent of the profits from trade. Also, he was to be permitted to invest one-eighth of the funds needed to initiate commerce and to receive a like share of the profits.

Might he have expected even more than that? Parts of the patent given Columbus were ambiguous.

> You, Christopher Columbus, are going by our orders to discover and gain, with certain
> light ships of ours and with our men, certain Islands and Mainland in the Ocean Sea,
> and it is hoped that with the aid of God there will be gained some of the said Islands and
> Mainland in the Ocean Sea by your hand and industry.

Did Columbus and Isabella expect to find the Indies or new territories? This question has never been satisfactorily answered. But from the above, the reader might conclude that today's venture capitalists would understand Isabella's actions, and a young entrepreneur would feel a certain kinship with Columbus. These were medieval people, to be sure, but at the same time, the quickening of the commercial instincts that took place in the fourteenth and fifteenth centuries was being felt.

At first, Columbus was rejected, but then one of the Queen's counselors, Louis de Santagel, keeper of the privy purse, noted that this was a small price to pay for the discovery of a new route to India and China. Besides, that business about new lands was a chimera, and so the title of admiral wouldn't cost anything.

This last matter would later pose a problem. Columbus made certain that his patent included the words ". . . that you enjoy the perquisites and salaries belonging to the said employments, and to each of them, in the same manner as the High Admiral of our kingdom does." Indeed, the section spelling out what Columbus and his descendants might expect from the voyages occupies a major portion of the document. At the time, the High Admiral collected one-third of the volume of the trade between Spain and the Canary Islands. Of course, no one could have predicted just how much would be found in the Americas, but one-third of that would have made Columbus and his heirs the wealthiest family in history.

Isabella was convinced of the merits of such an expedition and even offered to pawn her jewels to raise the needed amount, but Santagel said this wouldn't be necessary, that he would be able to raise the funds from investors. Ultimately, Isabella invested in a quarter of the shares of the enterprise; the rest came from courtiers, businessmen, bankers, and friends of Columbus in Spain. The Santa Hermandad, Spain's secret police, also had shares in the enterprise.

That Columbus sought wealth in the lands he came upon was manifest. He hoped for trade, to be sure, but more than anything else, he wanted gold. As did many in this period, Columbus believed that gold was to be found in places that were hot and silver in those that were cold. He, of course, was decamped in a hot area. In the ship's journal for November 21 is the entry: "Because of the heat which the Admiral says that he suffered there, he argues that in these Indies and where he was then, there was certain to be much gold."

The search for the metal began immediately. The October 13 entry said, "I was bent on finding out if there was gold and saw that some [natives] wore a bit of it suspended from a hole pierced in the nose, and by signs I learned that going to the south and making a turn about the island to the south there was a king who had large jars of it and possessed a lot." Then Columbus turned southward and two days later came across other natives who wore gold as bracelets, nose rings, and breastplates. More mentions of gold followed. The journal records just about all the gold he saw and learned about. Eventually, Columbus discovered some gold, and more was found in subsequent journeys.

Columbus located more items, which he brought back to Spain. He also took back some curiosities. In the first journal entry upon finding land on October 12, 1492, is recorded a chance encounter with a sole "Indian" who was traveling by open boat from the island of Santa Maria to Fernandina. He had food and water and "some dry leaves which must be a thing very much appreciated among them, because they already brought me some of them as a present at San Salvador." Columbus later noted that the natives of Hispaniola smoked a plant, "the perfume of which was fragrant and grateful." Thus was Europe introduced to tobacco, one of the first of the New World items that played a role in what was later called the "Columbian exchange," which included Columbus's introduction of citrus fruits to the West Indies, thus completing their transference from the Orient.

The Spaniards set about legalizing their claims. Madrid entered into negotiations with Lisbon and Rome. In May, the Pope granted Spain possession of all lands to the south and west not held by other Christians on Christmas Day, 1492. Two years later, Lisbon accepted a modified version of the papal contract. In the Treaty of Tordesillas, Spain agreed that Portugal would have all lands 370 leagues west of the Cape Verde Islands, and Madrid would control the rest. In effect, Spain was granted much of the Americas. Portugal received part of Brazil, and eventually the Viceroyalty of Brazil would comprise more than a third of South America, plus all of Africa. At the time, Lisbon seemed to have received the better part of the bargain. Consider that in 1513, the Portuguese would be in the Moluccas, south of the Philippines. Thus, the Portuguese overseas empire covered more than half the globe.

Columbus launched his second expedition in 1493 with an armada of 17 ships. These were not fighting ships like the ones the Portuguese sent to Asia. Instead, they carried a cargo of 1200 people who were to settle the lands, plant crops, and most important, mine for gold and silver. The hope was that the colonies established would be self-supporting in foodstuffs and send mineral wealth back to Spain. The major shortcoming was the lack of sufficient food and supplies to keep the colonies going until they became self-sufficient. The settlements were failures, but undeterred, Columbus embarked on a third voyage in 1498, that took him to South America. He was challenged by Francisco de Bobadilla, who gained control of the expedition, captured Columbus, and sent him and his two brothers back to Spain in chains, charging them with misconduct. A fourth expedition was mounted in 1502, but it was deemed a failure.

Columbus returned from that last journey in 1504. He was worn out and ill. Isabella had just died, and so his great protector was no longer there to assure that his rights were respected. He was a wealthy man, with more to come. In 1506, he would receive a chest with what today would be approximately a quarter of a million dollars in gold. Still, Columbus felt cheated. He had expected 10 percent of the wealth, but he only received 10 percent of Isabella's quarter share, which came to 2.5 percent, and he never was able to convince anyone in court that he merited the Admiral's third interest. A fallen hero, Columbus died in 1506, still believing he had discovered the outer reaches of the Orient.

Men like Columbus and da Gama would initiate a new order of things in the world, and in the process create methods of achieving wealth unimaginable to those knights who came home from the Crusades and the prelates and nobles who sent them.

Following up on Columbus's discoveries, the Spaniards took the lead in the race to the west, while Portuguese mariners concentrated on Africa and Asia. By mid-century the Spaniards had searched both coasts of North and South America and had sent exploring parties into the interiors of the continents. The Portuguese also explored the New World, sending Amerigo Vespucci, who previously had sailed for Spain, to search for wealth. Others would come after.

CHAPTER 6

Europe's American Empires

HE first empires in the New World and the Pacific were formed by Spain, Portugal, and the Netherlands. Each brought a different perspective to the enterprise, but all wanted to unearth wealth and bring it home to Europe. All of them looked on the world as a place to be looted. None was interested in settlement and cultivation. In the end, each succeeded; but embedded in their successes were the seeds of failure.

Initially, the Spanish monarchs, like their Portuguese counterparts, attempted to achieve a monopoly on exploration and exploitation. Unlike the Portuguese, after some initial failures and losses, the Spanish rulers were prepared to include merchants in their financing arrangements, and backed explorers in the Americas as well.

Most of the explorers came from Spain and Portugal, but their financing originated in all quarters of Europe. Some of the funds were derived from properties confiscated from the Jews and the Moors, but a good deal came from Italy and the German lands, where bankers who were involved with the Levantine and Asian trade now became interested in the Americas. In time, bankers in Seville would obtain leverage in the financing, but in the beginning, with the Italian banks plagued by invasions and poor leadership, their German counterparts assumed greater importance. The focus of their interest remained European and Asian, but they also were involved in syndicates that sent ships to the Americas and managed mines in Santo Domingo and New Spain. The Welsers, for their part, attempted unsuccessfully to create a settlement in Venezuela, while in 1528, the Ehringers purchased a monopoly of the slave trade to the West Indies. The religious wars of the Protestant Reformation, which involved the Spanish monarchs on the Catholic side, were costly, and were paid for by loans from German bankers as well as wealth from the New World extracted by conquistadores whose patents obliged them to set aside a large portion of the wealth they obtained for the Crown. German bankers also had leases on the Almaden mercury mines and the Guadalcanal silver mines in Spain.

The Conquistadores

The Spanish venture in the Americas was spearheaded by a group of adventurers known collectively as "the conquistadores," who, along with their English, French, and Dutch counterparts, engaged in a period of exploration that never has been equaled. Not until manned expeditions to the planets and beyond occur, perhaps late in the twenty-first century, will their exploits be surpassed.

The conquistadores would organize expeditions, put out what amounted to prospectuses, and seek financing. After a conquistador received his patent and financing, he would proceed to raise bands of soldiers, attract settlers, and purchase ships. Under most grants, one-fifth of the profits would go to the leader of the expedition, another fifth to the Crown. The rest would be taken by the bankers, the soldiers, sailors, and settlers. Any land seized in the expeditions would belong to the Crown, but the leaders received substantial land grants and also had the right to bestow parcels on their comrades-in-arms. Finally, the Church received generous land grants, and each expedition was required to take along missionaries whose task it was to convert the natives and make them more amenable to Spanish control.

From stations in the West Indies, the conquistadores fanned out to explore and plunder. Alonso de Ojeda founded a colony in 1508 on the east coast of the Isthmus of Panama, and from there, in the summer of 1513, Vasco de Balboa crossed the isthmus and became the first European to see the western coast of North America, this at a time when European mariners were already in the East Indies. Simultaneously, Juan Ponce de Leon sailed northward and discovered Florida. During the same decade, Diego Valasquez completed the conquest of Cuba, and other Spaniards landed on the eastern coast of Central America. Some ventured northward, and one, Lucas de Ayllon, may have gone as far as present-day Virginia before returning to the West Indies.

These northern expeditions might have continued had it not been for the exploits of Hernando Cortez in Mexico. Starting in 1519, Cortez and his band overran the Aztec empire of Montezuma and laid hands on vast hoards of gold. This was Spain's first great treasure find in the Americas. Cortez's conquests affected the course of world history. They made Spain the wealthiest country in Europe and ensured that Spanish efforts in the Americas would center around the search for precious metals, not for settlement sites. The vision of a passage to the Indies also faded from Spanish minds. Both of these would now be left to mariners, merchants, and monarchs of other European nations, especially those of the Netherlands, France, and England. And these countries, not Spain or Portugal, would conquer North America, while the Spaniards and Portuguese concentrated on lands to the south.

Whereas much of the literature of the Spanish and Portuguese conquest in the Americas focuses on what they took from the natives, most of the minerals came from mines discovered and exploited by these Europeans. In 1545, the largest silver mine ever known was discovered in Potosí in what today is Bolivia. In time, there were many mines in the area, the largest owned and managed by Spanish businessmen who organized joint stock companies and purchased rights from the Crown, which also received a share of the metal extracted, usually one-fifth. Nearly half of all the silver produced in the New World from 1521 to 1610 came from Potosí. These mines gave rise to a major Spanish problem: the need for more labor.

The Dawn of Mercantilism

By this time, a theory had developed to justify and explain the motives of Europe's newly powerful monarchs. In the sixteenth century, as the regionalism that survived the Middle Ages was starting to be supplanted by nation-states, the pursuit of wealth became a matter of national as well as individual and family concern. If the monarch were the father or mother to the people he or she ruled, did it not follow that all methods of enriching the state were desirable, while those that diminished wealth were to be averted? So it appeared to the rulers of this period, and to their subjects as well. Thus emerged an economic doctrine that informed many of the actions of the nation-states and those that followed. Known as *mercantilism,* it went virtually unchallenged in the sixteenth, seventeenth, and eighteenth centuries, was tested in the nineteenth century, and persists in some forms and among some groups to this day.

The mercantilists held that a nation's wealth could be measured by the amounts of precious metals it possessed. From this, it could be inferred that nations should seek gold and silver through explorations among peoples who had them or through the collection of taxes and tribute. Nations could seize the metals by force if necessary, mining if possible, and trade as well. Insofar as trade was concerned, mercantilists favored exports and discouraged imports, although they encouraged the import of raw materials, which could be turned into finished goods and then exported. This implied tariffs on imported finished goods, and government support and encouragement to those people and industries who produced goods that might be exported. In 1565, a law was passed in England prohibiting the export of sheep, and another forbidding the export of raw wool passed a century later, both to encourage the English cloth industry and deny wealth to rival nations. In *England's Treasure by Foreign Trade,* published posthumously in 1664, Thomas Mun wrote:

> Although a kingdom may be enriched by gifts received, or by the purchase taken from some other nations, yet these are things uncertain and of small consideration when they happen. The main thing is to possess goods; if you have them you will get money. "He that hath ware hath money by the year." The ordinary means therefore to increase our wealth and treasure is by foreign trade, wherein we must ever observe this rule; to sell more to strangers yearly than we consume of theirs in value. Behold then the true form and worth of foreign trade, which is the great revenue of the King, the school of our arts, the supply of our wants, the employment of our poor, the improvement of our lands, the terror of our enemies.

He went on to assert that England could increase its wealth by growing its own tobacco, flax, hemp, and other products, "which we now fetch from strangers to our great impoverishing."

Mercantilists favored the removal of barriers to internal commerce, such as tolls, taxes, harsh regulations, and the like. This policy was necessary in order to facilitate production. Yet they also supported grants of monopoly rights, the rationale being that monopolies were easier for the Crown to monitor and control, and recipients of exclusive rights would be more efficient than individuals obliged to compete with others. This implied the presence of a strong central government working hand-in-glove with prominent and affluent businessmen, bankers, and landlords. For the most part, mercantilists were unconcerned with the interests of small farmers and laborers. Indeed, the lower the wages and returns to these classes, the more resources there would be for the Crown and the wealthy of the land.

Mercantilists considered colonies necessary for national strength and wealth—but not all colonies. They favored colonies that produced items the mother country had to import from foreign nations; those that produced precious metals; those strategic for military or naval purposes; or those colonies that served as outlets for surplus domestic populations. They also supported the establishment of colonies to deny them to rivals. Mercantilists had a static view of the global economy, believing the amount of goods in the world to be finite, and that possession by one country diminished the wealth of the others. "The product of one man is the damage of another," wrote Michel de Montaigne in 1580. "No man profiteth but by the loss of others."

The New Europe of the Fuggers

The sixteenth century in Europe was an era of fierce religious and dynastic conflict. On October 31, 1517, Martin Luther—the son of a German miner, an Augustinian monk, a priest, and a professor of theology at the University of Wittenberg—nailed his 95 Theses to the door of the church in Wittenberg. Luther questioned several aspects of Catholic dogma and practice, but initially, Luther demonstrated no desire to leave the Church. The inability of Catholic leaders to deal effectively with him, combined with pressures from nationalistic German nobles, set into motion a chain of events which led to Luther's excommunication three years later and to the establishment of the first major Protestant sect.

A still more dangerous threat to the Church—and of consequence for the pursuit of wealth—came from John Calvin, who in 1536 went to Geneva in the hope of ending a religious quarrel there and at the same time established a new church. At the heart of Calvin's theology was the doctrine of predestination, the belief that man was born with original sin, and that all but a select few, who had been redeemed by Christ's sacrifice on the cross, were destined for damnation. The devout Calvinist might spend a lifetime seeking signs to determine whether or not he was one of the "elect." Such a sign might be seen in the acquisition of wealth, high status, or great power.

This created complications in business. Recall that during the Middle Ages, merchants, while they did not enjoy high status, were necessary and operated on the basis of trust. The Hanseatic and Rhenish Leagues, which traded throughout Europe and the Near East, and the Venetians and other Italians could not have engaged in the scope of trade they did without faith in their pledges. Trade in goods that took months and in some cases years to complete was made possible by the willingness of merchants to undergo hardships to preserve their reputations. Merchants were so trusted that they were asked to arbitrate squabbles between nobles and to provide assurance for treaties. The merchants of Brabant pledged to seize the properties of Emperor John I if he reneged on an agreement with a lesser noble.

Yet this code of honor limited competition and restricted profits, which Calvinism, in its more diluted forms, addressed. At the core of Calvinist theology were original sin, predestination, and the salvation through Christ of a small group of people, "the elect." Some Calvinist theologians came to believe God would indicate just who these people were by endowing them with intelligence, beauty, talent, and success in business. Achievement might be considered a sign of divine approval—and that ends justified means.

Calvin did not sanction the fast-and-loose business practices that eventually evolved. Indeed, while he was in power in the city-state of Geneva, he excoriated bankers and forbade the opening of new banks. Yet Calvinists often praised successful businessmen, overlooking their methods of achieving prosperity. "Whence do the merchant's profits come, except from his own diligence and industry?" Calvin asked. As sociologist Max Weber put it, "the *summum bonum* of this ethic [is] the earning of more and more money."

Europe had grown more worldly, and that included the Catholic Church, the avarice of which troubled Luther and Calvin, who through their new theologies were creating a form of Christianity destined to have great appeal to the middle class in many parts of western Europe. At the same time, nationalism was growing, a doctrine that fitted well with the new worldliness. The kings were consolidating their power in attempts to create strong states that would supercede the feudal dispensation. In some cases, the monarchs were able to work well with the Church, most notably in France, Spain, and Portugal. In others, such as England, Germany, and Scandinavia, revolts would take place leading the states to adopt the new Protestant faiths.

Concomitant with these religious developments and with the consolidation of monarchical powers was the decline of the Italian city-states. Lorenzo de Medici died in 1492 and was succeeded by his son, Piero, who proved reckless and inept. Florence clashed with its neighbors, and French King Charles VIII took advantage of this to invade Italy, which at the same time was struck with plague and food riots. The French attacked Venice as well, as did the Turks. Venice's power and cynical policies, which earlier had served it well, now prompted the Pope, France, and Spain to organize the League of Cambrai, which wrung concessions from the beleaguered city-state. Italy was in general decline, though at the time its problems seemed to come from Europe, the Near East, and the challenges of German banks.

The center for the latter challenge to Italian financial dominance came from Augsburg, a budding financial superpower. As in Italy, family banking firms predominated, with the Fuggers, Welsers, and Hochstetters among the most important, especially the Fuggers, which became the dominant bank in the sixteenth century.

The Fugger fortune began in what by now had become a familiar fashion: textiles. Johannes Fugger was a weaver who graduated to merchant status. Upon his death in 1409, he bequested to his son, Jacob, a sum that in today's funds would be approximately $500,000. Carrying on the commercial activities begun by his father, Jacob Fugger also became a moneylender and banker, and by the time of his death in 1469, the family had become one of the wealthiest in Augsburg. His sons, Ulrich, Georg, and Jacob II, became moneylenders to princes, extracting the rights to revenues from mines and cities in return for loans to nobles in Germany, Austria, and Hungary. The Fuggers lent the equivalent of several millions of dollars to Archduke Sigismund of Austria, receiving in return the entire yield of the richest silver mine in central Europe until the debt was repaid—with interest.

These banks were family affairs. A banker would dispatch a messenger from his headquarters in, say, Frankfort to a nephew in London, informing him of the needs of a client and of the terms that might be expected for a possible loan, along with information regarding individuals in the area who might be interested in being included in the undertaking. In the fifteenth and sixteenth centuries, such messengers criss-crossed Europe, in the process shaping what was to become our present capitalist structure. This was how the great merchant families, such as the Fuggers and, before them, the Medici, were able to finance their clients (often the rulers of nations and empires), by risking both their capital and that of other lenders interested in their ventures. When the client was less well known or deemed risky, the banker would make presentations to several potential lenders and even accompany the borrower to their offices for that purpose. Should the borrower be of high rank, the lenders might travel to his castle or estate for the same purpose. Either way, the concept was similar: the investment banker's function was to bring borrower and lender together.

While all the brothers were talented, Jacob II also was an original thinker. He conceived the idea of cornering the supplies of certain commodities, and in 1498, in concert with other Augsburg families, cornered the Venetian market for copper, an achievement no bank located in that city had ever managed to do. By the end of the first decade of the sixteenth century, then, this family was the most important force in European mining and textiles. The Fuggers conducted trade with the Orient, Europe, and Africa. They would provide the funds needed to outfit Ferdinand Magellan's circumnavigation of the world, which was profitable, even though only one ship and 18 men returned. By 1511, the Fugger family was by far the wealthiest in Europe, having amassed a fortune that today would be measured in the billions of dollars. More was to come. In 1515, together with the Welsers and Hochstetters, the Fuggers outfitted a major fleet that wrested control of Asian pepper from the Moslems.

The Price Revolution and Economic Stimulation

At one time, the conventional wisdom regarding the massive influx of gold and silver to Europe was that it caused a "price revolution" on the continent, particularly in Spain. This view was most effectively propounded by Earl Hamilton in his 1934 book, *American Treasure and the Price Revolution in Spain, 1501–1650*. Hamilton noted that between 1503 and 1660, 16.8 million grams of silver and 181.3 million grams of gold were imported into Europe. He concluded the impact on Spanish life was profound:

> For a season industry seems to have responded to the rise in prices precipitated by the influx of treasure. The resultant material prosperity, together with the effect of the specie on national psychology, played a part in the passage of Spain through her golden age of literature and art. But ultimately the importation of treasure (the exportation of which was retarded by legal restrictions) in exchange for goods sapped the economic vitality of the country and augmented the Price Revolution, which handicapped export industry. Historians have generally agreed that American gold and silver fanned the flames of Habsburg imperialism, added to the zeal with which Spanish rulers defended the Catholic faith against Protestant and Muhammadan, furnished sinews of war, and, in short, constituted an important factor in Spain's aggressive foreign policy.

Such a conclusion was supported by monetarist theory, which held that increases in the money supply result in price increases. As economist Alan Blinder put it, inflation "always and everywhere [is] primarily a monetary phenomenon."

More recent scholarship has pushed the price revolution farther back than the beginning of the influx of precious metals, and has assigned other causes. Several contemporary historians, most notably David Hackett Fischer in *The Great Wave: Price Revolutions and the Rhythm of History* (1996), have synthesized the works of others and added interpretations of their own in order to date the beginnings of the revolution to the early 1470s. They have concluded that the upswing in prices of a wide variety of goods, from food to fuel, was caused by population growth, which resulted in increases in demand. Fischer notes that England's population, which stood at 2 million in 1430 and the same in 1470, leapt to 2.8 million by 1541. Fischer cites contemporary sources to indicate that this was the case throughout Europe. Increasingly, Europeans were moving to towns. In the 1530s, one person out of ten in England was a town dweller; by the 1690s, it was one out of four. Fischer does not assert that the influx of bullion had no impact, but he does observe that prices nearly doubled before American silver had a significant effect on prices and economies.

Another result of the growth in population was the generally accepted view that there was insufficient room in Europe for so many people. In the early seventeenth century, Francis Bacon wrote that:

> When a State grows to an Over-Power it is like a great Flood, that will be sure to overflow. When the World hath peoples who will not marry or generate unless they know they have the means to live, there is no Danger of Inundations of People. But when there be great Shoales of People who go on to populate, without foreseeing their Means of Life and Sustenance, it is inevitable that once in an Age or two, they discharge a Portion of their People upon other nations.

Thus did Bacon, and others who felt as he did, support exploration, with the thought that it would lead to colonization that would draw off the surplus European population.

As the price revolution picked up steam, business was stimulated. As usually is the case during times of inflation, landlords and businessmen benefitted. "The real victims of economic forces in this age were the evicted agrarian smallholder, and the landless laborer of both town and country," wrote Peter Ramsay in *The Price Revolution in Sixteenth Century England*. Other losers included monarchs engaged in wars. Their need for increased revenues to pay for ordnance, ships, and men threw them into the arms of the bankers. Despite its vast empire, Spain likewise was in need of loans because of its many commitments, and soon was mortgaging its treasure fleet to the Fuggers and others. Taxes were increased, with the peasants bearing the brunt of the impact, since in many parts of Europe the nobility and Church were exempt from taxation.

The increased economic activity placed strains on the supplies of natural resources, none more than wood. Wood not only was the primary building material for homes, ships, and many other products, but in the form of charcoal it was used to smelt iron, tin, lead, and copper. Glass was coming into wider use, and charcoal was required in its manufacture. In colder parts of Europe, wood was used to boil seawater to obtain salt. It was used in brewing, at a time when beer and ale were commonly consumed in place of water. Prices of most commodities rose in the sixteenth century, the general increase being in the neighborhood of 230 percent, and for wood, 340 percent.

In 1548, a commission was established to investigate the destruction of forests by the

Sussex ironworks, and it reported that the problem was so severe that several port cities were threatened with a lack of fuel. A number of ironworks had to be closed due to the shortages. As the supply of local wood declined, England started importing wood, in competition with other countries experiencing the same shortfalls. Fearing the shortages would have an impact on naval construction, Queen Elizabeth prohibited the cutting of wood from Crown forests without special permission. When in 1584 the Countess of Rutland protested that lumber promised to her had not been delivered, the Queen's minister, Lord Burghley, replied that she was not using the lumber for intended purposes, and that her requests seemed far more than was needed for the repair of the castle and mills,

> especially whereas it has been informed unto me and complained of that the greatest number of the said trees have not been employed to the use they were allowed for but sold . . . for money and converted the same to the owners for private use, which . . . is a very foul deceit and abuse toward me and wrong to her Majesty. This shall make me more careful. For the better preservation of the wood there I mind to make a general stay without upon very special occasion.

Price increases, combined with crop failures toward the end of the sixteenth century, provided speculators with a means to wealth. They would attempt to corner foodstuffs and other materials, withhold them from the market, and then sell at substantially higher prices.

The Dutch Maritime Empire

Mention has been made of the rise of Antwerp, which accompanied the decline of some of the Italian city-states in the sixteenth century. Genoa thrived, in part because it was best prepared to make the switch from Mediterranean to Atlantic business, while others could or did not. In this period, the low countries were controlled by Spain, and that country's monarchs and merchants used Antwerp to help coordinate activities in its empire.

With an excellent port on the Scheldt River, Antwerp had easy access to the North Sea and the Atlantic. The city was an important center for the export of English cloth to the continent, and it developed a merchant class to rival that of Lubeck. By the mid-sixteenth century, it had emerged as the most active port in northern Europe, an important crossroads, and one of the most international cities on the continent. Much of the trade was managed by consortia of businessmen from several countries, whose members would borrow funds from local banks, pool their resources, contract for all of a specific commodity available, and then distribute portions to customers as far away as Russia. Out of all this came continuous, or nonstop, markets. There already was one for commodities on Wool Street, founded around 1460, and now a new one arose, established in 1531 for financial transactions, with an inscription over the door that read, "For the Use of Businessmen of Whatever Nation and Language." There, bills of exchange drawn on banks throughout Europe were bought and sold. Credit arbitrage was a major business. Merchants with excellent credit histories might be able to borrow funds at 8 percent, whereas monarchs with records for default might have to pay as high as 16 percent. Merchants might borrow at 8 percent and lend at 16 percent, thus realizing handsome profits for their willingness to assume risks. Rates for England soared during its wars with Spain, but those merchants who made loans on the eve of the victory over the Spanish Armada realized major profits when English loans rallied with England's triumph.

Some financiers became notorious for their activities. Piero Spino, a Florentine, served as prime agent for the French monarchy, while Francesco Erasso did the same for Spanish royal interests. During the reign of Queen Elizabeth, Sir Thomas Gresham worked with Flemish merchant Gaspar Schetz for the English ruler. As might have been expected, Antwerp became the center for intelligence gathering, both financial and political. There Spain learned of intrigues at the English court, and London found out what Spain intended to do in its worldwide empire. Despite Spain's control of the area, Antwerp became host to a lively trade in munitions. While Spain was preparing its assault on England, Gresham was able to openly purchase gunpowder and other supplies in Antwerp and have them transshipped. In his messages to the Queen, he spoke of the corruption of the city and the need for bribes. Alexander Bonvisi, a Genoese financier, assisted in this effort, while at the same time working with the Spaniards.

None of this was new. While Rome was fighting Carthage in the Punic Wars, the active trade between the two nations actually increased. The Muslims had been financed by Jacques Coeur and a host of Venetian bankers during the Crusades. The Bardis of Florence loaned money to both England and France during their fourteenth and fifteenth century wars, making possible the Hundred Years' War. In the seventeenth century, manufacturers and merchants in the city of Suhl sent its famous cannons to the French, Swiss, Venetians, Spanish, Prussians, and anyone else willing to pay. Oliver Cromwell feigned surprise on learning that Dutch firms were selling war supplies to his armies, even while England and Holland were at war. "They will sell arms to their enemies, and lend their ships to their enemies. They will do so," he told his countrymen.

Gaspar Ducci, an Italian financier, was the best known during the mid-sixteenth century. While other merchants tended to specialize in tangible products, such as shipments of cloth, pepper, alum, and the like, Ducci was more concerned with financial transactions, combining the activities of banker and merchant in ways resembling those of the Fuggers. Ducci represented several German states and Brussels in Antwerp, and he had alliances with the Florentines. He arranged for loans from German banks to the French monarchy at times when they were foes, and worked closely with German financiers Alexius Grimel and Hieronymous Seiler. Ducci lived in a palace and employed a score of bodyguards to protect him against retaliation from those he euchred. This crew was more like a private army than companions, and they would not stop at murder.

Antwerp's merchant-speculators were foremost in profiting from the inflation of the times. One of them, Pauwels van Dale, purchased a large amount of grain in 1565, a particularly poor harvest year, and stored it in his warehouse at a time when there was starvation in the city. A riot and looting erupted when news of his holdings became public. Similar developments occurred in other cities beset by famine. Toward the end of the century, almost all of Europe was struck by crime waves caused by hunger and the awareness that the rich were getting richer and the poor poorer. Such crime continued into the seventeenth century.

In the despair of the period rested the solution. The economic crisis stimulated businessmen to seek greater economies and markets. Moreover, as new players entered the fray, the exploration and exploitation of Asia, Africa, and the Americas continued.

Just as the sixteenth century saw the rise of Portugal and Spain, so the seventeenth was the Netherlands' century. By then, Antwerp had declined, with Amsterdam taking its place in the scheme of things in the Low Countries. The Netherlands had colonies in the Americas, and together with the Portuguese, opened Japan to trade. By 1566, when Holland revolted against the Spaniards, the Netherlands was a strong commercial nation. Dutch fishing fleets plied the North Sea, and the fish they caught were packed or dried and sold throughout central and southern Europe. Dutch merchants cut into the trade of the Hanseatic League and then entered the commercial life of the Mediterranean. In 1579, the Netherlands declared its independence from Spain. By then, the country's mariners, known collectively as the "sea-beggars," were helping enrich merchants and bankers in Amsterdam. Sea-beggars organized the East and West India Companies, the Amsterdam Stock Exchange, and the Bank of Amsterdam, the three legs upon which the country's greatness was erected. All the while, the Dutch carried on a series of wars with England and France, on occasion with both simultaneously. While costly in financial terms, they were far less so in human terms. Holland's leaders hired entire armies to fight for their country. As an English observer noted, "He that hath coin shall have strangers to fight for him."

The Dutch East India Company was organized in 1602 and given a monopoly of the Oriental trade for 19 years. The charter was renewed regularly. The company received enthusiastic support from the government—empowered to establish colonies, maintain armed forces, and assume sovereign power when it deemed this necessary to conduct business. Under the leadership of Jan Pieterszoon Coen, the company drove the Portuguese from the Indian Ocean and southeast Asia, displaced English traders in the region, and obtained a strong position in the spice trade. As a result, for many years the East India Company was able to pay large dividends, ranging from a high of 75 percent in 1606 to 50 percent in 1611, after which payments dropped off. For a long time, however, the Company was a stellar performer on the Amsterdam Stock Exchange.

The New Netherlands Company was organized in 1613 to conduct commerce in the Americas, with a three-year monopoly that was not renewed. The Dutch West India Company, which took over the New Netherlands Company's territory and more, was organized in 1621. It received a charter to trade and establish colonies in the Americas and the west coast of Africa below the Tropic of Cancer. This company established a small colony in New York harbor called New Amsterdam, another further up the Hudson River, and one in New Jersey, which were followed by settlements in South America and the Caribbean, including Curaçao. For a while it appeared the Dutch West India Company might seize Brazil from the Portuguese. While these settlements were not as important as those of the East India Company, Dutch shipping interests cut deeply into the trade of the English and French settlements.

The Dutch empire was always more commercial than political, in this respect resembling that of Portugal. The Dutch had little interest in agriculture, mining, settlement, or industry. What mattered to them was possessing trading posts through which they could attract items available in the areas they controlled using trade goods from elsewhere. For this, they mastered the art of naval construction. In the late seventeenth century, four of every five European vessels were Dutch, and they plied an area bounded by Japan to the east, South America to the west, the Cape of Good Hope and the Straits of Magellan to the south, and the Baltic and the North Atlantic to the north. Dutch ships could be found on every ocean and sea.

Insofar as Africa was concerned, Dutch traders and sea captains went first in search of gold. However, the growth of a Dutch foothold in Brazil changed this and led them into the lucrative slave trade. Entering the Gold Coast, Dutch traders established good relations with some of the African chiefs by offering superior trade goods at lower prices. In addition, they could provide cowry shells harvested off the coast of the Maldive Islands near Ceylon, which the West Africans used as currency. Olfert Dapper, a Dutch geographer writing in the mid-seventeenth century, noted, "The readiest merchandise . . . are certain shells called boesjies [cowries] . . . without them foreigners can drive but poor trade." According to him, cowries represented one-third of the goods exchanged for slaves.

The West African chiefs might have realized that competition with the Dutch would cause the Portuguese to offer better terms. Dutch successes prompted them to establish barracons of their own at Fort Nassau and on an island off Cape Verde named Goree. Then, in 1637, Dutch traders seized Elmina from the Portuguese. By then, they were the dominant force in West Africa, having supplanted the Portuguese in the slave trade.

By then, too, what historians have labeled "triangular trade" had come into existence, the key to which was the business of slaving. While there never was a template or pattern, generally speaking, this trade began in Europe, where merchants knew they would need trading goods to exchange for slaves. These were guns and ammunition, trinkets, pots and pans, and other such products. These would be sent to trading stations, or "factories," on the coast. Local chiefs would arrive there with their captives, and the bargaining would begin. In the end, the chiefs departed with the trading goods, and the Europeans had their slaves. The next step was to transport the slaves to the Americas, particularly the West Indies, where they would be exchanged for sugar, tobacco, and other agricultural products, which were taken to Europe to be sold. Large profits could be made with each exchange, the by-now familiar practice of taking products from areas where they are relatively inexpensive and selling or trading them in areas where they are more desirable.

Triangular trade did not last long. By the late eighteenth century, few ships followed the pattern. By then, the sugar trade in Cuba, Puerto Rico, Mexico, and other parts of the Caribbean was so important that London merchants engaged in it exclusively, sending their ships to the West Indies laden with trading goods and returning with sugar. The Dutch slavers who brought their cargoes to the Indies in this period often had to return home or back to Africa empty.

For all the profits to be made, few Dutch settlers were attracted to the colonies, and except for South Africa, that remained the situation for as long as the Netherlands was a substantial force in opening the world to commerce.

At home, meanwhile, the Dutch economy thrived. Immigrants fleeing from religious oppression elsewhere helped the Dutch create a major textile industry. Sugar refining, brewing, and distilling flourished in Rotterdam, while Amsterdam became a center for diamond cutting, lens making, and the production of mathematical and shipping instruments, as well as maps and charts. Amsterdam and several other Dutch cities were the publishing centers of Europe, and books from there were sold openly where permitted and smuggled into the places where they were banned.

The Dutch grew to be a powerful force in banking as well, offering superior services and highly competitive rates. The Dutch East India Company floated a 12.6 million florin bond issue at 3½ percent interest, and merchants could borrow at around that rate. While the German and Italian bankers often would lend for only short periods, the Dutch were willing to buy and sell the long-term bonds, which borrowers preferred.

The Dutch had a lively securities market and, in addition, several important commodity markets. The most sensational and famous of these was the market that sprang up to deal in tulip bulbs. The flowers had been introduced into Holland from Turkey, and they captured the fancy of the Dutch. In 1630, there were markets for bulbs in Amsterdam and Rotterdam, and others appeared later on elsewhere. Eventually, every western European nation had at least one tulip market. Bulbs even became a form of currency. By mid-1635, such species as the Semper Augustus, Admiral Liefken, and Viceroy brought fortunes on the market. The Viceroy, at its peak, cost 2500 florins on the Amsterdam market, at a time when a yoke of oxen could be purchased for 250 florin and a suit of clothes for 80. The market collapsed in late 1635, and within a week some of the bulbs were close to worthless. The Amsterdam market took a generation to recover from the tulip craze, but the new surge of expansion with dreams of wealth led to other manias.

Speculators and Bubbles

The tulip mania was the first of the modern "bubbles" that would mark western civilization from that time to the present. Bubbles occur when wild and unrealistic speculation arise around some product or financial opportunity, during which time participants entertain visions of great wealth achieved rapidly through the purchase of the right securities. Such speculation has existed in all western European nations, as dreams of the wealth to be obtained from overseas spread to the middle classes. On top of all this, the chronic wars of the period drove monarchs to ever-greater recourse to loans than had been the case earlier. In England the financial difficulties of the Crown resulted in the formation of the Bank of England in 1694, which advanced funds in return for a charter—and three years later the grant of a monopoly on joint-stock banking in the kingdom. The bank's prestige was based in part on its becoming the repository for tax and loan receipts and its close relationship to the treasury. A century later, Bank of England notes were the common tender for settling accounts, and the institution had become, for all intents and purposes, a central bank, providing England with greater financial stability than most other countries, and adding significantly to its power. The Dutch, too, had a central bank, the Bank of Amsterdam, which eased the financings by that country's merchants and those of the government. Commercial interests and foreign governments trusted bills issued by the banks, since—theoretically—each note was backed wholly by gold, available upon request. The French lacked such an institution, which added to the difficulty of competing in a period of colonial rivalries and wars.

Into this breech appeared John Law, one of the earliest "bubble makers," a financial genius and charlatan of a type that will be seen increasingly in this narrative. Law was a

Scots financier, the son of a prominent goldsmith-banker He had been instructed in finance by Thomas Neale, master of the mint, who had organized the first national lottery in 1694 and developed the paper currency for Scotland. In 1695, Law was imprisoned for having murdered his mistress's husband, but he escaped to the continent. He landed in Amsterdam and then wandered from country to country, trying to interest rulers in supporting his plan for a central bank in their countries, in the process accumulating a fortune through speculation and by writing a treatise entitled "Money and the Trade Considered," in which he argued for the creation of a paper currency that would expand the monetary base and create prosperity.

While Law was not the originator of reserve banking, which had existed even as early as the Hellenistic Age, he was one of its most successful practitioners. He demonstrated to the financial community of his time the feasibility of such a form of banking and the power that came with the ability to expand the currency.

Law suspected that the Dutch bank was investing gold deposits at a profit, realizing that so long as the investment public had confidence in the bank's ability to repay deposits, they would use its paper as though it were gold and not demand redemption. He recognized that the true backing for a currency was trust in its purchasing power, and not any special virtue of the gold backing. He was proposing to create an institution that at the same time would be a depository, a central bank, and the prime investing medium for the nation. It would be supported by the Crown, have prominent members, and be so respected that none would question the backing of its notes, thus enabling him to expand them at will. In this way the money supply of the country would be enlarged and the economy stimulated, but more important, Law would have at his disposal unlimited funds for investment.

In 1717, Law gained an important friend in the French court, Philip, Duke of Orleans, regent for King Louis XV. France was in dire financial circumstances, and the Duke was prepared to be convinced that the bank scheme could provide the court with large quantities of money with which to pay its debts. Orleans and his friends thus would receive enough funds to keep the ship of state on an even keel, Law would have power and prestige, and investors in the bank's stock would receive dividends and capital gains. Prosperity restored, interest rates would decline, assisting both governmental and private enterprise.

The bank was established, and Law was soon able to take control of many companies through the use of bills backed by bank deposits. The most important of these, the Compagnie des Indies (also known as the Mississippi Company), had been granted extensive rights in the Mississippi Valley. Law obtained for it the monopoly of tobacco concessions and control of trade with the French possessions in the East Indies, China, and Senegal. Then Law issued grandiose statements about the fantastic wealth of the region. "There one sees mountains filled with gold, silver, copper, lead, quicksilver," he proclaimed. "Since these metals are common there and the savages do not imagine their real worth, they exchange them for a swallow of brandy."

France was swept by a wave of speculation that in some ways resembled the tulip mania. The Rue de Quincampois, where stockbrokers and speculators assembled, was crowded with those hoping to double their holdings in weeks. Purchasers were permitted to take possession of shares with a payment of 10 percent of the price (margin), with the rest payable in 19 monthly installments. But in practice, when the shares rose, the speculators would sell to another group of speculators and pocket the profits, seeking profitable investments in other companies that sprang up. Real estate in the area increased in value, and so Paris had a financial district of sorts. An illusion of prosperity blanketed the city, as messenger boys converted tips into small purchases, then doubled and redoubled, and some emerged wealthy. According to one account, a wretched hunchback was able to make a good living renting his back as a portable desk. Expanding his influence, power, and reputation, in 1718 Law obtained the right to mint coins and collect taxes for the government.

Law's plans to assume the public debt appeared on the brink of realization in the autumn of 1719. Under his plan, the government would pay 3 percent interest on the portion of the 1.5 billion livres of debt the Mississippi Company assumed. The company had pledged to pay dividends at the rate of 12 percent, at a time when investments considered safe paid 5 percent. To accomplish this, Law would have had to show an annual profit of 200 million livres on operations, which was clearly impossible for a company whose only assets were raw land and a measure of hope. Some speculators, realizing this, started selling the shares short. In order to prevent a panic and boost morale, Law paraded a few thousand criminals through the streets, picks and shovels in hand, and announced they were on their way to New Orleans to mine gold. Shares shot up in value, the shorts were squeezed, and confidence was restored in Law's genius. In accordance with his plan, the Banque Royale issued 800 million livres in notes that further stimulated speculation. By November, Mississippi shares that had a par value of 500 livres were selling for more than 10,000 livres.

The fall of the Mississippi scheme came in 1720. The promises of wealth had not materialized, and after two years of illusion followed by dashed hopes, the market collapsed. Law was discredited, and the Paris market reorganized. The Bourse was chartered in 1726, and the appearance of a securities market provided France with a greater degree of liquidity. But this did not compensate for the lack of confidence in bank notes. The French were not to have the strong central bank enjoyed by the English. Loan rates there invariably were higher than those across the English Channel, an important factor in deciding which country would win the war for empire.

This is not to say the English were spared bubbles of their own. While the French were entranced with Mississippi, the English had their own version. The London money market had begun along the old Roman wall of Londinium. Merchants from Lombardy had settled in the area, giving the name of Lombard Street to what became the center of English finance. By the early eighteenth century, the street was teaming with brokers who traded shares of joint stock companies, some of which went back to the time of Elizabeth.

In 1711, several businessmen and nobles received a charter for the South Sea Company, which offered to assume the entire debt of England in return for trade concessions and grants that would make the company the most powerful economic and financial entity in the nation. It was to be done not through payments of cash but by an exchange of paper. Owners of government debt would be able to exchange their bonds for shares in the South Sea Company. To convince creditors of the soundness of the company, it was granted a monopoly on English trade with South America, and then another on the *asiento,* the African slave trade to Latin America as well. Finally, the government was to pay an 8000 pound annual management fee and 586,000 pounds in annual interest on the 9.5 million pounds of debt assumed by the company.

Even as Parliament debated the proposal, shares rose from 130 to 300. Members of both houses participated in the dealings, and were granted "favors" by South Sea directors. Prime Minister Robert Walpole later admitted to having owned shares during this period. Parliament agreed, and at once shares in the company soared. Dazzled by the French example, English investors stampeded into the market in droves.

By mid-year, South Seas shares were selling for more than 1000 pounds, and the success spilled over into securities of other companies. Some of these, firms engaged in construction and fabrication, were sound. Others, like one that planned to make planks from sawdust, might have been well-intentioned, but were not sound. Many were frauds, such as a company formed to produce radish oil, which had no known use.

The bubble burst within a year, wrecking the fortunes of hundreds and discrediting some English politicians. Parliament swiftly passed a law forbidding the issuance and trading of shares without legal authority, "either by act of Parliament or by Charter from the Crown." Another act, passed in 1734, prevented specific abuses by stockbrokers, and 40 years later, short-selling was forbidden. Few of these strictures were followed by the brokers and their customers, however. With or without regulations, the market thrived.

The rise of the London markets, which took place as the Paris Bourse stagnated, was due in part to the comparative lack of royal power in England and the solidity of the Bank of England. The Bourbons controlled much of France's domestic commerce and industry as well as overseas ventures. The English rulers, with limited exchequers overseen by an increasingly powerful Parliament, had to allow private enterprise to develop trade and industry. Faced with opportunities and possibilities, English investors were encouraged to risk their capital on new ventures as well as on established companies.

CHAPTER 7

The English Advantage

NGLAND was one of the first countries to enter the race for exploration and discovery, but initially, it found little of what was then considered wealth. Its efforts were complicated by the Crown's lack of funds to finance the kinds of expeditions that enabled Spain to tap the wealth of South America. At the time, England's monarchs were constantly in need of funds but were reluctant to ask the House of Commons for taxes and bequests, knowing that in return for providing capital the legislature would demand greater freedoms and rights. Paradoxically, the government's inability to act more forcefully than it did in this aspect of the pursuit of wealth and its need to rely on private capital, enabled England to become one of the most successful nations at colonization. Lacking the mineral wealth that the Spaniards discovered, England was obliged to turn to agriculture instead. The Spaniards found some of the world's most fertile soils in present-day Argentina, but they were there for gold and silver, not farming. As a result, they did not send families to Argentina, but rather conquistadores. The English sent families.

In order to appreciate the situation in which the English found themselves during the seventeenth century, one must consider that they hoped to find three things in North America: enormous amounts of gold and silver, or mines from which they could be extracted; large numbers of natives wealthy in trading goods that would fetch high prices in Europe; or, lacking these, fertile lands on which to grow the kinds of crops needed by the Europeans. Crops also would be required to sustain the original settlers. In retrospect, this was beneficial. It ensured that the English colonies actually would create wealth, not just transport precious metals and goods from one part of the world to another. The English in North America were settlers in families, not conquistadores concerned with plunder. All looked upon the New World as a potential storehouse of wealth. When the English North American holdings proved unpromising, the land became an appendage of European civilization and ultimately a major carrier of its traditions. Of course, none of this could have been imagined at the time. Clearly, this experience colored the development of what in time became the United States.

Europe's earliest American empires resulted from close collaboration between rulers and businessmen, especially bankers. The settlements required large infusions of capital, which the bankers stood prepared to provide—at a price. At the same time, as mercantilist sentiment grew and as the price revolution altered business activities, the power of the businessmen and bankers increased. In this period new ventures obtained their financing in several ways, one of which was the issuance of securities, which enabled those Europeans who were fascinated with the new world developing in the Americas to participate financially in the settlements. But it should be remembered that while the Americas were glamorous places for investment, larger profits were being made elsewhere—in Africa and Asia, for example. Also, as will be seen, the Indies were to prove more fruitful for investors than the mainland colonies, at least in the beginning.

In 1496, King Henry VII granted John Cabot, a Venetian mariner who had relocated to Bristol, a patent to explore the north Atlantic in search of a northwest passage. Cabot made two voyages and, of course, did not find that route, but he may have gotten as far as the coast of New England. Other voyages followed, with no impact on English life or fortunes. More important for England's exchequer were intrusions on Spanish commerce, adventures in slaving, and attempts to carve out a role in the Spanish colonial economy. As a matter of the official record, Queen Elizabeth did not openly support the pirates and slavers, but everyone in Europe knew she was the guiding force and went so far as to license privateers.

John Hawkins and the Slave Trade

John Hawkins was one of the first consequential figures in both areas. He spent his early career in the slave trade, following in the footsteps of his father, William, who had dabbled in the trade, transporting Africans from the Guinea coast of Africa to Portuguese settlements in Brazil. In 1562, Hawkins obtained financial backing from a group of London businessmen and set out for the Guinea coast, where he stole or purchased from natives more than 300 Africans. He then took them to Hispaniola, where he traded them for hides, ginger, sugar, and pearls. The settlers needed the slaves, and so Spanish strictures against such trade were overlooked. Besides, Hawkins' ships were well-armed and to not permit him to trade might invite violence. Alonso Arias de Herrera, president of the Audencia in Santo Domingo, wrote of this to the King:

> A Lutheran Englishman with a large ship and a shallop, both well-supplied with artillery, and a caravel and a large bark, both handsome vessels which they had taken from merchants as they left the Portuguese islands, arrived off the town of Puerta de Plata in this island. As soon as the captain and the mayor of this town saw them, fearing lest they march inland to pillage the country, they entered into negotiations with them to the end of procuring their departure and inquired of them what they wanted. The English said they would go if they were shown a port where they could careen a caravel and shallop. In order to get rid of them they sent them to the port of La Isabela, which is twelve leagues from here.

Hawkins got what he wanted and proceeded to La Isabela, where he sold most of the slaves and arranged for the disposition of those that remained. Other slaving expeditions followed, and his success led to royal favors and commissions. In 1588, Hawkins served as rear admiral against the Spanish Armada. Afterwards, he had a career as a privateer, raiding Spanish treasure fleets. By then, however, he was eclipsed by other English raiders, Sir Francis Drake in particular.

Commissioned by Queen Elizabeth in 1570 after serving an apprenticeship under Hawkins, Drake spent a quarter of a century plundering the Spanish Main. He struck at the Panamanian port of Nombre de Dios during a voyage from 1572 to 1573, capturing Spanish treasure bound from Peru. Later in the decade, Drake moved to the Pacific coast, attacking Spanish shipping as he went, and then turned west and circumnavigated the globe. In the 1580s, Drake sacked Cartegena, St. Augustine, and Santo Domingo, and he was alongside Hawkins in the contest against the Spanish Armada. English privateers continued to raid the Spanish Main in the seventeenth century, and for a while Henry Morgan, the leading English pirate of the time, actually governed Jamaica, which became the center for English contraband trade. In this period, as had been the case since the Mesopotamians, theft was an important means of obtaining wealth.

Other methods, slower and less direct, were agriculture and animal husbandry, which were the principal occupations of the settlers. These newcomers were Europeans, with European values and desires, who found themselves in what they saw as a virgin, savage land. Adjusting to the new dispensation and coming to terms with the environment would be among their major challenges, which would not be accomplished in a few years, or even a generation. More critical perhaps was that the settlers lacked capital, one of the first major problems they had to resolve.

They did so by resorting to the ancient method of pooling resources with others to limit risk and diversify investment. In England during the seventeenth century this took the form of joint stock companies: associations chartered by the Crown, often after the members made a substantial contribution to the royal exchequer. These companies were given the right to exercise authority over specified jurisdictions. They were outgrowths of a variety of guilds, known as regulated companies, which were comprised of guild members who were granted monopolies of trade with specified markets in return for their financial support of the sovereign.

The Joint Stock Companies

The East India Company, destined to be the most important of all the joint stock companies, obtained its charter in 1600. It was capitalized at 68,000 pounds and subscribed to by more than 200 merchants. The company was granted a 15-year monopoly for English trade between the Cape of Good Hope and the Straits of Magellan. Unlike those concerned with North America, it was not directly involved with settlements.

The initial activities were very much like those of companies that were formed to back specific voyages. Merchants would take shares in an enterprise, which would be dissolved following the return of the ship and the sale of the cargo. The East India Company had 12 such voyages between 1601 and 1612, going to such areas as the Red Sea and the East Indies, with only one showing a loss. The investors were repaid their capital plus a profit of more than 200 percent. Two years later, the East India Company had 19 facilities and was sending shipments of indigo, pepper, saltpeter, cottons, and silks from the Orient to England. It continued to thrive into the eighteenth century, and by

1717, the value of its shares came to 3.2 million pounds, ranking it third in size behind the flawed South Sea Company (10 million pounds) and the Bank of England (5.6 million pounds).

The East India Company and the other joint stock companies were run more efficiently and intelligently than their French and Spanish counterparts. A political appointee of the King of France might make careless mistakes that could cost the Crown a fortune and yet not suffer any undue personal loss. English merchants couldn't afford such slips; their own funds were at stake.

Later on, the company disposed of this arrangement and functioned as a unified enterprise, with proceeds from expeditions placed in the East Indies treasury to be dispensed to members in the form of dividends.

Some of the East India Company's earliest ventures were attempts to find the longed-for Northwest Passage to the Indies. None of these voyages was successful, and no gold was discovered either, but the explorers were able to report that the North American coastline was suitable for agriculture and related pursuits.

Sailing for the company in 1602, Bartholomew Gosnold returned to England with a cargo of sassafras. Two years later, George Weymouth arrived back in England with glowing reports of the New England coast. Merchants in Bristol, Plymouth, London, and other port cities applied for charters to explore and settle the region. In 1606, King James I granted several merchant groups a charter as the Virginia Company, to be governed from London by a council appointed by the Crown. The Plymouth merchants were given the right to exploit the New England area as far south as the fortieth parallel, while the London group was granted rights from the thirty-eighth parallel south to the Carolinas. The area between the two companies was to be a "no man's land," eventually to be opened to both circles.

Sir Thomas Smythe, a leader of the London group, at once set about organizing his resources. He hoped to learn from mistakes made by Raleigh and the Spaniards. The Roanoke settlement clearly had been undercapitalized; Smythe made certain that he had what he considered to be sufficient funds on hand before sending out the first ship. The Spaniards had been impatient, unwilling to engage in mining, and settling for whatever could be stolen from the natives. Smythe's men would be willing to work hard for their rewards, knowing that great profits could be had for such labors. At the same time, friendly relations with the natives would be established to facilitate trade, while an expedition was to be organized to search for the elusive Northwest Passage.

The following year, the *Susan Constant, Goodspeed,* and *Discovery* set sail for America from the London Company's docks. From the first, the expedition was doomed. The 120 passengers had convinced Smythe they understood the problems posed by settlement and were willing to persevere. In reality, they were still ignorant of the obstacles they would encounter, and hoped only to plunder the country and return as quickly as possible. In spite of Smythe's precautions, the expedition was understaffed and lacked sufficient financing. In fact, it differed only slightly from Raleigh's ill-fated Roanoke venture.

The ships arrived in Chesapeake Bay in May 1607, but not with the original complement of settlers. Some of the colonists who had begun the voyage with high hopes had second thoughts, and left the ships when they stopped for supplies. Others died on shipboard. Those who remained pitched tents along the James River and established the colony of Jamestown. They quickly fell out with the natives, were beset with disease, and quarreled among themselves.

The ships sailed back to England in early July. Upon their return the following January, only 40 haggard settlers were there to greet them. The venture seemed an unqualified failure.

Nevertheless, the London Company decided to continue the settlement for a while longer. Supplies were sent and additional colonists induced to make the voyage. Most important, Captain John Smith—a boastful, arrogant, yet charismatic veteran of several European conflicts—took command at Jamestown. Smith negotiated successfully with the natives (especially Chief Powhatan), established several new towns, and streamlined Jamestown's structure. In addition, he encouraged the pioneers to work by granting them a direct share of their production instead of having everyone draw from the common store. With that, production improved sharply, and Jamestown took a turn for the better. In the summer of 1609, some 500 additional colonists arrived and the settlement seemed on the verge of success. The search for a Northwest Passage had been abandoned, as had hopes of finding precious metals. Instead, Jamestown had become a thriving settlement of small landholders, sustaining itself by agriculture and trade with the natives, and returning some small profits to the London investors.

The most important event in Virginia's early history was the introduction of tobacco. According to tradition, John Rolfe brought tobacco to Virginia in 1611 or 1612, and from there it was taken to Maryland. At the time, the Jamestown settlement was still struggling. Tobacco provided it with a much needed cash crop. Farmers throughout the Virginia settlement now turned to tobacco culture, and soon the colony was economically viable. Maryland, too, became an important tobacco grower, and attempts to cultivate the crop in North Carolina also proved successful. But early efforts to plant tobacco north of Maryland ended in failure.

The first shipment of Virginia tobacco to London took place in 1613. Within three years, it had become the colony's chief export. Queen Elizabeth recognized the commercial potential of tobacco. It was an expensive indulgence, and a highly profitable one as well. In the early seventeenth century, tobacco was sold for its weight in silver. This encouraged growing, exportation, and taxation. So from the first, it was evident that the Virginians had found a cash crop that would enable them to obtain needed imports, while England would be able to free itself from dependence on the Spaniards for tobacco.

King James, who opposed the use of tobacco, acted on his belief by imposing a tariff of 4000 percent on tobacco. This had little effect, due largely to smuggling. By the early seventeenth century, the smoking and chewing of tobacco was prevalent in most parts of Europe. By 1614, there were some 7000 London establishments at which one might purchase tobacco, and England had come to realize that tobacco might become their version of Spanish gold.

Moreover, by 1614, it was believed the Virginia tobacco was every bit as good as that grown in Trinidad, at the time known for the high quality of its leaf. By 1615–1616, Virginia's planters were able to export 2500 pounds of tobacco, of which all but 200 pounds went to England. In this same period, 58,300 pounds of tobacco were sent to England from Spain.

The drainage of specie from England to Spain remained a matter of grave concern. In 1620, the House of Commons unanimously declared "that the importation of Spanish tobacco is one of the causes of the want of money within the kingdom." The following year, as the supply of Virginia tobacco increased, Parliament opted to end importation of Spanish tobacco, which by then took 60,000 pounds sterling out of England. In that year, England passed a law all but completely prohibiting the importation of tobacco from foreign countries.

Meanwhile, the fact that Europeans had taken to tobacco led to large-scale imports from the Caribbean plantations. Attempts were made to grow tobacco in northern Europe, but due to climate and soil, these early efforts failed to produce a satisfactory leaf. Belgium experimented with plantings in 1554, France in 1556, the Germanies in 1559, the Netherlands in 1561, and England in 1570. By 1700, tobacco was cultivated or used in western Europe, Italy, Russia, Persia, India, Japan, and North and West Africa. The only way Europeans could obtain satisfactory supplies in this period was through importation, which meant England had to take Virginia seriously as a source of wealth.

Virginia, envisaged as a gold mining and exploring colony and later as a place for homesteaders, now became a colony of small landholders, each family performing its own labors. Tobacco farming required large bands of field workers supervised by an overseer. Englishmen who agreed to become indentured servants and work in the fields were transported to Virginia and Maryland and served from two to seven years, after which they would be freed and given land. Demand still far exceeded supply. Nevertheless, for many years the majority of tobacco plantation workers were European.

By 1619, another labor source was made available. In that year a Dutch frigate landed in Jamestown and unloaded, as part of its cargo, 20 Africans. Most of them, and others who followed, worked in the tobacco fields. This was how the system of slavery was introduced into North America. But the English were not about to permit the Dutch to control the lucrative slave trade with Virginia. The previous year, King James I granted a monopoly in the commerce between Africa and the American colonies to a group of London merchants, who organized the Company of Adventurers of London Trading into Parts of Africa. By then, however, the Dutch grip on the trade was such that the English share was comparatively small.

The tobacco growers accepted slaves reluctantly. Indentured servants were less expensive. Slaves had to be purchased, and when they died, the planters suffered an economic loss, while none accompanied the death of an indentured servant. Then, too, the Europeans came voluntarily, the slaves against their wills, and so one might presume the former would be more docile and work more willingly. In time, these attitudes would change. During the early eighteenth century, the shortage of field labor spurred the trade, especially in males, but demand for females increased as well. After the middle of the century, Virginia planters had less of a need for imported slaves, the result of higher life expectancy and birth rates for slaves. The situation was different on the rice plantations in the low country in the Carolinas, where the life expectancy of slaves working in the rice fields was low. On the eve of the American Revolution, 35 percent of the South Carolina slaves had been born in Africa, while only 9 percent of the Virginia slaves were "imported."

The Sugar Trade

As important as tobacco would be in European-American commerce, sugar was becoming still more significant. Sugar cane was introduced into the West Indies around 1640, and within 20 years it had surpassed tobacco in importance as an American export, accounting for nearly half of England's imports from the Americas. This resulted in an increase in the demand for slaves. In 1672, the Royal African Company was organized to take over all of England's African affairs, and the Dutch were displaced. In 1713, the Spaniards recognized England's supremacy in the slave trade by granting the Guinea Company an *asiento* to supply the Spanish colonies with African slaves, supplanting a 1664 contract with the French African Company and adding to England's lead in this field. Under the terms of the contract, the Guinea Company was to supply the colonies with 144,000 slaves within a 30-year period, or 4800 annually. Spain was to receive 200,000 crowns for the privilege and a duty of 33½ crowns for each slave, while the English and Spanish monarchs each were to receive a one-quarter share of the profits. Even with such terms, the trade was highly profitable. By 1755, there were 237 licensed traders in Bristol, 147 in London, and 89 in Liverpool. The shops of Manchester, Exeter, and Chester were churning out trading goods. Sir John Clapham remarked toward the end of the eighteenth century that "Manchester lived on shirts for black men." The shipbuilders profited from the trade, as did sailors and candlers.

Without sugar, there would have been none of this. The price was high and the demand was growing. In 1720, England imported little more than half a million tons of sugar. By the end of the century, the figure was close to 2.5 million tons, and in the process, scores of millionaires were created. Some historians have asserted that in terms of economic importance, the West Indies surpassed India. The West Indies sugar planters were to the 1750s what the Arab petroleum tycoons would be two centuries later. "Rich as a Creole" was a commonplace way of indicating a person was wealthy. "Our tobacco colonies send us home no such wealthy planters as we frequently see arrive from our sugar islands," noted economist Adam Smith. In *The West Indian*, a play popular during the 1765 season in London, a servant for a reception for a West India planter remarked, "He's very rich, and that's sufficient. They say he has rum and sugar enough belonging to him, to make all the water in the Thames into punch." There were no such plays dealing with Virginia planters or Albany fur traders, simply because they were not so numerous or wealthy. When King George III spied an ornate coach on a London thoroughfare, he remarked, "Sugar. Sugar. Eh! All that sugar." Lord Chesterfield observed that it was impossible to purchase a seat in the House of Commons. "There was no such thing as a borough to be had now, for the East and West Indians have secured them all at the rate of three thousand pounds at least."

Consider the situation of one late eighteenth century Bristol businessman who had the good fortune to enter the sugar trade. William Miles worked as an unskilled laborer and managed to put together 15 pounds. He then signed on as a carpenter for a voyage to Jamaica, where he used his savings to buy "a cask or two of sugar." He brought the sugar back to Bristol where it was sold for a large profit. With this money he procured a consignment of English manufactured goods, took it to Jamaica, sold it again for a much higher price, and then purchased more sugar. He repeated the operation and, on his death in 1848, left an estate of more than 500,000 pounds.

New England

The Plymouth Company sent its first vessels to North America in 1607. Two ships landed near the Kennebec River in Maine early in the year, and a rude fort was thrown up close to the river's mouth. A handful of settlers remained in the colony during the winter, and George Popham, the leader of the expedition, visited Plymouth with tales of great wealth to be found in Maine. When the supply ship returned the following spring, it found only Popham's grave and a few starving settlers begging to be returned to Europe. During the next decade, the company continued to send ships to explore the area, but made no major move toward colonization. John Smith visited the region in 1614 and wrote a glowing report of it for potential settlers in his *Description of New England*, but no one volunteered to go to America. Several companies were organized on the strength of this report, among them the Adventurers, the Dorchester, the Laconia, and the New England. None was successful. When the Adventurers finally were able to arrange for a shipment to England, it was captured by French pirates. A second cargo was seized by the Turks.

Meanwhile, Smith's reports were read by a group of religious dissenters. These people, known as Pilgrims, had relocated for religious reasons to Leyden, in Holland. Representatives of the London Company offered to send the Pilgrims to Virginia as stockholders in the company, not as employees. After seven years, the venture was to be dissolved and a distribution made to all according to the number of shares they owned. The London Company would provide 7000 pounds and receive half the profits, with settlers dividing the other half among them. Thirty-five Pilgrims accepted the offer, and joined by 66 non-Pilgrims, left on the *Mayflower* from Plymouth in 1620.

The ship did not go to Virginia; instead it went to Massachusetts. Soon, a small town was established. The *Mayflower* remained for the winter and provided a haven for the colonists. By the time the ship left the following April, however, half the colonists had died.

The settlement was replenished the following fall when the *Fortune* dropped off 35 additional colonists and carried a cargo of furs back to England to the London Company. The settlement showed small profits almost immediately. In 1627, the Pilgrim leaders were able to buy out the London merchants and distribute all the land in the colony to its inhabitants. More towns were established, and the colony thrived. It remained independent until 1691, when it was annexed to the larger and more powerful Puritan settlements in Massachusetts. By then, however, the English had to face strong competitors from a country, which also possessed a vital merchant capitalist class and strong finances: the Dutch Republic.

The Dutch Challenge

In 1643, the English colonies north of New York united to form the New England Confederation. Its major ambition and accomplishment was to halt Dutch expansion from New Amsterdam and the Hudson valley. Dutch traders and manufacturers always had been interested in the fast-growing English markets in the Americas. The outbreak of the English civil war in the 1640s gave them their chance. Now that England was otherwise occupied, the Dutch moved to take over these markets. Since English shipping was disrupted and the price of English goods rose sharply—because of increased costs attending the fighting—the Dutch were able to undersell their competitors. Within a few years, operating with impunity on the high seas, the Dutch managed to displace the English in several colonial markets. Dutch dry goods, hardware, and beer outsold English products in New England and Virginia. By 1643, Dutch money was used in Virginia, and a decade later, it was common currency in other colonies as well. The Dutch took control of the trade in the English sugar islands and replaced the English as financial agents in Barbados. By 1655, four of every five trading ships engaged in African and American trade were Dutch.

Oliver Cromwell, who led the victors in the civil war, attempted to meet the Dutch challenge. London's Puritan merchants now had strong representation in government, and they meant to use it to drive the Dutch from the high seas. One indication of the new temper of the times was a sharp rise in ship construction after 1649. Another was passage of the mercantilist-inspired Navigation Acts of 1650 and 1651, which prohibited any foreign nation from trading with England's American colonies. Other restrictive legislation would follow.

Cromwell tried to avoid antagonizing the Dutch unnecessarily, for after all, they were Protestants like him and might be a useful ally in his planned attack on Catholic Europe. After passage of the Navigation Acts, he attempted to placate the Dutch merchants by negotiating a Protestant League, in which they would control the East Indies trade while England took North America and all of South America except Brazil. The two would unite in plundering Africa. But the Dutch, recognizing their strength, rejected this offer, insisting on free trade with North America and the Caribbean islands. Negotiations stalled and as noted, by 1651 anti-Dutch Puritans in Parliament passed a new Navigation Act that denied foreigners the right to carry goods between England and other nations. In effect, the only trade the Dutch were permitted with the English was carrying their own manufactured goods to English ports (but not to those of the colonies). The Act was tantamount to a declaration of trade war, and it was followed by a brief Anglo-Dutch naval war in 1652–1653. The New England Confederation planned to attack the Dutch possessions to the south, but at the last moment the Dutch agreed to respect the Navigation Acts and enter into a defensive alliance with Cromwell. It was clear at the time, however, that the Netherlands not only was England's equal but also wealthier, better prepared for war, and more aggressive. In addition, it was more advanced in the area of finance.

The Realization of Wealth in the North

Northern climate and soil were not suited for sugar and tobacco, no gold was found there, and there was little need for slaves. Settlers expected marginal existences as farmers, but they also hoped to find products to sell so they could use the funds obtained to purchase needed supplies. In addition, as in England, farmers required the services of specialists and of certain manufacturers of needed goods. All of these factors led the northern colonists down economic paths that differed from those of the southern colonies.

Most of the settlers became farmers, in some areas working in a community, in others on their own farms. This was an important consideration. Recall Francis Bacon's admonition regarding Europe's overpopulation. America seemed a vast wilderness to those early settlers. In Europe, they could hardly hope to become independent farmers working their own land. In America, land was not only abundant but virtually free for the taking. Simply by agreeing to come to New England, peasants were given land of their own. This was one of the most striking aspects of life in English North America. The other was the shortage of labor. In the late eighteenth century, Hector St. John de Crevecoeur arrived to see for himself the new nation that had just been formed, and he noted in one of his first "Letters from an American Farmer":

> The European does not find, as in Europe, a crowded society where every place is overstocked; he does not feel that difficulty of beginning. There is room for everybody in America. Has he any particular talent, or industry? He exerts it in order to procure a livelihood, and it succeeds. Is he a laborer, sober and industrious? He need not go many miles before he will be hired, well fed, and paid four or five times more than he can get in Europe.

What this inferred was that English North America presented unparalleled opportunities for those Europeans with sufficient daring to take the Atlantic voyage and work hard for themselves. Never before was access to capital in the form of land so available to common people, who quite suddenly realized that in America it would be possible for them not only to live better than they had in Europe but to actually become wealthy. In a memorable passage, historian Stanley Lebergott surveyed the European scene in the period prior to and immediately after the American Revolution:

> The daily tasks for virtually all eighteenth-century Europeans make today's concerns about alienation, unemployment, relative deprivation seem like a happy dream. In Scotland men sold themselves into slavery because of poverty, and worked in the salt and coal mines. In France travelers could describe the ragged peasant who yoked his plow with a donkey in one trace and his wife in the other. In Switzerland women filled buckets with urine and manure, yoked them across their shoulders, and carried them uphill to fertilize the fields. Highland women did the same in Scotland. In 1816 a traveler in France saw "washerwomen in the river, standing up to their waists in casks filled with water"; in what is now Czechoslovakia women "walking about without shoes or stockings on weekdays"; in Switzerland meat, even bread, "considered luxuries by the simple people, who had them only on holidays. In the most prosperous nation in Europe, thousands of young children made their living by sweeping the mud and horse droppings away from London streets in return for halfpennies from occasional passerbys. And the rest of Europe? A widely traveled farm expert described the "absolute slavery of the peasants in some parts of Germany, in Denmark, and in Poland and in Russia.

In America, where the free northern farmers had meat every day, starvation was virtually unknown. It was not a lawless country, but the severity of laws in the colonies was far less than in any part of Europe in this period. Little wonder that American farmers appeared so content with their lots, and at the same time so independent.

As for hired laborers, there were relatively few of them, for why become a craftsman when it was possible to be a landholding farmer? The farmers worked at crafts and professions along with growing crops and raising animals. They became shoemakers, brewers, and carpenters, while wives and daughters would spin yarn and weave cloth. Specialization was relatively rare.

Some of the specialists were itinerant craftsmen, who went from farmhouse to farmhouse offering their services in such areas as woodworking, bricklaying, and cooperage. Others were sedentary, such as candlemakers, glassmakers, and those who managed to scrape together sufficient funds to open gristmills, sawmills, and flourmills. But the latter were seasonal enterprises, and their owners and managers usually farmed as well.

Others, in areas of high population, might open shops. This was very much in the tradition of craftsmen who appeared in medieval Europe. They even had apprentices, with contracts not dissimilar to those written centuries earlier. In Chapter 3, there appeared one that involved William, barber of Sestri, in 1248. Compare that document with one written during the late colonial period in New York, in which the apprentice was bound to serve his master:

> . . . his secrets keep, his lawful commands gladly everywhere obey; he shall do no damage
> to his said master, not see to be done by others without letting or giving notice to his said
> master; he shall not waste his said master's goods, nor lend them unlawfully to any; he
> shall not commit fornication nor contract matrimony within the said term. At cards, dice,
> or any other unlawful game he shall not play, whereby his said master may have damage;
> with his own goods or the goods of those during the said term without licence from his
> said master he shall neither buy nor sell. He shall not absent himself day or night from his
> master's service without his leave, nor haunt alehouses or playhouses, but in all things as
> a faithful apprentice he shall behave himself toward his said master, and all during the
> said term.

Such restrictions became more unusual as time passed and distances grew. They were more often to be found along the seacoast than the interior, and in the seventeenth and eighteenth centuries, but not later. Guilds might be accepted in the restricted atmosphere of traditional Europe, but not in the far more open one of colonial and then national America. More often than not, apprentices would remain with masters through their terms of contract, but then they would move on, not becoming journeymen but selling their services on the basis of need and ability, not status.

England's rulers and owners of joint stock company securities bemoaned the absence of gold and silver in North America and wanted the colonies to produce cash crops to realize the benefits promised by the mercantilists. In the South, tobacco, rice, indigo, and sugar served as surrogates for precious metals. In addition, there were abortive attempts to grow olives and coffee, as well as to raise silkworms. The mother country offered bounties for their production, but all attempts failed. In the middle colonies, wheat, corn, barley, and other grains were grown, but in the seventeenth and early eighteenth centuries, these did not constitute major exports.

For a while, furs provided England with its desired export. Some Pilgrims set traps, skinned the animals caught, which ranged from squirrels to beaver to wolves, and then packed the pelts for shipment to England. Trapping was profitable at first, but by the late 1630s, costs outran financial returns. As the animals near the shore were depleted, trappers had to go deeper into the interior, and so this early attempt to find a viable export faded.

In an effort to revive the economy, New England offered subsidies to lure would-be entrepreneurs. These were made available to those who located mineral deposits, to weavers, and to those in the dying fur industry, but to little avail. The development of a triangular trade involving fish caught off the New England and Labrador banks met with greater success. English ships would land in New England and unload cargoes of goods for resale, and then take on a load of barrels of salted fish, which was carried to the Iberian peninsula or the Caribbean for resale. In time, the New England merchants would export barrels and other timber products to these markets as well.

Such activity required capital, and the settlers, with abundant land and scarce labor, also suffered from an absence of capital. This might be obtained from European bankers, but without credit histories, the colonists had to pay high interest rates, and even then, many were turned down as poor risks. Some Americans, who had relatives in European banks, might overcome this disability. For example, Henry Shrimpton was able to obtain loans through his brother, Edward, a London banker, as did John Cogan, whose brother Humphrey also was a London banker. This changed, as those New Englanders lacking such relationships established their credit. By the time of the American Revolution, scores of New England merchants had correspondent relationships with London.

As settlement moved inland, other opportunities for profit emerged. Peddlers might import tin or iron, which was used in the manufacture of utensils. These were then sold locally and eventually in wider areas. The peddlers would meet ships at the harbor and purchase pots, pans, cloth, needles, thread, and other manufactured products that settlers might find useful. They would pack the goods on their wagons and take off into the interior, stopping at farmhouses to sell what they could. These peddlers had to mark up their wares considerably in order to realize profits, and often it was necessary to barter with the settlers, who had little money themselves. It was not unusual for a peddler to return to the coast with a wagon filled with produce of various kinds—much of it whisky. It made little sense for settlers to send their wheat and corn to the coast, since such products were bulky and prices comparatively low. Converting grains to alcohol made more sense economically. The bulk was reduced, the whisky would become more attractive as it aged, and it would not spoil.

This was a period when most (except Quakers) believed rum, gin, brandy, and whisky were akin to foods, being nutritious, healthy, and even medicinal. According to W. J. Rorabaugh in The Alcoholic Republic, "Before 1750, nearly all Americans of all social classes drank alcoholic beverages in quantity, sometimes to the point of intoxication." Rorabaugh estimated that in 1710, the per capita consumption of alcohol for Americans over the age of 15 came to 5.1 gallons per annum, and rose to 6.6 gallons by 1770. Much of this was in the form of home-brewed beer and cider, with more than half being spirits. By way of comparison, in no year since the American Civil War has the per capita consumption of alcohol been as much as half the 1710 figure. Without the liquor trade, the frontier farmers would have had a difficult time earning funds to purchase needed supplies from the peddlers.

As towns appeared, general stores attempted to replace the peddlers. Their proprietors would travel to port cities several times a year to obtain stock, and often making special purchases for customers. Such individuals frequently had lines of credit in coastal banks on which to draw. By careful purchasing and a knowledge of their customers, storekeepers could do quite well for themselves, and might abandon farming to concentrate on mercantile interests. Such merchants stocked a wide variety of goods, from foods unavailable in the area, like condiments, tea, coffee, and chocolate, to tobacco, cloth and other products farmers earlier had obtained from peddlers. They might also invest their capital in land, insurance, and small loans. And they became clearinghouses for local, regional, and foreign information.

Shopkeepers and peddlers were natural rivals, each attempting to curb the sales of the other. In this, the shopkeepers, who were more substantial and had better connections in the legislatures—had a decided edge. One after the other, colonies passed legislation restraining the activities of peddlers. In 1717, Connecticut levied a charge on peddlers of 20 shillings for each 100 pounds worth of goods entering the colony. In addition, all peddlers had to have a license, which cost 5 pounds. In 1700, Rhode Island placed restrictions on what peddlers could sell, and in 1728, they were forbidden to enter the colony. Pennsylvania taxed peddlers for goods they sold that were manufactured in other colonies or overseas.

Southern Tobacco

The colonial economy, then, was dominated by two types of workers: farmers and merchants. This is to say it was agrarian, with the merchants' major task being to market the crops grown by farmers and use the proceeds to make purchases for them. In the mid-eighteenth century, the factors of production seemed to mandate this for America's future. In a world with cheap land, dear capital, and scarce labor, subsistence farming in the northern and middle colonies and the same, plus plantations, in the southern colonies seemed inevitable.

The high demand for tobacco and the yet-meager amount available from Virginia— combined with new legislation—caused prices to rise sharply. This encouraged a proliferation of small farms in North America and, eventually, the creation of plantations. The shortage of workers also spurred the slave trade, which, of course, increased the labor supply. These factors enabled the colonists to ship more and more tobacco: an average of 65,000 pounds per annum in the early 1620s, which rose to more than a million pounds by the end of the 1630s, and 20 million pounds by the late 1670s. By 1699, exports from Britain's North American colonies rose to 30,757,000 pounds, of which all but 113,000 came from Virginia and Maryland. That year, Britain imported 496,000 pounds from other areas, including Europe, Turkey, Africa, and the Caribbean. During the next three-quarters of a century, imports from other areas declined, spiking upward only in the early 1730s and the mid-1770s. Reexport of tobacco (from the colonies to England, and then to other markets) was generally steady during the first half of the century, but then rose in the third quarter, peaking at 97,000 pounds in 1773. By then, more than 80 percent of all exports from North America to England originated in the colonies of Virginia, Maryland, Carolina, and Georgia, with tobacco the chief product.

The leaf was shipped in hogsheads weighing approximately half a ton. Tobacco lost much of its moisture during shipping and so had to be moistened before handling. For the product to be used in smoking, the first operation was the removal of the stem and rib from the leafs to obtain what was known as "strips." This was done by women, using short, sharp knives. Next, flavorings such as sugar, glycerine, gum, and starch were added. These additives caused the leaf to ferment, and the tobacco was covered with cloth to help control the process. It was a tricky procedure. When successful, the leaf would be granulated for smoking purposes. When the process failed, the leaf would be pressed into plug, which might be chewed or ground into snuff.

The returns to all those involved in Britain were enormous. In addition, the British companies provided banking and related services to the planters, which added to their profits. In 1765, a French observer claimed, "the revenue from tobacco in Great Britain is esteemed to be about three hundred pounds sterling per annum—and the greater part of the profits of exported tobacco comes to the merchants, which brings nearly as great a sum every year into the Kingdom, the whole weight falling on the planter, who is kept down by the lowness of the original price and the extravagance of the Charges." He further observed, "how advantageous must this article be to Great Britain, for which the rest of Europe . . . pays her ready money, besides 200 large vessels and a proportional number of seamen, which are occupied in this trade. . . ."

While subsistence farming was the occupation of the majority of Americans in the north, those who could do so grew some tobacco as well. Fully half of all the American colonists obtained their cash earnings, directly or indirectly, from tobacco. Moreover, wages in Maryland often were paid in the form of tobacco, which functioned as a currency. Asked why the colonists grew tobacco rather than wheat, one official replied that labor occupied with tobacco was worth six times that used in wheat. In 1770, the value of tobacco exported from Britain's North American colonies alone came to 906,638 pounds sterling, and this did not take into account the leaf smuggled to places other than Britain and the Indies. In that year, the next most important export in terms of value was bread and flour, at 504,553 pounds sterling, followed by rice, which accounted for 340,693 pounds sterling.

Yet all was not well. Even prior to the American Revolution there were signs of trouble in the tobacco region. Soil depletion resulted in lower yield per acre. The tobacco growers faced a dilemma: in order to maintain income from the sale of a declining cost crop, they would have to expand their planting, bringing in a larger crop, which would then further depress prices. Indeed, prices fluctuated sharply. In 1713, the mean price for Maryland tobacco was 1 pence per pound. It fell to 0.71 pence the following year. By 1720, the price was up to 1.19 pence, only to fall to 0.65 pence by 1731. A generalized slump followed, then an advance to 1.48 pence in 1752 and a sustained rise to 2.23 pence by 1769. "Chronically low prices forced Tidewater [Virginia] planters to contemplate seriously the abandonment of tobacco in favor of wheat. Some gentlemen actually dropped the staple." Thereafter, the price declined, slipping to 1.13 pence in 1773.

One of the reasons tobacco growers in the "Bright Belt" supported revolution was their increasing indebtedness to English merchants. Approximately two out of every three tobacco planters owed money to their English agents. Thomas Jefferson was one of them, and he wrote that such debts "had become hereditary from father to son, for many generations, so that the planters were a species of property, annexed to certain merchants in London." The American Revolution brought an end to the Navigation Acts, but it did not alter the adverse circumstances many planters still had to face.

Northern Merchants

By the early eighteenth century some shopkeepers—most of them in coastal cities—had evolved into sedentary merchants. In part, the difference was a matter of scale. Shopkeepers purchased a relatively small quantity of selected items, which were sold from their shops to local clienteles. The sedentary merchant might purchase large lots of a widely diversified number of products, which could be warehoused, while some were sold from his establishment to a wider circle of customers than was served by shopkeepers. Other parts of the inventory might be resold to other merchants, shopkeepers, and peddlers. But there was more to the business than that—and more to the tasks of the sedentary merchant. These individuals were always on the prowl for business opportunities, such as taking a share in the insurance of voyages and in the ships, land speculation, and the brokering of loans. They acted as agents for customers, arranging purchases, payments, and financing for fees that might range from 2½ percent to 5 percent. As will be seen, lotteries were a big business in colonial America, with merchants organizing them or selling tickets. Some merchants ran factories, from which came metals, glass, candles, and the like. Others, in New England and New York, sponsored whaling expeditions and owned facilities that reduced the whale carcass to meat, bones, and whale oil. From the ranks of merchants would come the first true factory owners in the nation.

Sedentary merchants often had partners, or at least family members, who worked with them, whereas shopkeepers tended to be sole proprietors. Partners were desirable when each brought something to the business, such as capital, connections, experience, or knowledge. In some cases, one partner would remain in the shop while the other signed on as supercargo on one of the shipping missions and went from port to port making purchases. Or he might go to another city or part of the nation to explore business opportunities there. The corporate form, though known, was usually not employed. Colonial Americans were accustomed to sole proprietorships and partnerships, but not to corporations, which were not trusted. The concept of limited liability was troublesome to a people who had no experience with it, and shareholding and the separation of ownership and management posed another problem. Besides, in this period it was necessary to obtain passage of legislation in order to incorporate. In any case, few corporations were organized during the colonial period.

During the Middle Ages, banks would send relatives to capital centers to represent the family interests. There was relatively little of this in colonial America. Instead, sedentary merchants relied on agents, especially in London. Agents were expected to have a deep knowledge of the merchant's business and concerns, purchasing lots of merchandise when likely ones came to market. They would arrange financing and make investments if called on to do so. What this meant, in a period when communications were poor even by then-current standards, was that each had to trust the other. It also indicated that a merchant going to the docks to take possession of his cargo often had no clear idea of what it might contain. By the mid-eighteenth century, John Forster & Co., a New York merchant advertised as "Just Imported and to be Sold" at his store on Cruger's Wharf the following:

> A parcel of choice Irish beef and pork, Cork rose butter, dpt candles, fine green and
> Bohea tea, silk, cotton and Kenting Handkerchiefs, muslin cravats and Scotch gauze,
> choice old claret in bottles and hogsheads, with the following Scotch bonnets, women's
> stays, shoes, printed and broad cloths, silk and hair Button, oznabrigs, camblets and frizes
> of all sorts. Damasks of sundry color for vests, etc. Poplin, stock tape, cardinals, cloaks,
> cotton allapeens, flowered dimity plaid forrest cloths, kersey, duffels, baize, horn and ivory
> combs, metal and steel buckles, knives and forks, hinges and a parcel of choice barley.

The presence of such merchants and small manufacturers should not lead one to believe there was a thriving urban life in the colonies. There was no census in this period. The first such counting took place in 1790, at which time there were 3.9 million Americans, 3.7 million of whom lived in areas considered rural, which is to say they were farmers. Of the 202,000 who lived in "urban" areas, only 62,000 were in places with populations of between 25,000 and 50,000. A majority of Americans would live on farms in the nineteenth century as well. As late as 1900, there were three rural Americans for every two urban dwellers. The America that would emerge from the Revolution was populated by farmers, those who fabricated goods from farm products, and others who carried them to markets or created the means to do so. Such was America in its rural age.

CHAPTER *8*

The American Paths
to Wealth

 merican merchants were similar to those who once lived in Mesopotamia, Egypt, Greece, the Hellenistic Age, Rome, and the Middle Ages. Sedentary merchants were ever on the lookout for the main chance, the opportunity to turn a profit. In time, the world would become their marketplace. Merchants with good relations in London might learn of opportunities in the Caribbean and switch some operations there, and eventually the Orient as well. Since competent and honest agents in such areas were more difficult to locate than in London, partners shipping out as supercargo to Havana or Hong Kong became more common than before.

Wealth and the Background to the American Revolution

Ever more reluctant to call upon Parliament for grants, knowing the price would be to relinquish additional powers, the Crown sought other ways to raise capital. One was to oblige the American colonies to behave in a manner more in tune with mercantilist philosophy, that is, to perform so as to add wealth to the parent.

This thinking was present from the start, and the approach both assisted colonial enterprise and attempted to throttle those who might discourage the realization of the Crown's mandates. The matters of bounties and other encouragements to colonial exports of goods scarce or not found in the mother country already have been discussed. In response to the aforementioned conflict between the Netherlands and England, Parliament passed laws regulating commerce, most notably in acts passed in 1649 and 1651. These laws tacitly recognized that the Dutch were superior in finance, shipbuilding, and the carrying trade, and that the only way to compete was to exclude them from the English colonies Under the terms of the measures, goods could be carried to and from any colony in English ships with crews that were three-quarters English. Any products destined for non-English ports had first to be imported into England. These measures were consolidated in the Navigation Acts of 1660 and 1663, passed by the government of the newly restored monarchy under King Charles II, which also stipulated that certain colonial commodities could be exported only to England. These included tobacco, sugar, raw cotton, indigo, and ginger. Other products were later added, including lumber, furs, copper ore, naval stores, hemp, and iron. Further acts followed. In 1699, England prohibited the export of colonial woolens. Subsequent legislation forbade Englishmen with knowledge of woolen manufacture from leaving England and banned the export of tools used in textile manufacture. For their part, some colonies passed laws encouraging the manufacture of woolens, thus indicating a mercantilist view of economics that clashed with the interests of the mother country. The Molasses Act of 1733 placed a heavy duty on molasses, rum, and other products imported into the colonies from non-English possessions.

The colonists responded to all of this legislation by accepting the bounties and other encouragements to manufacture and trade while attempting to circumvent those that would limit their search for profits. Some of the provisions, which on the surface appeared to benefit England, actually worked to the advantage of colonists. The requirement that all goods be transported in English ships gave a boost to the northern shipbuilding interests, for example, and in the late eighteenth century, prior to the Revolution, shipping services of all kinds generated more revenues for the colonists than the earnings of any other product or service except tobacco.

In any case, the laws were for the most part ignored. This was not particularly difficult, since enforcement was sporadic, and bribery of colonial officials was quite common. In theory, the Board of Trade was in charge of such matters, but other bodies had roles as well, including Parliament, the Commissioners of Customs, the Privy Council, the Admiralty, the War Office, and the Treasury. Lord Carbury, Governor of New York from 1701 to 1708, wrote to the Board of Trade about the situation. He appeared to have mixed feelings regarding colonial manufactures and the way the colonies fit into the mercantilist scheme of things:

> I am well-informed, that upon Long Island and in Connecticut, they [colonial manufacturers] are setting up a woolen manufacturer, and I myself have seen serge made on Long Island that any man may wear. Now if they begin to make serge, they will in time make coarse cloth, and then fine. We have as good fuller's earth and tobacco pipe clay in this province as any in the world. How far this will be for the service of England, I submit to better judgements; but however I hope I may be pardoned, if I declare my opinion to be, that all these colonies, which are but twigs belonging to the main tree [England], ought to be kept entirely dependent and subservient to England. That can never be if they are suffered to go on in the notions they have. That as they are Englishmen, so they may set up the same manufactures here, as people may do in England. For the consequences will be that if once they see that they can clothe themselves not only comfortably but handsomely too, without the help of England, they who are not very fond of submitting to the government, will soon think of putting in execution designs they had long harbored in their breasts.

In other words, they would think in terms of separation from the mother country. Reports of northern and middle colonial violations of the Navigation Acts and other actions indicating an unwillingness to play their part in the mercantilist scheme of things appear throughout this period. Writing to the Board of Trade in 1743, Advocate General William Bolton complained:

> There has lately been carried on here a large illicit trade by importing into this province large quantities of European goods of almost all sorts from diverse parts of Europe, some of which are by the laws wholly prohibited to be imported in the plantations, and the rest are prohibited to be imported there unless brought directly from Great Britain. . . . One of these illicit traders, lately departed hence for Holland, proposed to one of the greatest sellers of broadcloths here (and how many others I can't say) to supply him with black-cloths from thence, saying the country might be better and cheaper supplied with broad-cloths of that color from Holland than from England; but to prevent or rather increase your lordships' . . . I need only to acquaint you that I write this clad in a superfine French cloth, which I bought on purpose that I might wear about the evidence of these illegal traders having already begun to destroy the vital parts of the British commerce; and to use as a memento to myself and the customhouse officers to do everything in our power toward cutting off this trade so very pernicious to the British nation.

Not surprisingly, the Americans felt otherwise regarding the regulations. In 1763, a Boston newspaper complained that "a colonist cannot make a button, a horseshoe, nor a hobnail, but some sooty iron-monger or respectable buttonmaker of Britain shall squall and bawl that his honor's worship is more egregiously maltreated, injured, cheated, and robbed by the rascally American Republicans."

During the period from 1668 to 1763, England and France engaged in what some historians have called the Second Hundred Years' War. Actually it was a series of wars, conducted in Europe but also in the two nations' colonial empires. There were The War of Devolution in 1668; King William's War (known in Europe as the War of the League of Augsburg) from 1689 to 1697; Queen Anne's War (War of Spanish Succession) from 1702 to 1713; the War of Jenkins' Ear from 1739 to 1742 (with Spain); King George's War (War of Austrian Succession) from 1740 to 1748; and the French and Indian War (Seven Years' War) from 1754 to 1763. England triumphed, but in the process expended a great deal of wealth. The nation had a debt of 130 million pounds, which required 4.5 million pounds annually for interest alone. It cost England 350,000 pounds annually to maintain its North American garrison. But there were benefits. Having the choice between annexing Canada and the French islands of Guadeloupe, Martinique, and St. Lucia, England chose Canada, not because it recognized the potential there, but not to anger the English West Indies interests in Parliament. The latter feared competition from the French sugar islands should they be annexed by England and thus exempted from the Navigation Laws. By then England's direct investment in the Indies came to 60 million pounds, six times that of investments on the North American mainland. The islands' financial backers were far more important in London's scheme of things than Virginia tobacco or New England's naval stores and fish.

In the eighteenth century, the French colonies in the Caribbean were more productive than those of England. Sugar flowed to France from Martinique, Guadeloupe, and Santo Domingo, the last producing more sugar than all of the English possessions in the region. After being refined, the sugar was sold throughout Europe. In exchange for sugar, the French sent their colonists tools, cloth, and other manufactured goods, as well as slaves. Thus France, like England, had accepted mercantilism. Part of this was encouraging trade with the English colonists. Bribery, collusion, and smuggling were in wide evidence along the Atlantic waterfront in the century after 1650, while the English generally looked the other way. Sir Robert Walpole, who was prime minister from 1721 to 1742, took note of the rapid economic growth in the northern colonies, and was reluctant to enforce laws he felt not only would cause economic problems in America, but also result in political friction. Walpole's successors followed the same course of action during the next two decades, as wars occupied most of their attention. This policy of nonenforcement started to change in 1762, when John Stuart, the Earl of Bute, a Tory, became Prime Minister, and in the following year, which saw the English triumph in the Seven Years' War, when George Grenville became prime minister.

Grenville thought the northern colonists had benefitted from the war through the elimination of French forces in Canada and the West and so should pay for part of the cost of the war and of maintaining armed forces in America. The Americans for their part seemed to believe the English had gone to war for their own reasons, not to assist the colonies, and in any case were not prepared to pay taxes when they had avoided and evaded them for so long. Moreover, the northern merchants had developed a lively trade with the French colonies in the West Indies, which they intended to continue.

According to the mercantile plan, New England was supposed to provide the West Indies with grains, fish, and other foods, and purchase sugar, molasses, and local products from the islanders. The New Englanders indeed did sell their products to the British West Indies, but insisted on payment in cash, even during the wars with the French. This gold was spent on sugar and molasses in the French islands, where the prices were lower and the quality better. In 1763, the French islands supplied more than 95 percent of the molasses imported into Massachusetts. The molasses was turned into rum, which was used as trading goods in Africa in exchange for slaves.

Grenville was not as concerned with colonies and mercantilist considerations as were some of his predecessors. While admitting the worth of the Indies, Grenville had doubts regarding the value of the North American possessions. Only tobacco and lumber seemed worthwhile products of these colonies. England could obtain its lumber elsewhere. Besides, the great lumber shortage had come to an end, as England and other parts of Europe converted to coal as fuel and for the most part had eliminated charcoal use in the reduction of metallic ores. Grenville was eager to enforce the regulations, not because he valued the northern colonies for their innate worth but rather the reverse. They were a burden on the Empire and needed to contribute their share to its upkeep.

The Economics of Protest

From 1763 to 1775, the path toward separation from the mother country deepened and widened. Parliament passed act after act to control the colonists, who protested vigorously against attempts to fit them into the mercantilist mold in ways that were disadvantageous to their interests. Of course, there were other reasons for protest and separation. Some historians believe the separation took place not in 1776, but when the English settlers first came to America. Others emphasize that the Americans, in the beginning at least, were fighting for the rights of Englishmen, a view held by a substantial group in the House of Commons at that time. And still others see the Revolution as the culmination of political concepts developed during the Enlightenment. In this section, however, only the economic explanations will be considered. Colonial protestors, many of them merchants, saw in the English actions attempts to force them from profitable occupations, while the English who supported a strong stand against them felt the Americans were negligent in their economic and political duties to the mother country.

Generations of American historians have traced the path to war and separation from 1763 to 1776, primarily concentrating on a series of acts on the part of England to force the colonists to meet their imperial and mercantilist obligations, and on the colonial responses. For many generations it was believed that the end of the Seven Years' War (which really lasted nine years) marked the start of this change in English policy. With the removal of the French menace in North America, England was now free to turn to colonial affairs with a singleminded determination, while the colonists, with the French no longer on their borders, were becoming less willing to bow to England's will. This approach ignores or plays down several factors. One is that France was hardly a spent force in this period. Another involves the stresses within English society, independent of whatever was happening in the Americas, that led to this perceived change in direction. Such issues will be discussed in the next chapter. For now, it is necessary to indicate how the matter played out in the northern colonies, which certainly caused tensions to grow.

The first actions that riled the merchants were the Sugar and Currency Acts, which Grenville intended to enforce vigorously. These acts, designed to break the trade with the French Indies and restrict the printing of paper money, were a one-two punch. To the colonists it seemed that England was taking gold from them under the provisions of the Sugar Act, while refusing the colonists the right to issue paper money to take its place. To the merchants in particular, the view was prevalent that Grenville meant to destroy their interests, but they were experienced at bribing English officials and meant to continue the practice. Besides, their trading partners in England, who had representation in Parliament, could be counted on to lead the fight against such legislation. Subsistence farmers on the frontiers were not overly concerned. These people had and needed little money. Whatever exchanges took place, they conducted by "bookkeeping barter," in which entries were made for credits and debits, with settlements made at irregular intervals. So there was no open break at that point. Writing in 1764, Governor Stephen Hopkins of Rhode Island said:

> The British ministry, whether induced by jealousy of the colonies, by false information, or some other alteration in the system of political government, we have no information. Whatever has been the motive, this we are sure of, the Parliament in their last session, passed an act, limiting, restricting, and burdening the trade of these colonies, much more than had ever been done before. As also for greatly enlarging the power and jurisdiction of the courts of admiralty in the colonies, and also came to a resolution, that it might be necessary to establish stamp duties, and other internal taxes, to be collected within them. This act and this resolution, have caused great uneasiness and consternation among the British subjects on the continent of America.

As Hopkins feared, the Stamp Act, which required the purchase of a stamp for most legal documents and paper products, was passed soon afterward, in March of 1765. It caused consternation in all the colonies among writers, printers, lawyers, and publishers, but not among merchants and farmers.

All the while, support for the colonists was growing among the merchants in Parliament. England's exports to America were declining, and those merchants felt the sting, and asked for repeal of the Stamp Act. The new prime minister, the Earl of Rockingham, was willing to seek repeal, but did not want the colonists to conclude he was acting because of their strength. In the end, Parliament repealed the Stamp Act, but it also passed the Declaratory Act asserting Parliament's right to pass such taxes. Parliament then repealed sections of the Sugar Act. When the Rockingham ministry fell and was replaced by one headed by William Pitt, the Earl of Chatham, who was considered a strong supporter of the colonists, the Americans concluded they were in a position of strength.

The Townsend Acts, passed in 1767, and named after Chancellor of the Exchequer Charles Townsend, caused them to reconsider. These acts placed taxes on colonial imports of tea, paper, paint, and glass, and the money collected was earmarked to pay the salaries of English judges and officials in America. This last provision was an attempt to eliminate the bribes paid to them by colonial merchants. The merchants responded with vows to end imports of English goods. There were more protests, and in June 1768, riots and pitched battles broke out between pro- and anti-English factions in Boston and New York. In the early spring of 1769, it was learned that the nonimportation agreements had caused English merchants to lose some 7.3 million pounds in trade, while only 3000 pounds had been collected in imposts. This caused a flurry of activity in London, ending when Grafton resigned in early 1770 and Lord North took his place. North stood with those demanding a hard line against the colonists.

North presented his plan to resolve the colonial problems on March 5, 1770. He would repeal all the Townsend duties except that on tea. Furthermore, he pledged that his government would not levy new taxes in America. But he also affirmed his intention to enforce all English laws in America. Given such a statement, the colonists naturally felt that once more they had obliged an English government to back down.

The Boston Massacre took place that same day and was followed by the Boston Tea Party, taken as another sign of colonial intransigence and unreasonableness. In reaction, in March 1774, Parliament closed the port of Boston until the city paid for the lost tea, and Lord North suspended the Massachusetts legislature and transferred powers to English officials. Other acts were passed to benefit Canada at the expense of the seaboard colonies. Taken together, these so called Intolerable Acts widened the breech between mother country and colonies. The following year came the conflict at Lexington and Concord. The road to separation had been entered, although this would not become certain for another year. In this period, however, major forces were sweeping over Europe, England in particular, which contributed to the growing tensions.

Sporadic wars, population pressures, the evolving nature of agriculture, and the chronic need for capital caused major imbalances in European society. Those who learned how to adjust were able to reap large economic rewards through speculation and investment, while others became impoverished. Speculation in securities and commodities abounded, becoming one of the ways for newcomers to achieve wealth. Sir George Colebrooke, a member of a prominent banking family, was one of the leading speculators, and attempted to achieve a corner in hemp. When this failed, in 1771–1772, he tried to do so in alum. He succeeded to the point that he was able to put the squeeze on those who used alum to dye textiles. Prices rose, but new supplies came to market, which drove the price down. In the end, Colebrooke was destroyed, causing a major panic, one of many that afflicted the financial markets in those turbulent times.

Thomas Jefferson later would suggest that in this period, every man had become either a hammer or an anvil, a sheep or a wolf, which is to say, the gain of one person was obtained at the expense of another. In 1766, an English pamphleteer put it this way:

> People not perceiving a scarcity, are apt to be jealous of one another; each suspecting another's inequality of gain to rob him of his share, everyone will be employing his skill and power, as best he can, to procure to himself the same plenty as formerly. This is but scrambling amongst ourselves, and helps us no more against our want, than the struggling for a short coverlet, by those who lie together, till it is pulled to pieces, will preserve them from the cold.
>
> The laborer's share being seldom more than a bare subsistence, never allows that body of men time or opportunity to raise their thought above that, or to contest with the richer for their's — unless when some uncommon or great distress, uniting them in one universal ferment, makes them forget respect, and emboldens them to serve their wants with armed force; and then sometimes they break in upon the rich, and sweep all like a deluge. But this rarely happens, but in the MALADMINISTRATION OF NEGLECTED AND MISMANAGED GOVERNMENT.

In the midst of this instability, and facing huge budget deficits, governments tried to raise additional revenues through taxes. In England, attempts were made to increase taxes on such commodities as cider, but these were resisted strenuously. English regiments were sent to Devon and Cornwall to put down insurrections there, and to Whitehaven when the press gangs rose up. Ireland was a continual source of insurrection. According to David Hackett Fischer, between 1740 and 1775, there were 159 major riots, and this did not include what might be categorized as scuffles. In most of these, English troops had to be called out to restore order. Some of the regiments who did so in England were to be dispatched to America to deal with riots that broke out in the 1770s. The Europewide turmoil is the backdrop against which one should consider the coming of the American Revolution and the conflict itself.

Alternative Paths to Wealth in the New Nation

It is not within the purview of this work to discuss the immediate events that led to the rupture between England's North America colonies and the mother country. It remains to be said that those who search for financial causation among the rebels will find little to sustain suspicions that they fought for pecuniary gain. Even the New England merchants, who chafed at English attempts to limit their illegal activities, would have realized that — given the distances, available technology, and successes at smuggling and bribery — the costs of battle and the uncertainties of initiating "a new order of things" in America were hardly worth going to war. Of course, there was the principle of "no taxation without representation," but much of England was not represented in Parliament, and these people paid their taxes. The concept that government rested on the consent of the governed was not a popular European, or even English, idea at the time. This was one of the signal creations and successes of the Revolution, a principle that not only would reverberate through history, but also would affect the concept of wealth, government, and the relationships between the two.

Lotteries As a Means to Obtain Wealth and Raise Funds

The colonists paid taxes reluctantly and rarely without being forced to do so. Yet they also recognized the need to support certain public improvements and education. They resorted to a familiar device to accomplish this, and at the same time offered those who participated a chance to enrich themselves: lotteries.

Lotteries were quite familiar in the Ancient World and Europe. They were used to select many public officials in the democracies of ancient Greece, as well as a means of gaming. Making selections through lot is even mentioned in the *Bible*, as in Proverbs 18:18, "The lot causeth strife to cease, and parteth asunder the contentious."

In order to understand why lotteries were so popular in the United States in the eighteenth century, it is first necessary to understand how different—economically and socially—the country was from what it is today. Government was minimal. Few companies issued stocks and bonds. Taxes were low and most were either excises or tariffs. So if a town wanted to raise funds to construct a bridge or a schoolhouse, officials would consider a lottery as readily as today's civic leaders would consider a bond issue or a new tax. In 1790, the *Salem Gazette* put the matter this way:

> Lotteries have been a very productive source of revenue in this state. The moral tendency of them has been supposed by some to be injurious to society; and government has been careful to grant them for such purposes only as that the probable benefit should outweigh the evil. By this means we have seen the interests of literature supported—the arts encouraged—the wastes of war repaired—inundations prevented—the burden of taxes lessened, etc.

Not only were lotteries more familiar than securities, but the question of honesty aside, most purchasers considered them safer. A bond would mature in several years, and by then the issuer might be insolvent. Stocks were even chancier, since their owners had no clear call on the company's assets. A lottery, on the other hand, collected funds through the sale of tickets to pay out prizes, and the drawing was usually held within a matter of months, if not sooner. To be sure, there might be delays because the lottery organizer would want to sell all of the tickets before the drawing. The matter of trust was also important, because it was always possible that the organizer might engage in fraud. Even so, lotteries were deemed the safest and surest method of collecting funds for worthy causes. Finally, they were much more popular than taxes, especially in a country where the battle cry of revolution had been, "No taxation without representation!," which really meant no taxation with *or* without representation.

What other method of raising funds pleased both the issuer and the purchaser? Most people pay taxes reluctantly, but no one obliges a person to purchase a lottery ticket. Lottery supporters made this observation time and again. In 1826, a member of Parliament put it this way:

> As it is at present conducted, the lottery is a voluntary tax, contributed to only by those who can afford it, and collected without trouble or expense; one by which many branches of the revenue are considerably aided, and by means of which hundreds of persons find employment. The wisdom of those who, at this time, resign the income produced by it, and add to the number of the unemployed, may surely be questioned.

The only opponents of lotteries protested on religious or moral grounds. Lottery supporters asserted the individual's right to participate in them. Thomas Jefferson did not consider lotteries dishonorable, but rather a useful part of the social scene:

> If we consider games of chance immoral, then every pursuit of human industry is immoral; for there is not a single one that is not subject to chance, not one wherein you do not risk a loss for the chance of some gain. But the greatest of all gamblers is the farmer. Yet so far from being immoral, they are indispensable for the existence of man. Almost all of those pursuits of chance produce something useful to society. But there are some that produce nothing, and endanger the well being of the individuals who engage in them, or of others depending on them. Such are games of chance with cards, dice, billiards, etc. There are some other games of chance, useful on certain occasions, and injurious only when carried beyond their useful bounds. Such are insurance, lotteries, raffles, etc. Money is wanting for a useful undertaking, like a school etc., for which a direct tax would be disapproved. It is raised therefore by a lottery.

Lotteries were conducted in most colonies in pre-Revolutionary America. According to one study, 158 were held between 1744 and 1774. Rhode Island alone ran 43 in the period from 1766 to 1775, and raised $106,000 in 1774, approximately $3.00 per person, a substantial amount of money at that time. Finally the American Revolution itself received support from lotteries.

The New Government

The Articles of Confederation, the first constitution under which the new nation operated, was a product of expediency. Under its terms, each state would have one vote in the new Congress, and the assent of nine would be needed before important decisions could be made. There could be no amendments without a unanimous vote. Congress lacked the power to collect taxes or regulate commerce. The right to issue money was shared with the individual states. It provided for the creation of new states out of the western lands.

This last point furnished the most important wealth-creating initiative under the Articles. Provision had to be made for land ownership in the West. Sales could supply the central government with capital, since requisitions on the states would not be honored. Under terms of the Land Ordinance of 1785, the public lands were to be divided into townships six miles square, containing 36 sections of 640 acres each. The sections were to be auctioned off to the highest bidders, with a proviso that the minimum price should be one dollar an acre.

As expected, speculators purchased large tracts of land for resale to settlers. One of the major firms in this business was the Ohio Company of Associates, organized by Manassah Cutler, a member of Congress from Connecticut, who was backed by European bankers and associates from other states. In time, the Ohio Company would take control of more than 1.5 million acres of land. Through lobbying, manipulations, and taking advantage of currency devaluations, Cutler's group was able to purchase the land at an average price of about eight cents an acre. The Scioto Company, founded by New York and New England speculators and Congressmen, and backed by Dutch and French bankers, obtained 5 million acres, while another million acres went to a group headed by New Jersey Congressman John Symmes.

Cutler, Symmes, and other speculators recognized the need for orderly government if settlement was to be achieved. Therefore, they supported plans for a modified version of Thomas Jefferson's Ordinance of 1784, which was designed to provide steps, which, if followed, allowed territories to become states. Cutler's plan would enable a territory to become a state in a three-stage process. Since the land companies had no interests in the southwest at the time, and not wanting to complicate matters, the new version was to apply only to the northwest. This would be crucial for the nation's future, for in the original Jeffersonian draft was a proposal to ban slavery in the new territories. Absent the southern territories, this plan, bound to have caused debate, was abandoned. The Northwest Ordinance of 1787 was passed with the support of the speculators and some disappointed Jeffersonians, and it provided the basic pattern for American continental expansion. As for the northwest, the legislation enabled the states of Ohio, Indiana, Illinois, Michigan, and Wisconsin to enter the nation in the next generation.

Even with the sale of western lands, the new nation and the states had financial difficulties. Repeated currency issues made to finance the Revolution, along with weak banks resulted in a distrust of paper money and a flight to gold and silver, that either went into hiding or was sent overseas. Several states found it impossible to collect taxes to pay for ongoing expenses; debtors demanded currency inflation and insisted that creditors accept the depreciated paper money as full payment for debts. The battlelines in this period were not between North and South, farmer and industrialist, but between creditor and debtor. When foreclosures were attempted in some communities, the debtors rose up and fought the authorities, and for a while it seemed that a new revolution, based on social and economic factors, was about to erupt.

In a last-ditch effort to prevent violence, several states issued more paper money, insisting as well that it be accepted as legal tender. This resulted in a rash of lawsuits in which creditors claimed they should not be obliged to accept the paper currency. One of the plaintiffs, a Rhode Island butcher named John Weeden, sued a customer, John Trevett, who tried to pay for meat with paper money. The case went to the Rhode Island Supreme Court in 1786, which decided in favor of Weeden. For the first time, the courts had declared an act of the legislature unconstitutional, at the same time deciding in favor of creditors. Formerly timid creditors elsewhere were now emboldened, and in six states they took power and ended the growing mania for currency inflation. Naturally, the debtors counterattacked, and in the summer of 1786 the possibility of outbreaks of violence seemed greater than ever.

Massachusetts underwent several strains in this period. Not only was it the home of American radicalism, but its farmers had suffered more than those in other states from the loss of trade with Europe. Foreclosures had begun in western Massachusetts, and there were more of them there than elsewhere. The poor debtor farmers demanded relief from the legislature, but received little attention. When the legislature adjourned in July 1786 without having taken action, protest rallies were organized in several western communities. By September the protestors united under the leadership of Captain Daniel Shays, a veteran of the Revolution, who led the hastily organized rebels against the state militia in several engagements. Governor James Bowdoin was alarmed. He castigated the debtor farmers as criminals and sent a reinforced militia under the leadership of General Benjamin Lincoln against Shays' small force. Shays and those who followed him were convinced they were fighting for the principles of the Declaration of Independence, while Bowdoin warned that unless Shays was put down, anarchy would follow and destroy the state, and eventually the nation as well. In time, Lincoln would crush Shays' Rebellion, forcing its leaders to flee and the "army" to disband. But before this happened, political and business leaders in all the states were obliged to consider whether governments that permitted such uprisings should not be strengthened or replaced.

The Road to the Constitution

The postwar economic depression reached its low point in the summer of 1786. From then on there was a slow, though irregular, advance in foreign trade and the domestic economy. This upturn was not prompted by actions of the Congress, which did not meet regularly and sometimes lacked a quorum for weeks at a time. Nor was it due to legislative or executive actions by state governments. Rather, the depression ended because Europe demanded more American goods and farmers and merchants learned to adjust to both peace and independence.

Part of this adjustment was the establishment of friendly relations among the states. This was as much a problem of international relations as were negotiations for treaties with European nations, since under the Confederation, the power over commerce was retained by the individual states. Few states attempted to erect tariffs and other barriers to trade, but there were commercial clashes between New York and her neighbors, and between Virginia and Maryland. Most states felt the need for better commercial guidelines. It was for these reasons that representatives from Maryland and Virginia met at Alexandria, and later Mount Vernon, to work out details for a trade agreement for the Potomac River. The conference, which was held in March 1785, was a success, and Maryland suggested that the Mount Vernon agreement be extended at a regional conference to include Delaware and Pennsylvania. In an expansive mood, Virginia's delegates countered by recommending that the invitation be extended to all the states. Maryland agreed. The conference was scheduled to be held at Annapolis in September 1786, and James Madison and others set about sending out invitations.

While this was happening, the Congress discussed means of amending the Confederation charter to make the government more workable. The need for a common front in dealing with foreign nations and the desire to end frictions between the states motivated several congressional delegates, while others felt the need for more efficient and binding means of obtaining revenues and controlling commerce. The movement came to a head that summer, when New York blocked a movement to amend the Articles to allow for a tariff, and New Jersey refused to accept an amendment to ensure payment of state quotas to the national treasury. On the eve of the Annapolis Convention, now scheduled to open on September 11, the outlook for interstate cooperation appeared slim.

Despite their conflicts and other indications that they would not support greater interstate cooperation, both New York and New Jersey sent delegates to the Annapolis meetings, along with representatives of Pennsylvania, Virginia, and Delaware. New Hampshire, Rhode Island, and Massachusetts also named delegates, but they failed to arrive in time to attend the meetings, which lasted only four days. The briefness of the sessions was not due to animosities or the lack of topics to consider. On the contrary, from the first there was a unanimity of opinion that a strengthened Confederation government would be needed. Alexander Hamilton of New York suggested that a general convention be held in Philadelphia the following year "to devise such further provisions as shall appear to them necessary to render the constitution of the Federal Government adequate to the exigencies of the Union," as well as to discuss those commercial problems which had led to the Annapolis Convention. Hamilton's recommendation was adopted by those delegates present at Annapolis and sent to the Congress and the various states.

During the next five months, state and Confederation leaders discussed the proposal, while Shays' Rebellion and other disruptive activities led to fears of a new social upheaval. Prompted both by the wish to have a stronger government able to put down such insurrections and by the desire to make the commercial clauses of the Articles more operable, the states consented to attend the Philadelphia meetings. Virginia and New Jersey were the first to accept. By the time of the convention, all but New Hampshire and Rhode Island had agreed to send delegates, and they soon fell in line. Recognizing the general desire for a strengthened government, the Congress agreed to accept the convention "for the sole and express purpose of revising the Articles of Confederation."

Not until May 25, 1787, were sufficient states represented in Philadelphia to call the convention to order. Some delegates left during that summer, but others arrived to take their places. The members of the convention represented a good cross section of commercial and agricultural leadership in the states. A majority had government experience of one kind or another; 39 of the 55 men who attended the convention had been or were members of Congress, eight had signed the Declaration of Independence, and seven had been governors of their states. They were a wealthy group, and although it often has been charged that they hoped to profit from their actions, there is no strong evidence that this was the case. Rather, the delegates wished to ensure a stable government in which the ideals of the Revolution could be preserved and the peaceful accumulation of wealth continue. If anything, the delegates were fearful that Shays and others like him would destroy their way of life and those freedoms that had enabled them to rise so high in society and politics. The members of the convention, for the most part, were more concerned with the preservation of values and property than with the extension of either. They were not interested in innovation so much as stability, and they cared less for representative government than for one that could maintain the law. Naturally, a few opposed these sentiments, but they were never in a position to do anything about their opposition.

In addition, each delegate had his own special interests to protect and his own ideas as to how they might best be served. For the most part, the delegates at Philadelphia differed primarily with regard to means; their ends were evident from the first. As the preamble to the Constitution would state, these were to form a more perfect union than had existed under the Articles of Confederation; to establish justice, which in the late eighteenth century meant rule by law; to insure domestic tranquility against those who would seek a social revolution; to provide for the common defense against those foreign enemies who might seek to harm the new nation; and to promote the general welfare, which in effect would grant these powers to the central government, and not to the states.

Some of the most important figures of the Revolution were absent. Jefferson was the minister to France and John Adams the minister to England. Tom Paine was on his way to Europe, where he would serve as a member of the French revolutionary government. Sam Adams had been relegated to the limited sphere of Massachusetts politics. Patrick Henry was named to the convention but refused to serve. Thus, some of the more radical Revolutionary leaders were not there.

In retrospect, it appears evident that the impetus for the convention came from those large farmers, merchants, and members of the creditor segment of the population who felt the need for a strong currency, a larger trading area, and other changes that would assist them in their work. In order to accomplish this, they were planning what amounted to a coup d'etat, which for some of them would be the second time they had done so in a dozen years. The first, which was to seek separation from England, was prompted by a wish to be free of governmental controls. It had succeeded, but in the minds of some who were to attend in Philadelphia, it had gone too far. Now they met once more, this time to create a stronger government, which was embodied in the Constitution.

The heart of the Constitution is found in Article I, Section 8, in which the powers of the Congress are enumerated. Since the delegates expected the legislature to dominate the executive and judicial branches, great care and much debate accompanied the hammering out of this section, which also reflects those failures of the Articles of Confederation most hoped to correct.

This section begins by stating that "the Congress shall have power to lay and collect taxes, duties, imposts and excises, to pay the debts and provide for the common defense and general welfare of the United States; but all duties, imposts and excises shall be uniform throughout the United States." The remainder of the section consists of 17 paragraphs, each stating another of the powers of the Congress. The legislature could call upon the militia to "suppress insurrections and repel invasions," and seven of the paragraphs deal with Congress's military and naval obligations and rights. Thus, the founding fathers sought to provide a stronger government to deal with foreign states and suppress rebellions. Five paragraphs deal with financial matters, such as giving Congress the right to borrow money, regulate commerce, coin money, and establish bankruptcy laws. This too rectified a perceived failure of the Confederation. Congress was given the power to establish post offices and post roads, to fix standards of weights and measures, to promote the progress of the arts and sciences and establish copyright laws, all of which were designed to assist the commercial interests. The final paragraph, sometimes called "the elastic clause," granted Congress the right "to make all laws which shall be necessary and proper for carrying into execution the foregoing powers, and all other powers vested by this Constitution in the government of the United States, or in any department or officer thereof."

This section—especially the elastic clause—led some delegates to fear a possible usurpation of power by the new government. Before they would sign the document, they demanded a bill of rights and other guarantees that the Congress would not rule tyrannically. Several delegates left without signing, saying they intended to fight for a bill of rights in the states. On September 12, 1787, each of 12 state delegations voted their approval, and the document was ready to be submitted to the states for ratification. Once the demanded Bill of Rights was added, ratification proceeded smoothly. On September 13, 1788, the Confederation congress adopted a resolution calling for the new government to take power. In the next few months this body organized the first elections under the Constitution and in other ways prepared for its own demise. Thus, constitutional revolution took place in America in 1787–1788, with the full cooperation of the institution to be overthrown.

The Jeffersonian Conception of Wealth

There was no question that George Washington would be elected President, and he selected Jefferson his Secretary of State and Alexander Hamilton his Secretary of the Treasury. This set the stage for the great philosophical debate between these two men, which often is presented as being between Jefferson's hopes for an agrarian America with a weak government, isolated from Europe and Hamilton's vision of an industrialized America with a strong central government providing assistance for industry, and sharing in European (or at least Western) civilization. This sweeping scenario is appealing, but in terms of the quest for wealth, it is not quite in accordance with the words and actions of Jefferson and Hamilton. Moreover, one should always keep in mind that Jeffersonianism appealed to the southern agrarians, while Hamiltonianism was in line with the northern merchant outlook.

The philosophical roots of Jeffersonian economic ideas may be found in the concepts of the physiocrats, a school of thought that often is traced to the writings of Francois Quesnay, who in 1756 published his first articles on economics in the *Grande Encyclopedia*. Quesnay and those who followed him believed true wealth was created by agriculture and mining, for they produced a surplus, a net product above the costs of production. For this reason they believed in minimal government, with taxes on the producers—wealthy landholders and miners—providing what little funds would be required. To them, commerce, banking, the professions, and manufacturing were useful but sterile, merely transforming raw materials into finished goods, financing them, or transporting them from one place to another. One of Quesnay's disciples, Anne Robert Jacques Turgot, who became France's finance minister in 1774, introduced physiocratic theories into that country on the eve of the French Revolution. In his *Reflections on the Formation and Distribution of Riches*, written in 1766, Turgot concluded:

> The husbandman is, therefore, the sole source of the riches, which, by their circulation, animate all the labors of the society; because he is the only one whose labor produces over and above the wages of the labor. . . . It is the earth which is always the first and only source of all wealth; it is that which as the result of cultivation produces all the revenue.

Pierre du Pont was a colleague of both Quesnay and Turgot, who became friendly with Jefferson when the American was minister to France. He helped negotiate the peace treaty that established the United States, and was active as a moderate in the early stages of the French Revolution. He escaped from France and came to the United States in 1797, at Jefferson's invitation, and remained there until the end of the revolution. His son, Eleuthere Irenee du Pont de Nemours, established a gunpowder mill in Delaware, which grew into one of the nation's premier chemical companies. Pierre du Pont was a physiocrat whose ideas reinforced those of Jefferson, while his son became a force in the creation of industrial America.

True to his physiocratic leanings, Jefferson opposed tariffs to protect manufacturers. "Cultivators of the earth are the most valuable citizens," he said in 1776. "As long therefore as they can find employment in this line, I would not convert them into mariners, artisans, or anything else. I consider the class of artificers as the panders of vice and the instruments by which the liberties of the country are generally overturned." As President, Jefferson would violate some of his basic principles by purchasing Louisiana, which he believed secured an agrarian future for the United States.

Such is the standard view of Jefferson, and it is correct as far as it goes—but it does not go far enough. Jefferson was not a believer in a simple, pastoral life, nor did he reject the quest for wealth. Rather, he perceived wealth in the land and believed his beloved farmers could do better economically by tilling the soil than through commerce or manufacturing. Had he not managed to get this idea across to the American people, he would not have gone as far as he did politically, because for the most part, they were deeply interested in becoming wealthy. As Alexis de Tocqueville wrote in 1840, "The love of wealth is therefore to be traced, as either a principal or [an] accessory motive, at the bottom of all that the Americans do; this gives to all their passions a sort of family likeness." It was a conclusion many visitors to America noted. Another of these, Felix Grund, wrote in 1843, "There is, probably, no people on earth with whom business constitutes pleasure, and industry amusement, in an equal degree with the inhabitants of America."

As has been noted, in the late eighteenth century sugar in its various forms had become more valuable than tobacco as an American export to Europe. We also have seen how the growth in the European populations created a greater demand for foodstuffs than previously had been the case. The early national economy was being reshaped by the growth in the European population and the inability of European agriculture to meet the increased demand for foodstuffs. By the mid-eighteenth century, the balance of trade among grain and all other commodities shifted decisively in favor of grain. In a broad swath from Virginia to Connecticut, farmers were switching to grain production. Their markets were in the Iberian peninsula and the West Indies. In 1789, an English commission reported that the country would experience shortages of all grains except barley, and for 27 of the next 30 years, England was a net importer of wheat and flour, much of it from the United States. After the post-Revolutionary War depression, the increase in grain and livestock prices resulted in economic growth for that 30-year span.

The founding fathers were quite explicit in the goal to leverage political freedom through economic liberalism: "The spirit for Trade which pervades these states is not to be restrained," George Washington wrote to James Warren in 1784. Writing in his *Notes on the State of Virginia*, Jefferson advocated a switch in southern agriculture from tobacco to wheat. Tobacco yields "a culture productive of infinite wretchedness," he said, adding that the cultivation of wheat "feeds the laborers plentifully, requires from them only moderate toil, except at harvest, and diffuses plenty and happiness among the whole." He advocated the building of canals and land freeholding and wrote to Washington, "Since all the world was becoming commercial, America too must get as much as possible of this modern source of wealth and power." Washington himself switched to wheat farming at Mount Vernon. Jefferson, then, was not as much concerned about the independent, self-sufficient farmer who, because he produced his own food, clothing, and shelter, might be free from commercial constraints. Rather, he postulated a nation that was capitalistic and commercial, based on agriculture. He did not oppose internal improvements as such, but rather saw in them a means to further his vision of an agrarian America. These notions were the very definition of *Americanism*, a term coined by Jefferson that he counterpoised to *aristocracy* throughout his writings. He argued continually against the dominance of a new elite of wealth and privilege, and gave high priority to laws that would prevent the concentration of landed wealth. Jefferson's genius lay in integrating a program of economic development and a policy for nation building into a radical moral theory. His policies helped create an economic base to support the early democratic republic. He was concerned with policies that would expand the landholding population, largely through opening the public lands to all citizens at low prices. Then the territories could be admitted to statehood in the belief they would be controlled by independent farmer-capitalists who would come to dominate the legislature in opposition, as will be seen, to the Hamiltonians. Jefferson favored the elimination of primogeniture and entail to break up large estates. He did not entertain Malthusian fears; rather, he thought there might be more people than work to occupy them productively. Moreover, he did not denigrate those who found employment in areas other than farming. Historian Joyce Appleby believes too much is made of Jefferson's physiocratic inclinations and not enough regarding his experience with agriculture itself:

> In England and America commercial farming was a progressive economic force, suggesting to some that the future would be far different from the past. But, equally important, we now know that these advances occurred in some countries and not others, despite similar physical characteristics. No such breakthrough, for instance, took place in France. Indeed, the Physiocrats enthusiasm for agricultural improvements and free trade represented as much as anything a longing to replicate the miracle of abundance across the Channel.

Jefferson insisted that the new democratic nation could not be based upon existing property owners alone. To du Pont de Nemours, he complained, "You set down as zeros all individuals not having land."

Alexander Hamilton and the Creation of the National Credit

As indicated, Hamilton is often presented as the antithesis of Jefferson, although they agreed on such important concepts as *laissez faire*. But even on this matter, there were some differences. Jefferson opposed most governmental influences in the economy, whereas Hamilton supported many aids to the private sector. Some writers have attempted to place Hamilton in the classical school which, spearheaded by Adam Smith and David Ricardo, accepted and even promoted manufacturers and merchants over farmers and miners as productive elements in the economy. There is some justification for this point of view, but as will be seen, Hamilton was eclectic and pragmatic, drawing inspiration from others, including John Law and those who developed the concepts of central banking. More often than not, however, he worked out his own solutions to problems. In *An Inquiry into the Nature and Causes of the Wealth of Nations*, published in the revolutionary year of 1776, Adam Smith argued in favor of specialization according to the distribution of the factors of production, indicating that free trade benefitted all. Unlike the physiocrats, he saw value in the efforts of workers and businesspeople other than farmers and miners.

> The prejudices of some political writers against shopkeepers and tradesmen, are altogether without foundation. So far as it from being necessary, either to tax them, or to restrict their numbers, that they can never be multiplied so as to hurt the public, though they may so as to hurt one another. The quantity of grocery goods, for example, which can be sold in a particular town, is limited by the demand of that town and its neighborhood. The capital, therefore, which can be employed in the grocery trade cannot exceed what is sufficient to purchase that quantity. If this capital is divided between two different grocers, their competition will tend to make both of them sell cheaper than if it were in the hands of only one; and if it were divided among twenty, their competition would be just so much the greater, and the chance of their combining together, in order to raise the price, just so much less.

Smith opposed government intervention on behalf of business interests and was particularly critical of bounties and tariffs. Hamilton thought otherwise. Like Smith, Ricardo supported the concept of free trade and production according to the distribution of the factors of production. "Under a system of perfectly free commerce, each country naturally devotes its capital and labor to such employment as are most beneficial to each," he wrote. "The pursuit of individual advantage is admirably connected with the universal good of the whole. By stimulating industry, by rewarding ingenuity, and by using most efficaciously the peculiar powers bestowed by nature, it distributes labor most effectively and most economically; while increasing the general mass of production, it diffuses general benefit, and binds together by one common tie of interest and intercourse, the universal society of nations throughout the civilized world." It is this principle, said Ricardo in his familiar argument, that determines that wine shall be made in France and Portugal, that grain shall be grown in America and Poland, and that hardware and other goods shall be manufactured in England.

Hamilton accepted the concept of division of labor and was interested in the expansion of the markets for American grain. He would encourage emigration to America in order to obtain additional workers for factories and farms. He broke with Smith and Ricardo on the matter of comparative advantage, arguing that government intervention is necessary to lend support to those in industry who are in competition with nations that had head starts and more capital than did the Americans of his period. Hamilton also disagreed with Ricardo in that while he wanted America to produce grain for world markets, he also wanted to encourage the manufacture of those goods Ricardo assigned to England.

Hamilton's prescription for wealth was to set down a financial infrastructure to complement that envisaged in Article I, Section 8 of the Constitution. He saw the creation of public credit as crucial. Without a sound currency and strong banks, capital access would be limited to those who wanted to enter manufacturing. Along with Jefferson, Hamilton was concerned with opening opportunities for those with skills, fortitude, and ambition, but he didn't limit this to farmers. For him, merchants and manufacturers were to be vital forces in the American economy.

At the time he assumed office as Secretary of the Treasury in 1789, the United States had debts of $54 million. Confederation bonds were selling for around 15 cents on the dollar. Interest rates were high and the political situation dicey, so capital for continuing and new ventures was hard to come by. Lenders were unwilling to assume political and financial risks, and borrowers were unwilling or unable to pay the high interest rates demanded under the circumstances.

Hamilton refused to consider default or bankruptcy, insisting that either course would close world capital markets to the new nation. Instead, he proposed a program to establish the national credit on a firm foundation. All agreed to the repayment of the foreign debt of $11.7 million, which was accomplished by issuing new certificates in place of the old ones. The Secretary's plan to repay the domestic debt was more controversial. Much of this debt had been issued to soldiers and suppliers of war material, many of whom sold the paper to speculators. Hamilton recognized this but went ahead anyway, arguing that those who had confidence in the government by purchasing depreciated debt might well be rewarded. Besides, if they were given long-term bonds in place of the old ones, it would give them a stake in seeing the new government succeed.

He then recommended that state debts be assumed by the federal government (to bind the states to the Union), which outraged states that had little or no debt. Of course, it pleased those who relished the opportunity to have others pay their bills. This plan also angered Hamilton's opponents, who organized to defeat the program. They were disarmed when he worked out a deal with the Jeffersonians whereby the new nation's seat of government would be located in what became Washington, D.C. Hamilton won the substance, while Jefferson and his followers gained satisfaction from a symbolic victory. Hamilton didn't mind this concession, figuring such a site would assist in winning additional southern support for the new nation.

Hamilton recommended the creation of a Bank of the United States to serve as the government's depository and fiscal agent. Four-fifths of the BUS's stock was to be sold to private individuals, another way of tying the monied classes to government. More important, however, was the fact that the bank, through its branches, would provide a national currency in which borrowers and lenders alike would have confidence. In addition, the Mint Act, passed two years later, established a bimetallic standard and was meant to ensure the government would pay its debts in legal tender and not the feared paper money.

Finally, Hamilton searched for other means whereby government might obtain funding. Given the economic climate of the time, it was not surprising that he thought lotteries the obvious and most efficient method of raising the needed capital.

These lotteries, he believed, should be understandable and accessible so that purchasers would see "fewer obstacles between *hope* and *gratification*." The tickets should be low-priced to make them available to as many people as possible. "Everybody, almost, can and will be willing to hazard a trifling sum for the chance of considerable gain." Hamilton also thought there should be many prizes, so that the odds of winning would be more attractive. To raise $30,000, he recommended the sale of 50,000 tickets at $4.00 each, which would bring in $200,000. The top prize would be $20,000; the lesser ones would descend to 400 at $100 each. This was one part of the Hamiltonian program that was not introduced, much less put into practice.

Taken together, the Hamiltonian program would provide the United States with the sound credit required to support large-scale borrowings, without which industrial capitalism would be difficult to develop. This was stated clearly in his *First Report on the Public Credit* (1790).

> The advantage to the public creditors, from the increased value of that part of their property which constitutes the public debt, needs no explanation. But there is a consequence of this, less obvious, though not less true, in which every other citizen is interested. It is a well-known fact, that, in countries in which the national debt is properly funded, and an object of established confidence, it answers most of the purposes of money. Transfers of stock or public debt are their equivalent to payments in specie; or in other words, stock, in the principal transactions of business, passes current as specie. The same thing would, in all probability, happen here under the like circumstances.

In his *Report on Manufactures*, Hamilton wrote of the "deficiency of pecuniary capital" and the need to excite "the confidence of cautious, sagacious capitalists, both citizens and foreigners."

As might be imagined, Jefferson and his followers were wary regarding such talk. Jefferson believed wealth consisted of land and its products, and would use government to make land accessible to all and so "democratize" wealth. Hamilton asserted wealth consisted of more than land. He extended it to capital, labor, and the businessmen. A strong currency, stable and trusted, together with credit, would enable entrepreneurs to have access to capital at low interest rates. Being trusted as a debtor would permit the government to borrow funds needed for the kinds of internal improvements entrepreneurs required for their manufacturing and commercial activities. This is to suggest that the powers granted Congress in Article I, Section 8 of the Constitution could not be realized easily without a sound national credit, which was what Hamilton provided in his financial program.

Ultimately, the answer to the question of whether the American people's future rested with the Hamiltonian or Jeffersonian vision was not to be decided purely by economic factors, as important as those might have been. Rather, it was a product of the entrepreneurial nature of the population. To quote de Tocqueville again:

> America is a land of wonders, in which everything is in constant motion and every change seems an improvement. The idea of novelty is there indissolubly connected with the idea of amelioration. No natural boundary seems to be set to the efforts of man; and in his eyes what is not yet done is only what he has not yet attempted to do.

As will be seen, the Americans' desire for change and their pragmatic willingness to enter new fields—to embrace the new—militated against the bucolic kind of existence the Jeffersonian alternative envisioned, different as it was from the earlier European model. When, a century later, those Americans who remained on the farms became entrepreneurs, and as Jefferson had suggested they do, began to feed the multitudes, they did so with more business acumen than was possessed by a good many of those in manufacturing and allied businesses. In the beginning and throughout much of the nineteenth century, agriculture, the servicing of agriculture, and other extractive industries represented the path to wealth in the United States.

CHAPTER 9

Industrial Wealth

 ECENT scholarship has emphasized the need to consider English settlement in North America not as a whole but rather as the product of four waves, each from a different geographic, religious, cultural, and economic part of the diverse British Isles. Those Englishmen who emigrated to the colonies from East Anglia created the Puritan commonwealth in New England based on Calvinist precepts, and that heritage was visible until well after the Civil War. Emigrants from southwest England, the Anglican Cavaliers who lost out in the English civil war—went to the American South, where they attempted to recreate the kind of existence they knew in the old country, and this, also, lasted until the American Civil War. The Quakers of the north midlands provided Pennsylvania with its unique cultural flavor in the colonial and early national periods, and represented an intriguing contrast to the Calvinist approach to business. The Scotch-Irish, who emigrated to the back country of colonial America, were the quintessential frontier dwellers. Of course, these are, in part at least, caricatures, but caricatures contain elements of the truth.

Jefferson's concepts of socioeconomic organization and endeavor appealed to southern Cavaliers, while Hamiltonianism was more in line with much of the northern, Puritan tradition. The plantation economy of the South, the early industrial economy of the Northeast, and the grain-based economy of the Midwest all were founded on concepts of what constituted wealth and the search for it.

Increased Population and Agriculture

As has been seen, the path the United States took from colonies to nation may be analyzed as another chapter in the quest for wealth. However, there are other perspectives that should be considered. The western world—and the eastern as well—experienced seismic demographic and economic changes in the late eighteenth century. There were many consequences of these mutations, among them three significant revolutions: the American, the French, and the Industrial. This was a period of major population growth in Europe, which was noted by prescient observers who argued for massive emigration to the Americas to ease the stresses in the old world.

In 1700, the population of Europe was approximately 100 to 120 million; by 1800, it had risen to almost 190 million. This was what prompted economist David Ricardo to come forth with his theory of rent, which held that increases in the demand for food-stuffs led to the cultivation of marginal land, whose lower output placed upward pres-sures on prices. The difficulties of workers and farmers in a world of increased population troubled Ricardo and absorbed much of his energy.

The same perceived problem was addressed by Ricardo's contemporary, Thomas Malthus, who believed that population was expanding geometrically and production arithmetically, a theme adumbrated in his 1798 work, *An Essay on the Principle of Pop-ulation*. The challenge of growing sufficient food for this large population engaged the interests of Jethro Tull, an Englishman who had studied agriculture in England and on the continent for more than 30 years. While he had often spoken and written about the subject, only in 1731 was his influential book, *The New Horse-Houghing Husbandry, or An Essay on the Principles of Tillage and Vegetation*, published. Tull pioneered in the field of intensive farming, recommending deep hoeing and plowing, crop rotation, and the cultivation of such roots as turnips and beets. Most important, he emphasized the necessity for observation and experimentation and the need to discard outmoded tradi-tional ways of cultivation.

Tull's methods were taken up avidly by many English nobles, among them Lord Townshend, the former ambassador to the Netherlands, who withdrew from public life in 1730 to cultivate his large holdings in Norfolk on Tull's principles. "Turnip" Towns-hend, as he came to be known, read one of the first copies of Tull's book, which became his bible on the subject. Others followed, among them Arthur Young, who traveled through Europe in the 1760s publicizing the new methods. King George III became an ardent convert, advocating the new agriculture so enthusiastically that he became known as "Farmer George." Farm production increased, but even so, the population problem, combined with a series of poor harvests, led to distress throughout Western Europe and prompted the continuing search for more advanced agricultural practices. In the meantime, prices continued to rise, causing consternation for debtors and delight for creditors. In addition, there was a search for economies that might bring down costs—in manufacturing as well as on the farm. As Joyce Appleby has noted:

> It is now generally recognized that the first capitalists were farmers and landlords—then men who revolutionized English agriculture in the seventeenth and eighteenth centuries. Far from being the stronghold of conservatism, the countryside witnessed dramatic changes in the working and holding of land. The breakthrough in agricultural productivity not only freed the English from famine; it liberated their imaginations as well. With old assumptions undermined, radical theories about individual freedom acquired plausibility.

Taken together, these factors were at the heart of the great debate in the new United States regarding the country's economic destiny.

The Industrial Revolution

Concomitant with the changes in agriculture were developments in industry, which may be seen as handmaiden to the extractive occupations in this period. Usually referred to as "the Industrial Revolution," this transformation affected virtually every aspect of society, from commerce and banking to religion, literature, and art. Industrialization was to have a major impact on the way people obtained wealth. Since earliest history, the most common means was to acquire large tracts of fertile land and the labor to work it. Merchants were those who in the main transported agricultural production for sale in distant markets. The Industrial Revolution would change this basic pattern for all time. Manufactured goods would come to dominate production and commerce. Even agriculture itself would be altered beyond recognition. Prior to the Industrial Revolution, farmers could still benefit by reading the Roman agricultural writers Varro and Columella. After the Industrial Revolution, these works, like so many others, became the province of historians, classicists, and antiquarians.

Traditionally, this momentous change is traced to developments in the textile industry, which at the time was an adjunct of wool harvesting, an ancient English occupation. The pioneers in textile technology were seeking a less expensive, more efficient method of transforming wool into cloth. Likewise, innovators in ironmongering sought to produce better and cheaper iron for the production of farm implements. Later, developers of the steam engine thought it would be used primarily to pump water from coal mines (extractive), so that coal could be obtained more easily and cheaply for the production of iron.

The Industrial Revolution began in England. Why this was so is a matter of conjecture, and of course the causes of so large and complicated a movement are varied. Part of the reason may have been the relative freedom the English enjoyed. This left room for individual initiative. The pressures of the state were not as stifling there as on the continent. Then there was the shortage of wood and population pressures, the kinds of factors that stir creativity and innovation. Iron ore and coal were present and close to the ports, which meant water transportation was accessible. England was a major producer of wool, a key ingredient in the early Industrial Revolution. But there are individual factors to consider as well, which cannot easily be comprehended. Why, for example, did nineteenth and twentieth century Hungary produce more atomic researchers and scientists per capita than any other country? Why did the Caribbean produce a disproportionate number of baseball players, or the American inner cities more Jewish-American basketball players in the 1940s and 1950s and African American players in the 1980s and 1990s?

In the early eighteenth century, English farmers would shear their sheep and transform the wool into yarn—or sell it to someone who would do so—then weave it into cloth. From that, they would make their clothing or sell the product to others who would produce garments. In Lancashire during the 1740s, a group of middlemen appeared, known as "fustian masters." They would purchase the raw material—linen, wool, and cotton from suppliers in the Americas—and provide it to housewives, who would transform it into yarn. The yarn would then be taken to women who were adept at weaving it into cloth, and so on down the line until the final product was sold to merchants. Thus, the fustian masters were developing a highly specialized division of labor.

Technology and the Textile Industry

In the early 1730s, John Kay, a Colchester clothier, experimented with devices for making cloth weaving simpler and less costly—in effect, for mechanizing the process. Out of this came the "flying shuttle," which was invented in 1733. The flying shuttle was quickly adopted, throwing many weavers out of work. This is an early example of a phenomenon that would recur many times thereafter. A new technology would be introduced, creating wealth for its discoverer and those who capitalized on it, and distress among those whom it displaced. The result is a disparity of wealth that often brings calls for income redistribution and talk of inequities in the system. It has happened with regularity, but on three occasions the impact has been significantly greater: in the late eighteenth century, with the Industrial Revolution; in the late nineteenth century, with the emergence of national and international markets; and in the late twentieth century, as the information revolution got into full swing.

Kay was one of the first individuals to benefit and suffer from this phenomenon. Although supported by manufacturers and businessmen, he was set upon by angry weavers and in 1753 was forced to flee to France. It was too late to stop the march of mechanization. Soon, other inventors came forward with additional contributions. John Wyatt and Lewis Paul invented a spinning machine about the same time as Kay's flying shuttle appeared. It was patented in 1738. James Hargreave's "jenny" was developed in 1765 and patented in 1769. Initially, this machine allowed 16 spindles of thread to be spun simultaneously, but by the end of the century, the capacity had been increased to 120 spindles. Richard Arkwright's water frame, which appeared at the same time, was a water-powered device that permitted the manufacture of cotton fabric.

All of these machines wreaked havoc in the labor force. In the early 1760s, weavers found it difficult to get enough thread, since the mechanization of weaving had stepped up productivity, lowered costs, and increased demand. Thirty years later, the mechanization of thread manufacture reversed the situation. At that time there developed a shortage of weavers to handle the large amounts of yarn being produced. The demand for operators of weaving machines caused their wages to rise. In his classic, *The Industrial Revolution in the Eighteenth Century*, Paul Mantaux described it thus:

> While spinning was now done by machinery, weaving was still done by hand. About 1760, weavers found it difficult to get enough thread to keep themselves in constant employment. Thirty years later the opposite was the case: there was a scarcity of weavers and their wages rose rapidly. Those who wove fancy muslins at Bolton were paid in 1792 as much as 3s. or 3s. 6d. a yard, while the weavers of cotton velveteen earned 35s. a week. So they gave themselves great airs, and could be seen parading about the streets, swinging their canes, with 5 pound notes ostentatiously stuck in their hatbands. They dressed like the middle class and would not admit workmen of other trades to the public houses they patronized. It is true that their prosperity was short-lived.

But this soon ended, as improvements in the machines led to an oversupply of weavers. From being a labor-intensive industry, textiles were becoming capital-intensive. In addition, there were some unanticipated problems resulting from the inability of the weaver to absorb all of the yarn being produced. The disproportion between the output of spun yard and material became so great that spinners were forced to export. This gave rise to some alarm. Many people feared that a weaving industry supplied by English cotton thread might be set up in neighboring countries, particularly in France. A vigorous campaign was conducted against the export of cotton thread, and there was even some talk of prohibiting it altogether.

Initially, none of these inventions altered the practices of the fustian masters, who simply purchased the equipment and placed it in the cottages. For example, the spinning wheel was replaced by the spinning jenny. But the water frame and some other inventions dictated that the production of textiles take place in central locations, so the idea of the factory developed in various places at the same time. In addition, several inventors generated the concept that the machines might be united. In 1779, Samuel Crompton joined the jenny and the water frame to produce a machine known as the "mule." From the water frame, the mule borrowed the rollers through which the thread was drawn, and from the jenny, the moving carriage that slid backwards and forwards. The thread produced by the water frame was strong but coarse, while that turned out by the jenny was fine, but broke easily. The mule united the good points of both and produced thread that was at the same time strong and fine. It also speeded up the production of thread. With a single machine, one operator in 1792 produced 212,000 yards of yarn. In the last two decades of the century, cotton fabric output had increased by more than 800 percent. Fifty years after these inventions, textiles accounted for half of England's exports.

The Steam Engine and Its Impact

The replacement of human labor by machines generated both problems and possibilities. The possibilities included a higher standard of living for many, a higher level of productivity, and, in time, a longer life span. Among the problems were a disruption of ancient trades and crafts, unemployment among those displaced by the machines who were unable to adapt to the new dispensation, and an increase in the pace of change, to which some were unable to adjust. Of immediate need in the late eighteenth century was a source of power to run the new machines. As indicated, water power was one answer, windmills another, but neither was dependable or portable. What appeared to provide the solution was the steam engine, that device developed by Hero of Alexandria in the first century B.C., which at the time was used as a toy.

Thomas Newcomen experimented with a crude steam engine in the early eighteenth century, and in 1711, a company was formed that attempted to produce and market the device. One Newcomen engine developed power equivalent to 50 horses (a sensible and conventional method of measuring power, which is still used today) at one-sixth the cost. By 1767, there were 70 such engines in the Newcastle area, most of which were used to pump water out of coal and tin mines.

During the 1760s, James Watt, a Scots engineer, experimented with the Newcomen engine and came up with a superior design. Watt patented his engine in 1769, but there were difficulties in the finance and manufacture of the device. In order to overcome these, he formed an alliance with John Roebuck, who owned and operated coal mines and knew these engines could be used to pump water from them. When Roebuck went bankrupt, he introduced Watt to Matthew Boulton, a large manufacturer and metalworker who also recognized the engine's importance. Boulton had an even grander vision; he wanted to open a factory to manufacture the engines for sale. By 1776, the new engine was ready for production. Its use spread slowly because, at first, Watt refused to make modifications that his potential customers wanted. He gave in reluctantly, whereupon sales increased and the revolution in power began.

The appearance of the steam engine enabled steel makers to improve their methods of production, since the engines could be used to power blast furnaces. At the same time, the need for iron and steel to produce engines created shortages of the metal, which the engines helped rectify.

In 1784, Henry Cort introduced a new method for melting and stirring molten iron ore. With Cort's process, more of the impurities could be removed. In addition, Cort developed a superior rolling mill that continuously shaped the molten metal into bars and other forms.

Most of these innovators were English, and England led the way in the Industrial Revolution. Oliver Evans was one of the non-English contributors, though technically he was English, since he was born in America while it was still a colony. In 1778, Evans invented a machine for making teeth for carding machines. Seven years later, with his brothers, who were flour millers, he developed several laborsaving devices for use in flour milling, out of which came an automatic mill that cut labor costs in half. By 1808, an improved version of the system could grind nine bushels of wheat in an hour.

Evans also improved upon the Watt steam engine, one use of which was to power printing presses, making possible the modern newspaper, among whose first readers were people seeking business information. The pioneers in publishing were not journalists in the current sense of the term. Instead, they were businesspeople who perceived the need for information and acted to provide it. Early on, they functioned as combination entrepreneur-journalist-financier-laborers. They would organize a company, raise money, purchase machinery, write copy, set type, and publish their "broadsides," which were then taken to the marketplaces or wharfs and sold to businessmen in need of information on prices, ship arrivals, and other news. Usually there was no need for the presses on a full-time basis, so the owner utilized them to print playing cards, lottery tickets, political broadsides, and job printing assignments that came along.

Perhaps the most famous of the early journalists was Benjamin Franklin, much of whose printing income derived from publishing official notices for the political powers-that-were. One of his major tasks was to accustom Americans to reading newspapers for news as well as commercial information. Out of this, in time, came a robust political press. But in the beginning, the function of newspapers was to assist business.

The innovations in textiles, iron, and coal transformed the English economy from one based on agriculture to one founded on industry, to the point that England was obliged to import foodstuffs and pay for it by exports of machinery, coal, and other products of its factories. This did not occur quickly, or even over a few decades, but over the course of the century. Coal consumption rose from 11 million tons in 1800 to 100 million tons in 1870; iron production from less than 0.2 million tons in 1806 to 6.6 million tons in 1873. There were 2400 power looms in England in 1813 and 250,000 in 1850. Steam capacity as late as 1840 stood at 0.6 million horsepower and rose to 13.7 million horsepower in 1896.

Eli Whitney and the Emergence of the Cotton South

Need wealth be extracted from the economy only by Jeffersonian or Hamiltonian means? Was it not possible for a combination to develop: small farmers producing crops for sale to manufacturers? In fact, this is close to what happened, due largely to industrialization, however, and not agriculture.

The mechanization of spinning and weaving initially affected wool, the traditional fabric of England, but soon it spilled over into other fabrics, including cotton. Although cultivated in the South during the colonial period, it was not an important crop, or to be more precise, crops. Sea island cotton, with long, smooth fibers and small seeds, was grown (as the name indicates) on islands off the Georgia and South Carolina coasts. Green seed cotton, which was hardier and relatively easy to grow, had short fibers and larger seeds, which were difficult to remove. Workers were able to extract little more than a pound of fiber a day by hand. Farmers interested in cotton knew that the future of the crop rested with the green seed variety, and that a more efficient and economical means of separating fiber and seed was needed. Therefore, farmers and others throughout the 1790s were at work attempting to develop just such a device.

Credit for inventing the first practical cotton gin (or engine) belongs to Eli Whitney, who was typical of the inventor-businessmen of the time in that he straddled several industries and inventions. The son of a poor Massachusetts farmer, Whitney demonstrated an early talent for mechanics. In 1779, at the age of 14, he installed a forge in his father's workshop and manufactured nails. When that market started to decline, he turned to hatpins and walking sticks. For a time, he taught school while attending secondary school himself. Whitney finally entered Yale, from which he graduated in 1792 at the age of 28, whereupon he left for a post as private tutor on a Georgia plantation owned by Catherine Greene, the widow of Revolutionary War general Nathaniel Greene. The plantation grew cotton. In addition to his teaching duties, Whitney helped manage the plantation and came to recognize the need for a cotton gin. His answer was a very simple device, a set of rolling cylinders with wired teeth that brushed the cotton from the seeds and deposited it in a hopper. Using a gin, a worker could extract more than 50 pounds of cotton per day.

Whitney and attorney Phineas Miller formed a partnership to apply for patents on the gin, intending to produce and market it throughout the South. While Miller attempted to obtain financing, Whitney secured a patent in Philadelphia, returned to New Haven, set up a machine shop, and started to produce the gins. Miller obtained six orders, which were paid for 60 percent in cash and 40 percent in farm produce. By then, however, the simple machine had been copied by others, often with improvements, and sold for lower prices. Whitney and Miller filed infringement of patent suits and tried to win royalty awards, and while they won some cases, the costs of litigation were greater than the awards. The suits indicated that, absent the Whitney gin, a device of that sort soon would have been developed by some other inventor. Such was often the case with the other inventor-businessmen discussed in this chapter. As they were working on their concepts, others were doing the same. Some inventors and businessmen, in their search for wealth, are uniquely original, but they are rare. Most function in an environment that encourages their plans; that is, a need arises for which they seek a solution.

Discouraged, Whitney turned to other inventions, in 1798 winning a government contract to manufacture small arms for the federal government. Although he failed to live up to the terms of the contract, he did deliver 500 muskets in 1801, and his New Haven armory continued to produce arms until Whitney's death in 1825. By then, cotton had become the dominant American cash crop. Output went from 10,000 bales in 1793 to 209,000 in 1815 and to more than 530,000 in 1825. The million bale mark was passed in 1835, and the 2 million mark in 1850. On the eve of the Civil War, in 1859, more than 5.3 million bales were produced.

Jefferson had thought the independent small farmer also could be a businessman, but he could not have foreseen the impact cotton would have on the southern economy and planter psychology. While a large majority of southerners remained small farmers, the plantations dominated the larger economy, and the planter had to be business-oriented. Generally, planters would borrow needed funds from a bank or a factor, the collateral being the future crops, with interest rates fluctuating according to the market, usually from 8 to 12 percent. Any amount of cotton produced beyond the contract would be sold by the factor or bank, which received a commission on the sale. If insufficient cotton was delivered, the planter would have to go into the open market and make the necessary purchases. As might be imagined, there was a lively futures market in cotton.

The demand for slaves increased as well. Field hands generally sold for around $300 in 1790; by the 1850s, they might command as much as $5000. During the constitutional debates, the delegates discussed the future of slavery in the United States. Article I, Section 9 forbade the government from regulating the slave trade before 1808, and in 1807, even as the cotton gin had started transforming the southern economy, sufficient southern votes were cast to henceforward end the importation of slaves. That there were violations of the law became evident later in the century, and there was a vigorous and important domestic slave trade. This matter and the business of plantations will be discussed in Chapter 10.

One might have expected white southerners to become cotton manufacturers and garner wealth from processing as well as growing cotton. Some of them did, but in 1810, most American cotton textiles still were produced by household manufacturers. Of the 14.8 million yards produced that year, more than 9 million were turned out in South Carolina, Georgia, and Virginia. Rhode Island produced 461,000 yards that year, and Massachusetts so little it wasn't even reported. But this situation was changing. By 1840, there were 248 plants in the southern states capitalized at more than $4.3 million. In 1850, however, the number of plants had dwindled to 166 capitalized at $7.2 million. In the same period the number of northern plants went from 674 to 564 and their capitalization from $34.9 million to $53.8 million. Six times as many northerners were engaged in cotton processing as were southerners. The reason was machines and motivation. The slaveholders of the South scorned those "in trade," in much the same way the English Cavaliers derided the tradesmen who supported Oliver Cromwell.

Samuel Slater, Francis Cabot Lowell, and the Emergence of the Industrial North

The arrival of new textile machines did not mean the day of the fustian master in England was over. Despite the clear advantages of the new methods, change came slowly, as is usually the case. In addition, capital was lacking, and individuals skilled in the use of the machines were scarce. As late as 1803, only one-sixteenth of the cloth produced in the English town of West Riding was produced in factories; the rest was produced in traditional ways by weavers. This scenario would replay itself many times in the next two centuries, in everything from railroads, steamships, and telegraph to electrification and on to computers and the Internet. Part of the explanation is that young people (the pioneers in new industries are usually young) who possess the requisite knowledge and skills are in short supply, as are those with the imagination and daring to supply them with capital.

In the late eighteenth and early nineteenth centuries, the English manufacturers guarded their industrial knowledge with the kind of care a future generation would employ to safeguard atomic secrets. The government enacted regulations that forbade the export of technology. Skilled mechanics were not permitted to leave the country, and officials in the port cities stayed on the lookout for skilled mechanics and machinists attempting to flee with their secrets and talents. But then, as now, keeping industrial secrets was close to impossible. Twenty-one-year-old Samuel Slater, who was an apprentice at the factory of Jedediah Strutt, one of Arkwright's close associates, had learned how to make yarn. Slater disguised himself as a farm laborer and slipped out of the country in 1789, bound for America. For a while he worked in New York, but no one there seemed to appreciate how his knowledge could transform business methods. In 1790, he learned that Moses Brown and his son-in-law, William Almy of Providence, Rhode Island, leaders in the Baltic and Oriental trade, were attempting—without much success—to create a textile factory. Brown had visited several small shops in Massachusetts and Connecticut to learn all he could of the ways of manufacturing. In them, he saw some machines that had been smuggled out of England, but most were broken and discarded, since the owners did not know how to repair and maintain them. Moreover, the Americans lacked the knowledge base that would enable them to make improvements and develop new machines. In this period only England possessed that kind of human capital. Thus, Brown and Almy had the funds and the zeal for manufacturing, but they lacked knowledge and technology, both of which remained in England.

Slater contacted the two men in a letter: "A few days ago I was informed that you wanted a manager of cotton spinning & co. in which business I flatter myself that I can give the greatest satisfaction, in making machinery, making good yarn, either for stockings or twist, as any that is made in England." Brown and Almy sent for him, and Slater started work. Within three months he was named a partner. Unlike the merchants and bankers, he lacked capital and credit. Slater's capital was in his head. The new developments in textile technology were giving the edge to knowledgeable workers.

In Providence, at Almy, Brown & Slater, Slater supervised the construction of what some consider the first American factory. There, the machines he created spun yarn, which was woven into cloth by handweavers the same way it had been done prior to the invention of the Cartwright weaving machines. The venture was a success, but at the time Brown and Almy viewed it as an adjunct to their textile trading business and did not consider switching their main business from trade to manufacturing—or, for that matter, how wealth might be derived from manufacture rather than commerce.

Other factories were started in New England, but not until the War of 1812 did the movement become significant. At that time English textiles were denied to the American market, and Americans had to make do with more expensive, yet inferior, handwoven fabric.

This situation appealed to Francis Cabot Lowell, a Boston merchant who also engaged in a variety of other occupations. Lowell was a sedentary merchant with offices on a wharf, from which he dealt in insurance, land purchases and sales, lottery tickets, and anything else that might turn a profit. He was a global entrepreneur, engaging in commerce with ships owned by his father and other family members. As his name indicates, Lowell was a member of the city's aristocracy, and his wife was a Jackson, another of the blue bloods. His partner was his brother-in-law, Patrick Tracy Jackson. Together, they took shares in ship cargoes, and Jackson occasionally would ship out as supercargo to make trades in the ports the ships visited, as was done in Hellenistic times and later. The business was prosperous, and Lowell was doing well.

All of this ended with the Napoleonic Wars. First, President Jefferson embargoed American shipping, and then, when the United States entered the conflict during the War of 1812, business dried up completely. Lowell had gone to England on a family visit in 1810. He rented a cottage in Edinburgh and from there visited merchants in Bristol, iron foundries in Lancashire, and cotton mills whenever he could obtain invitations to inspect the facilities. While there, he met fellow Bostonian Nathan Appleton, who later wrote, "We had frequent conversations on the subject of cotton manufacture, and he informed me that he had determined, before his return to America, to visit Manchester, for the purpose of obtaining all possible information on the subject, with a view to the introduction of improved manufacture in the United States."

The Lowells went to Paris in late 1811, and then on to London in early 1812, where Francis Lowell learned of the imminence of war between the United States and England. They then decided to return home. The customs inspectors went through their baggage and found nothing dealing with textiles. All of the information was stored in Francis Lowell's head. The war began while they were on the high seas, and their ship was captured by an English frigate. Lowell did not disclose what he had learned, and the family soon was released. When he arrived home, Lowell found his transoceanic shipping interests were no more. He had to find another occupation. Textiles were an obvious candidate.

As already noted, there was no textile industry of any size in Massachusetts in 1810. Virtually all the cotton cloth used in the state was produced by handicrafters or imported from England. The War of 1812 changed this. Lowell and Jackson were among just a handful of Massachusetts men who saw the possibilities. The state had adequate water power, a good labor force, and most important, sufficient capital accumulated from commerce and an entrepreneurial class prepared to use it.

Lowell approached some of these individuals with his ideas for a factory based on the English model. It is not certain when he began to do this, or whom he approached initially. Jackson was involved from the start, as was Nathan Appleton, and it is fairly clear that Lowell received advice and assistance from two of his uncles who had attempted, unsuccessfully, to start a mill of their own. Sometime in mid-1813, they decided to form the Boston Manufacturing Company, to be located in Waltham. Appleton, who later wrote a memoir, said that Lowell and Jackson "came to me one day on the Boston exchange, and stated that they had determined to establish a cotton manufactory, that they had purchased water power in Waltham, and that they had obtained an act of incorporation, and Mr. Jackson had agreed to give up all other business and take the management of the concern."

The act of incorporation requires some explanation. In this period corporations were rare and little trusted. Sole proprietorships and partnerships seemed more solid and trustworthy, especially since the partners did not have limited liability, as did the corporation, and ownership and management were united more firmly. In order to form a corporation, the promoters had to have a bill introduced and passed in the state legislature, and that would remain the case in most states until the 1830s. Why did Lowell have to incorporate? Because he was proposing to raise the prodigious sum of $400,000, and no one in the Massachusetts of that time was prepared to assume so large a risk. Presumably, the merchants who were involved with the initial offering had experience in this kind of venture, having taken shares in voyages and land speculations, but this was not the same. In those commercial and land ventures, the understanding was that the capital and profits would be divided once the venture came to fruition. Boston Manufacturing was more like the joint stock companies of the colonial period in that shares could be transferred and the company would be long-lived. But there was a difference. The joint stock companies operated with royal patents which could be extended or terminated as the monarch pleased. Such was not the case with Boston Manufacturing.

The company issued 100 shares, each with a liability to the buyer of $4000. The understanding was that $1000 would be called initially, with the owner responsible for providing additional funds up to the $4000 limit when called upon to do so. There were 12 original shareholders, with half the shares taken by Jackson, Lowell, and their relatives. Israel Thorndyke, Sr., a prominent Boston merchant who was friendly with the Lowells and Jacksons, took 10 shares, and his son, Israel Thorndyke, Jr., came in for another 10. In sum, Boston Manufacturing was the creation of a closely knit group of businessmen. This was the dawn of the age of incorporation and modern securities underwriting and investment. The shareholders might not have considered purchasing shares were it not to demonstrate support for a relative and friend. This personal consideration can be added to the quest for the wealth they perceived Boston Manufacturing might bring them.

Lowell did not intend to create another mill like the one in Rhode Island. At this factory raw, ginned cotton would enter on one end of the building and be processed, spun into yarn, and then woven into cloth, all by operators at machines. And there would be other operations at Waltham. There would be a mill, houses for the workers, and a machine shop.

Lowell then set about hiring a labor force. He decided to offer employment to young girls, the daughters of nearby farmers. They were to work in the factory for several years and save their money for dowries. They would live in housing provided by the mill under the supervision of a chaperone.

The machine shop was a key element in the enterprise. Lowell hoped to take on Jacob Perkins for the task of creating textile manufacturing machinery. He wanted it not only for use in his own factory but for sale to others. Perkins, a highly regarded inventor who had a successful nail factory, was not interested, but he recommended Paul Moody, a 34-year-old mechanic who had helped construct some of the nail-making machines. Moody became superintendent of the facility in October 1813. He constructed a Cartwright machine according to the specifications set down by Lowell. At first, they relied upon the original version, plus some others purchased from local inventors. But when Moody became more experienced, he added improvements. In the planning period, Lowell and Moody visited inventors throughout the New England region in search of ideas and possibly to license patents. Just as Lowell had had no compunctions against pilfering English concepts, likewise he did not waver when doing the same in America. At one point, he and Moody tried to purchase a patent for a winding machine from a Mr. Shepherd of

Taunton. At first, Shepherd tried to drive a hard bargain: "You must have them, you cannot do without them, as you know, Mr. Moody." Turning to Lowell, Moody suggested an improvement on their existing model, inspired by the Shepherd design. "I am just thinking I can spin the cops direct on the bobbin," he mused. Shepherd jumped to accept Lowell's original offer. "No," said Lowell. "It is too late." Writing in 1858, Appleton recalled their efforts. With "admiration and satisfaction," they would sit for hours, "watching the beautiful movement of this new and wonderful machine, destined as it evidently was, to change the character of all textile industry."

In December 1814, the Boston Manufacturing Company was ready to start producing cloth. Lowell placed his first order for cotton. Everything went smoothly, and by 1817, there were some 125 workers at the factory. Because of good sales, Lowell was able to lower the price of his cloth to stimulate demand. In 1815, Boston Manufacturing showed sales of less than $3000. By 1817, the figure was well over $34,000, and the company paid a dividend of 17 percent. Even Lowell was surprised at this showing. As Appleton put it, "The only circumstance which made him distrust his own calculations was that he could bring them to no other result but one which was too favorable to be creditable."

As had been the case in England, the obvious advantages of machine manufacturing of textiles did not persuade many others to enter the field. As far as the fustian masters were concerned, it was too novel, too unusual, and far too risky. They could see the advantages of yarn-making equipment, but not of cloth fabricating machines, in the light of inexpensive English cloth. Not until 1816 did production increase significantly. By then, Lowell had become a major supplier of machines to other would-be manufacturers. Sales came to $8700 in 1818 and leaped to $28,800 in 1819, returning a profit of $14,000, far more than textile sales. The company also began licensing its patents, and business in all three areas—manufacture of cloth, manufacture of machines, and licensing—were doing moderately well.

Lowell functioned as a combination manager, research director, employment officer, foreman, and salesman, for he also traveled to stores selling his textiles. Early in 1816, he traveled to Rhode Island to sell weaving machines to yarn manufacturers. He met with little success. The Rhode Island manufacturers did not feel they could compete with English exports. Lowell then proceeded to Washington, where he lobbied for a high tariff on imported textiles to keep English textiles out of the American market after the war. A measure was before the House of Representatives calling for a 33.3 percent tariff on all cotton products, and New England mercantile interests were attempting to push it down to 25 percent. Lowell presented a report to Congress:

> The articles whose prohibition we pray for, are made of very inferior materials, and are manufactured in a manner calculated to deceive rather than serve the consumer. No part of the produce of the United States enters into their composition. They are the work of foreign hands on a foreign material. Yet they are thrown into this country in such abundance as to threaten the exclusion of more useful and substantial manufacture.

He then presented "the Lowell Proviso," under which the customs office would assume that cotton cloth from overseas cost 25 cents a square yard to produce, and would be taxed accordingly. In the end, the tariff was set at 25 percent for three years and 20 percent thereafter, with the Lowell Proviso to go into effect in three years. While this appeared to be a defeat, it actually was not, for while the nominal tariff was to be at 20 percent, the actual was at least 10 percent higher.

The protective tariff worked wonders for Boston Manufacturing. As noted, total revenues for 1817 came to $34,000. In 1825, they were $345,000. By 1826, Massachusetts had 135 factories, 25 more than Rhode Island. Lowell lived long enough to see the early success of Boston Manufacturing, but he was not there for the boom years. He died in August 1817, less than half a year after passage of the tariff, at the age of 42.

Lowell may be considered one of the earliest American industrialists or, alternatively—or perhaps concomitantly—as the person who devised a more efficient method of processing an agricultural commodity, cotton. The latter was the view of South Carolina Senator John C. Calhoun, who became the spokesman of the agrarian South and favored an alliance of southern planters and northern manufacturers, since each was dependent on the other. Calhoun believed that just as the southern economy was based, in part at least, on the labor of black slaves, so the northern economy was coming to be founded on the labor of white workers. In the 1820s and 1830s, Calhoun visited Waltham and surrounding towns to see what the Yankees were doing with his region's cotton. Just as a previous generation of Boston traders had carried and sold the products of agrarian America overseas and had imported goods and Africans for sale to southern farmers, Calhoun saw their sons and grandsons now processing the raw materials of farms into finished goods, much of which would be consumed by southerners and sent to foreign markets. Industry existed to serve agriculture and depended upon it, thought Calhoun and others like him. The American business tradition had its roots in the soil.

The Quaker Alternative

Consider, too, that Lowell's business practices included the piracy of English manufacturing secrets and the appropriation of the ideas of others to use in his machines. Such actions might be justifiable in the Calvinist atmosphere of early nineteenth century Boston. Lowell was true to his colleagues, but he was a ruthless competitor, prepared, among other things, to use the power of the federal government to stifle foreign cloth manufacturers. Lowell did indeed bow to the dictates of Calvinism in his search for success and wealth.

Given the intensity of competition, it must have appeared easier to take the Calvinist route, especially in industries in which large amounts of money could be obtained in a very few transactions. Retailing was one such industry. The clerk in an early nineteenth century dry goods store would lead the customer to pile after pile of goods, praising his wares as he went. The hard sell predominated. Items did not sell at uniform prices; haggling was standard procedure. The clerk was always careful to size up the social and economic status of his customer before quoting prices. In speaking of his experiences in a Connecticut dry goods store in the 1820s, P. T. Barnum said, "The customers cheated us, and we cheated them. Each party expected to be cheated if it was possible." *Caveat emptor* is as good a motto for Calvinist business as any.

Even so, there existed at the time an alternative theological base for capitalism, which offered a more honest and forthright approach and managed to bring forward the code of honor merchants had to hew to during the Middle Ages. While Calvinists proselytized and prospered, George Fox spoke out for the Society of Friends, more commonly known as the Quakers. Like Calvin, Fox admonished his followers to "strive to be rich in the life, and in the kingdom and things of the world." This was to be done with prudence, honesty, and respect for order. "True Godliness doesn't turn men out of the world," wrote William Penn, one of the most prominent Quakers, "but enables them to live better in it, and excites their endeavors to mend it."

The Quaker ethic was accepted by many who never saw the inside of a meeting-house. While not a Quaker or practitioner of any organized religion, Benjamin Franklin, no mean businessman himself, admired their honesty and sobriety. He liked to quote Proverbs 22: "Seest thou a man diligent in his business? He shall stand before kings."

Quakers were urged to deal equitably with employees, customers, and clients. As Fox put it, "When people came to have experience of Friends' honesty and faithfulness, and found that their yea was yea and their nay was nay, that they would keep to a word in their dealings, and that they would not cozen and cheat them, they would come to trust them." Bound by religious vows, they could be counted on to give fair weights and prices. Quakers would not misrepresent products and services, no small matter when distances were long, communications poor, and trust necessary for many dealings. This, of course, entailed an appreciation of the need for a fairness and honesty that would engender trust. Quaker business practitioners made certain those with whom they dealt understood what they meant by fairness, lived up to their avowed precepts, and so earned that trust.

As might have been expected, Quakers conducted business without lawyers; disputes were settled among the parties or at the Quaker meetings. In an honest community, the Quakers reasoned, there would be no need for lawyers, whose very presence indicated societal breakdown. Fox had contempt for them and spoke of "the lawyers black, their black robes as a puddle, and like a black pit, almost covered over with blackness." Until 1722, it was illegal to practice law for fees in Pennsylvania.

So it would appear that both Calvinist and Quaker believed capitalism to be like a jungle, but their reactions differed sharply. The Calvinist took the attitude that in such an environment, everyone was for himself. The Quaker believed that if all worked together, difficulties could be surmounted to the benefit of both buyer and seller, individual and society.

From their perches in Philadelphia ("The City of Brotherly Love" in Greek), a Quaker business aristocracy directed a web of relationships that extended around the world. Philadelphia became the busiest commercial city in the colonies and the young nation. Chestnut Street, not Wall Street, was the most important securities market. The Second Bank of the United States, chartered by Congress in 1816, was more powerful in the 1820s and 1830s than the Federal Reserve is today. Quakers were leaders in commerce, retailing, and land speculation, all areas in which sharpsters might easily trap the unwary. Yet the Quaker ethic of fair dealing was profitable. Fairness paid dividends.

CHAPTER 10

The Mechanization
of Agriculture

wo northerners, Eli Whitney and Francis Cabot Lowell, helped to make cotton the king in the South. A southerner, Cyrus McCormick, developed the technology that created emperor wheat, first in the East, and then the Midwest. If Lowell was the father of the American factory, McCormick was the precursor and model for American big business— and big profits. Lowell thought in regional terms insofar as markets were concerned. McCormick's reach was national and then global. Lowell pioneered the industrial corporation; McCormick developed it several steps further, and dealt with business problems that Lowell had no need to consider. Both men, however, created products and enterprises that served agrarian America.

Cyrus McCormick and the Reaper

Cyrus McCormick is generally credited with inventing the reaper, a device that cut wheat in such a way that the grain would not fall from the stalks, leaving it in the field for a binder, a worker who would gather it and arrange the stalks in orderly sheaves. Later, McCormick helped develop a machine that would bind the stalks as well, and his name is associated with a variety of other devices used in wheat harvesting. But even his most ardent champions concede that he was just one of dozens of inventors and farmers at work on such machines at the time. McCormick's abilities were not primarily inventive, at least when it came to his accumulation of wealth. Rather, his most original work rested in sales and distribution, servicing and credit, popularization and education. Without these, and even armed with a superior machine, McCormick might have failed. His task was much more difficult than Lowell's. Once the cloth was manufactured, Lowell would attempt to sell it to retailers. Or he might have taken orders prior to making the cloth and then would make deliveries. Unable to sell the cloth, he could place it in inventory. In contrast, McCormick was selling a machine, a capital good rather than a consumer good. He had stiff competition, in terms of both price and quality. The wheat farmer needed the machine for only a few days a year; the rest of the time it remained in the barn. And if it didn't operate efficiently on those days, the investment would be a waste. The machines were costly, and many farmers couldn't afford them. McCormick had to devise a way for them to pay with relative ease. He had to instruct the farmers in the operation of the reapers and his other machines. Without meeting all of these extra requirements, McCormick's reaper would have failed. What it came down to was that McCormick realized, quite early, that he was not selling a machine so much as a service. This was a lesson other manufacturers would learn from his time to the present. Today's manufacturers of desktop computers know—almost without having to be told—that their machines are merely the devices needed to run the software placed in them and not ends in themselves.

That McCormick and others in Virginia were developing their reapers in the 1830s vindicated Jefferson's concept of a food-based capitalist economy. Indeed, work on such machines began even earlier. Cyrus' father, Robert McCormick, a farmer in the small town of Walnut Grove, invented a thresher which he sold to neighbors for $70, and in 1816, he, too, had produced a reaper. It was one of several versions used on farms in the early nineteenth century, produced by such now-forgotten men as William Manning of New Jersey, Enoch Ambler and Alexander Wilson of New York, and Maine inventor Samuel Lane. There were two reasons for their interest: the short harvest season and the high cost of occasional labor. Farmers with their families might till the soil and care for the crop, but in the short harvest period for wheat, family labor might not suffice, and so they would have to hire local workers, who, since the demand for their services was great, could charge high fees.

In 1816, when Robert McCormick had Cyrus harvest a neighbor's field with his reaper, one observer said the machine was worth at least $100,000 if it could be marketed well, and another ordered a machine for the next year's harvest. "Since the year 1818, farmers have very sensibly felt that labor has been much dearer than produce," wrote Jonathan Roberts of the Pennsylvania Agricultural Society in 1823. "We can not speedily look for their equalization; a mitigation of this effect may be sought in some degree by improved implements. Nothing is more wanted than the application of animal labor in the cutting of grain." Indeed, so pressing was the need that de Tocqueville thought that unless some means were found to lessen the costs of harvest, many farmers would abandon the soil. "To cultivate the ground promises an almost certain reward for his efforts, but a slow one," he observed. "In that way you grow rich little by little and with toil. Agriculture only suits the wealthy, who already have a great superfluity, or the poor, who only want to live." As for the great mass of farmers in the middle, "His choice is made; he sells his field, moves from his house, and takes up some risky but lucrative profession." In other words, only those who could afford to hire gangs of workers in harvesting crops, and subsistence farmers, working with their families at harvest, would survive. So much for the Jeffersonian dream.

The experiments continued, and while they did, the price of farm labor rose, going from an average of $0.78 a day in the period from 1811 to 1820 to $0.88 in the 1831–1840 decade. Meanwhile, the price of wheat declined irregularly. Then, in 1836, there was a large-scale crop failure, and the price of wheat and flour rose. Some farmers did quite well for themselves that year, while others simply abandoned their farms and headed to the cities.

In this atmosphere Obed Hussey, a Virginian who knew the McCormicks, seized the main chance. Developing a reaper, he took it to New York for trials, which went quite well. This spurred Cyrus McCormick to action, and he produced a new reaper, too, advertising in 1843, "They all give satisfaction, allowance being made for defects which I had afterwards to correct." Soon after, he warranted that his machine would cut from 15 to 20 acres a day.

Both Hussey and McCormick sold machines in the early 1840s. They would receive an order and then turn out the reaper. There were no inventories in those days. Neither man had the capital that would require. Farmers were divided on the merits of each machine. Emboldened, Hussey challenged McCormick to a competition in 1842. McCormick won the first round, Hussey the second. There were other competitions, with other entrants. No conclusive winner emerged, but farmers attending the contests left believing that they had to buy one or another of the models they had seen.

McCormick emerged the clear winner by 1849, selling 1500 machines in all parts of the East, while Hussey was a distant second with only a hundred or so. McCormick owed his success to several factors. In the first place, his sales agents offered to teach the farmers how to use the machines. Second, he provided farmers with a written guarantee that the machines would work when needed, and agents were on call to make those guarantees good. He sold the reapers for a down payment of $30, with the rest of the price payable within six months, on condition that the machine cut 1½ acres an hour. If the machine failed to live up to that standard, the $30 would be refunded. Unlike the others, McCormick refused to haggle over price; the farmers were told to take it or leave it. It was a dangerous tactic, but it worked, and it provided McCormick with greater credibility.

One may wonder why McCormick didn't take the next step that would be considered automatically today: sell the service, not the machine. McCormick might have kept his machines, hired gangs of labor, and moved from region to region, following the harvest season, charging farmers who, as indicated, wanted the service, not necessarily the machine. Recall Francis Cabot Lowell's difficulty in establishing Boston Manufacturing: the problem was not brainpower or energy, but lack of capital. McCormick was the largest factor in the new industry, but he lacked sufficient capital for such an approach. The matter of capital appeared again when he made an audacious move. In the late 1840s, upper New York state was the nation's largest producer of wheat. By then, McCormick had experimented with using parts manufactured by others, and he found some suppliers unreliable. He had several licensees in areas difficult to reach from Virginia, and he was distressed with the quality of the machines they were selling under his nameplate. Furthermore, his early sales agents proved irregular in their operations and reporting.

McCormick thought the time had arrived to move closer to his customers and consolidate his operations. The Erie Canal—which we soon will consider—was by this time in operation, and western Pennsylvania and Ohio had evolved into important farm areas. A McCormick factory in either state, or New York, might have seemed plausible. So would a factory in such places as St. Louis or Cincinnati, the former dominating the Missouri-Mississippi, the latter the "Queen of the Ohio." And there were other cities as well. McCormick had witnessed the strong drive to the West, however, and he became convinced Chicago was the place to be. In 1848, Chicago was a dusty town of around 18,000 beset by smallpox and cholera epidemics. Its economy was based on small farms, lumber, and grain—little more. That year, Chicago shipped more grain than any other midwestern city. Although the Chicago River hardly compared to the Hudson, Missouri-Mississippi, or Ohio, it was being dredged so it would be navigable. To McCormick it appeared the nation had a watery spine, with Chicago at one end and New Orleans at the other.

McCormick had visited Chicago as early as 1844, and had even formed a partnership with C. M. Gray of that city to produce and sell reapers for the 1848 harvest. He also struck up friendships with William B. Ogden, the city's leading booster and wealthiest businessman, who was willing to bankroll a factory for McCormick, and with Stephen Douglas, who, elected to the Senate in 1847, spoke glowingly of new railroads running out of a Chicago hub and the possibilities of the city displacing New York as a financial center. Finally, McCormick was devoutly Presbyterian, and Chicago possessed a strong and active Presbyterian community that he found hospitable. So Chicago it was to be.

With $40,000 borrowed from Ogden, McCormick was able to establish his factory in time for the 1849 harvest season. McCormick manufactured 1500 reapers, the average production cost for each machine coming to less than $65, including agent's fee and an allowance for bad debts. The reaper would be sold for $115, or if purchased on credit, $120. The product run sold out, making McCormick a successful and wealthy man. By 1856, his factory was turning out more than 4000 machines annually.

Cyrus McCormick was the first really big manufacturer in American history, a major innovator, and, of course, a very wealthy man. In its time, the McCormick works became the largest factory in the world. Yet his machines were not necessarily superior to those produced by some of his competitors. In fact, at one time he was embroiled in legal actions charging him with having stolen ideas from them, which he won. What accounted for his success and the failures of the others was McCormick's uncanny ability to understand his customers and meet their needs. As a salesman-distributor, he had no peer.

Reapers were linked to the growing of wheat, which in turn depended on the price. The higher the price, the more was grown and the greater the need for reapers. As will be seen, a similar situation existed in the American South, where there was a strong correlation between the prices of cotton and slaves. The labor shortage caused by farmers leaving the Midwest during the California Gold Rush in the late 1840s and early 1850s also increased the demand for reapers. The McCormick works turned out 4600 machines in the 1851–1854 period, making McCormick Chicago's leading citizen, not only a symbol of the city's growing power but also a major purchaser of wood and iron from local establishments and an employer of local labor. A credit report filed on him in 1853 read:

> Been here 6 or 8 years. Has a very fine property, a large brick building with steam engine. Can't have less than 100 hands to work—is considered worth $200,000. We think him with $150,000 clear. His patent is worth a fortune though it cost him a good deal of money to defend it. He manufactures from 12–15,000 reapers a year, which he sells at $120 each.

By 1848, the report raised the estimate of McCormick's net worth and conjectured he was the wealthiest man in the Midwest.

The Need for Transportation

McCormick sent his first reapers from his Walnut Grove facility to the Midwest in 1844. They were placed on wagons and taken to Scottsville, Virginia, then loaded on a flatboat and sent by canal to the James River, which flowed to the Atlantic. They then were put onto a ship that headed south, around Florida to New Orleans. There, the machines were reloaded and sent upstream to Cincinnati. Transporting the machines from Walnut Grove to Scottsville cost more than all the rest of the voyage. A few years later, during the gold rush, a traveler could go from China to San Francisco faster and at a lower cost than from St. Louis to San Francisco. In this period, water transport was by far less expensive than land transport, sometimes startlingly so. During the War of 1812, the government purchased cannons from a facility near Washington for $400, then spent another $1500–$2000 to have them shipped to northern Ohio. At a time when flour and pork cost $10 a barrel in the East, flour and pork imported to the western garrisons cost $100 and $127 respectively.

While Hamilton's successes in providing a financial infrastructure for the new nation eased the path for those seeking wealth, much more was needed from government. Throughout American history, governments have assisted in creating both the transportation and communications infrastructures. This was needed, for without them, individual and corporate businesses would lack mobility, information, and access to markets. Some historians have suggested that private concerns might have built the roads, canals, and railroads to satisfy pecuniary interests. Perhaps so, but there is no clear record of the private sector's willingness to do so, since hopes for profit were slim. Instead, the partnership between public and private interests resulted in a form of mixed capitalism, pragmatic to the core, that typified American business throughout much of its history, certainly in the early years.

The need for faster, more reliable, and less expensive transportation was not lost on the founding fathers. For them, such transportation was to be for agricultural goods, not finished products of the sort later turned out by Lowell and McCormick. For this reason, despite their many differences, Jeffersonians and Hamiltonians could agree, generally, on the need for a federal role in the improvement of roads and waterways.

George Washington, both before and during his presidency, was a canal advocate. In 1784, he promoted the Potomac Canal, which would begin at the Potomac River and extend inland. Five hundred shares were offered at 100 pounds each. Washington and others hoped this would enable them to start work and that by the time the money ran out, sufficient mileage would have been created to offer services to shippers, with the tolls collected paying for further digging until the line was completed. When share sales to private investors fell short, the states of Virginia and Maryland stepped in to purchase approximately half the shares.

The going was difficult. Canal technology was relatively undeveloped, especially in the matter of locks, and the promoter, David Ramsey, was inexperienced. The company was close to bankruptcy in 1792 when the states agreed to provide additional funds, making the canal navigable for 220 miles. When toll revenues fell short as well, lotteries were held to provide even more funding. Another project, the James River Canal, experienced similar problems, and both canals fell into bankruptcy and were merged into other projects. Although financial failures, the canals provided major benefits to the regions they served. Economic development resulted in more traffic, and by 1811, the restructured Potomac Company was able to show a slight profit, having transported close to $1 million worth of goods that year and taking in $22,542 in tolls.

By then, the federal government had formulated ambitious plans for internal improvements. Indeed, it might be claimed that from the first, with the Hamiltonian program, one of the chief goals of the central government (and of the states and localities, too) was to ease the way for people to become wealthy. Politicians eager to unite the country supported internal improvements, as did the farmers and manufacturers whom the roads and canals would serve. Owners of land in remote areas were ardent backers of projects. All were willing to make investments, even if they proved unprofitable.

When Presidents Washington and John Adams asked for federal grants, the Jeffersonians questioned their propriety and criticized the costs, even while they conceded the need for them. Once in power, however, they too supported projects. It was during Jefferson's presidency that the first large-scale, unified program was developed. In 1803, he purchased the Louisiana Territory for some $15 million, selling $11.25 million in government bonds to help in the financing. That same year the state of Ohio, chafing at the underfunding of internal improvements, set aside 5 percent of the new proceeds from the sale of public lands for roads. Well aware of the pressures for such activities and of the need to provide transportation in the states to be carved from the Louisiana Purchase, Jefferson, in his second inaugural address in 1805, recommended that revenues "be applied to rivers, canals, roads, arts, manufactures, education, and other great objects within each state." The following year, Congress authorized construction of the National Turnpike, designed to link Ohio to Maryland and Virginia. This caused some consternation in the Northeast, but two years later, Secretary of the Treasury Albert Gallatin met these objections with his comprehensive program to fund transportation throughout the United States.

Gallatin's *Report on Roads and Canals* was a key document and benchmark in opening an unprecedented period of road and canal construction. In it, the Secretary stated: "The general utility of artificial roads and canals is universally admitted." In England and other countries, he said, "these improvements may often, in ordinary cases, be left to individual exertion, without any direct aid from government." But the private capital for such projects wasn't present in the United States, according to the report, and so government would have to play an important role. Canals, in particular, would suffer losses. "Some works already executed are unprofitable; many more remain unattempted, because their ultimate productiveness depends on other improvements, too extensive and too distant to be embraced by the same individuals."

Gallatin's report proposed a "tide water inland navigation" from Massachusetts to Georgia that would consist of canals and turnpikes. The most ambitious part of the program involved east-west connections. Gallatin knew canals could not traverse the Appalachians "in the present state of science." He called for river improvements from New Jersey to Georgia and roads across the mountains. New York might best be served by a canal from the Hudson River to the Great Lakes. To fund these projects, Gallatin proposed the authorization of $20 million, to be spent over a 10-year period. Of this amount, $4.8 million would be earmarked for the Massachusetts-Georgia projects.

River and harbor improvements would cost another $1.5 million. Canals in all parts of the country would receive $7.3 million in federal funds. Gallatin thought much of this could be raised through surpluses in the federal revenues, land sales, and new taxes. Completed projects might be sold to "individuals, or companies, and the proceeds applied to a new improvement." Since few at the time believed canals would ever be sufficiently profitable, it would appear that Gallatin was forecasting substantial federal ownership of the means of transportation and support for businessmen and farmers.

As it turned out, Gallatin's proposals inaugurated a period of governmental economic activity unparalleled in American history. For the next generation, the federal and state governments spent a larger proportion of the gross national product on these and similar enterprises than ever before or since. Not even during the 1930s and after would the percentage be exceeded.

Gallatin's plans could not be implemented at once, since foreign difficulties intervened, especially the War of 1812. Federal aid to road and canal construction fell from $68,000 in 1812 to $31,000 in 1813. The war, however, demonstrated the importance of transportation to the interior of the country, and after the return of peace there was little difficulty convincing the public of the need for these projects. Most of the money expended went for turnpikes and river and harbor improvements. By 1829, less than $2 million had been invested in shares of canal companies, and of this amount, fully half went to the Chesapeake & Ohio Canal Company, the successor to the Potomac Company.

As might have been anticipated, these programs, originated and instituted by Jefferson, James Madison, and James Monroe, Virginians all, were for the most part in the South. The next President, John Quincy Adams, was a nationalist, and although more funds were expended in the North than before, the southern bias remained. The meaning of this was not lost on land speculators in the North and Midwest, who came to understand they would have to make plans of their own for developing their holdings. The going was slow. Planning which began in the late 1780s would not receive the kind of consideration required for close to 40 years, during which time land became a major American speculative medium.

In 1788, Nathaniel Gorham and Oliver Phelps, two of the leading land speculators, had accumulated a large tract in western New York, setting off a boom in that part of the state. Gorham and Phelps thought western New York was the key to development in the Northwest. One might sail up the Hudson to Albany and then enter the Mohawk River as far as it could be taken. Then a long portage was necessary to get to Lake Ontario, and another from Niagara to Lake Erie, the gateway to the Northwest. Alternatively, the Ontario might be bypassed by a road or canal to what today is Buffalo, on the eastern end of Lake Erie. Might a canal eliminate those portages? One could draw upon the waters of the Finger Lakes, so water was not as much of a problem as it was elsewhere. Such a canal would open the commerce of the Midwest to New York City, making it the leading American port. More to the point, as far as Gorham and Phelps were concerned, such a canal would serve farmers in the land they owned in western New York and make it far more valuable. By 1790, they held 2.6 million acres and calculated that if they could sell half of it at $10 an acre—not an unreasonable price given a canal—their net worth would come to around $13 million, a huge fortune in this period.

Robert Morris also was aware of the value of the land if a canal could be dug. As the head of a combine of several wealthy speculators, he purchased land from Gorham and Phelps and others in 1790, accumulating 5 million acres. He then arranged a meeting with Theophile Cazenove of J. Henry Cazenove & Company, a Dutch firm, which had helped finance the American Revolution and was interested in investments in the new country. Morris, who did not believe in holding investments for long, tried to sell Cazenove some of his land. Cazenove sent agents to the area, and they reported back that the land had good soil and was rich in timber resources. Convinced Morris was correct, Cazenove purchased 1.5 million acres for 75,000 pounds, and additional land from New Yorkers Alexander Macomb, William Duer, and Andrew Craigie. Within a few months Cazenove and his Dutch associates had 3 million acres. They formed the Holland Land Company and prepared to retail the land to European settlers. Few were interested. With no easy access, the land was of limited value. Thus far, all who had bought and then sold the land, like Gorham, Phelps, and Morris, had made profits. It looked as though the Dutch were left holding the bag.

Infrastructure and Wealth: The Erie Canal

Whether there was any correspondence or relationship between the Cazenove group or other land speculators and New York Governor George Clinton is unknown. But in January 1791, Clinton delivered a message to the legislature calling for a transportation linkage, preferably a canal, between Albany and Lake Erie. Without this, he said, New York could lose out to Boston and Philadelphia for commercial leadership, and he spoke of how the farmers of trans-Appalachia might send their produce down the Mississippi, even though at that time New Orleans was a French city. A survey was made, and the work was monitored carefully by those with western land interests.

Elkanah Watson was one of them, but unlike the others, he actually relocated to western New York and lived on the land. A multifaceted individual, Watson was a sheepman who had introduced merino sheep to the United States. He also sponsored state fairs that were somewhat akin to those held in Europe during the Middle Ages, where he attempted to win over others to sheep husbandry, without much success initially. The reason was familiar: although merino wool was more expensive than any other, the high cost of transport made cultivation uneconomical. Watson was in a position to do something about this.

While in Europe during and after the American Revolution, Watson had studied the English methods of canal construction. He had visited with Washington in 1785, and they spoke of the Potomac project. Afterward, he went to upper New York and mapped the area, in the process of which he plotted a system of canal-lake-river connections he asserted would be fairly inexpensive to construct and operate. He conceded that even so, the system would be uneconomical initially, but this would soon change. Should his plan be adopted, "a vast wilderness will as it were by magic, rise into instant civilization." Just as Lowell was to lobby for his interests in Washington later on, in 1791 Watson lobbied in Albany for his waterway scheme. He found an ally in General Philip Schuyler, who represented Albany in the legislature and owned considerable land in Duchess County.

In March 1792, New York incorporated two companies, the Western Inland Lock Navigation Company and the Northern Inland Lock Navigation Company, to actually construct the waterway. Neither was able to raise much money, and nothing came of the Northern project, while the Western Company made a careful survey but did little more. With the coming of the War of 1812, everything was put on hold.

After the war the New York congressional delegation lobbied in Washington for federal support for a canal. They managed to get passage of a measure that would have provided the state with $1.5 million in seed money, but President Madison vetoed the measure on March 3, 1817. Six weeks later, the New York legislature, realizing that any waterway would have to be financed by the state, adopted a measure providing for a new canal to follow the route set down by the Western Company. Fittingly, the project was to be headed by Governor De Witt Clinton, the nephew of Governor George Clinton. In 1809, Clinton had served on a commission to explore the route, and six years later he had petitioned the legislature for canal funds. Clinton had Presidential ambitions. He had been defeated in the 1812 election by Madison and wanted another crack at the post. He was opposed by the New York Tammany organization, which, shortsightedly, fought the canal measure as not being helpful to the city. Clinton marshaled support in upper New York, knowing that a successful canal would enable him to crush Tammany and perhaps lead to another presidential nomination.

Clinton saw the canal as a joint project between the state and private capital. Soon he was able to create a Canal Fund, which would receive income from state taxes on salt and other goods, on steamship travel, and on land within 25 miles of the proposed canal, as well as from lotteries and bond issues underwritten by the state and purchased by those who would benefit from the canal—land speculators—and foreigners. Those same investors would purchase stocks as well, shares of which were attractive, as will be seen, due to the liquidity provided by trading facilities in most large cities. It was assumed that tolls, which would be collected even before the entire canal was in operation, would supplement these sources and in time be sufficient to enable the state to pay off the bonds and eliminate the taxes. Clinton estimated the canal would cost $7 million, this at a time when the banking and insurance capital in New York was less than $21 million.

The subscriptions did better than anticipated. The New York banks and insurance companies came through with purchases, disagreeing as they did with Tammany. The bonds and stock sold well in London and Amsterdam, and the Holland Land Company made a large land grant to the state, the land to be sold to speculators at the highest price it had fetched thus far. To sweeten the situation, the legislature voted $1 million a year for two years as a supplement.

Work began soon after on what was to be called the Erie Canal. The middle section, which connected the Mohawk and Seneca Rivers, was completed in October 1819, and traffic began the following May, by which time the engineers were pushing on to Lake Erie. As construction proceeded, the price of canal securities rose and new issues were marketed. Toll revenues were higher than anticipated, and the Canal Fund swelled.

The Erie was completed in 1825, and on November 4, Clinton celebrated by pouring a keg of Lake Erie water into the Atlantic at New York City. As one contemporary put it, "They have built the longest canal in the world in the least time, with the least experience, for the least money, and to the greatest public benefit." The Erie ran 363 miles and cost little more than the anticipated $7 million. Even before completion, toll revenues exceeded interest on the bonds, which were liquidated much earlier than anticipated.

The cost of shipping freight from Buffalo to New York in 1818 had been $100 a ton. With the Erie in operation, the figure fell to $15 and the time required from twenty days to eight. The prices of farm products to consumers in New York fell, and the price of land soared. Business at the port of New York reached a frenetic pace, with products unloaded at the Hudson wharfs, transported across town to the East River wharfs, and reloaded for shipment to Europe. East River ships from Europe did the reverse.

The success of the Erie spurred the federal government to increase financial aid for road and canal construction from $363,000 in 1825 to $1.2 million by 1835. While the funding was welcome, it was hardly needed. The huge success of the Erie had helped New York City beyond the claims of its promoters. In the words of Oliver Wendell Holmes, the Erie made New York "the tip of the tongue that laps up the cream of the commerce of a continent." Within a relatively few years, Manhattan was boosted into commercial preeminence over the likes of Boston and Philadelphia. It became the port of choice for immigrants, who swarmed into upper New York and from there traveled to the Midwest. It made the New York financial markets the leaders on the continent. But for the moment, the Erie sparked the creation of a canal mania that was greater in scale and scope than the Mississippi and South Seas bubbles, and which became a template for manias that followed.

Canal Mania

As has been seen, success breeds imitation. This was true during the Middle Ages, and it was true in nineteenth century America. Recall the competition in cathedral construction. The building boom that began in the eleventh century and lasted through the thirteenth century wasn't that different from the canal mania of the first half of the nineteenth century. If the cathedral in the next town drew many pilgrims and added to its luster, your town would have to have one as well. During the 1820s and 1830s, Philadelphia and Baltimore made plans for links to trans-Appalachia, hoping to arrive there before the trade of Ohio, Indiana, and Illinois was irretrievably lost to New York. Their problem—and that of Boston as well—was how best to accomplish this. Pennsylvania already had a fine turnpike system, which in the early 1820s carried more than 30,000 tons of goods annually. The state's mountain barrier to the West was more difficult to conquer than the relatively flat lands of central New York. Likewise, Baltimore and Boston would have to build their canals through hilly territory. Any canals constructed by these states would have to have many locks, which were balky, time-consuming, and expensive to use for shippers. There soon would be the alternative of railroads. For the time being, however, the success of the Erie led Philadelphia to construct its Mainline Canal, which originally cost $12.1 million and then an additional $4.5 million. Baltimore fared similarly. Building on the experience of the Potomac Company, the city planned a canal to run from Georgetown to Cumberland, and from there by tunnel to the Youghiogheny River and the West. The Chesapeake & Ohio Canal never went beyond Cumberland. It was completed in 1850 at a cost of more than $11 million, of which Maryland contributed $7 million and terminal cities another $1.5 million. Both were failures. The canals were sold in 1857 to the Pennsylvania Railroad for $7.5 million. Canal construction for Boston never went beyond the planning stage.

The desire of these port cities for canals of their own may be understandable. Less so was the mania that swept the rest of the country.

It began in Ohio. Clinton's secretary, Charles Haines, had initiated a correspondence with Governor Ethan Allen Brown in 1820 in which he wrote of the impact the Erie would have on Ohio and suggested canals for his state. "The commencement and completion of the Ohio Canal excite anxious and deep considerations in this state," he wrote. "We see and feel the importance of this work, not only to the great western section of the Union, but to the country that stretches from the mouth of the Hudson to the lakes." An Ohio canal system would be an extension of the Erie, "into the heart of a fertile territory, capable of sustaining from 10 to 15 millions of people. When Ohio resolves to make her canal from the lakes to the Ohio River, and is willing to pledge her credit for the means of accomplishing the undertaking, it will be done."

How? Ohio's credit was low, and the state hadn't recovered completely from a minor financial panic in 1819. Brown thought "the aspect of affairs rather gloomy" insofar as canal financing was concerned. Still, the early success enjoyed by the Erie encouraged him and others interested in canals for Ohio. In 1825, as the Erie neared completion, the Ohio state legislature authorized the construction of two canals, both of which would pass through the most heavily settled parts of the state. The names indicate the hopes of the promoters: the Ohio & Erie, which would extend from Portsmouth on the Ohio River to Cleveland on Lake Erie, and the Miami & Erie, which would link Cincinnati to Toledo, also on Lake Erie. Governor Clinton agreed to act as consultant to the Canal Board, while Simon Perkins, the Ohio agent for the Connecticut Land Company, which had extensive holdings in the state, headed the board.

Clinton recommended that the canal bonds to be issued be secured by the state's credit. That way, potential purchasers would be assured of repayment and the interest charges would be lower. The board followed his advice, and the issue was sold to the New York bank of Rathbone & Lord, which resold the bonds to New York and London investors. Haines had predicted that "New York capital would sustain the enterprise," and he was right. In all, $4.5 million of Ohio canal bonds were sold in the city from 1825 to 1832. Prime, Ward & King took $770,000 for resale in Europe through the London bank of Baring Brothers, and John Jacob Astor, the nation's leading landlord, purchased $800,000 of bonds in 1826 and an additional $342,000 two years later, as well as odd amounts of bonds issued by other Ohio canal companies.[1]

Clinton traveled to Ohio to turn the first spade of earth on the Ohio Canal in 1826, and construction proceeded smoothly. The waterway was completed seven years later. Although not as dramatically successful as the Erie, since Ohio's population was smaller than New York's, the canal was profitable, and others were initiated. By 1833, Ohio had more than 400 miles of canals, with most of the bonds owned in New York and Europe.

---

[1] Baring Brothers, established as a bank in 1763, had started out as a cloth manufacturer, expanded into the import-export business, and then entered finance.

Fearful that a New York-Ohio nexus would dominate the Midwest, and aware of the enthusiastic reception for canal bonds, Indiana entered the competition. In 1832, construction was begun on the Wabash & Erie. This canal, more than 450 miles long, was completed in 1843, but it was never profitable. Overly ambitious, late in coming, and the wrong kind of transportation at the wrong time in the wrong place, it failed. No matter. Speculation in canal paper expanded in an early version of a bull market.

During the late 1820s and into the 1830s, dozens of canals were initiated in the area between New York in the north, Virginia in the south, and Indiana in the west. The canal mania, originating in the desire of political leaders to unite the country in a transportation network, was assisted by Washington throughout. The Bank of the United States helped the states market their bonds, and acted as agent for foreign banks and investors. Congress did what it could to encourage settlement. After 1820, one no longer could purchase public land on credit, but the price per acre at auctions was lowered to a minimum of $1.25 and the minimum tract to an eighth of a section. A person with as little as $100 could buy 80 acres of land from the government. This helped fuel the westward movement, and so assisted the canals—and the land speculators.

This policy changed in 1828 with the election of Andrew Jackson to the Presidency. Jackson's policies and programs differed sharply from those of his predecessors. Opposed to the increasing power of the federal government in economic matters and considering federal aid to a particular economic interest (in this case farmers who wanted to send their products to market) as a possible threat to individual freedom, Jackson made it clear he would reverse several key aid programs. In 1830, Congress passed a measure to assist in the construction of a road from Maysville to Lexington in Kentucky. Jackson vetoed the measure, saying the road was really a private venture and not within federal jurisdiction. Other, similar vetoes were handed down. This did not mean Jackson intended to halt all programs. During his two terms in office, federal public improvements accounted for more than $25 million in spending, of which $6.8 million went to turnpikes and canals. But the atmosphere in Washington had changed.

As a result of cutbacks in spending and increased tariff and land sales revenues, the government was able to pay off its national debt, and by 1836 it was showing a surplus in the Treasury. In June 1836, Jackson decided to distribute this surplus to the states, beginning on January 1, 1837. At the time, some of the states that had funded canals and roads were deeply in debt, having floated so many internal improvement bonds. These states used the distribution to inflate their debts further, thus feeding a speculative fever that continued to gain momentum, especially in New York and London.

This was reflected in land purchases. Public land sales, already on the rise, now soared. In 1836, 20 million acres of government land were sold, bringing in $25 million in revenue. For the first time, land sales surpassed customs as the U.S. Treasury's chief source of income. The money was deposited in local banks, much of it then borrowed by speculators to buy more land, and then the cycle repeated itself. Most of the land sales occurred in the Midwest, but all parts of the country shared in the mania. Chicago became the boomtown that attracted Cyrus McCormick in this period. New York's assessed real estate rose from $300 million in 1831 to $600 million in 1837.

Jackson frowned on all of this. Arguably the only American President who was consistently opposed to the influence of business, even agrarian business, in all of its manifestations, and ever suspicious of speculation, in July 1836, Jackson issued the "specie circular," directing that sales of public lands would have to be paid for in gold or Virginia land scrip.

The specie circular put an end to the wild speculation in land and its effects soon spilled over into the paper issued by the canal companies and states. But even before the circular, the mania showed signs of abating. In 1834, less than $3 million in new bonds and stocks were purchased, and some issues had to be withdrawn for lack of buyers. One reason for this was the failure of several of the more heavily promoted canals to show profits and pay interest on their bonds or dividends on stocks. Another was the growing number of canals that made no economic sense, built simply because the money was there and the land companies that wanted them held sway in state legislatures.

As can be seen, absent federal and state financing, these canals could not have been constructed. This is not surprising. Private capital was lacking. Between 1815 and 1860, some three-quarters of the $188 million invested in canals came through the sales of municipal and state bonds alone.

In 1834, largely as a result of canal construction, the Pennsylvania state debt had reached $34 million, of which English investors owned $20 million and the Dutch, $1.8 million. When there was a run on the Philadelphia banks in 1842, several were forced to close down, including the Bank of the United States in Pennsylvania. The repercussions led to the collapse of the state's credit and defaults on bonds. European investors and speculators were outraged. Sovereigns weren't supposed to default, although the record of such happenings is long and chronic. Writing in the *London Morning Chronicle*, the Reverend Sydney Smith, who owned Pennsylvania bonds, complained. How could any American sit down to dinner in London knowing he owed two or three pounds to every person in the room?

> Figure to yourself a Pennsylvanian receiving foreigners in his own country, walking over the public works with them, and showing them Larcenous Lake, Swindling Swamp, Crafty Canal, and Rogues' Railway, and other, dishonest works. The swamp we gained (says the patriotic borrower) by the repudiated loans of 1828. Our canal robbery was in 1830; we pocketed your good people's money for the railroad only last year. All of this may seem very smart to the Americans; but if I had the misfortune to be born among such a people, the land of my fathers should not retain me a single moment after the act of repudiation. I would appeal from my fathers to my forefathers. I would fly to Newgate for greater purity of thought, and seek in the prisons of England for better rules of life.

Holders of Pennsylvania bonds were not lost, however. Aided by the Barings and other London houses, Pennsylvania was able to put its affairs in order and make payments in 1848. By then, however, its refinancing bonds could not be sold.

Maryland suffered a similar fate, and Indiana also defaulted. In both cases, restructuring was made by London banks, but canal paper could no longer be sold to investors there or in the United States.

Three more aspects of the canal mania deserve to be noted. One is that the canal boom was real enough in its early years, namely the mid-1820s. By the 1840s, it was all but over—for several reasons. First, the best sites were taken by then, and second, the failures of several later canals sounded a warning to promoters and investors that funding would not be available. Finally, the arrival of the railroad, a promising new technology, provided promoters and investors with a viable, attractive alternative. The second aspect is that those early canals *did* have available funds, in the mixed capitalism of the Erie and with bonds and shares capable of being sold to investors and speculators. Given such paper, an aftermarket became necessary, and so securities exchanges appeared and grew. This is to say that by the early nineteenth century, a capital market had come into existence. Those inventors who appeared during the early years of the Industrial Revolution had to scrape to obtain financing. Lowell and Whitney had to improvise. McCormick had to rely on wealthy Chicago investors. The time had not yet arrived when manufacturers could obtain the funds they needed from markets. Such was the nature of the society of the North and Northeast in this period. Insofar as the South was concerned, the cotton culture had developed in a manner quite unlike anything in the other sections. The quest for wealth there took a different form, and there was some question whether this quest was paramount in the eyes of the plantation South.

John Jacob Astor and Real Estate

Regarding the third aspect of canal fever, the development of infrastructure illustrated the way the quest for wealth was intimately tied to real estate speculation and dealings. More money has been made by more Americans in real estate than any other medium. The land speculators involved in canal building were operating in the grand tradition, and their successors would earn even greater fortunes from their real estate dealings. And the wealth from real estate has been much more widespread than that of any other medium. It continues to this day. A family who in the 1980s purchased a home in the suburbs for $100,000, with a $70,000 mortgage, and then sold it for $200,000 less than a decade later, is in that same tradition. This form of investment (and speculation) has even been encouraged by government through tax laws and made possible by banks and savings and loan societies that provided mortgages. If many of the homebuyers of the 1920s had been told that they, like stock market speculators, were buying on margin, they would have been horrified. A century earlier, John Jacob Astor would have understood perfectly.

The opportunities presented in America attracted many immigrants, some of whom became important businesspeople. Astor, who was the wealthiest American prior to the Civil War, leaving an estate of more than $20 million, had been a merchant, speculator, financier, and trader in a wide variety of businesses, and he performed well in all of these endeavors.

Astor was born in Waldorf, a small German city, in 1763, and worked there and in London making musical instruments before emigrating to America. He arrived in Baltimore in 1784, his only possessions being seven flutes and $25 in cash. Astor then went to New York to work for his brother, a butcher, and there he sold his flutes. While on shipboard, Astor had listened to some passengers talking about the fur trade. After a while, he quit his brother's employ and started trading furs. Within a year he was back in London selling furs he had purchased in America and buying trading goods to take back with him. Astor continued dealing in musical instruments and other items, but increasingly he concentrated on furs. By the early 1790s he had become a major force in this field, but in addition, he invested in banks and an insurance company. By 1800, he was worth around $250,000, had a ship, and was importing arms, ammunition, and wool. Fur remained a constant in his operations. In 1808, Astor organized the American Fur Company, which achieved domination in its field.

Astor next entered the China trade, and by 1809, with five ships in his fleet, had become a major factor in this area. When the cargoes were unloaded, Astor would sell part in the domestic market and export the rest to Europe.

In 1835, weary and ill at the age of 71, Astor decided to concentrate on New York real estate, buying raw Manhattan land, selling it when settlement reached the area, and then repeating the process. This was not a wholly new venture; Astor had purchased his first New York properties as early as 1789. In 1797, he bought a farm in the middle of Manhattan for $25,000, considered quite high at the time. He held on to the property, however, and at the time of his death, it sold for that amount per square yard. Once, upon selling a lot on Wall Street for $8000, Astor was told that in a few years it would go for $12,000. He agreed, but added that he had used that $8000 to purchase 80 lots above Canal Street, and that when the Wall Street lot sold for $12,000, those holdings would be worth $80,000. During the financial panic of 1837, Astor was instrumental in saving the City Bank from failure, and he used his connections with that institution to help finance his real estate operations. Just before he died, Astor said, "Could I begin life again, knowing what I now know, and had money to invest, I would buy every foot of land on the Island of Manhattan."

CHAPTER *11*

Infrastructure and Wealth

HE pursuit of wealth called attention to the need for transportation improvements in the early years of the United States, and as we have seen, most of the goods that traveled down the canals and on the turnpikes were products of the farm, not the factory. This would continue throughout the rest of the pre-Civil War period. The demand remained for swift, dependable transportation to perform what by now were the quite familiar tasks of taking goods from areas where they were in abundance to those where they were scarce. In the North this brought to center stage a new form of transportation, the railroad. In the South it took a bizarre turn, transporting slaves from agricultural sections in which they were no longer needed to those in which the demand was growing. Also in this period, the need for capital resulted in the creation of a financial marketplace. What began as an appendage of European markets by the 1850s had gained a measure of independence.

Small Beginnings on Wall Street

Stocks and bonds were not bought and sold in the English colonies, although there were banks, pawnbrokers, and other financial intermediaries. Some colonists purchased English bonds, but the colonies did not issue them on their own. Tobacco planters and others who exported to Europe utilized the services of London and Hamburg bankers. Large-scale undertakings such as voyages were organized by sedentary merchants, among those Francis Cabot Lowell and others in Boston, and their counterparts in coastal cities such as New York, Philadelphia, and Charleston. These men knew of the concepts of limited liability and incorporation, but the joint stock companies of the time had royal charters that had to be renewed. They also must have known of the Mississippi and South Sea bubbles, and of the speculation in London and Amsterdam. There was none of this in America during the colonial period. Investors were people who purchased interests in land or other property that could be seen, touched, and held for long periods. Most important, of course, were farms, livestock, and outbuildings. Businesses

151

such as ship's candlers, hardware, dry goods, and the like were also sought for investments. Speculators were focused on a short time horizon and bought with the idea of selling soon after. For this group, lottery tickets and colonial paper currencies had to suffice, especially lotteries, whose popularity expanded during the early national period. By 1820, they were firmly established, and most had reputations for honest dealing. In 1824, according to a contemporary account, there were eight or ten ticket sellers in New York. Nine years later, there were 147 of them.

By the mid-eighteenth century some merchants had started to specialize in marine and fire insurance. There were a few banks, but they did not accept deposits or deal in commercial paper. Rather, they made loans in the form of paper money issued by the colony, which were collateralized by property. Thus, a person might purchase a farm with a bank loan collateralized by the farm itself.

With the onset of the Revolution came the need for financings, and the government, under the Articles of Confederation, issued paper money and borrowed heavily. This currency and the government bonds were bought and sold in the larger coastal cities. These paper assets became items for speculation, and lively markets for them developed quickly. After the Treaty of Paris was signed, the new states and the central government sold bonds, which also were bought and sold by merchants.

With the Constitution, interest in investments grew. When in 1790 Congress authorized three bond issues to fund the Hamilton financial program, the new vehicles became objects of speculation. Merchants with offices on Wall Street in New York and their counterparts elsewhere stood ready to buy and sell the bonds, and attempted to maintain inventories and seek information that would help them in their pricing. This was difficult, and it wasn't unusual for a potential buyer or seller to visit several merchants in order to determine where the best prices could be obtained. In 1791, with the establishment of the quasi-private Bank of the United States (BUS) and the Bank of New York (organized in 1784 and chartered in New York in 1791), the merchants also could deal in common stocks. With five securities to price, the merchants realized their old methods would not do, and so they organized to have public auctions, which began in the summer of 1791 and were held into the spring of 1792. Some of the buyers meant to hold on to the securities and so obtain a stream of dividends. Others were speculators, not unlike those in land except that the bonds and stocks were more easily purchased and sold. The securities could be used as collateral for loans, so, in effect, they were being purchased on margin by those dreaming of making a killing in a short period. Writing of the speculation, James Sullivan observed:

> The rage in the present day [is] for acquiring property by accident. Some men are supposed to have made large fortunes by speculations in the stocks and banks. And they who have not been thus fortunate, can discover no reason why their neighbors should be thus favorably distinguished from them. And too many are ready to lay aside their ordinary business, to pursue chance as the only goddess worthy of human adoration.

For the moment, stocks and bonds replaced the lotteries for those seeking to take a chance. The colonies had been spared the Mississippi and South Seas bubbles. Now one was developing in the young United States. BUS stock, issued in July 1791 at $25, stood at $280 a month later, fell to $110, and rose once more. In August, one observer wrote: "The scriptomania is at full height," while another said, doubtless with exaggeration, "A frenzy runs through all of the nation." Writing to Jefferson of the scene in New York, Madison said, "Stock-jobbing drowns every other subject. The coffee house is an eternal buzz with the gamblers."

The interest in securities prompted promoters to organize other banks. In January 1792, the Million Bank of the State of New York made its appearance, capitalized at $1 million, with shares priced at $500. It was oversubscribed by a factor of 10. So were the shares of the Tammany Bank, offered the next day, also at $500 a share. Then it was the turn of the Tammanial Tontine Association, an insurance scheme. Rumors of additional financial institutions caused excitement at the auctions. While speculators reveled in such activity, so did those interested in achieving wealth through the initiation of new businesses.

The craving for wealth was assisted greatly by the creation of a secondary market in securities. Of course, it developed slowly over time. From government paper to that of banks and insurance companies, to canals and railroads, was a course that took more than a generation to traverse. As will be seen, it would take even longer for Americans to become familiar and comfortable with the stocks of industrial concerns. The Tammanial Tontine Association might attract investors and speculators in both the primary and secondary markets. Francis Cabot Lowell, on the other hand, would have to seek financing from friends and relatives for Boston Manufacturing, shares of which certainly would not have attracted customers in Boston, much less New York. The advent of the market for stocks and bonds in New York marked the beginning of securities-based capitalism, but it was not yet the norm for financing businesses and speculation.

The New Nation's First Major Stock Speculator

It also resulted in the appearance of the nation's first securities market manipulator and the first financial panic. William Duer, the manipulator, had been a member of the Continental Congress, but he resigned in 1779 to follow his business interests. He obtained a government post supplying the army with provisions, promptly lining his own pockets taking some plum contracts, and emerged from the war a wealthy and influential man. Duer was honored for his public services and admired for his business acumen. Seeking new opportunities, in 1786 he became secretary to the Board of the Treasury, while continuing his land speculations in partnership with Andrew Craigie and Brissot de Warville, who represented several European banks interested in investing in the new nation. When Hamilton became Secretary of the Treasury in 1789, he selected Duer as his undersecretary. Duer resigned after six months in his post, but retained close friendships at the Treasury and used them to obtain inside information.

Duer learned Hamilton intended, when necessary, to enter the market to support bond prices. Provided with these facts, he would know when to buy and when to sell, using funds supplied by Andrew Craigie and Brissot de Warville, who backed him financially for a share of the profits. "The public debt affords the best field in the world for speculation," wrote Craigie to his European clients. "But it is a field in which strangers may easily be lost. I know of no way of making safe speculations but by being associated with people who from their official situation know all present and can aid future arrangements either for or against the funds." He was referring to Duer, of course.

Duer's successes with the BUS and Bank of New York stocks attracted the attention of Alexander Macomb, who could provide Duer with two important things: money and secrecy. Duer would contribute the information regarding Treasury purchases and sales, and Macomb the funds to act upon it. All transactions would be made in Macomb's name, thus assuring Duer of anonymity.

Not satisfied with this, Duer approached Walter Livingston, scion of one of the state's wealthiest families, and formed a financial relationship with him as well. On one occasion he told Macomb to purchase BUS stock, saying there would be a merger of the BUS and the Bank of New York, and he simultaneously arranged for Livingston to sell the stock short. Thus, Livingston was selling shares to Macomb, without whom the market would have been too thin for sizable transactions. When the merger failed to take place, BUS stock plunged. Macomb, having provided the funds for the purchases, lost heavily, and when Livingston covered the short position, Duer reaped a large profit.

On his own Duer maintained his interests in land speculation and helped organize the Society for Useful Manufactures, which hoped to enter that field. He formed at least four partnerships that engaged in brokerage. By then, Duer planned to use the large profits made in securities to organize commercial and manufacturing businesses that would make him the most powerful businessman in America.

Duer plunged in with passion. He borrowed from friends and associates. According to one Wall Street observer, he paid interest of 3 to 4 percent per month to "persons of all descriptions . . . Merchants, tradesmen, draymen, widows, orphans, oystermen, market women, churches." How could they lose, given Duer's reputation and those high interest rates? He even sold his father-in-law's home to obtain more capital. Constantly cash poor, he was skating close to the edge of disaster.

It was the rapid rise in the market for those bank stocks, caused in part by rumors Duer planted, that led to his downfall. By March 1792, Duer made an altogether common mistake of such plungers: he came to believe his own lies. Duer started purchasing large blocks of stock, some on a deferred basis, meaning that he made purchases with contracts to pay for them in a short period, usually two weeks. It was a usual practice at the time. Duer did not have the money, but he expected the shares to rise in price, whereupon he would sell, pocket the profits, and then pay for the shares. Just how much he invested is unknown, but we do know Duer borrowed more than $200,000 from Livingston in early March, presumably for use in the market.

Had prices risen, Duer might have emerged from this project with the power he sought, but they declined instead. While still wealthy, Duer faced what today would be considered a liquidity crisis. Had he attempted to cash out his holdings, his sales would have depressed the markets even more.

At around this time, irregularities were discovered in Duer's books while he had been in government; Comptroller of the Currency Oliver Wolcott informed Duer he owed the government almost a quarter of a million dollars from the time he served on the Treasury Board. Duer tried to put Wolcott off, while scurrying around trying to borrow money to meet his market obligations. In desperation, he attempted to contact Hamilton for aid, but the Secretary had moved to Philadelphia when the capital was switched to that city and could not be reached.

On March 22, Duer met with Livingston and assured him all was well. It was another lie. The following day, Duer was taken to debtors' prison. The news sent ripples of fear through the small New York investment community. Stock prices collapsed as speculators rushed to become liquid. Twenty-five failures were announced that week. From his cell, Duer tried to calm his creditors, promising that if released he would make a full set-tlement—in 90 days. There were no takers. Livingston confessed he could not honor the notes he had cosigned with Duer and more panic followed. The panic spread to other cities. Standish Ford of Philadelphia wrote to a friend, Peter Anspach, in New York, "The whole of our misfortunes we may certainly charge to the New York failures, for no person would have stopped here if it had not been for their endorsements on the notes of New Yorkers. Their own losses on stocks could have been born."

At this point Hamilton returned. He was saddened to learn of Duer's activities and incarceration, but was more concerned by the financial panic. He ordered his agents to enter the market and start purchasing government bonds so as to support their prices. Hamilton then announced that if necessary, the government was prepared to float a large loan in Amsterdam and use the funds obtained there to support the market. He instructed the Customs House to accept 60-day notes in lieu of cash from those merchants in financial binds. Then additional Treasury purchases were made, as well as some for BUS and other bank stocks. It was the first time a leading member of the federal establishment intervened to halt a Wall Street panic. Macomb and Livingston recovered. Brissot and Craigie prospered in land speculation. As for Duer, he remained in prison, trying to salvage his holdings from there. He died in 1799 while still incarcerated, bringing to a close the career of the young nation's first major securities speculator who had almost singlehandedly caused Wall Street's first financial panic.

The New York Stock and Exchange Board

The eruption of activity affected the securities auctions. The New York state legislature, suspecting the auctions were being rigged, moved to ban them on April 10, 1792. The brokers and auctioneers, learning of the legislature's intent, had halted them voluntarily eight days earlier. They did not intend to leave the business, however, and on May 17 they gathered at Corre's Hotel and signed what came to be known as the "buttonwood agreement," because of a nearby buttonwood tree. From then on, this private organization, which came to be known as the New York Stock and Exchange Board (NYS&EB), traded only those shares accepted to the list, only among themselves (and so excluded outsiders), at fixed commissions (which meant they would not try to undercut each other in seeking customers). This did not mean the members would cease their business of buying and selling shares from their offices. The agreement applied only to those transactions at the auctions.

The existence of a secondary market eased the way for banks that hoped to enter the primary market, which is to say the underwriting of securities for a client and the sale of those securities to a customer. This, in essence, was the function of the investment banker: to create a security that would fulfill the needs of both client and customer.

In those early days, the obvious clients were banks and insurance companies, since customers were familiar with them and willing to accept the securities that were issued for them. Of the two, the banks were more important. From 1792 to 1801, the number of chartered banks increased from 3 to 23; at the turn of the century, their total capitalization exceeded $33 million. By 1817, more than a third of the issues traded at the Stock & Exchange Board were those of banks. Insurance companies expanded at a slower rate at first, but their underwritings accelerated, and by 1818 the number of these issues exceeded banks for the first time. Next in importance were chartered firms engaged in local transportation and manufacturing. The canal, road, and dock companies were traded irregularly. Until the 1820s, only Boston dealt with shares and bonds of manufacturing companies, largely because in this period there were more manufacturing companies in New England than anywhere else.

Far more important than the securities of companies were the government debt obligations, which were auctioned in greater numbers than company shares and bonds. In addition, there were bonds of states and municipalities. The New York city and state governments floated bonds each year from 1812 to 1817, and in the same period, as a result of war needs, the federal debt increased from $45 million to $123 million.

The attitude toward wealth remained essentially Jeffersonian, however. Farmers and merchants alike considered themselves capitalists in their own right, and rather than invest surplus funds in shares of companies or government obligations, they would plow them back into their own businesses. A good deal of the buying of debt and trading of shares was done by agents of foreigners, especially the English and Dutch banks and individuals. American bankers, such as Stephan Girard in Philadelphia and Prime, Ward & King functioned primarily as agents of European correspondent firms. Thus, a goodly number of canal bonds and shares purchased by European interests were done so through these banks and others like them.

The Importance of Railroads

That the construction of railroads echoed some attributes of canal development is not surprising. Entrepreneurs and governments often seek templates from the past which they hope will serve in the present and future. Like the federal and state governments during the canal era, those who assisted the early railroads did so in the hope of creating wealth in the service areas, and in this way they were serving constituent interests.

There was a regional pattern to governmental aid. Except in Massachusetts, where aid was given to railroads when the landed and commercial interests there realized a canal was not possible, little was provided in New England. The situation was different elsewhere. Substantial assistance was available in New York, Maryland, Virginia, Pennsylvania, South Carolina, Georgia, and Michigan, among others. In the case of Georgia, not only was the railroad from Atlanta to Chattanooga financed by the state, it was operated by state officials until after the Civil War. The New York & Erie Railroad received a $6 million loan from the state. The Baltimore & Ohio Railroad sold $3 million worth of common stock to Maryland. From 1825 to 1840, states floated more than $90 million in bonds for railroad construction, and municipalities contributed at least that much.

The federal government did not offer such aid, blocked by constitutional objections from legislators and the executive branch. But the tariff on iron was lowered to enable the railroads to purchase inexpensive metals, this over the objections of the young domestic iron industry. The government provided surveys to the railroads, and beginning in 1850, large land grants, starting with 2.5 million acres to Illinois along the proposed route of the Illinois Central on the condition it would receive 7 percent of the railroad's earnings. Grants to other states followed.

While the canal systems proved important to those who used their services—which is to say the shippers along the waterways—they had obvious limitations. These were overcome with the arrival of the railroad. Railroads were faster than canal boats; in 1832, steam-powered freight railroads went at 6 miles per hour, while canal speeds were less than 4 miles per hour. Ten years later, passengers on the steamships that plied the Mississippi would travel at 10 mph, while steam railroads took them to their destinations at 15 mph. In 1817, a sloop could reach Albany from New York in 36 hours; in 1841, a railroad took 10 hours to traverse the same distance. Canals could be crippled by lack of water and were useless in the winter in areas where they froze. This was not a problem with railroads. Canals could not be constructed economically in hilly areas, a difficulty many railroads could overcome. On the other hand, railroads usually were more costly to construct per mile than canals and involved more complex technologies. They shared another problem. Like canals, railroads helped create their customers in that settlers would go into areas opened by the railroad. This meant that at first, they would tend to be uneconomical. The canals had been strongly supported by land companies, whose leaders tended to look to them as a means of making the land more valuable, and thus increasing their wealth. This was even more the case with the railroads. So what if there were losses from services? The railroads would grow rich by granting construction contracts to companies in which they had interests and selling land to settlers. After carrying them to their new homes, they would transport the goods they produced to markets.

The most important of the early railroads were the New York Central and the Pennsylvania, and while both had terminuses in Chicago, they were strikingly different in origins and technology.

The New York Central

The New York Central originated in 1825 to solve a problem with the Erie Canal. For most of its stretch, the Erie ran through fairly level countryside, but the land was hilly between Schenectady and Albany, and a series of locks were required to get the flatboats through. The route was 40 miles long, but the trip took more than a day. For this reason, on December 18, 1825, George Featherstonhaugh, who lived in the outskirts of Schenectady, advertised his intention of organizing the Mohawk and Hudson Rail Road Company, which was to construct a railroad between the Mohawk and Hudson Rivers. He planned to raise $300,000 and hoped the state would come up with another $200,000. Featherstonhaugh had read about railroads but knew little more about them than did most Americans. Indeed, the first true railroad, the Stockton and Darlington, went into operation in England only three months prior to Featherstonhaugh's announcement.

Featherstonhaugh was convinced that sufficient Schenectady business people were interested in such a line and would purchase the shares required to get things moving. He obtained a charter from the state legislature, despite attempts on the part of Erie Canal interests to block it. The canal people failed, but they did manage to attach a rider limiting the Mohawk and Hudson to passenger traffic and obliging it to rebate funds to the canal equal to the losses it would suffer.

Featherstonhaugh then attempted to sell shares with a par value of $100 and an initial call of $30. He did not attract enough purchasers, and the idea of selling shares to outsiders and overseas appears not to have been considered. This was, after all, a new technology, untested and unproven. Moreover, in this period Americans not only were unaccustomed to investing, but were reluctant to do so in ventures they could not see, which is to say, those far from where they lived and worked. Nonetheless, some New York City merchants and speculators were interested in the new railroad. Prominent civic leaders, including Nicholas Fish, James Duane, and John Jacob Astor, took shares, but the going was difficult, and not until 1828 did the company begin operation. Construction began the following year.

Mohawk and Hudson shares were traded at the NYS&EB in October 1830, and at the initial trade sold for $110, a 10 percent premium over the original price, indicating optimism now that construction had begun. The stock rose and fell on news from the construction gangs, but in the autumn of 1831, as work neared completion, it sold for $174. The first horse-drawn cars made their appearances soon after, as did passengers. As Featherstonhaugh had predicted and promised, the Mohawk and Hudson returned a profit from the start and soon was paying dividends. With this, many of the original investors took their profits and sought other railroads in which to invest. Given the availability of capital, these were not long in coming. The Saratoga and Schenectady, the Utica and Schenectady, the Syracuse and Utica (capitalized at $800,000 and oversubscribed), the Tonawanda, the Auburn and Rochester, the Schenectady and Troy, the Rochester and Syracuse, the Rochester, Lockport and Niagara Falls, the Buffalo and Rochester, the Attica and Buffalo, and the Buffalo and Lockport—all were formed and constructed within the period of two decades, and their shares were featured at the NYS&EB. In 1843, the state, recognizing that railroads would replace canals, removed the penalty paid to the Erie Canal and permitted the railroads to carry freight. One might travel or ship goods from Buffalo to Albany by railroad, which by then had locomotives, but this required changing several times to different lines.

In 1853, several of the lines came together to form the New York Central Railroad, with the members turning in their paper for Central securities. The new railroad had 650 miles of track, much of which would have to be replaced and harmonized with the other lines. Passengers and freight could then be loaded into Hudson River ships or placed on other railroads to reach New York City. Later on, when the Central entered Chicago, passengers wishing to travel there could leave New York, transfer at Albany, and transfer again at Buffalo. Meanwhile, goods from the Midwest had little difficulty being sent to New York. The Erie Canal had made New York the nation's premier city for business. The New York Central confirmed that position.

Erastus Corning, the moving force in creating the Central, was to be its first president. Corning was a sedentary merchant, but with a difference. From his offices in Albany, Corning directed the efforts of what for the time was a major interconnecting set of interests. He was Albany's leading merchant, the president of Erastus Corning & Company. He owned the Albany Nail Factory and the Albany Iron Works, which supplied the nail factory with iron, and both sold their wares through Erastus Corning & Company. The iron works produced wheels and the nail factory spikes that were sold to the railroads that Corning controlled, and they would become the providers of these products to the Central. Corning was the guiding force at the Albany City Bank, which financed his other enterprises. He had interests in several New York banks—in Binghamton, Batavia, Buffalo, and Cazenovia. In order to serve his banking interests, Corning became involved with Democratic politics, supporting President Andrew Jackson's campaign against the Second Bank of the United States, which was his major competitor in upper New York State, and he contributed to Martin Van Buren's 1828 campaign for the governorship. Van Buren's campaign was a tactical move, for he intended to become Jackson's Secretary of State, which he did two months after Jackson was sworn in. Van Buren's only significant act as governor was to support legislation to create a safety fund for the state's banks, a measure Corning wanted badly. Later, Corning would serve in the state legislature and the House of Representatives, but these were essentially part-time posts for him. In addition to all of this, Corning owned large tracts of land in western New York and potentially valuable land in Michigan. He intended to expand the Central to western New York and then take it into Chicago, and he assumed an equity position in the Michigan Central to better serve his interests there.

Each part of the Corning empire served the other parts, and the Central tied it all together into one neat bundle. Yet it was not the centerpiece of the empire. That role was reserved for Corning himself. Like the other shareholders, he turned in his stock in other lines for Central paper and in the process realized a profit of $100,000. Then he announced a major renovation program, which would cost $1 million over a two-year period. His Albany bank would act as agent in raising that sum. Almost $750,000 would be expended on rails, which would be imported from England by Erastus Corning & Company, and for which he would receive a 2.5 percent commission. The bill for spikes from the nail factory came to $84,000, and the iron works provided $71,000 worth of axles and wheels. The Central purchased land from Corning. How much did all this come to? By some estimates, the Corning interests profited by about $250,000 a year. Corning saw nothing wrong with any of this. He asserted he charged fair prices, and on occasion permitted other manufacturers and merchants a share of the business.

The Pennsylvania Railroad

Recognizing how much the Erie Canal contributed to New York's success, Philadelphians tried to develop a canal of their own, but due to the hilly nature of the landscape, it failed. Then the Baltimore & Ohio, a thirteen-mile line, was initiated by Baltimore business leaders fearful that the Chesapeake & Ohio Canal, then being extended, would divert inland trade to Virginia. The B&O was completed in 1830, which led the owners of the C&O Canal to abandon construction plans. Aware that canals and railroads were helping Baltimore and New York develop, Philadelphians feared for the future of their city. Meanwhile, western Pennsylvanians, seeing the New York railroads expanding rapidly, demanded a line of their own, believing that without one, the midwestern business—and their own as well—would be drained to New York City. If a Pennsylvania equivalent could not be arranged, they said, branch lines from the B&O might do.

In December 1845, a group of prominent Philadelphians met to discuss the possibilities of a railroad, and by the time the state legislature met in early January, they had several drafts to offer. One of these, introduced by prominent Whig William Haley, who had opposed Jackson and Van Buren, was "an act to incorporate the Pennsylvania Central Railroad Company." Almost immediately, it became the focus of attention and debate. Canal proponents opposed the measure. Western farmers spoke out in favor of a connection with the B&O, which might be constructed in less than a year. Some Democrats, fearing the new railroad would be a failure, insisted no state funds be committed to it. Others, who expected success, did not want private interests to profit from what they felt should be a state project. A much-amended measure, backed by the anti-Jacksonians and Whigs, passed by slim margins in March, while a second bill, supported by Democrats, which provided for the B&O connection, failed by a single vote. The measure was signed into law on April 10, 1846, and the Pennsylvania Railroad Company was born.

Under terms of its charter, the line was to be constructed from Harrisburg to Pittsburgh, with feeders to be added later on. It would be denied entry into Philadelphia. The Philadelphia and Columbia, a part of the Main Line and state-owned, would retain control of the Philadelphia-Harrisburg route. As a concession to the western farmers who still supported the B&O connection, the charter contained a provision granting that line a right of way into Pittsburgh if the Pennsylvania was unable to sell $3 million worth of stock and construct at least 30 miles of track along the route within little more than a year.

The Pennsylvania was to be capitalized at $7.5 million, but that figure soon was raised to $40 million. The stock was to be sold privately; the state would not take shares. Should the company fail, the taxpayers would have lost nothing, and the assumption was that the B&O would then take over, draining western Pennsylvania's commerce to Baltimore. But if the line was a success, the state would have the right to purchase it after 20 years at the initial construction costs plus 8 percent, but minus profits. Furthermore, if the option was not taken up in 1866, it could be renewed for another 20 years, and so on into perpetuity.

The Philadelphia Whig politicians and merchants were determined to control the Pennsylvania and in time take it into their city. The only way to accomplish this would be to purchase shares, and so they did. They committed to purchase 30,000 shares at $50 each for a total of $1.5 million. By early February of 1847, 30,570 shares had been purchased by 2634 individuals, most of whom were Philadelphia residents.

Samuel Merrick was named the Pennsylvania's first president. A prominent merchant, Merrick knew next to nothing about railroading, and in any case was unable to devote his full attention to the line. This might not have mattered had he possessed any interest or aptitude in railroad management, but he lacked both. In 1850, J. Edgar Thompson took over. As a surveyor for one railroad and chief engineer for another over a period of two decades, Thompson, at the age of 39, was considered one of the most experienced railroaders in the nation. Thompson proved as good as his reputation. The Pennsylvania was both an economic and financial success. It paid a dividend on the common in 1847, which continued on into the mid-twentieth century, and even more than the New York Central, it became a blue-chip stock. It was not traded on the NYS&EB list, however. Fearing New Yorkers would gain control of the company, the directors listed it on the Philadelphia Stock Exchange instead.

Boston, which had shunned canals, also became a railroad power, with the construction of the Boston & Providence and other lines, while Connecticut and Rhode Island built the New York, Providence, and Boston.

Some $1.2 billion was invested in American railroads between 1830 and 1860. A large part of this came from governments, a substantial amount from overseas via American banks, and a small share from American investors. A large percentage of this group were farmers and others with holdings along proposed routes. Increasingly, however, railroads came to dominate activity at the NYS&EB.

By the time of the Civil War, railroading had become big business, with $1.25 billion invested in the lines. More even than turnpikes, canals, and steamboats, the railroads expanded markets for goods. Some historians have asserted that the Midwest was the key to the Civil War, in that during the 1840s and early 1850s, more goods from there reached markets via the Mississippi River to New Orleans than via the Great Lakes and Erie Canal to New York. The railroad links that bound the Midwest to New York, Boston, and Philadelphia were important factors in deciding which way the region would go. In the process, Chicago, with its railroad ties to New York, became the largest city in the Midwest, and not St. Louis, a great Mississippi port in its own right, with connections to New Orleans. There are historians who claim that without the railroads, the Midwest would have been wedded to the South by Mississippi River steamboats, and the Confederacy would have won its independence. During the Civil War, the New York brokerage firm of Jerome, Riggs & Co. took note of the importance of railroads in the country's future:

> Although only about thirty years have elapsed since [the railroad] came into use, it now includes all the operations of society. It has created by far the greater proportion of the value of the property of the country. Without it there could be neither domestic nor foreign commerce to any considerable extent. It brings together the producer and consumer, who could be united by no other tie. Every day increases its usefulness and power. Society cannot now put forth a single great effort in which the railroad is not the chief agent and actor.

The Telegraph

Running a railroad is much more complex than managing a canal. Schedules have to be worked out, and communication between various points along the line is vital. Without such contacts, the lines could not hope for the efficiencies they required. Fortunately, the telegraph appeared and filled this need. If the railroad was indispensable for transport, the telegraph was the key invention for information distribution. Both, of course, were essential components of the national infrastructure.

Thus, the telegraph was an important part of the railroad business, but it was far more than that. Not only did it provide instant communication, which was a boon to business, but without the telegraph, anything but very short-distance railroads would have been impossible to manage. Just as the railroad enabled business people to expand their markets and sources of supply, so the telegraph eliminated the time factor in the transmission of information. It was the first in a long line of communications inventions that transformed the world of business in the nineteenth and twentieth centuries.

There is such a thing as a technological imperative. The business and political leaders of the mid-1850s already had the telegraph, but they thought of it in conventional terms. Initially, its full potential was not utilized. The telegraph would not be denied, however, and in the end all competing systems had to bow to it.

In Article I, Section VIII of the Constitution, the founding fathers had provided for assistance to business by giving Congress the right to create a postal service. The mail in this period was needed more by business interests than by farmers and others. Merchants had to have information. Mail was one means of obtaining it, newspapers another, and tales from travelers a third. One might imagine, then, that anything that would speed the transmission of information would be seized upon. Not so with the telegraph, however.

It should be clear by now that businessmen and others in search of wealth during the early Industrial Revolution often were shortsighted and reluctant to abandon the old and outmoded for the new and appropriate. Consider the need for information collection and distribution during the California gold rush. The swift development of California in the early 1850s prompted Congress to consider several plans for the creation of a transcontinental railroad. Politics intervened and construction would not start for another decade. Concomitant with the call for a railroad was the need for better mail service from California to the rest of the country. In 1857, Postmaster General Aaron Brown solicited bids from companies involved with information. Adams Express, American Express, and Wells Fargo, all businesses in transport, were not interested. Why carry mail when there was gold to be transported? Nevertheless, John Butterfield, one of the founders of American Express, submitted a bid, and formed a company, Butterfield Overland Express, which carried passengers and mail from Tipton, Missouri to San Francisco in the then-amazing time of just 24 days. The operation was financed in part by the government, which paid Butterfield $600,000 a year, for a 2800-mile operation that cost $1 million to create.

Joseph Holt succeeded Brown in 1859 and supported a faster postal service. He awarded William Russell the contract. The organizer of the freight firm of Russell, Majors & Waddell, Russell agreed to form a company that would deliver mail from New York to San Francisco in 22 days. The plan was to send letters from New York to St. Joseph, Missouri by train, and from there to San Francisco by horseback. The telegraph, incidentally, was in operation by then along the New York to St. Joseph route. If telegraphed, the letter could have been delivered in nine days.

In 1859, Russell organized the Leavenworth & Pike's Peak Express Company to operate the business, which soon after was reorganized twice and emerged as the Pony Express. Russell purchased 500 horses, established 190 stations, hired 200 attendants, and for a total investment of $100,000 had his line equipped and ready to go. The service began on March 23, 1860, and although it charged $3.00 for a half-ounce letter to be taken from San Francisco to Salt Lake City, and $5.00 beyond that, it did not make money. In October 1861, the Pony Express sent out its last rider, having lost out to a far superior competitor. The telegraph line from New York to San Francisco had just been completed. "The pony was fast," wrote one historian of the venture, "but he could not compete with lightning." By then, the telegraph was nearly two decades old.

While traveling home from Europe in 1832, Samuel F. B. Morse, an artist and professor, met Charles Jackson, a Bostonian who dabbled in electromagnetism. Watching a demonstration Jackson held for the passengers, Morse hit upon the idea of the telegraph. For the rest of his life, Jackson would complain bitterly that Morse stole his idea.

Morse devised a crude telegraphic device, which was ready for a trial in 1835, but he still lacked a source of power. In 1831, Michael Faraday, an English scientist, had noted that the motion of a magnet in the vicinity of a circuit induced a current in the latter. Since engines could be used to move magnets, in this way Faraday developed the basic theories behind the first dynamo. In time, the dynamos would produce electricity for industries and houses, but in this period they were not consequential, since the implications of the dynamo were not understood or appreciated. More important for Morse's purposes was the development in 1836 by Joseph Henry, an American, of the "intensity battery." Powered by batteries, the telegraph was ready for commercial exploitation.

The technology was quite simple. A key would interrupt the flow of electricity, and by holding it down for longer or shorter periods, the operation would create a stream of "dots" and "dashes," to be recorded on a printer or interpreted orally. Aided by assistants, Morse developed a working model late in the year. Further modifications were required before he was able to demonstrate it before a group of scientists in 1837. The following year, Morse filed a caveat for the machine at the Patent Office. He further perfected the device, organized a corporation to produce and market it, and traveled to Washington seeking federal support for a demonstration line. Fortunately, that year the government revised the copyright law and Morse was able to safeguard his invention better than he might have done otherwise.

Telegraphy interested Congressman Francis Smith of Maine, chairman of the House Committee on Commerce, who became an ardent supporter of the Morse telegraph, which he hoped would be purchased by the government and used in post offices. It seemed so simple. A letter was a piece of paper on which a message was written by the sender, who then placed it in an envelope and dispatched it to the addressee. Both the sender and receiver of the letter were interested in the message, not the paper on which it was written. The telegraph enabled the sender to transmit the message, not the physical paper, to the addressee instantaneously. There was no problem of lost messages. It could be considered the first step toward e-mail, but of course Congressman Smith would have thought in terms of physical and electric mail.

Smith tried to obtain an appropriation of $30,000 for the construction of a demonstration line between Washington and Baltimore by a company known as Magnetic Telegraph of Maryland. The bill failed to pass, but Morse finally received his appropriation in 1843 and went to work. He proved a poor technician and businessman. Morse tried to lay the wires underground, an expensive and time-consuming method. He hired Ezra Cornell, who had invented a trench digger, to perform the job, but after laying eight miles of wire, half the money was gone. With only $7000 left, they switched to above-ground wires. By May 1, they were within fifteen miles of Baltimore, where the Whig Party had just nominated Henry Clay for the Presidency. The news was wired to Washington, arriving there an hour and a half before the news reached the Capitol by rail.

Now Morse opened the telegraph to the public, but the response was disappointing. A Baltimore merchant wired a Washington bank to inquire whether a check drawn by a depositor was good. A Washington family wanted to know whether a rumor of the death of a relative was true. Some merchants used it to inquire about deliveries, but the traffic was slow, perhaps because it was so revolutionary an invention, and its potential was insufficiently recognized.

Dismayed, Morse offered to sell rights to the telegraph to the government for $100,000. There was opposition, however, and with the coming of the Mexican War, all discussions ended. Were it not for these developments, the telegraph doubtless would have become a government-operated system. This was not to be, but Postmaster General Cave Johnson wanted government to regulate the telegraph: "The use of an instrument so powerful for good or evil cannot with safety to the people be left in the hands of private individuals uncontrolled by law." So there would be private ownership but public regulation.

Now Morse acted to capitalize on his invention by licensing operating companies. For $15,000, Magnetic Telegraph was given the right to construct a line from Washington to New York. By early 1847, companies were being formed throughout the East and Midwest. It was a romantic business, attracting young men as space travel would a century and a quarter later. In their youths, both Thomas Alva Edison and Andrew Carnegie were telegraph operators. What better education in commerce was possible than to send and receive business dispatches for some of the nation's most astute business leaders?

By this time, rival machines and systems had made their appearances. Royal House was awarded a patent for his telegraph in 1846. Two years later, Alexander Bain, a Scots scientist, received his patent. Others would follow, as did companies that acquired licenses. The result was that individuals in an area using the Morse system could not communicate with those with a different system. Clearly, this was intolerable.

A start toward resolving this situation arose when Hiram Sibley, a man who dabbled in many enterprises, met Samuel Seldon, who held the House telegraph rights. In 1849, Seldon proposed that they construct a line in an area already served by the Morse interests. Sibley agreed, and they formed the New York State Printing Telegraph Co. Sibley came to understand that the rivalries were wasteful and conceived the idea of uniting all the telegraph companies into a single system, using the House patents. By then, the telegraph had been accepted by businesses, and it was vital for the railroads by the 1850s, and a major force in tying the country together commercially. Like the railroads, the telegraph would make national companies possible.

It was a long battle, during which Sibley gradually came to believe the Morse system was superior, and he approached the Morse people, asking for a truce to be followed by an alliance. In 1856, Western Union, the realization of Sibley's ambitions, was organized. In 1861, the telegraph poles reached the West Coast. National telecommunications was now possible.

By then, retired merchant Cyrus Field had abandoned an earlier plan for a rival network and was concentrating on an Atlantic cable, which was successfully completed in 1866. Other cables followed, and in the process, virtually instantaneous communication between businesses and even individuals was theoretically possible. A powerful tool had been provided to those seeking to obtain wealth. Together, the railroad and the telegraph gave farmers and manufacturers the means to conduct business much more easily and with lower costs than ever before, while the creation of investment banks and securities markets did the same for raising capital.

CHAPTER 12

Emperor Wheat
and King Cotton

hile the Northeast and Midwest adapted to the factory system, the new farm implements that made farming more of a business than it had been earlier, along with transportation and communications improvements, were drawing the sections closer together. The plantation South was undergoing changes in a different direction. While there were canals and railroads in the South, there were far fewer of them there than in other parts of the country. Southerners argued that their fine river systems made them less necessary than in the North, but this was true largely because the South was not engaged in the kinds of activities that were developing in the Northeast. There was little manufacturing, so the South did not require the imports of iron and steel and items made of these metals as was the case up north. Northern banking flourished and so did the securities markets. Southerners in need of banking services more often than not relied on northern and English institutions.

To visitors, it might appear the cotton South was prosperous and offered more promise than did the industrialized North. Cotton exports were the largest moneymaker for the United States in the antebellum period. Cotton production rose from 73,000 bales in 1810 to 178,000 bales in 1820, and 335,000 in 1830. It crossed the million bale mark in 1835 and the 3 million level in 1852. On the eve of the Civil War, more than 4.5 million bales were produced, with some of the crop going to the northern textile mills, but more to Europe, England in particular. During the 1850s, cotton exports accounted for from one-third to one-half of the dollar volume of exports. Wheat production also increased, especially in the new lands opened in the West, and a good deal of this was for sale in the Northeast and, when Europe's crops were bad, there as well. By then, each region of the country had developed specialized products—cotton, rice, and tobacco in the South, wheat, corn, and hogs in the Midwest, and manufacturing, financial services, and shipping in the Northeast. In all sections, however, independent subsistence farmers accounted for substantial portions of the population. Visitors to the United States in the antebellum days often commented on the differences between the grain-based farms of the North and the cotton-based ones in the South. The former seemed to them to be more efficient and better maintained, the people more industrious. For want of a better term, they inclined more toward capitalist incentives.

Northern Wheat

While it would appear that cotton had become the dominant American crop, bringing great wealth to some and less to others, wheat was affording its cultivators large profits as well. As Jefferson had predicted, American farmers—far more than their European counterparts—tended to be in the business of agriculture. While it was true that American farmers viewed urban dwellers as unnatural and preferred the hardships and rigors of the countryside to the squalor and crush of the cities, they nonetheless expected that their efforts would bring material rewards in the form of high incomes, economic abundance, and the ever-increasing value of their land, equipment, and cattle.

By 1850, the average American farm was 203 acres, larger than its European counterpart. Many western farms, owned by families who did not consider themselves wealthy, ran into the thousands of acres, or at least so it seemed, for their owners were not certain where their holdings ended and the next farm—or wilderness—began. Europeans who visited them were surprised at what they witnessed. One wrote that land in America was not farmed as much as it was mined. Crops were extracted from the soil, with little regard to maintaining its fertility with fertilizers. Why bother, since there was so much land to be had for little or no price. Alexis de Tocqueville remarked on this in the 1830s.

> It is unusual for an American farmer to settle forever on the land he occupies; especially in the provinces of the West; fields are cleared to be sold again, not to be cultivated. A farm is built in the anticipation that, since the state of the country will soon be changing with the increase of population, one will be able to sell it for a good price.

This was one instance where Tocqueville misunderstood what he was witnessing. By the 1850s, it had become evident to observers that waste was the American rule when it came to western lands. One writer estimated (without indicating his methods) that from the first settlements to 1851, Americans had wasted a half billion dollars worth of soil. Another writer, a reporter for the *National Intelligencer*, estimated that of the 125 million tilled acres in the United States, four-fifths were being depleted at a rapid rate and only one-fifth sustained or improved. "There are whole counties, and almost whole states, which would once have yielded an average of twenty bushels of wheat or forty of Indian corn to the acre, yet would not (unmanured) average more than twenty of corn and five of wheat," wrote the *New York Tribune* in 1851. "The virtue has gone out of the land. They have been robbed of their fertility by false, miserable, wasteful culture."

What all of these writers failed to understand was that on the American farms, the maintenance of land was not the paramount problem. That would be the shortage of labor and capital, which implied the need to increase production with fewer workers. For this reason, American farmers rushed to mechanize, and in the process—because of the virgin land and plentiful rainfall—they became the most efficient and productive in the world.

"Hands are always scarce in harvest and demand good wages," grumbled an Indiana wheat farmer in 1852, sounding much like a Massachusetts factory owner complaining of labor shortages in busy seasons. "Machines are being introduced now for harvesting wheat, and some of them are designed to thresh, and partially clean it, also. They are truly labor-saving. The sickle has been laid aside, and the scythe and cradle will most probably soon give place to this machinery, worked by horse or steam power," he continued. Such a person may have loved his land, but it shared his affection with the machine. In time he might move on, leaving the land with scarcely a backward glance and taking his carefully tended machines to the next farm.

In a Europe that still harbored traces of feudalism, his counterpart would have had little land and cheap labor; the availability of resources was switched in capitalist America. In 1820, agricultural workers could be had for $13 a month; midwestern machine operators could expect as much as two dollars a day. The higher price was more than compensated by the much higher productivity. In 1820, it would have taken 14 men armed with hand reapers to cut 15 acres of wheat in a day. Given the equipment available in 1856, nine men could do the job, and in the process harvest more wheat, since machine harvesting was less wasteful than doing the task by hand. Writing in the *Country Gentleman*, a midwestern farm journal, in 1855, one farmer catalogued his experiences with both hand and machine harvesting:

> In the first place, in this section of the country, for several years past, no good mowers could be hired for less than $1.50 a day and board, and I never saw five mowers together that would average over one acre each, daily, and seldom that when they would yield two tons of dry hay. For years before we had mowing machines, I often let my mowing by the acre, and paid from $1.25 to $1.50, besides board. Now I could get any quantity I ever had, or ever will to cut, done for 62½ cents per acre by horses and they will cut 10 acres per day. The difference of board of 10 men in place of one man and one pair of horses, is no small item.

Such a farmer might own his own equipment or, as was becoming more the rule in the Midwest, would use the services of a jobber, a person who owned a variety of machines, and hired gangs of men to go from farm to farm, servicing the farmers at planting and harvest times.

Other implements followed the McCormick reaper. Disk harrows, seeders, and field cultivators, among others, made their appearances in the 1850s. John Deere's steel plows were the standard for excellence in the upper Midwest. In 1856, he and his 65 employees were producing them at the rate of 13,400 a year at the Deere plant in Moline, Illinois, and had no trouble selling them, despite competition. There was even more competition in the field of threshers. In the 1840s, John and Hiram Pitts, farmer-inventors like McCormick, produced a model that became quite popular in the Midwest. They organized J. B. Pitts & Co., erected a factory in Dayton, Ohio, and produced several models there in the 1850s. One of these, a giant powered by eight horses, was advertised as being capable of threshing 300 bushels a day. The *Ohio Cultivator* reported in 1856 that "almost all the grain is threshed and cleaned, if not in one operation, at least by one machine, so that a fanning mill, as a separate machine, amounts to little else than a superannuated implement." The Pitts brothers, in turn, had competition from another firm headed by Jerome I. Case, which produced mechanical threshers in Racine, Wisconsin. Not only were the Case machines superior to the Pitts models in several respects, they were also better advertised and merchandised. Without such machines as the reaper and those that followed, the large-scale farms of Pennsylvania and upper New York—whose harvests were processed and taken to market by way of the Erie Canal, and later by the New York Central and the Pennsylvania Railroads—would not have been possible to work economically. As farmers there moved on to Ohio and Indiana in the 1840s, and to Illinois and Wisconsin in the 1850s, they settled on still larger farms and needed even more and better machinery. The wheat growers recognized this more than any other group. The *Prairie Farmer* took note in 1850:

> The wheat crop is the great crop of the Northwest, for exchange purposes. It pays debts, buys groceries, clothing, and lands, and answers more emphatically the purposes of trade among the farmers, than any other crop. The corn is the main crop in home feeding, the pork and beef, butter and cheese, all go to enrich particular districts, but the wheat is the reliance of the democracy of agriculture.

Most New York wheat growers considered a yield of 50 bushels an acre quite good, while 70 bushels was the norm for Pennsylvania and 85 for Ohio. In contrast, returns averaged more than 130 bushels in Iowa, 160 in Illinois, and 220 in Wisconsin—or so it was claimed by writers of the period. In 1849, the nation raised slightly more than 100 million bushels of wheat; in 1859 it produced 173 million bushels. The leading wheat states in 1849 were Pennsylvania, Ohio, New York, and Virginia, in that order. Ten years later, they were Illinois, Indiana, Ohio, and Wisconsin. In this decade Illinois' production rose from 6.2 million bushels to 16.8 million. The upper Mississippi Valley had become the nation's granary, tied to the Northeast by rail and even more to the South by the Missouri-Mississippi-Ohio river system. In the process, Chicago became the largest miller of flour in America. In 1850, grain and flour shipments from the city came to less than 2 million bushels. By 1860, they were in excess of 31 million bushels. By then, too, the value of farm machinery in the nation came to $246 million, with the large majority of this in the North and Midwest.

Profits on the Plantations

Was the cotton South dominated by the kinds of plantations portrayed in such novels and motion pictures as *Gone With the Wind*? Were the southern cotton plantations profitable? If they were not profitable, why did the planters persist in their activities? Finally, did cotton make the South prosperous? The answers might appear self-evident.

We know of large plantations owned by wealthy planters, supervised by overseers, and worked by slaves. The slave census of 1860, taken on the eve of the Civil War, was the most extensive and accurate in the counting and classification of slaves. According to the census, there were 3,950,513 slaves in the United States and 383,637 slaveholders. The slaveholder of that year owned an average of 10 slaves, 2 more than his 1850 counterpart, but this figure is somewhat deceptive, since 275,681 of the slaveholders owned fewer than 10 slaves, and almost 1 million of the slaves lived on small family farms. There were 2292 slaveholders who owned more than 100 slaves, and one might assume these were the plantation owners familiar to readers of romantic novels.

Other statistics and information indicate that a great deal of cotton was raised by small farmers, who planted and sold it as a cash crop while producing foodstuffs much of the time. Their slaves were engaged in a variety of tasks besides planting, cultivating, harvesting, taking the cotton to the gin, and helping with the baling and transport to market. The records of some of these small farmers have survived. One of them, Moses Waddell, owned a farm near Abbeville, South Carolina, on which 23 slaves worked, most of them as field hands. The largest amount of cotton picked on it was 20 bales. Waddell had his own gin and a press in which to bale the cotton. He would send the cotton to market via flatboat, paying one dollar per bale to do so. Besides cotton, he raised oats, wheat, and corn. When they were not engaged in planting and harvesting, the slaves maintained the farm, cleared new ground, and split rails for fences. The women harvested fruit, picked peaches and apples, and did the mending and sewing.

In considering the matter of profits, one must take account of opportunity costs involved in the cotton culture on southern plantations. Indeed, opportunity costs (the costs of not being able to utilize capital employed in one occupation in others that might be more profitable) is a key to appreciating the plantation South's quest for wealth.

Let us start with the fact that the southern planters believed they were making large profits from cotton cultivation. Throughout the antebellum period, articles and studies were done to demonstrate this, and planters (especially in Louisiana and Mississippi) offered statistics that would appear plausible. To this, abolitionists and other critics replied that those two states had some of the finest soil and rainfall in the world, and that this, more than any other factor, accounted for the profits. Nor did the planters spend much time on the question of whether or not they would have been better off employing free labor rather than slaves. Thus, the opportunity cost of not using the land for other purposes should be considered, but even more important are the large sums the planters had tied up in their slaves. If individual planters could have sold them and then invested the money elsewhere, their profits would have risen sharply. Moreover, the premature death of a slave would be a large capital loss, while the death of a free worker would not. Then too, there were "pension costs" for slaves, who traditionally were cared for if they lived beyond their productive years, and none for free labor. A Virginian living in France in 1860 wrote to a relative of this:

> Please, let me know the condition of the old negroes at Cherry Grove, and whether there is the remotest likelihood of their closing this life. They must be very helpless; and will soon, if not now, require the personal attention of a young negro. Suggest some mode of making them comfortable the balance of their lives; and at the present or less expense.

The cotton South understood this. When it came to labor for canal and ditch digging in malarial areas, free labor rather than slave was employed invariably. The English actor, Tyrone Power, visited America in 1835 and watched hundreds of newly arrived Irish immigrants digging a canal through a swamp to Lake Pontchartrain in Louisiana. Later he wrote, "Slave labor cannot be substituted to any extent, being much too expensive; a good slave costs at this time 200 pounds sterling, and to have a thousand such swept off a line of canal in one season would call for prompt consideration." When Irish laborers died, they were replaced by others, but the death of a slave would have cost the contractor some $900 each, the average price that year.

In the last half century, scholars have examined the surviving plantation accounts in order to determine the matter of profitability. One of these is for Hopeton, on the Altimaha River in Glynn County, Georgia. Hopeton had been started by John Couper, a Scots immigrant, shortly after the War of 1812, about the same time Lowell was planning Boston Manufacturing. It fell into bankruptcy in 1827 and was taken over by creditors, with Couper remaining as overseer until 1852. Hopeton grew cotton, experimented with sugar and rice, and in time came to be seen as a well-run, profitable enterprise. Charles Lyell, the English scientist, visited Hopeton in 1845 on his American journey and commented favorably on what he saw. Couper kept a set of books while he ran the plantation, which, although incomplete by today's standards, do give some idea of how much money had been invested and earned. From 1840 to 1850, gross sales of crops were as high as $41,162 (1846) and as low as $18,906 (1842). Profits in 1842 were $1479 and in 1846, $23,917, and the rate of profits on what Couper considered invested capital ran from 0.4 percent in the former year to 6.9 percent in the latter. Couper did not take depreciation into account, nor did he consider the death of a slave as a loss or the birth of an infant slave an asset, a matter that will soon be explored. Nor did he take account of expenses, not even his own wages. What we do know, however, is that Couper and his employers believed these figures reflected the return they were receiving. How did this compare with alternative investments? The average return for Hopeton from 1840 to 1850 came to 3.6 percent by these figures. In the same period, 60–90 day commercial paper in New York returned 8.1 percent, and three to six month paper in Boston, 7.8 percent. In no year of this span did Hopeton do better than the New York and Boston rates. In addition, investments in such paper were virtually risk-free and required no effort on the part of the owner. On a purely economic basis, then, plantations were not good investments.

Did this matter? Certainly it should have, in a civilization concerned with profits and wealth, but there are reasons to believe this did not describe the cotton South. One historian, Eugene Genovese, in some of his works, most notably *The Political Economie of Slavery*, has argued persuasively that the southern frame of mind was precapitalist. While northern businessmen were concerned with maximizing their wealth, southern cotton planters, while hoping to live graciously, were more interested in preserving their way of life. If so, this would go far toward explaining the attitude of the slaveholders toward their plantations. What is more, some southerners recognized this. Albert Pike, a leading cotton planter, complained in 1855:

> From the rattle with which the nurse tickles the ear of the child born in the South to the shroud that covers the cold form of the dead, everything comes to use from the North. We rise from between sheets made on northern looms, and pillows of northern feathers, to wash in basins made in the north, dry our bodies on northern towels, and dress ourselves in garments woven on northern looms; we eat from northern plates and fishes; our rooms are swept with northern brooms, our gardens dug with northern spades, and our bread kneaded on trays or dishes of northern wood or tin; and the very wood which feeds our fires is cut with northern axes, helved with hickory brought from Connecticut and New York.

There was a movement in the South, small to be sure, to change all of this. Six textile factories were organized in Mississippi in 1850, and another twenty in Alabama between 1849 and 1854. But capital invested in manufacturing in the South was about 20 percent of the national total in 1840, 17.6 percent in 1850, and less than 16 percent in 1860. Furthermore, little of the growth in southern manufacturing was in textile and related factories, or iron and steel. Rather, it was in lumber, tobacco processing, and flour milling.

The Economics of Slavery

What of the slaves? On a well-managed plantation in the deep South, cotton production per capita could run as high as eight bales, each weighing 383 pounds. In 1839, a prime field hand cost approximately $1000, and on such a plantation he could have produced 3064 pounds of cotton, which at that year's average price of 13½ cents a pound would have returned $413.64 to the master. From this must be deducted processing costs of $4 and marketing costs of 70 cents per bale. No other maintenance, such as the costs of farm animals, fertilizers, and the like, were taken into account. Slave upkeep was generally thought to be $20 a year by plantation owners, too low considering the costs of food and clothing, which were produced on the plantation. With these items added, the cost of upkeep would have been more on the order of $60. When all the costs are deducted, according to the slaveholders' own calculations, the net return amounted to $356.24, or approximately a 36 percent return on the slave.

These were the kinds of figures slaveholders produced when they wanted to demonstrate the profitability of their businesses. Andrew Jackson was convinced the southern economy could not thrive without slaves. To free the slaves, he asserted, would cut the value of southern lands by three-quarters, because white people could not cultivate the lowlands where cotton, rice, and sugar were grown.

The "rental price" for slaves provides a more realistic method of determining return on investment. As a rule of thumb, planters computed the hire of a slave for a year at one-eighth the purchase price, so a slave costing $1000 would be rented to a planter for approximately $125, to which should be added the costs of food, clothing, and shelter. The contract would be voided should the slave die, but if he fell ill or ran away, the lessee still had to pay. The year in the upper South was calculated at 51 weeks, for the slave was permitted to go home for the Christmas holiday. On such a basis, the return might be figured, with maintenance, at around 12 percent. Even if depreciation is taken into account, the return would be 10 percent, a respectable figure perhaps, but not when other factors are considered.

Take the matter of motivation. Those Irish laborers Power saw in Louisiana had to perform or be dismissed. Since there was an oversupply of unskilled workers, especially in the 1850s, free labor had an incentive to be productive. Not so the slave. Southern white narratives are filled with tales of simpleminded, lazy, and irresponsible slaves. There even was a theory that held that in people of African descent, the pineal gland placed pressures on the brain so that they did not develop beyond a childhood level, hence this behavior. What such analysis does not take into consideration is that slaves had little incentive to be resourceful, and in fact, might have a positive incentive to be unproductive, since that might mean less work. Resentment, too, probably played a role in slave behavior. One visitor to a plantation wrote of the slaves he saw: "Nothing can be conceived more inert than a slave; his unwilling labor is discovered in every step that he takes; he moves not, if he can avoid it; if the eyes of the overseer be off him, he sleeps; the ox and the horse, driven by the slave, appears to sleep also; all is listless inactivity." Thomas Cooper, an English economist who traveled in the United States during the 1820s, estimated that the "usual work of a field slave is barely two-thirds what a white day laborer at usual wages would perform." He concluded that free labor was preferable except in areas where whites might become incapacitated during the summer, neglecting the aforementioned matter of the deaths of slaves compared to those of hired laborers.

Frederick Douglass, who was born into slavery but escaped in 1838 and went on to become a leading abolitionist, published his *Narrative of the Life of Frederick Douglass, an American Slave*, in 1845, in which he explained how this circumstance came about:

> To make a contented slave, you must make a thoughtless one. It is necessary to darken his moral and mental vision, and, so far as possible, to annihilate his power of reason. He must be able to detect no inconsistencies in slavery. The man who takes his earnings must be able to convince him that he has the perfect right to do so. It must not depend upon mere force: the slave must know no higher law than his master's will. The whole relationship must not only demonstrate to his mind its necessity, but its absolute rightfulness. If there be one crevice through which a single drop can fall, it will certainly rust off the slave's chains.

What this implies is that the South's labor force was to a large extent uneducated, lacked incentive, and was not particularly productive. In order to economize, the master generally fed field hands as cheaply as possible, which meant a diet of fatback pork and cornmeal, and their clothing was inferior as well. The lack of respect for and confidence in their slaves meant the slaveholders had low expectations of their productivity. The presence of slaves discouraged the introduction of labor-saving machinery such as was being introduced in the North. In all, this meant the South, as a result of slavery, was becoming a backward part of an industrializing America. No matter, said southern apologists. We have cotton, and cotton rules.

The price of slaves fluctuated according to the dictates of supply and demand. The cholera epidemic of 1833 caused the deaths of slaves worth $4 million at current market value and resulted in a sharp increase in the price of slaves in those areas affected. The spread of the cotton culture to the West also increased the prices of slaves, which in any case rose irregularly throughout the antebellum period. Since the slave trade had ended in 1807, imports were no longer permitted by law, although there was some smuggling, especially when prices rose. In November 1856, Governor James Adams of South Carolina called for the reopening of the slave trade, and the following month the matter was debated at a commercial convention in Savannah. The British consul in New Orleans reported to London in May 1857 that some 15 slave trading vessels had been sent from the city within the past two months. Baltimore- and New York-based ships plied the sea lanes between the Congo and the lower South. The following year, Charles Lamar, the scion of one of the most prominent Georgia families, imported 420 Africans into Brunswick, Georgia, and took no pains to hide the fact. A slave ship with a large cargo was captured off the South Carolina coast. The Africans were detained in Fort Sumter until they could be sent back to their homes. The slave population did rise as a result of natural forces, going from some 1.5 million in 1820 to the 3,950,513 recorded in 1860. This was a sizable increase, but insufficient to meet the growing demand.

One might think this situation would encourage the breeding of slaves. Was this the way to wealth in the slave business? Scholars have scoured the literature and found little evidence that breeding was a practice, much less a business. This can be seen in the fact that invariably males sold for higher prices than females. In 1842, the Reverend Jesse Turner, a slaveholder, told a Richmond audience:

> I keep no breeding woman nor brood mare. If I want a negro, I buy him already raised to my hand, and if I want a horse or mule I buy him also. . . . I think it is cheaper to buy than to raise. At my house, therefore, there are no noisy groups of mischievous young negroes to feed, nor are there any flocks of young horses to maintain.

There is anecdotal evidence that some breeding did exist. In 1838, the *Charleston Mercury* ran an advertisement that illustrates this:

> A GIRL about 20 years of age (raised in Virginia) and her two female children, one four the other 2 years old. She is . . . remarkably strong and healthy, never having had a day's sickness, with the exception of the small pox, in her life. The children are fine and healthy. She is very prolific in her generating qualities, and affords a rare opportunity for any person which wishes to raise a family of strong and healthy servants for their own use. Sold for no fault.

In 1856, a southern farmer told landscape architect Frederick Law Olmsted that in the South, "as much attention is paid to the breeding and growth of negroes as that of horses and mules." Statements such as this fueled the erroneous belief that breeding was widespread. In an attempt to address the matter through the use of statistics and economic models, economists Alfred Conrad and John Meyer assumed that a female slave who cost $800 and produced five children at two-year intervals, worked land that yielded 3.75 bales of cotton per acre, at 7.5 cents per pound. If the children were sold for $875 each at the age of 13, the yield would be $6012.50 in net proceeds, over 30 years, an average of $200 a year, for a net return on investment of approximately 25 percent. Of course, such assumptions are hardly realistic. Would any of those children—or the female slave herself—die in childbirth or from other causes, or escape to freedom? Even in the Conrad and Meyer model, the slave would not show a profit until the fifteenth year. The verdict is still out on this matter, as it was in 1958 when Conrad and Meyer attempted their calculation.

The Domestic Slave Trade

What is certain is that there was a lively and profitable domestic slave trade based on a practice that has been familiar throughout recorded history: the transport of items from areas in which they are in plentiful supply and low in price to areas where demand and prices are both higher. What was true for spices two millennia ago was so for slaves in the mid-nineteenth century. That these were human beings did not deter the traders, sellers, and purchasers, although there is some evidence that several of them had twinges of conscience. Not many, however. To the dealers in slaves, they were commodities, the prices of which were determined by supply and demand.

By this time, slaves were in oversupply in the states of the old South, such as Virginia and the Carolinas. Much of the tobacco land had been leached of its fertility, and the climate was not right for cotton or rice. Land values were falling in these states and rising in the newer ones, such as Texas and the cotton growing areas of the lower South, such as Mississippi. During the decade of the 1820s, 124,000 slaves were sent from Virginia, Maryland, Delaware, North Carolina, Kentucky, and the District of Columbia to South Carolina, Georgia, Alabama, Mississippi, Tennessee, and Georgia. The prosperous years of the early 1830s caused the movement to expand, and large numbers were sold to Floridians as well. Some 265,000 slaves were sold in interstate traffic in the 1830s, the peak for such activity. The hard years of depression slowed the sales during the 1840s, when only 146,000 were transferred. During the 1850s, some 207,000 went south and west to new homes. According to one estimate, Virginia exported an average of 9400 and Kentucky 3400 slaves annually, while Mississippi purchased 10,000 or so.

It made sense to take slaves from Virginia to the auctions at New Orleans. By 1860, prime field hands could be purchased in Virginia for $1250 and taken to the auctions and sold for $1800. So they were.

Tradition has it that while southerners defended slavery, they held slave traders in contempt. The reason for this, so it was said, was that white southerners involved with slavery believed the labor of the slave supported their way of life but disdained the commerce in them. Addressing the Mississippi Supreme Court in 1832, a southern lawyer expressed this point of view.

> I can imagine a man who would hold slaves, who would think it perfectly right to own such property, and cultivate his cotton field by their labor, and yet scorn to make a business of buying and selling human beings for speculation; nay, who would abhor and detest both the speculator and the dealer, and who would shun his society. And I can imagine a community of such men. . . . I do not attempt argument before this court to prove the wide difference between a slave holder and a slave trader; such an attempt before this court, who are slave holders, I would consider insulting to their feelings.

Some might see this as a distinction without a difference, but there were those in the antebellum South who believed in both the distinction and the difference. After the war, a former plantation owner, writing of the status of the slave trader, explained it this way, conceding the contradiction.

> In the South the calling of slave-trader was always hateful, odious, even among the slave-holders themselves. This is curious, but it is so. A trader's children recovered, to some extent, but there was ever a thin cloud resting on them, which they could not get rid of. We had two or three slave-traders in this section, and, although their children were taken into society, it was no uncommon thing to hear the sly remark—"his or her father was a slave driver."

One suspects that this uneasy attitude rested on the knowledge that the slaves were truly human beings, and to work them on the assertion that the master was protecting childlike creatures was one thing (even when punishing them for running away and other breeches), but buying and selling was another matter. If the slaveholder was indeed precapitalist and held "money grubbers" in contempt, this might make sense.

William Reynolds, a merchant who defended slavery, described an auction in Memphis during which 23 slaves were sold:

> One yellow woman was sold who had two children. She begged and implored her new master on her knees to buy her children also, but it had no effect. She then begged him to buy her little girl (about five years old) but all to no purpose, it was truly heart rending to hear her cries when they were taking her away.

An awareness of this prompted more than a few slaveholders to stipulate in their wills that their slaves should be sold only in family groups. One Transylvanian slaveholder, William Little Brown, sold his slave to obtain funds for his tuition. In his diary he wrote:

> "Necessity compels me to sell Abram. I have told him so and he acquiesces. Justice forbids slavery and traffic in human flesh. The money, therefore, which I may receive for him I shall esteem so much borrowed from Abram. In consideration of which, I do promise should heaven prosper me at some future date to redeem him and give him his liberty."

Louisiana and Alabama prohibited the sale of a child under the age of 10 from its mother, but not the sales themselves. Such was the divided mind of the cotton South as the Civil War neared.

Yet as in so many matters dealing with slavery, there exists contrary evidence. Nathan Bedford Forrest of Memphis, the future Confederate general, became wealthy in slave trading. He not only was respected, but the people of Memphis, even with this knowledge of his activities, elected him mayor. Thomas Gadsdon and Louis de Saussure of Charleston came from aristocratic families, became slave traders, and their reputations do not appear to have suffered.

Lured by the promise of profits, large numbers of businessmen entered the slave trade. They were clustered in such port cities as Charleston, Richmond, and New Orleans, where the greatest number of active slave markets were located. Montgomery, Alabama, was the most important inland center for the trade, with 164 registered traders in the 1839–1860 period. They would wait until the crops were harvested in the exporting area, after which slave prices would decline. At that point they would come in with their offers, make purchases, and then walk, drive, or most often, ship the slaves to the areas where the prices were higher.

Many of them operated on a small scale, because a good deal of capital was required. Even so, there were several large factors in the business. One of these was organized by John Meek, a Tennessean, and Samuel Logan and C. Haynes of Virginia. Meek was a veteran in the business in 1835, and Logan and Haynes were wealthy lawyers. It was Logan who had the idea of buying slaves in Virginia and shipping them to Tennessee, and he sought a partner from that state. He did so surreptitiously, not wanting his neighbors and clients to know what he was up to. Meek had been recommended by mutual friends, and they soon came to terms. After the crops were in that year, the Virginians purchased 47 slaves for $19,800, an average of $421 each. They pledged the "shipment" would be ready on August 10, but there were troubles. Logan and Haynes originally arranged for payments to be made several months after they took possession, but the sellers changed their minds and insisted they be paid on delivery. Logan and Haynes lacked sufficient funds, and while they bargained, some of the slaves learned they were to be sent to the West, and escaped. The others were dispatched, and in the end the partnership made a good profit on the deal.

This attracted other firms to the area, and the competition for slaves caused their prices to rise. In 1836, Logan purchased 61 slaves for $42,420, an average of $695 each, and all of them but one were shipped to Meek for sale, the lone exception being a slave who cut off his hand in the hope this would prevent his shipment. So it did. Logan informed Meek of what had happened, adding that he would try to exchange him for a whole slave. In addition, a few slaves escaped while in transit. Even so, the partners realized a profit on the transaction.

The partnership was shaken by the financial panic of 1837, which hurt Logan's other interests and sources of borrowed funds used to finance purchases. Logan asked Meek to forward him $5000 to $10,000 in gold in order to pay for several batches of slaves. He also complained that several of his legal clients had learned of his dealings in slaves and had dismissed him for that reason. "We are among the damnest population upon the earth for the slander of men's circumstances," he wrote. What followed for the partnership is unknown, for the correspondence ended on this note. Other firms did survive the depression and went on to become even larger.

We know most about Franklin & Armfield, which left extensive records, including advertisements, incorporations, and stories that appeared in contemporary newspapers. Isaac Franklin, the founder, was born in a frontier community in western Tennessee in 1789. In 1807, at the age of 18, he was employed by his brothers as a trading agent and sent to New Orleans, where he learned the rudiments of the slave trade. After service in the War of 1812, he entered the business. He would wander the Tennessee countryside, inquiring from house to house whether there were any slaves for sale. When he had sufficient slaves, or when his money ran out, he would take them to Natchez, the center for slave dealing in that part of the country, where they would be auctioned. Franklin did well, and the time arrived when he needed help in the work. He found this in 1824 in the persons of John Armfield and Rice Ballard, young men who were, if anything, more aggressive than Franklin in their activities. For a few months they cooperated but remained independent, and in 1825 they formed Ballard, Franklin & Co. Ballard left the business in 1828, and the firm became Franklin & Armfield, which in the beginning concentrated on the Natchez trade. It continued in the business until 1841.

Within a few years, it became evident that Natchez was declining as a trading center, and being replaced by New Orleans. The partners relocated to Alexandria, Virginia, and their agents would each have territory in the upper South from which to purchase slaves. Armfield managed affairs from there, while Franklin moved to New Orleans, where he would arrange for the sales.

In May 1828, Franklin & Armfield advertised for "150 likely young Negroes of both sexes between the ages of 8 and 25 years." Other, similar advertisements followed, indicating the business was good and expanding. Armfield erected a slave pen in Alexandria where the slaves were housed until ready for shipment. Not content with this, he contacted several independent traders and offered to advance them funds for their operations on the understanding they would supply him with prime slaves, leaving the others to his competitors. Some agreed to this arrangement and became satellite firms to

Franklin & Armfield. One of them, George Chaffered & Co. of Frederickstown, Maryland, abandoned its business of purchasing slaves and then driving them to New Orleans and devoted itself to supplying Armfield—and in the process became wealthy. In time, slave pens were established in five cities in Virginia and Maryland. On July 2, 1833, the syndicate advertised for slaves in the *National Intelligencer.*

CASH IN MARKET. We pay Cash for any number of likely Negroes, of both sexes, from 12 to 25 years of age. Field Hands. Also Mechanics of every description. Apply to:

R.C. Ballard & Co.	Richmond, Va.
J.M. Saunders & Co.	Warrenton, Va.
George Chaffered & Co.	Frederickstown, Md.
James F. Purvis & Co.	Baltimore, Md.
Thomas M. Jones	Easton, Md.

Or to the subscribers at their residence in Alexandria.
Persons having likely servants to dispose of, will do well to give us a call, as we at all times will pay higher prices in cash than any other purchaser who is now or may hereafter come into the market. All communications promptly attended to.
FRANKLIN & ARMFIELD

Armfield purchased four ships, the *Tribune, United States, Isaac Franklin,* and *Uncas,* which sailed regularly from Alexandria to New Orleans, carrying paying passengers as well as slaves. Passengers were encouraged to visit the slave quarters while en route to see their good care. Armfield's men stressed that, unlike other slave traders, Franklin & Armfield would not break up families. Armfield proved a genius at this kind of merchandising. Some of the passengers were plantation owners in the market for slaves. When attending the auctions, they might seek out Franklin & Armfield "merchandise," for they were considered "prime." Armfield did for slaves what Frank Perdue would do for chickens more than a century later: he made them a branded item that commanded a premium price.

In 1834, the firm sent between 1000 to 1200 slaves from Virginia and Maryland to New Orleans, and the numbers increased over the next three years. There is no way of determining just how profitable the business was, but at the time Armfield, a driver 10 years earlier, was said to be worth half a million dollars, while Franklin was even wealthier. By then, the senior partner was tired of the business. He yearned for a respectability that could not be had in the slave trade. In 1841, he informed Armfield of his intentions to marry a Presbyterian minister's daughter and raise a family. He built one of the finest estates in the South, Fairvue, near Nashville, and became a planter. Franklin died in 1846, leaving an estate of $750,000. Armfield continued for a while on his own, but in time he too left the business.

By then, another major trading company had appeared. Hughes & Downing, established in Lexington, Kentucky, began small, sending a parcel of 13 slaves from there to Natchez in the autumn of 1843. The slaves cost $5292.50 and were sold for $8695. After deductions for transport of $257.72, the profit came to $3144.78, high by almost any measure. One of the slaves was a boy, purchased for $440 and sold for $540. Generally speaking, this was the order of profits the partners expected.

Like Franklin & Armstead, Hughes & Downing was considered respectable, if such could describe any trading company in the view of contemporaries and the present. Lewis Robards, on the other hand, who was the biggest trader in Kentucky in the 1850s, also was the most unscrupulous by the standards of the business. He would sell sick slaves and when they died soon after, refuse to offer compensation, as did Hughes & Downing, Franklin & Armfield, and other firms. He made a specialty of selling young girls for concubinage and advertising them as such, contrary to the antebellum South's code of public conduct. Robards mistreated his slaves, considered wrong in itself but also a detriment to business. Before purchasing a slave, the buyer had the right to examine him. Whip marks detracted from the price, because they indicated the slave was recalcitrant and might run away. At least, this was the case with slaves purchased from most companies. In Robards' case, such marks might be considered the result of his rage.

Robards' dealings continually landed him in trouble, both with buyers and the law. In the end, he was forced from the business, and few mourned his passing. Were it not for the great demand for slaves in the 1850s, he could not have lasted as long as he did.

The reason for the increased demand—and higher slave prices—in this period was the rush to the southwest, Texas in particular, following the successful conclusion of the Mexican War. It came as something of a surprise. In 1844, a Virginia newspaperman deplored the low prices of the time, thinking "it will be a long time before slaves recover their former prices." By 1855, a Georgia commentator remarked on the "upward sweep" which he thought could not be sustained.

> The old rule of pricing a negro by the price of cotton by the pound—that is to say, if cotton is worth twelve cents a negro man is worth $1200, if at fifteen cents then $1500—does not seem to be regarded. Negros are 25 percent higher now with cotton at ten and a half cents than they were two or three years ago when it was worth fifteen and sixteen cents. . . . A reversal will come soon.

There was no decline in prices, which continued to rise out of relation to the price of cotton. A New Orleans writer in 1860 tried to justify the high price of slaves in a way that sounds strikingly reminiscent of that adopted by financial writers in 1929, or 1999, in discussing the high prices of securities:

> The theory that the price of negroes is ruled by the price of cotton is not good, for it does not account for the present aspect of the slave market. . . . Nor do we agree with our contemporaries who argue that a speculative demand is the unsubstantial basis of the advance in the price of slaves—that the rates are too high and must come down very soon. It is our impression that the great demand for slaves in the Southwest will keep up prices as it caused their advance in the first place, and that the rates are not a cent above the real value of the laborer who is to be engaged in tilling the fertile lands of a section of the country which yields the planter nearly double the crop that the fields of the Atlantic states do. The Southwest is being opened by a great tide of emigration. The planter who puts ten hands to work on the prolific soil of Texas and Western Louisiana soon makes enough money to buy ten more, and they have to be supplied from the older states—hence the prices which rule in Virginia, the Carolinas, and Georgia. A demand founded in such causes cannot fall off for a score or more years, and the prices of negroes must keep up. They will probably advance somewhat.

Slavery may or may not have been an uneconomical institution when compared with free labor, but the fact remains that profits were to be made from the internal slave trade, and more than a few southerners took advantage of this opportunity for wealth. Nor is it any wonder that in the 1850s, buyers began to consider the breeding aspects of slavery. Even so, the thought was not universal and was not reflected in the prices of slaves at the New Orleans auctions, where females continued to fetch less than males.

There can be no doubt that slavery was a big business in the late 1850s. If a value of $1000 per slave is assigned to the slave population of that period—a reasonable sum that takes into account the lower prices for females and children—the net worth of American slaves was on the order of $4 billion. Using the same method of calculation, the net worth 10 years earlier was $1.6 billion. As a result of natural increases in the slave population, but due more to the sharp rise in prices, the southern financial stake in the institution more than doubled in the pre-Civil War decade.

Slaveholders would argue that such a great investment had to be protected, even at the risk of war and the survival of the Union itself if need be, though they did not couch their public arguments in such terms. Indeed, some southerners were coming to realize the moral and economic drawbacks of slavery. But as already noted, they were not businessmen in the same sense as eastern manufacturers and railroad men and midwestern farmers. Unlike them, southerners did not judge a civilization or society in terms of profits and assets. At a time when such matters were becoming increasingly important, the South's leaders seemed to prefer to retain their attitudes. Isaac Franklin, who made a fortune in the slave trade, wanted nothing more than to be a plantation owner, although there was little profit to be made from such a life or endeavor.

The fact remains that while castigating the slave traders, respectable white southerners put up with them. They provided goods and services for which there was great and growing demand in the late 1850s. Slave trading declined when the Civil War began in 1861, and half a year into the fighting, all the visible companies had disappeared. After Appomattox, there were many white southerners who bemoaned the passing of antebellum civilization, and some who defended slavery. There were none to justify the slave trade, which at best was considered a necessary evil. Many decades would pass before they would concede that the evil was not in the trade and the profits made from dealing in human beings, but in the system that made such profits possible. Well into the twentieth century, there were those who argued that slavery might have ended peacefully were it not for the cotton culture. It is true that in the early years of the nineteenth century, there were individuals and organizations, in the South as well as the North, working for manumission. There were few in the South who spoke openly of such matters in the late 1850s.

"Cotton is King"

In 1856, it appeared the United States would have a difficult time avoiding civil war. Fighting was already taking place in Kansas. In retrospect, we can see that in effect, the war had already begun.

While the question of the morality of slavery was everpresent, at this time, except for abolitionists in the North and "fire eaters" in the South, it was not yet a central national issue. A more important concern in that election year was the related matter of the extension of slavery into the territories. Many southerners understood that unless slavery were permitted to spread, when the territories became states they would vote with the North on such issues as the tariff, banking, and internal improvements, and in time might even attempt to end slavery where it existed. They also knew the matter of prerogative of secession had never been resolved. As far as they were concerned, leaving the Union was a constitutional right.

Could the region prevail if it did secede and war came? The South had a smaller population than the North, few factories to produce the tools of war, and inadequate internal transportation. But it did harbor hopes of intervention by European countries, which realized after the Mexican War that the United States could become a continental power. If the South seceded successfully, other regions might follow. Half a dozen or more countries in North America would pose less of a threat to the European powers than a large united one. How best to win European support, then, was a major issue after the 1856 election. The answer came the following year, and not from London or Paris, but rather from Wall Street.

At the time, the U.S. was in the midst of an economic boom. England's acceptance of free trade in 1846 had resulted in export-driven growth. Then came the American victory in the Mexican War, followed by the annexation of the Southwest and the discovery of gold in California. The outbreak of the Crimean War in Europe in 1854 caused foreign gold to come to America for safekeeping. All of which boosted the money supply, which had been $6.79 per capita in 1845 and rose to $12.93 by 1857. Little wonder the bulls on Wall Street celebrated.

There were signs of an economic slowdown that summer. The Crimean War had ended, and with this, demand slackened for American grain, so the price declined. Northern and midwestern farmers, who had been expecting higher prices, suffered. But speculation in cotton caused its price to rise, so the outlook in the South was better. Textile manufacturers were faced with the situation of having to try to pass on higher raw material prices. The market for textiles was weak, however, to the point that northern mills were dismissing part of their work force.

That summer, farmers in all sections of the country began drawing against their deposits and borrowing in anticipation of the need for funds during the autumn harvest. In itself, this should not have been a serious matter. The banks were accustomed to large withdrawals that season of the year, and most of the time were prepared to meet demands. But the situations in wheat and cotton were critical and causing distress in a country where the banking system had been vulnerable for two decades. By late July, strains in the system had developed.

Shortly before noon on August 11, N. H. Wolfe & Co., a large grain and flour company, declared itself insolvent. Wolfe was a very conservative house. If it could fail, what of the others? With this, prices turned downward at the Stock & Exchange Board's afternoon auction. On August 19, Edwin Johnson, president of the Michigan Central, resigned "in order to spend more time on personal matters." No one believed him and that stock plunged. Five days later, Charles Stetson, president of the prestigious Ohio Life Insurance & Trust Co., announced his firm's failure. Ohio Life had speculated in western lands and channeled eastern and foreign funds into Ohio and Illinois. It had also invested major sums in railroad securities.

As they always did at such times, depositors rushed to their banks to withdraw funds. Other banks failed. DaLaunay, Iselin & Clark, a private bank, was shuttered on August 25. Many speculators announced an inability to honor contracts. More banks failed.

But there seemed to be hope. The steamer *Central America* was due in the harbor in late September, bringing $1.6 million in California gold to ease the situation. However, even nature conspired against the bulls. The ship sank in a hurricane off Cape Hatteras on September 12. Now the panic extended to Philadelphia and Baltimore banks and markets. By October, a dozen railroads were in receivership.

New York was in turmoil. The depression extended into the autumn and winter. The 1857–1858 winter weather was unusually harsh, and the city's citizens suffered. There was looting in the streets. Mayor Fernando Wood called upon wealthy New Yorkers to help the poor, warning of the possibility of added violence. An East Side gang, the "Dead Rabbits," seized City Hall, ejected the mayor and his staff, and held it for an hour.

All of this news was received in the South as a sign of northern weakness. The cotton planters did much of their banking with European houses and so did not suffer losses. Although a few southern banks failed, this did not result in panic. The price of cotton rose still higher, this time due to increased European demand. American cotton exports earned $132 million in 1857 and $131 million in 1858. In 1859, the figure would rise to $161 million.

Southern newspapers were jubilant and jeered the prostrate North. The Charleston *Mercury* asked on October 14, "Why does the South allow itself to be tattered and torn by the dissensions and death struggles of New York's money changers?" "The wealth of the South is permanent and real, that of the North fugitive and fictitious," said Georgia Governor Herschel Johnson. After the panic seemed to be ending and recovery taking place, Senator James Hammond of South Carolina—who in 1856 had cautioned against a sectional war which he thought the South could not win—now trumpeted a new doctrine: "Cotton is King!" Hammond told the North, "Fortunately for you it was the commencement of the cotton season, and we have poured upon you 1.6 million bales of cotton just at the crisis to save you."

Southern newspapers took up the cry. In the event of sectional war, the North would be devastated financially, they asserted. Dismissed workers there would revolt and side with the South. The anti-Catholic Know Nothings and Republicans would oppose the workers, leading to class warfare in the North. Northern banks and railroads would go under. Meanwhile, the South could withhold cotton from the market, causing distress in Europe, and obliging governments there, already hoping for the dissolution of the United States, to recognize the new southern government and even come to its aid.

The scenario may seem overdone in light of what we know happened, but at the time, it appeared quite plausible, especially considering the events of 1857. The panic of that year certainly did not precipitate the Civil War, but it did provide southern anti-Union politicians with another arrow for their quiver.

CHAPTER 13

Gold, Silver, and the Civil War

INCE the beginning of recorded history, and probably before that, individuals have made fortunes during wars. Armies must be supplied, weapons procured, loans contracted, taxes increased, and black markets supplied. Transportation facilities have to be made available. Wagers on the outcome can be made by dealing in the paper debts of each side. This is not to suggest that wars are profitable enterprises. Even the victors can be bankrupted by warfare. Rather, individuals and companies can prosper by engaging in the activities described above.

The American Civil War was no exception. Fortunes were made backing both the Union and Confederate causes, though not many in the latter case, and those who did amass wealth in the Confederacy lost all if they placed it in Confederate currency and bonds. Much more was made in the Union. Affluence was achieved by many of those who supplied the government with needed provisions and services, by raising the money needed to pay for them, and in speculation in securities and currency.

In addition, part of President Abraham Lincoln's agenda had little to do with war and much to do with the nation's economic future. The foundation was set during the war for a network of railroads that would run from the Mississippi to the Pacific.

Then too, the Civil War opened a Pandora's box in the matter of currency. The question of currency had been an issue in America since Hamilton argued for the creation of the Bank of the United States—and on a wider scale since the appearance of civilization in the Fertile Crescent. Gold and silver had been considered measures of wealth, but over time, paper came to signify it as well. The assumption in John Law's day was that behind the paper rested those precious metals. During the early national period of the U.S., banks would issue paper money that could be redeemed for metals. There arose a class of "note merchants," who would purchase bank paper at discounts in areas distant from the bank and then take the bills to the issuing bank for redemption. There had been paper money issues without metallic backing, such as the *assignats* printed during the French Revolution, which theoretically were backed by land seized by the new government, but actually they were unsupported. There is ever the temptation to print increasing amounts of paper, which ultimately results in the dilution of its value and—in some cases during the twentieth century—financial chaos and revolution. One of the most notable experiments with paper money came during the Civil War, and repercussions from it would be felt for the rest of the century.

Jay Cooke: Financing the Union Cause

By the 1840s, scores of investment banks sought clients and customers. Most were located in New York, Philadelphia, Boston, and Baltimore, but there were such banks in other northern cities as well. As had been the case earlier, the larger ones had relationships with European banks with significant customer bases that were seeking to invest in American government and business paper. In addition, the American banks acted as agents for wealthy Americans who were interested in European securities, but in this period there were few in this category. Prime, Ward & King, a New York firm, remained the agent for Baring Brothers & Co. N. M. Rothschild & Sons started dealing heavily in American securities in 1835, doing so through S. I. Joseph & Co. When Joseph went bankrupt in the financial panic of 1837, the Rothschilds dispatched August Belmont to New York, where he organized August Belmont & Co., which served as their new agent. George Peabody of Boston went the other way, settling in London that same year and entering the financial world as agent for the state of Maryland, selling its bonds to English investors. Peabody opened an investment bank in his own name in 1852, and in 1855 he took on as his junior partner Junius Spencer Morgan, formerly a dry goods merchant. When Peabody retired in 1864, Morgan took over at the firm, which became J. S. Morgan & Co., and did much business with the Philadelphia firm of Drexel & Co., which began its existence as a note merchant. Other prominent American investment banks of the period were Corcoran & Riggs in Washington, D.C., Duncan, Sherman in New York, and Lee Higginson in Boston, among many others. E. W. Clark, a Philadelphia firm, was one of the more significant of the period. Established in 1837, Clark opened branch offices throughout the east and became an important seller of government bonds during the Mexican War. Clark later recognized as Clark, Dodge & Co.

In 1842, the man who was to become the first major American investment banker, Jay Cooke, was a partner at E. W. Clark & Co. When Clark suspended operations due to losses in the 1857 panic, Cooke decided to go off on his own, doing so in an unusual way that presaged his later activities. Without bothering to establish a banking house, he approached several railroads that required capital and offered to raise funds for them through bond underwritings. He proposed to be compensated either by a commission or by shares of common stock. At the same time, Cooke reorganized several defunct railroads and canals, taking shares and bonds in payment for services and selling them for profits once the enterprises were recognized as viable. On January 1, 1861, Cooke formed Jay Cooke & Co., and in the early summer of that year comanaged with Drexel & Co. a $3 million Pennsylvania state issue. While not as large or well-known as several older banks, when the Civil War began Cooke was better situated and more experienced than anyone else in the marketing of large issues of securities. He had deepened his relationship with Anthony Drexel, the renowned Philadelphia banker and an intimate of Secretary of the Treasury Salmon Chase. In 1860, Cooke had contributed to and helped finance the Chase campaign for the Republican Presidential nomination.

Fort Sumter fell on April 13, 1861, and the undeclared (because it suited Lincoln's plans not to recognize the Confederacy) war was on. After consultation with Chase and others, Lincoln decided to do what he could to make the war "a short and decisive one." He wanted an armed force of more than 400,000 and $400 million to pay for it. Chase did not agree wholly with the plan and intended to raise, initially at least, $320 million, of which $240 million was to be borrowed through the sale of paper. He knew that his predecessors, Secretaries Howell Cobb and John Dix, who had served under President James Buchanan, had failed to sell all of a $10 million and an $8 million offering. Further, the Secretary was a lawyer, not a financier, and realized he needed help, which in time he received from Cooke, who was then in the process of completing the distribution of the Pennsylvania debt issue.

During the war, the Union's expenditures rose from $66.5 million in 1861 to $1.3 billion by 1865. In this period, the national debt rose from $90.6 million to $2.7 billion. Some of the money needed to fight the war came from taxes and the issuance of a quarter billion dollars in paper money. The rest came from borrowing, $2 billion worth, much of it through the efforts of investment bankers.

Initially, Chase relied on traditional methods of raising revenues for the government. He announced a bond issue of $150 million, offered at par, sending notices to bankers in New York, Boston, and Philadelphia that the Treasury was prepared to accept bids. This was the way Cobb, Dix, and their predecessors had raised money. The trouble was that Cobb and Dix had failed, and so did Chase. He received insufficient bids, and many of these were for below par.

On July 12, 1861, Cooke wrote to Chase of his plans to open an office in Washington with Drexel & Co. In a letter to his brother, Cooke instructed him to "tell Governor Chase that I hold myself at his service and, pay or no pay, I will do all I can to aid him in Treasury matters. I feel, however, that if he would give me a chance I could show him a way to raise the money."

What Cooke was suggesting was that his experience, and that of Drexel, had equipped the combination to distribute securities efficiently and effectively. Essentially, investment bankers are financial intermediaries who seek to satisfy the needs of both clients and customers. In this case, the client was the United States Treasury and the customers that network of banks, trust companies, insurance firms, and private individuals in the market for debt obligations.

Cooke's office was opened in February of 1862. This was a period during which, as a result of the seizing of two Confederate envoys from the English ship *Trent* and military setbacks on the front, it appeared the United States might find itself at war with England and defeated militarily by the Confederacy. In such a situation, the purchase of American bonds seemed quite chancy. In December 1861, the nation's banks suspended specie payments and the Treasury did the same the following month, further signs of government weakness and hardly encouraging to bond buyers.

To meet pressing financial needs, in February Congress passed the Legal Tender Act, which authorized the Treasury to issue $150 million in bank notes—in effect, paper money, that soon came to be called "greenbacks"—not backed by gold or silver, but by the credit of the government. They were to be legal tender, and creditors were obliged to accept them in payment of debts. In addition, $500 million in 20-year, 6 percent bonds, callable in five years, could be issued. The public could pay for them in greenbacks, and the bonds would be redeemed in gold. At the time, they were being traded against gold at below their face value, meaning that with $100 in gold coins, one could purchase as much as $120 in greenbacks. Since the bonds would be redeemed in gold, this meant that the purchaser would receive much more than 6 percent interest—if, of course, the Union won the war and the government survived and was able to redeem the bonds in five years or at maturity. It was the first round in what came to be known as "the money question," which became a central issue in politics and finance for the rest of the century.

The bond sales went poorly, not only denying the government the money but sending negative signals to the markets and the world, England included, where as a result of the *Trent* affair, investors shied from the bonds. With this, Chase turned to Cooke for assistance.

Cooke realized that the placement of government bonds with the large institutions would be difficult if not impossible. Drawing on his experience with the Pennsylvania issue, he decided to attempt to do something that was most unusual for the time—sell bonds to small investors who had little or no experience with such paper. He advertised extensively in newspapers and through correspondent banks in Boston, Baltimore, New York, and Philadelphia and employed an army of 2500 commission agents to scour the back country, offering the securities first to country bankers, and eventually to almost anyone else considered a potential investor. Cooke's salesforce made placements as large as $300,000 and others as small as $50. Without the telegraph, which enabled the banks to keep in touch with each other regarding their placements, this kind of syndicate would not have been possible.

Cooke's salespitch appealed to investors' financial self-interest, and also to their patriotism. Without this latter ingredient, the effort might not have succeeded. In a typical broadside, directed at "farmers, mechanics, and capitalists," he wrote:

> You have a solemn duty to perform to your government and to posterity! Our gallant army and navy must be supported by every man and woman who has any means, large or small, at their control. The United States Government, to which we owe our prosperity as a nation, security of person and property of every sort, calls on each individual to rally to its support—not with donations or gifts—though who would withhold them—BUT WITH SUBSCRIPTIONS TO HER LOANS, based on the best security in the world, the untold and scarcely yet tried resources of this mighty continent, which were developing rapidly when the rebellion broke out, and to maintain which, AS A PRICELESS HERITAGE TO POSTERITY. This defense against rebellion is made.

It went on in this vein for several paragraphs, ending with, "Your nearest patriotic bank or banker will supply this loan, on which so much depends!" Such patriotic appeals would be made during bond sales in both world wars, the difference being that in the twentieth century wars, the interest rates were nowhere near as appealing as they were during the Civil War.

The Cooke strategy proved successful. By early 1864, his syndicate had sold more than $360 million in bonds, while the Treasury sold the rest. Cooke extracted only a small commission for his efforts, one-sixteenth of 1 percent, but he made much more in trading and through his new relationship with the Treasury.

The Treasury employed Cooke in early 1865 to sell an issue of 7.3 percent debt, a figure chosen because it accrued one cent per day on the $50 notes. Once again, Cooke assembled a large syndicate and opened "Working Men's Savings Banks," which were really sales offices with evening hours to accommodate workers who could not get there during daytime. And as Hamilton had done in the early national period, he entered the market on the buy side when their prices slipped.

The Wall Street Scene

The coming of war did not please Wall Streeters, who saw the conflict as a disruption of business at best and a prelude to the dissolution of the country itself at worst. The fears that accompanied the 1857 panic were still palpable. Stocks sold off at the beginning of the war. Southern merchants owed their northern suppliers almost $300 million; nearly all of this was a total loss. Business slumped due to the uncertainty. Approximately 6000 northern firms, with liabilities of more than $5000 each, went into bankruptcy, and a like number failed that owed less than that amount. The banking structure was seriously damaged. For example, 89 of Illinois' 110 financial institutions were in the hands of receivers by the end of 1861.

As noted previously, at the beginning of the war, the federal debt was $90.5 million, much of which was closely held by wealthy investors both in the United States and overseas, with England and the Netherlands the most important foreign investors. The same was true of state and municipal bonds, the former coming to $191 million, the latter to $79 million. This was a small fraction of the amount of paper issued by American corporations. Just prior to the coming of war, there was $433 million in par value in railroad stocks alone, and another $363 million in railroad bonds. Bank stocks accounted for $266 million, canal stocks $25 million, and stocks in insurance companies $13 million. Not all of these issues were traded at the NYS&EB. Despite the coming of the telegraph, many of the smaller local and regional exchanges continued on, and while statistics were not collected on such matters, in the aggregate they must have traded far more shares than did the NYS&EB. Nor did the Board have a monopoly in the city. Issues not considered suitable for listing were traded in an outdoors market known as the Curb. After the 1837 panic, some brokers went indoors with a new exchange, called the New Board. After the California gold rush began, shares in mining companies, also not qualified for listing, were traded at one of several mining exchanges that sprang up. After the war began, the exchanges proliferated. Literally dozens of them appeared during the war, some open evenings after the rest of them had closed, and there was one at Republican Party headquarters at night.

Gilpin's New Room, also known as the "Coal Hole" because it was so dark and gloomy, was the most famous of these exchanges. To serve brokers who were not that patriotic, Gilpin's membership was open to all who would pay a $25 annual fee. There, only one item was traded: gold, which sold against greenbacks. Gold trading began in the city shortly after the northern banks and then the federal government stopped gold payments. Immediately, some members of the NYS&EB suggested trading gold against greenbacks at their exchange. The majority seemed to feel it was wrong to wager against

Union victories, and in 1862, several resolutions were passed condemning the gold traders. For the next two years, despite charges that its members lacked patriotism and regulations and legislation aimed at curbing gold speculation, Gilpin's prospered.

Its operations were based on Gresham's Law, which holds that bad money drives good money out of circulation. The law was named after Sir Thomas Gresham, an advisor to Queen Elizabeth I, who pointed out that due to the debasement of English coins, and because other coins were withdrawn from circulation leaving the degraded currency to circulate, English foreign trade was suffering. This happened almost instantly when the greenbacks appeared. Individuals hoarded their gold coins and used greenbacks to settle accounts and make purchases.

The value of the greenbacks immediately fell below 100 cents on the dollar, then rose when there were reports of Union victories and fell again on news of defeats. On April 18, 1862, at the beginning of General George McClellan's advance into the South in what came to be known as the Peninsula Campaign, gold was at 101½. At the time, it appeared McClellan might be successful, which explains the small premium given gold. But as the campaign wore on, and it became evident Confederate Generals Joseph Johnston and Thomas "Stonewall" Jackson were outmaneuvering him, gold rose in value. On July 1, the price stood at 108¾, and by July 21 had gone to 120. After the Union defeat at Fredericksburg in December, the price rose to 134. Not until General U.S. Grant's victory at Vicksburg on July 4, 1863, was there any decline. In the interim, gold rose to a high of 190, retreated to 145, and continued to slide to 122½ before halting. In the process, fortunes were made and lost by those who guessed right or wrong.

In order to be better informed about the war and so make the right wagers on gold, speculators had operatives stationed in the telegraph offices, which meant they might get news minutes before it reached Gilpin's. Other, more aggressive traders, hired agents to travel with the armies and send information as soon as possible, usually by means of coded telegrams. In 1863, several private wires brought the news to Wall Street. By 1864, speculators had spies in the Confederate camp to report on news and rumors. Thus, Wall Street learned of the plans of both sides before officers in the field were informed. Lincoln knew of this and realized that the best source of news about the war was not from his generals, but from Wall Street. By following the gold price by the minute, he could learn of Union victories or defeats. He was disgusted, as were others. "What do you think of those fellows in Wall Street who are gambling in gold at such a time as this?" he asked. "For my part, I wish every one of them had his devilish head shot off."

Trading in gold against greenbacks served no direct economic purpose. Secondary markets in stocks and bonds were useful, since they provided liquidity without which the securities might not have been sold to the original purchasers. Gilpin's did nothing like this; it didn't even stimulate gold mining, which in any case never needed encouraging.

The existence of Gilpin's did ease the plight of American merchants who dealt with foreign customers. The American importer who had to pay an English exporter $100,000 in gold would be able to go to Gilpin's and make the purchase for $120,000 in greenbacks. To students of markets and today's fluctuating currencies, it may seem strange that the speculators and merchants did not organize a futures market, in which an importer might have purchased a contract to buy pounds sterling at a specified price on or before a specified date. This did not happen, or if it did, it was not reported in the press of the time or mentioned in contemporary accounts elsewhere.

In February 1863, Congress attempted to curb the gold gamblers and made it a crime to offer loans on bullion above par, but this did not affect coins and so the trading continued.

In early April of 1864, in an attempt to put an end to the speculation, Secretary Chase announced that each morning gold would be sold at the Subtreasury at an announced price, this at a time when gold was at 189. The price that first day, Monday, April 18th, was to be 165. This prompted panic selling at Gilpin's, as bulls tried to bid up the price while the bears hammered it down. It was possible, for example, to buy government gold at 165 and then sell it to the bulls, who were vainly attempting to support the price, for an easy profit. The crowd at Gilpin's departed, while prices fell at what by now had been renamed the New York Stock Exchange, as both bulls and bears struggled to make sense of the situation. Prices continued to fall until Friday, when the bulls finally realized that the lower prices posted at the Subtreasury had resulted in a run on that institution. On Monday, April 25, the government was forced to bow, and the gold sales ended. With this, the speculators returned to Gilpin's, and the price of gold rose at once to 182.

In May and June of 1864, after Grant failed to outflank General Robert E. Lee at Spotsylvania and seemed to have been bested at Cold Harbor, the price of gold rose yet higher. An angry Congress debated a proposal declaring gold transactions to be penal offenses unless they took place in the offices of the buyer or seller. Some Congressmen warned that this would be interpreted as a sign of weakness and so increase the price of gold. Following the debates, speculators purchased gold, betting the law would pass. And so it did, on June 20th.

Gilpin's closed down, but the law was a failure in that it did not stop trading. The brokers and dealers would meet in offices or on the street, where conversations like this one took place:

If I were in your office, I would sell you $20,000 gold at 175.

If I were at my office, I would bid you 170 for the lot.

If I were at your office, I would let you have it for 173, and that is the best I can do.

Then I would take it.

Memos changed hands and the deal would be consummated the following day. All the bill did was to close Gilpin's and help the price of gold to rise to 250. Within a short period, the measure was repealed, and the brokers formed the New York Gold Exchange in October 1864, shortly before the Presidential election. At that time it appeared that Lincoln might lose.

The "Gold Room," as it was called, was the most informal and certainly the wildest in American history. At the far wall was a large, clocklike apparatus on which was indicated the last sale price for gold. Describing the Room shortly after the end of the Civil War, an observer wrote:

Imagine a rat-put in full blast, with 20 to 30 men ranged around the rat tragedy, each
with a canine under his arm, yelling and howling at once, and you have as good a com-

parison as can be found in the outside world of the aspect of the Gold Room as it strikes the beholder on his first entrance. The furniture of this room is extremely simple. It consists of two iron railings and an indicator. The first railing is a circle about four feet high and ten feet in diameter, placed exactly in the center of the room. In the interior, which represents the space devoted to rat killing in other establishments, is a marble cupid throwing up a jet of pure Croton water. The artistic conception is not appropriate. Instead of a cupid throwing a pearly fountain into the air, there should be a hungry Midas turning everything to gold and starving from sheer inability to eat.

On July 11, with Confederate General Jubal Early's army within five miles of Washington, the price of gold soared. James Medbury, who was on the scene and later wrote of what he saw, did not think the cause was Early's progress, but rather manipulation. He reported:

On July 11 gold reached its highest quotation, selling at nightfall for 285. War had nothing to do with that excessive price. It was simply the culmination of a well-concerted corner. Even these figures, which will probably go down in history as the extreme point reached in gold sales, were really below the prices paid at the Room after the regular adjournment. One transaction at least on that day was for 289½. And a lot of gold amounting to $100,000 was bought at the extraordinary rate of 310!
After that the corner was broken and gold fell in price.

At the beginning of the war, gold was transferred by messengers carrying coins in canvas bags. Robbers descended on the district, and throwing red pepper in the eyes of the messengers, they would steal the gold. After several of these raids, the brokers arranged for a central depository at the Bank of New York and the issuance of private certificates, drawn upon the bank, to settle accounts. In order to participate in this plan, each broker had to maintain a large balance at the bank. Edward Ketchum, of the firm of Ketchum, Son & Co., recognized in this situation an opportunity to enrich himself. Forging $1.5 million in certificates, he absconded, but was soon captured.

The Gold Ring

The Gold Room continued to operate after the war, although the action was not as wild for the first few postwar years as it was when the fighting raged. Now greenbacks rose or declined, depending on which way the political and economic winds happened to blow.

There were some $400 million in greenbacks outstanding at the end of the war. Hard money forces, meaning those who opposed an inflation that would drive down the value of legal tender and cause hardship among creditors, favored the gradual elimination of paper and the return to a gold standard. Inflationists, who feared deflation more than inflation, argued that an increase in paper money would stimulate economic activity, and their ranks included many debtors. During the Presidential campaign of 1868, Republican U.S. Grant favored the gradual return of the gold standard, which would be accomplished by regular auctions of gold by the Treasury. The Democratic platform attempted to straddle the issue, as did candidate Horatio Seymour. Grant won the election, but before he was sworn in, Congress voted to halt the further redemption of the greenbacks. The issue was taken to the courts, and in 1869, in the case of *Hepburn v. Griswold*, the Supreme Court declared the greenbacks were not legal tender. In 1871, with a changed Court, the decision was reversed. Speculation at the Gold Exchange continued, but now prices were not dictated by military victories or defeats, but by export and import figures, political and legal maneuvers, and bull and bear pools.

The most infamous of these, the so-called "Gold Ring," began soon after Grant's ·inauguration. At the time, the Jeffersonian dream of America supplying foodstuffs to Europe had been realized; the United States was the world's largest producer of wheat. Foreigners purchased that wheat with dollars, often selling gold to acquire them. When the gold price was high, they could get more dollars, and when the price fell, they received fewer of them. Thus, a low gold price meant expensive wheat, a high one, inexpensive wheat, and the latter would stimulate the economy. If this happened, the railroads carrying wheat to market would be among the beneficiaries.

Jay Gould was a railroad tycoon and one of the cleverest speculators in history. He arranged with Jim Fisk, another speculator, to meet Abel Corbin, the President's brother-in-law, who dabbled on Wall Street. Gould argued that if the nation's gold supply were constricted, prices would inevitably rise and this would assure prosperity to all. Lower gold prices, in contrast, would lead to lower commodity prices and hardship. Since he controlled the Wabash Railroad, an important line in the transportation of grain, he would benefit. But Gould had larger ambitions. If he could purchase gold at low prices and then force it up, he would become very wealthy indeed—and could claim to have done it all in the name of patriotism.

Gould indicated that if Corbin could explain this to Grant and win the President to the plan, he might be included in the gold-buying syndicate. Corbin did speak with Grant of the idea and the impact of a higher gold price on the economy, but the President was not impressed. Undeterred, Gould and Fisk went on anyway. All that was needed, they thought, was for the government to remain out of the market once the price of gold rose. They started with Corbin planting a story in the press to the effect that Grant had become a fiscal expansionist. Next, they managed to have Daniel Butterfield, who was involved in the Ring, appointed to the post of assistant treasurer in New York. Finally, Corbin arranged for a meeting between Grant and Gould at which he pointed out to the President the benefits of a higher gold price. Whatever the results, news of the meeting was leaked to the Street, and the impression there was that the government would remain out of the market.

All the while, the Gold Ring accumulated gold and contracts for future delivery of the metal. On September 1, the Treasury ended its regular gold auctions, undertaken to gradually reduce the circulation of greenbacks, and this was seen as a sign that no further gold would come to market for the time being.

Stock prices had declined in late August, and the sell-off continued into September. The price of gold remained steady—in the mid-130s. The Ring continued its accumulation and started to squeeze the shorts. On September 3, the New York Times reported, ". . . a very decided, and in point of wealth strong Bull movement was inaugurated in the Gold Room today, and advanced the price of gold by main force." The price rose slowly but steadily, crossing the 140 level on September 22. By then, the Ring had accumulated some $40 million in gold futures contracts, twice the available supply in the city. The corner was completed the following day. Amid signs of wavering on the part of the Treasury, Gould acted swiftly. The market opened at 143½ on September 24th and soon was at 150. In order to obtain funds to purchase gold and so make good their contracts, speculators sold stocks, which caused distress at the Stock Exchange. The gold price continued upward, reaching 161⅜, with Fisk openly predicting a price of 200.

At this, Grant acted, instructing the Treasury to commence gold sales. Congressman James Garfield, the future President, was dispatched to Wall Street with the news. Standing on the steps of the Subtreasury, he proclaimed, "Fellow citizens. God reigns and the government in Washington still lives! I am instructed to inform you that the Secretary of the Treasury has placed ten million in gold upon the market!"

The Gold Room was in pandemonium when the news arrived there. On one end of the floor gold was selling for 160, while on the other it had collapsed to 135. It ended the day at 131¼. The ring had been smashed, but not Gould and Fisk, who managed to wriggle out of several costly contracts. The price continued to drop and finally settled at 120.

Resumption of Specie Payments

Gold exports in the face of financial stringencies was one of the causes for the Panic of 1873. Inflationists responded by saying more money would alleviate the distress. Clearly, this situation was resulting in large speculative gains and losses in which nothing constructive for the nation was being accomplished.

Washington concluded that a decision on the nature of the currency no longer could be delayed. This was driven home by the results of the 1874 congressional elections, when impelled by the depression and inflationist elements, mostly Democrats were swept into office, who pledged not only to maintain the greenbacks but to issue more of them. However, before the new Congress could meet, the lame duck session passed the Resumption Act of 1875.

Sponsors of the measure refused to answer questions about the implications of its provision. But one of its leading champions, Senator John Sherman of Ohio, conceded that it placed "the whole credit and money of the United States" in the hands of the Secretary of the Treasury. As it turned out, the next Treasury secretary was to be Sherman himself.

All sides believed the battle lines would be clear in the 1876 Presidential contest, when Republican Rutherford B. Hayes, a bullionist, won a disputed election. Meanwhile, the economic depression continued as "resumption day" approached. In anticipation of the event, the price of gold rose in New York, so that by mid-December 1878, it was close to par with greenbacks. Still, that Christmas, the Treasury feared a run on the banks as greenback owners rushed to exchange them for gold, a preview of what today's antigold forces believe would happen if we return to a gold standard.

January 1 was a bank holiday, but the banks opened on schedule the next day, with bags of gold coins at the ready. The anticipated rush to gold didn't materialize. Convinced the government's pledge was trustworthy, the public remained calm. Before the Subtreasury closed that day, $132,000 in greenbacks had been redeemed, but some $400,000 in gold had been exchanged for greenbacks. Greenbacks were now preferable to gold for ordinary transactions. Wall Street celebrated what seemed a victory for the hard money forces. Undersecretary of the Treasury J. K. Upton reported to Sherman: "By five o'clock the news was all over the land, and the New York bankers were sipping their tea in absolute safety."

The gold standard was no panacea. Contrary to the optimistic forecasts of the bullionists, there was no influx of gold from abroad, and the depression deepened. The *Commer-*

cial and Financial Chronicle, which had predicted a boom with gold, lost faith: "Where is the prosperity promised with that event? Wheat is no higher. Corn is no higher. There is no money in any of the earth's products. Where is the promised prosperity?"

The writer didn't have long to wait. Europe experienced massive crop failures in 1879 that continued into 1880. Meanwhile, the American crops were excellent, and huge amounts were shipped overseas. "It is the American supply alone, which has saved Europe from general famine," wrote the *Economist*. During the last quarter of 1879, Britain sent $20 million in gold to America to pay for wheat, France contributed $30 million, and Germany, $10 million.

As a result of this, plus domestic changes, gold reserves rose from $119 million in June to $157 million by September. As the bullionists had theorized, the depression came to an end with the arrival of foreign gold. Interest rates fell, and the economy recovered. As might have been expected, the Republicans credited the recovery to resumption and the gold standard and to falling interest rates. "It has lifted the credit of the nation from the point where 6 percent bonds sold at 86 to where 4 percent bonds are eagerly sought at premium," they proclaimed in 1880. "The United States notes are now, in form, security, and convenience, the best circulating medium known," said Secretary Sherman. In rebuttal, the inflationists noted that it was wheat, not gold, that ushered in prosperity, and they cited manipulation of the greenbacks by Sherman and expansion of the money supply through gold imports as evidence of this. The debate had just begun, and it would reach a climax in the election of 1896, when, with a host of other problems besetting the country, the gold standard became the dividing line between the parties, another round in the struggle between the Jeffersonians and Hamiltonians regarding the nature of wealth.

The Silver Bonanza

Noting that westward expansion continued during the Civil War, one writer grumbled that while the rivers of the East ran red with blood, those of the West ran yellow with gold. He might have added white with silver, or to be more precise, bluish-black with argentite and other silver ores. From the California Gold Rush of 1849 to the Alaska Gold Find of 1896 and the rush to the Yukon that followed, miners roamed the West seeking bonanzas in gold and silver. In the process, they drove out Indians, created small towns, encouraged the development of the railroads, and enriched the nation. There were two unusual things about these settlers. In the first place, they weren't really settlers, but rather tended to go from one find to another. They sought wealth in what to farmers and ranchers would be considered unattractive places, and so they opened areas for others. The second uncommon fact about them is that unlike other "frontiersmen," most miners came from the West, not the East or Europe. The largest contingent was made up of Californians who, after seeing gold was hard to come by there, sought wealth elsewhere.

There was a gold strike in Pike's Peak, Colorado, and a major silver find in Virginia City, Nevada, in 1858, based on the famous Comstock Lode. Other finds would follow—Silver City, Idaho, in 1862; South Pass City, Wyoming, in 1867; Leadville, Colorado, in 1870; and the famous Deadwood City finds of 1875, distinguished for giving America the legendary figures Wild Bill Hickok, California Jack, Poker Alice, and

Calamity Jane. Then there was the Tombstone bonanza, from which emerged Wyatt Earp, Doc Holliday, the Clantons, and the dramatic showdown at O.K. Corral.

All followed the same pattern—discovery, the rush to seek wealth, the formation of towns, the creation of large mining companies, foreign investment, the petering out of veins, and the migration of miners to new sites, leaving ghost towns in the wake.

This is illustrated in the Comstock Lode silver find, the greatest in history, eclipsing that of Potosí during the Age of Discovery. Half a billion dollars worth of the metal was extracted in two decades from what was known as the Washoe region of Nevada, and while not as famous as some of the others, Comstock was equally important financially and politically.

The tale of the Comstock began in 1857, when two brothers, Allen and Hosea Grosch, arrived in Gold Canyon, Nevada, named for a small gold find, after wandering through California and Mexico seeking gold. They found some bluish-black mud in streams, which they ignored, and in 1856 located two veins of silver. Hosea died of a foot injury and Allen perished in a storm, and nothing more happened until 1857 when Henry Comstock purchased their cabin and came upon their papers and some of that congealed mud. Comstock wasn't interested in silver; like others in the area, he sought gold.

Meanwhile, another prospector, James Fennimore, who came to Nevada after knifing a man in California, happened upon an outcropping of yellow quartz, wrote the location on a slip of paper, and put it under a nearby rock—the method of posting claims. Then he moved on. He returned the following year with some other prospectors and one of them, John Bishop, washed some gold specks from an outcropping. Two others, Patrick McLaughlin and Peter O'Reilly, dug for a while, found nothing, and then deepened a spring to obtain additional water for their washings. By chance, they threw some of the mud from the stream's bottom into their rocker. When the dirt washed away, they found gold. They named the area Gold Hill and continued working. News of the find spread, and within weeks the area was inundated with hundreds of miners, armed with pans, filling the streams.

Learning of this, Comstock returned to Gold Canyon and declared the gold was on land belonging to him, Fennimore, and another miner, Emmanuel Penrod. His claim was accepted, whereupon Comstock bought Fennimore's share for $40 and started working with Penrod.

Within days, they had washed several hundred dollars of gold from the stream. But the going was rough, for that blue mud made recovery difficult. They thought that without the mud the Ophir, as they called the stream, would be very valuable.

Rancher B. A. Harrison was interested in the Ophir. He convinced the prospectors it might be worthwhile to have an assay on the mud, which they commissioned. They received the findings in late June 1859. The blue mud contained $876 worth of gold and more than $3000 in silver. The news couldn't be kept secret. Within weeks, miners rushed to what Comstock promptly dubbed "The Comstock Lode." Fennimore, who came from Virginia, poured some liquor on the ground and shouted, "I baptize this spot Virginia Town." At least, that is the legend. The mining West had many such myths. Virginia City became the hub of the Comstock region of Washoe.

As was customary, the original owners of the Ophir sold their holdings early in the game, and at the time thought they had bilked the buyers. Penrod received $3000 for his shares. He took the money and left Washoe for richer diggings, which he never found. Comstock sold his for $11,000 and opened a supply store in nearby Carson City. The store failed, and Comstock returned to mining, with little success. In 1870, he fatally shot himself and is buried in an unmarked grave in Bozeman, Montana. McLaughlin sold his holdings for $3500, couldn't find gold elsewhere, and took employment as a cook for $40 a month. He died a pauper in 1879. O'Reilly held his shares longer than the others, selling for $45,000. He, too, never found another bonanza. In the attempt, he was trapped in a cave-in and taken to a hospital. He recovered his physical health, but ultimately went mad. Like McLaughlin, he died poor. All lived long enough to realize how mistaken they had been to sell.

The true nature of the wealth of the Comstock Lode unfolded gradually, as one shallow mine after another was sunk into the hills of the region, especially Mt. Davidson, not far from what is now Reno.

Winter came early in 1859, sealing the passes to miners who wanted to start digging and washing. The passes opened in March 1860, and now began the biggest mining boom since California. George Hearst, the father of publisher William Randolph Hearst, was one participant. He parlayed a $450 investment into more than $1 million.

Then there were those who hoped to make fortunes servicing the miners. It was very much like the mining towns pictured in movies about the Old West (this was one of the few accurate portrayals of western life provided by the motion pictures). The towns were magnets for those seeking fortunes: prostitutes from the East and Europe, gamblers from the Mississippi, saloon keepers from New York, Boston, Chicago, and San Francisco, desperadoes from all points on the compass, Mexican gunmen, cowboys, and laborers.

Carpenters and masons charged exorbitant rates for their services, often doing better than those who hired them. Before winter in 1860, there were more than a hundred wooden buildings in Virginia City. The International Hotel was the center for social activity, but Berry's Tavern, Nick's Tavern, and other saloons did a good business. The cost for services was high. A bunk for the night was a dollar, or $4.50 a week. One lodging house, the Astor, placed 18 cots in a 20 by 12 foot room and had no trouble finding occupants. Carpenters making $6 a day didn't mind such charges. Miners, who received from $4 to $6 a day at the Ophir and Gould & Curry mines, had quarters provided at group rates, while cooks ($50 to $100 a month) slept in kitchens.

By November, Virginia City had a population of 2200, while several nearby towns had 1200 or so. The Civil War would begin and end with little disruption in the daily routine. Mississippians worked alongside New Yorkers, and no one cared. Silver, not slavery, was the issue at Washoe, and would remain so for a generation.

Some of the miners made fortunes; most did not. The real winner was the city of San Francisco, whose leaders financed the mines, lent money to operators at high rates, and sold them lumber, foodstuffs, mine equipment, and other provisions, all of which yielded good profits. Lawyers did well by filing claims and defending them in court. In 1860, there were more than 50 lawyers in Virginia City prepared to litigate. By 1863, the city had a population of less than 10,000, of whom 215 were lawyers. As one miner put it, "I made a small fortune with pick and shovel. My damn San Francisco lawyer made a bigger one with his quill and ledger."

In order to regularize trading in mining securities, the San Francisco Stock and Exchange Board was organized in 1862. Patterned after the NYS&EB, it held two auctions a day, with brokers trading among themselves between calls. It was packed day and night. Howard Cobb, the leading auctioneer of the time, bought and sold more shares in terms of dollar value than any New York broker of the period. During the next 10 years, there were many sessions during which volume in San Francisco exceeded that in New York. At a time when New York was the scene of a gold mania, San Francisco was the silver capital of America.

Almarin Paul, who arrived in Washoe in 1860, was by then a legend. One of the few men in the area with an academic knowledge of geology, he watched the miners trying to pan for silver as they might for gold and knew they would find little that way. Paul believed that deep mines, not the shallow ones then being dug, would be needed. He erected a large mill in Gold Canyon, bringing machinery from San Francisco at $400 a ton and lumber at $300 per thousand feet. In 1861, he constructed a second mill, and both were profitable. By 1870, mills costing more than $10 million had been constructed, and the deeper they went, the more silver they found.

They also found heat. Temperatures increased three degrees for each hundred feet, and miners were working in 100-degree heat. Ice and snow were brought down from the nearby mountains and sent into the shafts to cool the workers. In 1877, the Consolidated Virginia alone purchased 3.4 million pounds of ice, setting up "ice rooms" beneath the surface, where miners rested between 15 minute shifts. But even this was only a palliative. That year, at a cost of more than $2.2 million, some of the operators banded together to erect a 25-mile pipeline from the mountains to the mines to bring ice water to the miners. By late 1878, some shafts were more than 3000 feet deep, and miners found water at a temperature of 180 degrees. Several miners were scalded to death by the superheated water. Soon after, former President Grant visited the mines and went down one of the shafts. "That's as close to hell as I ever want to get," he remarked.

Getting water out of the mines was another problem. At one point, the Ophir was closed for two years before the water could be removed. Huge Hale & Norcross and Savage pumps, some capable of removing 640 gallons a minute, were brought to Comstock at great cost. These were the largest to be had, but they could not cope with the rushing underground springs. Nor could huge fans and air pumps bring sufficient fresh air to the miners. Mules—called Washao canaries—balked at going underground, and some had to be killed to prevent them from stampeding 2000 feet below the surface.

Engineer-businessman-promoter Adolph Sutro thought he could conquer all of these drawbacks. He proposed to construct a four-mile tunnel through Mt. Davidson, which would drain millions of gallons of water, ventilate the mines, and in the process uncover new veins. It seemed prudent and brilliant, and the Nevada legislature gave its approval to the scheme in 1865. The Sutro Tunnel Company was formed soon after. According to the terms, each mine would ante $2 per ton for all ore brought to the surface as payment for Sutro Tunnel's services, and an additional 25 cents per ton for ore taken through the tunnel.

But before anything could be done, the act was declared invalid by the courts, and Sutro had to go to Washington to seek aid. With the help of San Francisco bankers—led by William Chapman Ralston—who had major interests in the mines, Sutro lobbied through Congress a measure to assist his company. It was signed into law by President Andrew Johnson in 1866. Next, Sutro set out to collect the funds—between $1 million and $4 million—he thought would be needed for construction.

Sutro was able to raise $600,000 in Europe, and eastern bankers, including August Belmont, assured him they could get the rest. Little was done on this front, however, and Sutro went back to Europe to see if he could sell other investors there on the tunnel. Mark Twain, who was in the mining area, reported on Sutro's return to America in the *Alta Californian:*

> Mr. A. Sutro of the great Sutro Tunnel scheme arrived yesterday on the *Russia*. He brought his tunnel back with him. He failed to sell it to the Europeans. They said it was a good tunnel, but they would look around a little before purchasing; if they could not find a tunnel to suit them nearer at home they would call again.

Sutro gradually obtained enough money to start construction in 1869, and the work continued for 10 years, with many interruptions. When completed in 1879, it was hailed as one of the great construction feats of all time. New York and London investors were excited, expecting instant profits, and the share price of Sutro Tunnel rose. But the bonanza days were over by then, and Sutro realized the tunnel could never be profitable without a major new ore discovery, which was unlikely at that stage. So he rushed to New York to sell his shares before others learned of this. He began selling when Sutro Tunnel was at $6.60; by the time he was finished it was at 6 cents. Sutro did manage to show a profit of $900,000 on his small investment, but most of the others were wiped out. McCalmont & Brothers, a London establishment, closed its books on the deal with a loss of $755,000. Later on, an American investor wrote, "Mr. Sutro has accumulated a large fortune, a very large portion of which came out of me."

Large corporations, not the lone prospectors of legend, became the rule in the mining camps. The Black Hills Placer Company, a $10 million concern, was a major force in Deadwood in the 1880s. Flush with success in silver, George Hearst became a big player in the gold fields there. In 1878, he organized Homestake Mining, which erected a mill in Lead City, the largest in the territory. Homestake still exists, one of the very few mining concerns that survived the silver and gold rushes.

The mining boom in Washoe was over by the 1880s. During the previous three decades, scores of miners made millions, but most lost all they earned. Only a handful, like Hearst, went on to greater things. Some had greatness thrust upon them. John Mackay was one of these. Dublin-born, he arrived in Virginia City in 1859 and made $5 million from his ownership shares in the Kentuck Mine, a seemingly worthless operation he nursed back to health. He did the same with several other mines, leaving Washoe a multimillionaire. He relocated to San Francisco and organized the Postal Telegraph Company in the early twentieth century. This rival to Western Union helped lay the Pacific cable and for a while was a major force in telecommunications. Mackay represented the United States at the coronation of Tzar Alexander III and even helped one of his former employees, "Gentleman Jim" Corbett, to become world heavyweight boxing champion. At the time of his death, Mackay was worth between $20 and $30 million. But his real claim to fame came through his daughter, Ellen, who married songwriter Irving Berlin over her father's objections.

Nevada was established by silver, and the territory became a state in 1864. But the real winner in the silver bonanza was California, whose leaders now entertained visions of becoming the New York of the Pacific. That city dominated Nevada, providing all of the state's U.S. Senators from the time of statehood to 1903. It was not the first time that wealth was amassed by people far from the scene, and they were prepared to venture still further. By the time Nevada achieved statehood, a yet greater engineering effort had been mounted, that of completing transcontinental rail lines from the Pacific to the Mississippi.

CHAPTER *14*

The Impact of the
Transcontinentals

ARREN Harding, who occupied the White House from 1921 to 1923, was born on a farm in Caledonia, Ohio, in 1865. He was the last President to be born during or before the Civil War. Consider the changes witnessed by a person born in the same year who lived to see Harding's accession to the Presidency.

Outside of home remedies, medicine was almost unknown in towns like Caledonia. Hospitals were few, and most small towns lacked them. Besides, more often than not, they were places one went to die, not to be cured. Mortality rates were not calculated in most parts of the country, but in Massachusetts from 1865 to 1869, there were 146 deaths per 1000 live births. It was a world without telephones, electric lights, typewriters, or cameras, not to mention automobiles or subways. The elevator had been invented just before the war, but few were in operation. There were no concrete sidewalks. Few houses had indoor plumbing; Harding's wasn't one of them.

Most goods consumed by Americans of this period were produced locally. Department stores and mail order houses were in the future. Itinerant peddlers were quite common. The small factories turning out consumer goods would sell them to commission agents, who would travel from one dry goods store to another, taking orders and then shipping the wares by rail. It was an agrarian country, very much in the Jeffersonian mold. There were some 35 million Americans, 27 million of whom lived in areas the Census Bureau identified as rural. There were 3.5 million more Americans in such places in 1870 than in 1860, and only 2.7 million more urban dwellers. Fewer than 1.5 million lived in cities with populations of more than a million, and more than 4 million in towns of less than 25,000. It was a country of farmers and those who worked to serve their needs. It also was Jeffersonian America triumphant.

All of this would change, and the agency of change was the railroad. Already the nation's major industry, it began to serve agrarian America. This was a time when the sound of a railroad whistle in the night was romantic. The railroad was glamorous and magical to that generation, just as the airplane would be to a later one and space travel is today. It was to take people from farms like those in Caledonia to large cities—Cincinnati, Columbus, even Chicago and New York—places the young Harding read about but never expected to see.

Railroaders provided local businessmen, and especially farmers, with the opportunity to sell their goods in many markets. The farmer might not be able to go to the cities, but in time, cities could come to the farmer via the Sears Roebuck and Montgomery Ward mail order catalogues, and the salesmen from McCormick, Deere, and Case, who were eager to sell their farm implements. The same railroad that carried grain to market also transported meat from the Midwest to eastern markets in refrigerated cars. So it was for a wide variety of products, from beer to shoes to machine tools. In time, the creation of the railroad network would prompt many businesses to look beyond local markets to regional and even national customers. With the costs of transportation and communication lowered so sharply, customer bases expanded.

Wealth in the Western Rails

Transportation is a key factor in all wars, but during the Civil War, the situation was complicated by needs that had little to do with the conflict. While new lines were created in the Northeast and old ones enlarged and improved, a major construction effort began in the drive to the Far West, where inhabitants' lives hardly had been touched by the war.

Before the war, large railroads had begun absorbing smaller ones, and this continued during and after the war, often with government urging. The Pennsylvania, for example, acquired the Pittsburgh, Fort Wayne and Chicago, which took the line into Chicago. It obtained the Marietta & Cincinnati, which formed a link to Cincinnati. The Springfield, Mt. Vernon & Pittsburgh took the Pennsylvania into Columbus. By 1861, there was scarcely an important section of southern Ohio, Indiana, or Illinois that was more than a short distance from a line in which the Pennsylvania had an interest or was about to acquire one. Shortly after the end of the war, Commodore Cornelius Vanderbilt, who had taken control of the New York Central from Erastus Corning, united the many small lines of upper New York State with his New York & Harlem Railroad. He also purchased the Lake Shore & Michigan Southern which had access to Chicago as well.

The Atlantic and Great Western was constructed during the war. Running from Dayton, Ohio, to Salamanca, New York, it was the longest line erected in this period. With the Erie, it linked New York to St. Louis, providing New York with the first track all the way to the Mississippi. The Philadelphia & Erie, completed in 1864, connected the new oil fields of western Pennsylvania to Philadelphia.

All of these railroads, and many others, prospered during the war. In addition, construction in the cities accelerated. According to the *Chicago Tribune* of October 8, 1863, "On every street and avenue, one sees new buildings going up, immense stone, brick, and iron buildings, blocks, marble palaces and new residences; everywhere the grading of streets, the building of sewers, the laying of water and gas pipes are all in progress at the same time."

As had been the case with the earliest railroads, and before them the canals and turnpikes, internal improvements increased the value of the land through which they passed, which in turn provided goods for the railroad to carry. Just before the Civil War, English observer James Sterling noted:

> The prairies absolutely make their own railways without cost to anyone. The development of the country by the means of a railway is such that what was yesterday a wasteland is today a valuable district. There is thus action and reaction: the railway improves the land; the improvements pay for the railway.

The eastern and southern canals and railroads were supported by land companies whose holdings would increase in value given better transportation. Leaders at such companies lobbied for internal improvements, purchased stocks and bonds in the companies that would provide them, helped settlers who wanted to farm the areas, and in other ways acted to achieve their goal of great wealth.

Any western railroad would lack such sponsorship, as Asa Whitney understood. A prosperous merchant who had taken to railroading in the 1830s, Whitney offered in the 1840s "to give my country this great thoroughfare for all nations without the cost of one dollar." In 1844, he proposed to Congress that it charter a railroad from Lake Michigan to Oregon and finance it through the sale of public lands along the right of way. The line would cost approximately $65 million to build, which would be raised from the land sales and charges to users. Whitney would own and manage the railroad until it earned back the costs, whereupon he would turn it over to the federal government. He would receive compensation from unsold land after all costs had been paid. Whitney got nowhere with his plan, but the debate regarding a transcontinental railroad had begun.

During the 1850s, the issue of a railroad from the Midwest or South to California was a subject of heated political debate as both sections jockeyed to defend their interests. Now that the South was out of the running, and it was clear that the road would go from the Midwest to California, the question was which city would be the eastern terminus. Then, too, convincing political leaders in the East of the priorities for such lines in time of war was a problem.

There was no need to convince the Lincoln Administration of the need for such a project. While most of the 1860 Republican party platform dealt with issues originating out of the debate on slavery in the territories, there was this as well:

> . . . That a railroad to the Pacific Ocean is imperatively demanded by the interests of the whole country; that the federal government ought to render immediate and efficient aid in its construction; and that, as preliminary thereto, a daily overland mail should be promptly established.

Another section of the platform called for "the passage by Congress of the complete and satisfactory homestead measure, which has already passed the House." There was nothing novel about this. Ever since passage of the Land Ordinance of 1785 and the Land Act of 1796, the government had provided assistance for settlers in the form of low-priced land. Other acts followed with regularity, such as the Preemption Act of 1841, which permitted would-be settlers to purchase up to 160 acres for a minimum price of $1.25 per acre. The construction of the railroad and the provision of land were companion pieces. The land would enable eastern free farmers to settle the West with government assistance, and the railroads would provide them with a means of getting their crops to market.

One of the first major pieces of legislation passed by the Civil War Congress was The Homestead Act of 1862, which entitled any citizen over the age of 21 to 160 acres of the public domain by settling on it for five years. Lincoln also signed the Morrill Act, which granted each state that had not seceded 30,000 acres of land for each senator and representative for the purpose of endowing at least one agricultural college. In his first annual message to Congress, Lincoln expressed the philosophy that informed such action, and indicated he considered himself clearly in the Jeffersonian tradition. "Capital is only the fruit of labor, and could not have existed if labor had not first existed. Labor is the superior of capital and deserves much higher consideration." Lincoln spoke of

> Men with their families, wives, sons, and daughters, who work for themselves on their farms, in their houses, and in their shops, taking the whole product to themselves . . . asking no favor of capital on the one hand not of hired laborers or slaves on the other. . . . The prudent, penniless beginning in the world who labors for wages while, saves a surplus with which to buy tools or land for himself . . . and at length hires another new worker to help him. This is the just and generous and prosperous system, which opens the way to all. No men living are worthier to be trusted than those who toil up from poverty. Let them beware of surrendering a political power which they already possess, and which if surrendered will surely be used to close the door of advancement, and to fix new disabilities and burdens upon them till all of liberty shall be lost.

Theodore Dehone Judah, the guiding force in what was to become the Union Pacific, the first transcontinental railroad, had spent the 1840s and early 1850s working on eastern railroads, and in 1854, he was hired as chief engineer for a 21-mile railroad to run from Sacramento to the mines in the Sierra Nevada foothills. Working at a furious pace, Judah surveyed the land, hired crews, purchased supplies, and had the railroad up and running by February 1855. Judah next explored the possibilities of a wagon road to Washoe, and in the process he became interested in a railroad across the mountains and into Washoe—and then on to the Mississippi. There was some interest in his idea, and in September 1859, he appeared at a Pacific Railroad convention in San Francisco. Judah then traveled to Washington to lobby for the proposal. Next, he went to San Francisco and attempted to raise money for his scheme, which he called the Central Pacific Railroad of California. When he was unable to obtain the necessary funds, Judah moved on to Sacramento in 1861, where he located backers in the form of wholesale grocer Leland Stanford, dry goods merchant Charles Crocker, and Mark Hopkins and Collis P. Huntington, partners in a hardware store. Understanding by then that unless he could convince them of the immediate return they would have on their investments, they would not be interested, Judah spoke not of transcontinentals but instead of the railroad to Washoe. With this, he won their support and began his survey. Soon afterward, construction began in Sacramento. Needing more financing, Judah returned to Washington seeking support for his Pacific Railroad bill. With the coming of war in April, Congress was more amenable. When Lincoln signed the measure on July 1, Judah had the needed backing.

The act provided for not one, but two companies to construct a line between the Pacific coast and the Missouri River. In addition, there would be a telegraph line along the route. The second company, the Union Pacific, was incorporated with an authorized capital of $100 million. The Central Pacific was to build a line within California's boundary and then head east. The Union Pacific would build from Omaha, Nebraska, and then head west. The lines would be funded by government loans in the form of 5 percent bonds in amounts ranging from $16,000 per mile in areas where the terrain was flat, to $48,000 per mile for lines in the mountains, to $32,000 per mile for sections in between. The companies would be given land grants of ten alternate sections per mile. Railroads received generous subsidies and land grants, in return for which the government received preferential rates. In this way, land development, which was a major spur for canals and the eastern railroads, was put in place. Without transportation, the western lands were of little value. Given the railroad and an active colonization effort, the lands could be very valuable indeed. The funds would not be made available until the first 40 miles of track were laid. Finally, the act did not specify just how many miles each company would construct, and this was done deliberately, as a spur to each. In time, the two lines would meet, and the one that constructed the most miles would receive the greater amount of money.

Work in Omaha began on December 2, 1863, but then things stalled, even though contracts had been let to construction companies. Peter Dey, chief engineer, did not like the way the business was being managed. He had estimated the costs of the first 100 miles to be $30,000 per mile, and the contract was for $60,000. Dey resigned on December 7, 1864, writing to Union Pacific President John Dix, "I do not approve of the contract for building the first hundred miles from Omaha west, and I do not care to have my name so connected with the railroad that I shall appear to endorse the contract." Dey was replaced by Grenville Dodge, who, as it turned out, proved a superb organizer and engineer.

Work began in California on January 8, 1863, and dissension immediately broke out between Judah and his partners regarding the nature of the construction. For Judah, quality was important as well as speed; Huntington and the others cared mainly about speed. On this issue, the partnership dissolved, with Judah agreeing to be bought out for $100,000, and he was succeeded as chief engineer by Samuel Montague. Once again Judah traveled east, hoping to find financial backing for a plan to mount a hostile takeover and oust the Huntington group. But he died of yellow fever shortly after arriving in New York.

The building of the transcontinental is one of the great stories of American engineering and business. The construction was frantic and was followed closely in the press as though it were an athletic event. Hostile Indians, harsh weather, difficult terrain, and labor shortages: were all surmounted, and toward the end of the project, the two companies were laying two miles per day. On May 10, 1869, the two lines celebrated their coming together at Promontory Point, Utah, with Leland Stanford driving the last spike, which was made of California gold. Between 1862 and 1871, more than 125 million acres were granted to assist in construction. In the process these railroads, and those in other parts of the country, started to transform the tenor of American life. They would add to the wealth of a wide variety of economic interests. But while the railroads, for the most part, did quite well financially (although almost all suffered bankruptcy at one time or another in the late nineteenth century and some were put out of business), the construction companies made immense profits (Dey was right about that contract).

Unsurprisingly, the enormous amounts of money and power involved with railroad construction created opportunities for corruption. The actual building cost for the Central Pacific was $58 million, but the construction companies, including Charles Crocker & Co., controlled by the four partners, received $120 million. Later it was discovered that much of the work was shoddy, requiring extremely costly renovations. An even more scandalous situation existed at the Union Pacific, whose prime builder was Credit Mobilier, which was ruled by Thomas Durant, the Union Pacific vice president. Durant, who in time bowed to a rival group, planned to give outpriced contracts to Credit Mobilier, which was controlled by prominent owners of Union Pacific stock. What they would lose in Union Pacific earnings they would more than make up in dividends from Credit Mobilier. The net proceeds from the government came to $50.9 million. Credit Mobilier received stock, bonds, and land grants, along with $23 million in cash, for a profit of 48 percent on capital. The company's agent, Congressman Oakes Ames, was provided with 343 shares of company stock to be distributed among Congressmen where it would "do the most good." A subsequent investigation revealed the existence of bipartisan corruption, and the abuse reached to Vice President Schuyler Colfax.

Railroads would enlarge the markets for Jefferson's farmers and add to their prosperity. But at the same time, the farmers were outraged by rates. The railroaders responded that rates had to be in line with costs and that their profits were hardly exorbitant. Complaints from shippers led to the creation of the ICC in 1887, which forbade collusion. In themselves, the railroads would not have sufficed for farmers and processors of farm goods who wanted to send perishables to market. They needed another technological advance: refrigeration. The development of refrigeration is a classic account of how a merchant benefitted from taking products where they were plentiful to areas where they were in short supply, or to be more precise, nonexistent.

Selling Ice

A contemporary of Francis Cabot Lowell, Frederic Tudor was born into a patrician Boston family in 1783. His father had been George Washington's judge advocate general during the Revolution. For a while, he too seemed destined for a career in law, but soon Tudor found other, more commercial interests. He apprenticed himself to a dry goods merchant in order to learn the business, and perhaps his exposure to spices and condiments led him to consider food preservation. In 1805, Tudor and his brother William speculated on the viability of cutting ice from nearby Fresh Pond in winter and then taking it to southern ports where it could be sold at high prices. Tudor learned of an American captain who had taken ice from Norway to London. In addition, he discovered that others had had the same idea. "Ice-creams were carried to Trinidad by the English when they were in possession of that island in pots packed with sand from Europe," he wrote to a friend. Writing to a cousin, Tudor said, "The idea of carrying ice to tropical climates will at first no doubt startle and astonish you, but when you take into consideration the following circumstances, I think you will cease to doubt the practicality of the thing and adopt the proposal I shall presently make to you."

With the encouragement and financial support of his cousin, James Savage, Tudor invested $10,000 in a shipment of 130 tons of ice to Martinique. The event was noted in a local newspaper. "No joke. A vessel has cleared the Customs House for Martinique with a cargo of ice. We hope this will not prove a slippery speculation." But the ice arrived safely, and was deposited in an insulated ice house Tudor had contracted for before the ship left port. Tudor went to the market to display some of his wares to the astounded natives, most of whom had never seen ice. He took some orders, one of which was for 40 pounds, which sold for $300. There were other sales, but the going was difficult. After six months, what remained of Tudor's shipment had melted, and he had a loss of $4000. There were more shipments, more partial successes, and then in 1807 — when President Jefferson imposed an embargo to keep the United States out of Europe's wars—the business came to an end. Tudor returned to Boston, where he learned his father had lost his fortune. Unable to pay his creditors, Tudor narrowly escaped debtors' prison and remained on his family's farm for the duration of the embargo. He then went to Cuba and successfully won a monopoly on the ice trade to that island. Before he could make his first voyage, however, the War of 1812 intervened, and once more Tudor returned to the farm.

All of this gave him time to think. Why was that first voyage not more successful? Tudor concluded that before he could make sales, he would have to educate potential customers on the benefits of ice. In addition, he thought that while the Caribbean islands could become a good market, even better sales might be realized among wealthy southerners, some of whom had experience with ice on their trips to the North. He opened small shops there where he sold iced drinks at low prices to develop a market. Selling ice for 10 cents a pound, when there were 16 glasses to a gallon, Tudor calculated the iced drinks would cost no more than half a cent each. Tudor planned to sign a contract with a prominent bar keeper who would be provided with free ice.

> The object is to make the whole population use cold drinks instead of warm or tepid and it will be affected in the course of three years. A single conspicuous bar keeper having one of the jars and selling steadily has liquors all cold without an increase in price, [would] render it absolutely necessary that the others come into it or lose their customers—they are compelled to do what they could in no other way be induced to undertake.

Business was improving, but Tudor was still struggling to make ends meet. In addition, he was now facing competition. The prospect of selling ice that cost 30 cents a ton to cut, and carrying it a thousand miles and to sell for 10 cents a pound was appealing. Tudor tried to lower his costs and at the same time improve his product. The ice was difficult to cut and the pieces were irregular in shape, prompting sea captains to complain that the shifting cargoes were harming their ships. Then there was the problem of melting. If he could resolve these problems, his costs would decline, his profits would rise, and his competitors would leave the business.

In the mid-1820s, Tudor ran into Nathaniel Jarvis Wyeth, who owned a hotel with an ice house. Wyeth had an interest in ice harvesting and some mechanical skills. In 1825, he invented and patented an ice cutter whose revolving blades could sweep across the surface of a frozen pond, cutting deep, regular grooves in a checkerboard pattern. Then the blocks of ice could be taken to the ships and stored tightly in the holds so they would not slip and slide, ending the possibility of damage. Tudor obtained exclusive rights to the device and named Wyeth manager of his ice company. At the same time, he experimented with insulated ice houses, and finally had some success.

The Wyeth harvester and the insulated ice houses enabled Tudor to undersell his competitors and drive them out of the business. But then some of them infringed the patent and competition revived, with prices falling steadily as sales increased. Boston shipped 1200 tons of ice in 1816, and the figure rose to 4000 tons in 1826 and 65,000 tons in 1846. Meanwhile, Tudor turned to other pursuits, among them coal mining and an attempt to create the first American amusement park. He tried coffee importing, just as the market turned downward. He lost more than $200,000 on this venture, which practically wiped him out.

All the while, the demand for ice continued to increase. Seeking new markets, Tudor sent a ship with 180 tons of ice to Calcutta, where he erected an ice house and made and sold small refrigerators to the English stationed there. Encouraged, he started to export fruits and dairy products as well. In 1841, to further effect economies, Wyeth persuaded the legislature to charter a railroad to run between Fresh Pond and the dock at Charlestown, known as the Charlestown Branch Railroad. Later, Tudor purchased extensive rights to buy ice on Walden Pond, near which Henry Thoreau lived, and his new Fitchburg Railroad absorbed the Charlestown Branch. To Thoreau, the railroad was the symbol of a changing world (and not for the better). In *Walden*, he wrote of the train whistle in the night, the new importance of time in a period when people really didn't know how to occupy themselves effectively. "The sweltering inhabitants of Charlestown and New Orleans. Of Madras and Bombay and Calcutta, drink at my well," he wrote. "The pure Walden water is mingled with the sacred water of the Ganges."

In 1856, the year Wyeth died, Boston exported 146,000 tons of ice around the world. Tudor ice sold in China and the Philippines. Refrigeration was altering the way people lived in America. In 1860, as war clouds appeared in the South, New Orleans imported 24,000 tons of ice; in 1837, the imports had been a mere 375 tons. As important as ice was as a product, however, it was to prove even more significant, as, together with the railroad, it enabled farmers and processors of farm goods to conquer new markets.

The Revolution in Meatpacking

Americans always were a meat-eating people. While other countries had grain staples, such as wheat and rice, Americans ate enormous quantities of meat. In the 1850s, an Irish immigrant to New York wrote to his parents that he ate meat twice a week. His wife, seeing the letter, asked why he didn't tell the truth: that he had meat at every meal— breakfast, lunch, and supper. "They would never believe me," he replied.

American meat in that period, as earlier, came from cattle and pigs raised locally. Butchery was a simple enough proposition. The butcher would raise or purchase a steer or pig, carve it up, and then sell the parts for more than the price of the whole. Profits depended on a number of variables, the most important being the cost of the animal, the speed with which it was processed, the amount of waste, pricing, and marketing. The meat was sold from butcher shops and meat wagons that went door to door. In both instances, the butcher would try to keep the meat on ice so that his offerings would remain fresh.

This changed somewhat with the coming of the railroad. Butchers in areas where farm animals were plentiful still relied on local supplies. The railroads made it possible to purchase cattle raised a distance from the eastern cities, especially the Midwest, where they were plentiful and inexpensive. The problem lay in transportation. Before the Civil War, the cattle would be loaded into railroad cars and then sent on to the cities, where they would be unloaded and moved to the central meat packing plants that recently had come into existence, slaughtered, dressed, and from there delivered to the butchers. Everyone involved in the business realized that this process was uneconomical. The butchers and their customers did not want the entire animal, just the meat, and so the transport of live animals was wasteful. Also, the animals lost weight en route, and some of them died. It would make more sense—and return higher profits—if the animals could be slaughtered in the Midwest, dressed there, and then sent east. The problem was how to keep the meat fresh, and the answer was refrigeration.

Shippers started experimenting with refrigeration during the Civil War, but nothing came of it. In 1871, G. H. Hammond, a Chicago butcher, used freight cars in which the meat was kept on ice, with poor results. Three years later, another Chicago firm, Morris & Company, tried out air-cooled freight cars that could be used only in the dead of winter. Morris hung carcasses on frames built within the cars, and through slits in the sides, cold winter air circulated and kept the meat cool—some of the time.

Another butcher, Gustavus Swift, moved to Chicago in 1875 from Sandwich, Massachusetts on Cape Cod because he realized the attractiveness of the inexpensive meat available there. In addition, Swift had a mania for efficiency, calculating that if he could improve meat packing methods even slightly, profit margins would rise dramatically. He purchased a slaughterhouse and formed partnerships with several New England butchers, setting out to rectify the problems of earlier methods of shipment. Initially, he tried the Morris approach, but quickly recognized its drawbacks. Then Swift experimented with mechanical refrigeration, with disappointing results. Together with engineer Andrew Chase, he developed the first workable insulated car. Ice would be packed in compartments under the car's roof, with a system of pipes drawing off the water when the ice melted. Swift arranged for ice depots along the railroad's route so the compartments could be refilled when needed. The next difficulty was distribution, which he took care of by constructing cold storage buildings at the rail terminals. Carts would carry the meat to butchers who had signed up with Swift.

Interested in better methods of processing, Swift was the first to use overhead conveyers to "disassemble" the carcass, which would be hung on a moving belt that took it from butcher to butcher, each assigned a specific task. The combination of the division of labor and the conveyor belts trimmed labor time, and so increased profits. Swift also was concerned with the disposal of those parts of the animal that were not fit for human consumption. At the time, only the meat and hides were salable; the head, feet, liver, tongue, heart, and tripe were sold separately at giveaway prices and the fat was thrown away. Swift searched for uses for these waste products. First came oleomargarine, followed by glue, beef extract, soap, fertilizers, and later, pharmaceuticals. Shinbones were employed in making knife handles. The saying at Swift was, "We use all of the hog but the squeal."

Railroads and Wealth from Beer

The railroads affected virtually every agricultural product, and their derivatives, by providing them with larger markets, which in turn led to greater profits. Brewers, who—prior to the coming of railroads—were limited to local markets, could now consider larger ones. This was particularly true of those German-American brewers in the Midwest, St. Louis and Milwaukee in particular, who wanted to send their beers to the hotter parts of the country, where sales were bound to be good. Before the coming of railroads, they had to use water transport to get their products to distant customers. The midwestern brewers would send ice-packed barrels by river boat to New Orleans, where they would be deposited in ice houses and later transshipped via the Gulf of Mexico to Galveston. The Missouri, Kansas and Texas, along with the Texas Central, provided an alternative link—from St. Louis to Dallas and Houston, and from there to San Antonio, and ultimately to Galveston. Other railroads followed. After some time in a local ice house, the beer would be sent to the interior. Most of the ice available in New Orleans came from Boston, where it was cut from nearby ponds, sent by rail to the port, loaded on ships, and moved down the coast and into the gulf to New Orleans. This method clearly was uneconomical; not only were the costs high, but the chances of beer spoilage were substantial.

The railroad changed all of this and the numbers illustrate the story best. In 1860, the nation had more than 30,000 miles of track. By 1870, the mileage had grown to 53,000; in 1880, to 93,000; in 1890, to 167,000; and at the turn of the century, 193,000. The rate of growth had slowed by 1900, but mileage continued to expand into the twentieth century, doubling by 1920.

Prior to the rapid expansion of the railroad, St. Louis appeared destined to become the premier city of the heartland, due to its location on the Mississippi River and the importance of that waterway. America's future lay in the Midwest, it was believed, and the traffic there would be from north to south. In the middle of it all was St. Louis. That the city would not have so central a position in the railroad age was obvious, though, because economic and political requirements dictated a network whose major lines would generally run from east to west. Yet St. Louis did entertain hopes of achieving a dominant position in the railway age, with the city fathers encouraging several lines to construct terminals there. Some of them did. As its name indicates, the pre-Civil War Pacific Railroad Company, headquartered in St. Louis, aspired to become the first railway to run from the Mississippi to the west coast. While this was not to be, St. Louis did become a major rail hub, second in the Midwest only to Chicago. The coming of the railroad, which was both faster and more predictable than river boats and coaches, meant that brewers might hope to ship their wares more quickly to distant markets.

By 1870, Adolphus Busch, head of the Anheuser-Busch Company, was completing his new brew house complex and knew he would have more capacity than he needed, even given the expansion of St. Louis. He also could observe construction of the Eads Bridge across the Mississippi River, which would ease east-west commerce. In 1874, St. Louis' businesses shipped 307,878 tons of goods to the West. In 1880, the figure came to 818,182, a rise of 166 percent, while total St. Louis trade rose by 85 percent. More significant, the bridge and railroads meant the city's business interests could look to both the east and west for customers and suppliers. As one contemporary put it, "a much larger traffic passes over the great bridge than is transported on the river."

Busch was one of the first brewers to understand the implications of such changes, and to expand his business horizon to meet the challenges of new technological, demographic, and geographic developments. He would move to become a regional and then a national brewer. It was a daring innovation in approach. While the railroad could carry his beer to nearby cities and towns far more efficiently than could the riverboats and ferries, he had to concern himself with the difficulties as well as possibilities. What about shipping costs, the establishment of depots, dealings with agents and customers in relatively distant places? All that would present problems, but Busch could address these matters later on. At the time, the important consideration for Busch was that the opening of the Eads Bridge and the development of St. Louis' railroads meant he could contemplate enlarging his markets.

By itself, the new bridge hardly sufficed to impel expansion, since the beer had to be kept cool if it were to survive shipment. This necessitated the establishment of ice houses along the shipping routes, similar to those used by Swift, but Busch considered this unsatisfactory. Fortunately for Busch and other brewers, there were people working on the problem and solutions were soon to arrive, among them an offshoot of the work on refrigeration done by Swift.

Even before the Civil War, experiments with manufactured ice were being conducted. A Florida physician, John Gorrie, did some pioneering work in the field in the 1850s, but it was not until 1862 that a French inventor, Ferdinand Carre, was able to demonstrate a workable device. American Samuel David Lount and German scientist Franz Windhausen conducted further experiments, but progress was slow. One machine, developed by Charles Tellier, was tried by a New Orleans brewer in 1869, and a Carre machine was installed at the S. Liebmann's Son Brewery in Brooklyn the following year, but there were few other trials. "Mechanical refrigeration" machines were demonstrated at the Philadelphia World's Fair in 1876, and now the entire beer industry became entranced with the apparatus. Not until the 1880s would mechanical refrigeration become widely accepted, however.

In 1881, Anheuser-Busch installed an artificial refrigeration system at the brewery, doing so after Busch investigated several systems, studied economies, and calculated the risks and potential rewards. Busch could see that efficiency and the shortage of storage space demanded the change. Ice machines also would provide the brewery with dry rather than wet cooling, which would be uniform throughout the year and so better enable the company to maintain quality controls. Moreover, the machines would permit the company to operate without the services of a large cadre of ice haulers, and this alone might have justified the installation. In addition, the machines freed large plant areas formerly used for ice storage.

Also, like Swift, Busch sought to sell everything he could produce. This led him to become a purveyor of ice. His machines turned out more ice than was needed at the storage facilities, and he marketed the surplus, cutting his costs considerably. Some went to local businesses, but even more to the railroads for use in their refrigerator cars. Busch celebrated warm weather throughout the year: it helped the sale of his beer, and mild winters often affected the ice harvest on the lakes, ponds, and rivers near his ice-houses, so he could sell the ice at $2 to $3 a ton.

By 1876, Busch was sending his beer to Texas by railroad. "The E. Anheuser Company's Palace Refrigerator Car reached here on Tuesday evening, only four days from St. Louis," observed the *Galveston Daily News* on January 18 of that year. "It came over the St. Louis and Iron Mountain and the International and Great Northern roads. This is the quickest trip ever made through from St. Louis by any but a passenger or express car." The newspaper went on to observe, ". . . this enterprise is truly characteristic of the E. Anheuser Company Brewing Association. Having first secured beyond all cavil or question the reputation of making the best lager beer in the country, they are now determined that it shall be supplied in all its purity to their numerous customers in every city of the United States." The firm made certain all knew of the event, celebrating it with an open house. "Capt. E. E. Parker will officiate as master of ceremonies, which is equivalent to saying that the contents of that car will be freely sampled for the benefit of his thirsty friends, and perhaps a Galveston sandwich or two will be thrown in to help its flavor." Thus Texans came to drink Missouri-brewed beer, just as Bostonians were consuming meat slaughtered in Chicago, which came from animals raised in even more distant places. It was expansion such as this that made the breweries among the fastest growing and most profitable companies in the nation. By 1900 brewing had become America's fifth largest industry, with revenues of $280 million. By then, too, refrigerated freight cars made it possible for California fruit and produce to be sent to the east coast cities. Agribusiness boomed in California, with one local writer saying it was nothing less than "the gold rush relived."

Wealth from Cattle

In 1860, when there were 31.5 million Americans, the nation had 17 million head of cattle. Texas, with a population of 604,000, had more than 2.9 million head of cattle, leading all other states. The east Texas range provided cattle for other parts of the country, though in this period, most fresh meat eaten by Americans was raised locally. Cowboys would drive herds to Galveston and send them to New Orleans by ship. A few enterprising ranchers made the long trek to Chicago or California, and some provisioned Cuba with the tough longhorns. It was a good and profitable business. The cattle roamed the range freely, and then were rounded up by the cowboys, who sold them for $6 a head at the terminals.

The cattle business languished during the Civil War, as the cowboys joined the armies and the cattle were left to roam the range unmolested. This was the situation in 1866, when the cowboys returned to Texas. The range was swollen with fat, mature beeves, ready for the roundup. The oversupply of east Texas cattle meant they could be purchased at low prices. At the same time, northern prosperity resulted in a higher demand for beef. A mature steer sold for more than $85 in Massachusetts and almost $70 in New York—and $9 in Galveston. Anyone able to transport cattle from Texas to the East could make a fortune.

So thought Joseph McCoy, a Springfield, Illinois, cattle dealer, who in 1867 decided to take steers to Kansas, where they would be fattened, and then transporting them east by rail for sale. With this in mind, McCoy selected Abilene as the town. Later, he would refer to Abilene as a "small, dead place . . . of about one dozen log huts," but with plentiful water and grass for grazing. Starting in July, he set about a building program that made Abilene into the first of the cowtowns which became so familiar to readers of fiction and viewers of movies and television westerns.

For a while, McCoy was deterred by three forces. One was the Indian Wars. The second problem was the buffalo that dominated the range. With the destruction of the great buffalo herds, the way was open for cattle. The third problem was the farmers, who fought the ranchers for land. In the beginning the ranchers had the advantage, but the introduction of barbed wire in 1874 denied cattle entry to the range. In addition, the costs of transporting cattle were high, and weight loss and death in transit were major problems. These problems were resolved when Swift developed the refrigerated railroad car. This meant the steers could be slaughtered and the carcasses sent east by rail, saving space, preserving weight, and enabling the packers to make larger profits.

The combination of these factors helped change the industry's locale. In 1865, it appeared the demand for meat would benefit east Texas. Because of the circumstances just described, the range moved north and west into the Texas panhandle, Colorado, Wyoming, the Dakotas, and Montana. McCoy did not wait for all of this to fall into place. In 1869, 75,000 head were driven to town for transshipment. The following year, the number was 350,000, and it rose steadily thereafter.

McCoy's early success led other Texas drovers to take their herds to Abilene, and higher profits led to overproduction. Cattle prices now dictated production and encouraged speculation. This was fueled by reports of the riches to be reaped, many of which were churned out by publicists working for railroads hoping to profit from greater traffic. One article, "How Cattlemen Get Rich," was typical:

> A good sized steer, when it is fit for the butcher market, will bring from $45 to $60. The same animal at its birth was worth $5. He has run on the plains and cropped the grass from the public domain for four or five years, and now, with scarcely any expense to his owner, is worth $40 more than when he started on his pilgrimage. A thousand of these animals are kept nearly as cheaply as a single one, so with a thousand as a starter and with an investment of but $5,000 in the start, in four years the stock raiser has made from $40,000 to $45,000. Allow $5,000 for expenses which he has been going on and he still has $35,000 and even $45,000 for a net profit. That is all there is of the problem and that is why our cattlemen grow rich.

Many factors were ignored in such presentations. One was disease. In 1867, for example, an epidemic took the lives of tens of thousands of cattle in east Texas, and similar maladies struck with dismal regularity. Then there was the problem of gluts, which could depress cattle prices so that transport charges were higher than those fetched at markets. Bad weather, especially in the northern ranges, could kill off herds. Water shortages in the South could do similar damage. Moreover, newcomers to the range, along with investors, had to buy from old timers who knew the market and values far better than they did. Invariably, they were taken for financial rides. To be sure, there were ranchers in the late 1870s and early 1880s who made fortunes, but there were many more who lost all they had. Even so, one cannot deny the allure of the range. Theodore Roosevelt, settling in the Dakotas in 1883, said he was going there to hunt buffalo before they all disappeared, and he remained to live the life of a rancher for two years.

Roosevelt invested in land and cattle and lost about $25,000. Twenty years later, he visited the Dakotas again, this time as President. Looking about him, Roosevelt remarked, "Here, the romance of my life began."

Ranching became the glamour industry of 1883, as radio and motion pictures would be in the 1920s and computers and electronics in the 1960s. Most of the investments were partnerships, so no ranch was listed on the eastern securities exchanges. Speculators and investors who had never been west of Cleveland spoke knowingly of ranching, their conversations studded with "facts" gleaned from reports written by analysts who themselves might never have gone that far.

Such arrangements rarely worked out well. The investors knew little of the cattle business or the Plains and had to trust cattlemen to serve as their agents. The latter, realizing they were dealing with novices, milked them for what they could get. "When we agreed to associate, you said we could establish a company with $40,000," wrote James Gardner, an Albany, New York, businessman to his Wyoming cattleman partner, George McClellan, in 1881. "You now have expended almost $48,000, and still you have the bravery to tell me the end is not in sight." McClellan sent assurances all would turn out well, asked for more money, and got it. The partnership failed, as did most of them, to be replaced by syndicates. By the 1880s, the cattle industry was big business, with million-dollar ranches not the least unusual. It followed the same pattern as mining. In the beginning there was the lone gambler. But ultimately, leadership fell to the large companies.

The further one got from the Plains, the fewer and less troublesome seemed the problems involved. If the eastern gentry purchased participations in syndicates, wealthy United Kingdom bankers and investors eagerly organized them, and poured money earned from textile ventures in India into the American ranches. It seemed sensible. All they had to do was look at the foreign trade figures. In 1873, the United States sent $71 million in beef overseas, along with thousands of head of cattle. Meat exports topped $100 million in 1877, $32 million more than the value of American wheat and flour exports there. Between 1877 and 1879, cattle shipments increased threefold, with 60 percent going to the British Isles. American beef was becoming a major factor in foreign trade, and the English and Scots wanted to profit from it.

Especially the Scots. William Menzies, an Edinburgh lawyer and financier, visited America in 1864, 1867, and 1872, and was impressed with what he saw. In 1883, Menzies gathered nine of his associates and organized the Scottish-American Investment Company, capitalized at 1 million pounds. Scottish-American purchased shares in 11 midwestern and western railroads, and by the 1880s, was involved with ranches. Other companies followed, and the Scottish financial invasion of the Plains was underway. By 1880, four Edinburgh trusts had some 2.2 million pounds invested in American securities, while a Dundee-based trust provided an additional 2 million pounds.

These early syndicates did well and encouraged others to enter the field. All the reports were encouraging. The Earl of Airlie, chairman of the Scottish-American Mortgage Company, visited America in 1880 and the following year told his stockbroker, "It is not uncommon for a cattle breeder to clear 80 or even 100 percent a year on his capital." Scottish-American organized the Prairie Cattle Company that year, capitalizing it at 200,000 pounds. The Texas Land and Cattle Company was organized in Dundee in 1881 to take over the assets of the Matador Cattle Company, a Texas ranch. Matador had been valued by its owners as worth between $1.2 and $1.3 million. They received a substantial premium from English and Scots investors. Seeing this, other ranchers tried to sell to the foreigners, and succeeded.

Now informal exchanges appeared, the most important being in Cheyenne, Wyoming. The investment mania was contagious, for the profits were there, as were the dividends. Prairie paid a 20½ percent dividend in 1883, and 10 percent in 1884 and 1885. Western Land's dividends in these years were 15 percent, 15 percent, and 10 percent. Swan, one of the largest ranches, paid 9 percent, 10 percent, and 6 percent. Funds could be borrowed at 4½ percent in Scotland. The arithmetic was appealing.

This rush of investment from abroad troubled some Americans, who feared foreigners soon would control the cattle industry and own most of the Plains. President Chester Arthur agreed that foreign holdings should be limited. In 1884, Secretary of the Interior Samuel Kirkwood of Iowa said, "It is contrary to national policy, and would be antagonistic to the sentiments of the country, to permit the appropriation of public lands in large quantities, by individuals or corporations, whether native or foreign." Running for the Presidency that year, Republican James G. Blaine had as his slogan "America for Americans," and Democrat Grover Cleveland promised action to end "appropriation" of American resources by foreigners, while the Democratic platform accused the Republicans of having "given away the people's heritage till now a few railroads, and nonresident aliens, individual and corporate, possess a larger area than that of all our farms between the two seas."

Cleveland won the election and delivered on his promises. He ordered ranchers to remove their cattle from Indian and government land. This meant relocation to overgrazed ranges, where thousands of head died. It was the beginning of the end for the romantic visions of raising cattle.

Adding to the problems was a new outbreak of tick disease, which appeared in 1885 in Kansas. To overproduction, disease, and these political problems were added demands on the part of cowboys for higher wages. Rustling increased when they were not granted, and profits sank.

By autumn of 1886, beef prices had fallen to new lows. Hard economic times cut back on demand. In 1882, steers had sold for $9 a hundredweight; four years later, the price had gone to $1.80. Then came what was purported to be the final blow. Snow fell on the Plains in October and continued into November. The freezing weather took its toll. Some ranchers told reporters of seeing cattle struggling along on stumps of legs, the hooves having frozen and snapped off. One put his thought down in verse:

I may not see a hundred
Before I see the Styx,
But coal or ember, I'll remember
Eighteen-eighty six.
The stiff heaps in the coulee,
The dead eyes in the camp,
And the wind about, blowing fortunes out
As a woman blows out a lamp.

Now the foreign investors were told of the destruction of their herds. Headlines spoke of the hundreds of thousands of cattle lying dead on the Plains.

Had it really happened? Later, it would be learned that the figures were inflated. American agents sold foreigners herds that didn't exist, or were much smaller than represented. A herd of 10,000 head would be sold as being 50,000. Fewer than 5000 died, but the investors would be told 45,000 had perished. Thousands of cattle did die and scores of American agents escaped prison as a result of the blizzard of '86.

When the Agriculture Department released its estimate of the cattle population for 1886, it came to 56.6 million head, up from 54.9 million the previous year. For 1887, the estimate would be 58.6 million, 2 million *more* than in 1886, and the figure would rise to 60 million by 1890 before declining. This does not mean, however, that no one suffered. There were pockets in the West where times had never been so bad, though the overall picture was not as severe as is often portrayed.

Even so, there were problems, which some thought might be resolved with new funds. A tale was told of a group of ranchers who entered a saloon after viewing the range. "Cheer up," said the bartender. "The cattle may be dead, but they haven't frozen the books." Show a good report, he implied, and the easterners and foreigners will shower you with new funds.

This didn't happen, and for a while a large number of ranchers faced difficulties and some ruination. Many were saved by credit extended by agents, especially John Clay and Joseph Rosenbaum. On learning of distress in the Helena area of Montana, Rosenbaum went there and called a meeting of his clients, who expected to be foreclosed, since they couldn't make payments on their loans. Instead, Rosenbaum told them he would carry their notes until better times and loaned them $1 million to help restock the range. The cattlemen never forgot Rosenbaum's help. During the 1907 financial panic, when he faced ruin, the Montana cattlemen raised a million dollars to help cover his losses.

In time, the range recovered. Larger fortunes were made there in the early twentieth century than in the 1880s. By then, however, the romance was gone, surviving only in legends.

The Farmer and the West

Ultimately, the farmers would seize much of the West and derive the greatest amount of wealth from the region. The miners represented no problem. They had no use for the virgin soil, and in any case, they moved on when the diggings petered out. The Indians were a hindrance, to be resolved by the Army and the decline of the buffalo population, upon which the Indians relied for their sustenance. The cattlemen were a major obstacle, but they could be dealt with. As noted, President Cleveland was no friend of the cattle interests. The farmers usually owned title to the land, obtained through the Morrill Act of 1862, and when justice arrived in the form of federal marshals, their rights could be asserted. Too, the farmer had an ally in the railroad interests, who wanted to take crops to market and bring supplies to the homesteads. In time, however, the farmers would view the railroads as their enemies, setting the stage for the political battles of the 1890s.

The farmers also were aided by inventors and manufacturers. Joseph Glidden received a patent for an inexpensive means of producing barbed wire in 1874, when the Secretary of Agriculture estimated the net worth of farm fences at $2 billion, often costing the farmer more than the land they encircled. Nearly 3 million pounds of barbed wire were sold in 1876. By 1880, the figure was 80 million, and the price had fallen from $15 a hundred pounds to less than $10. It would go to $4 in 1890.

Water was another problem in the arid Plains, but here, too, there was a solution. Where possible, the farmers would dig wells, and no farm was without a cistern to capture rain water. The Great Plains was windswept, and so the farmers redesigned eastern windmills, which powered pumps to dredge water from beneath the surface. In addition, they developed methods of dry farming, husbanding resources carefully. Finally, there were the invention and production of machinery. The harvester had appeared before the Civil War, freeing thousands of farmers for service in the Union armies. Now came improved plows, grain drills, disk harrows, threshing machines, and combines. The 61 hours of labor per acre required to grow wheat was reduced to 3 hours, while oats went from 66 hours to 7, and corn from 39 hours to 15. Labor costs also fell, in most cases, by 70 percent and more. The machinery was expensive, however, and the economics of farming dictated large holdings, not the 160 acres obtainable under terms of the Morrill Act. Farmers in the Great Plains needed 360 to 640 acres to practice extensive agriculture.

Always, the farmer was plagued by forces similar to those that troubled the cattlemen — overproduction, reliance on good weather, foreign competition, and the costs of transportation. Of these, the main problem was overproduction, prompting debt-ridden farmers to plant even more to compensate for lower prices, whereupon prices fell once again.

Due to increased production and growing foreign competition, the prices of agricultural products fell steadily in this period. Corn went from $0.78 a bushel in 1867 to $0.21 in 1896, and in the same period, wheat went from $2.01 to $0.72 and oats from $0.59 to $0.18. The price of farm machinery fell, as did interest rates on money the farmers borrowed. Still, farmers railed against railroad charges, which at times exceeded the value of the crop sent to market. "There are three great crops raised in Nebraska," wrote a farm newspaper. "One is a crop of corn, one is a crop of freight rates, and one a crop of interest. One is produced by farmers who by sweat and toil farm the land. The other two are produced by men who sit in their offices and behind their bank counters and farm the farmers."

The bankers and railroaders protested. They noted that railroads were capital intensive. In 1860, they had $1.8 billion in stocks and bonds outstanding; by 1897, the figure was $10.6 billion, at a time when the federal debt was $1.2 billion. Those loans had to bear interest and the stock dividends, for without these, additional issues could not be marketed. The railroads agreed rates went up during periods of peak demand and declined when demand was low, but that was the way to earn sufficient funds to pay their substantial borrowings. That so many railroads went bankrupt in those years indicates they were not as profitable as the farmers thought they were.

Furthermore, the image of the struggling farmer borrowing heavily to keep body and soul together is deceiving. Banks generally did not make loans to marginal farmers, preferring those who were prosperous and more likely to repay the loans. Most of the borrowing was for expansion — more land, more machinery, and more livestock.

Little wonder, then, that the farmers, like some of the labor organizations, turned to politics. They had some goals similar to those of labor. Farmers tended to blame many of their problems on urban America, especially banks. Several farm organizations blamed their trouble on Jews, who they felt controlled banks, and on foreigners allied with Wall Street. Farm organizations supported immigration restriction and the nationalization of railroads and banks. In general, farmers wanted lower tariffs to enable foreign firms to compete with American companies and so decrease the prices of domestic manufactured goods. Farmers often joined with labor organizations in seeking to curb the power of business. Of paramount concern was the money question. Since farmers tended to be debtors, they wanted currency inflation, which would enable them to repay loans with devalued dollars.

Several farm groups organized the Greenback Party in 1876 and ran candidates for the Presidency in the next three elections, but did not win a single electoral vote. The Greenback Party favored the reissuance of greenback currency and the remonetization of silver, which would lead to inflation, enabling debtor farmers to repay their borrowing with depreciated dollars. It was issues such as these that concerned voters in the post-Civil War era. In 1892, the People's Party, better known as Populists, nominated James Weaver for President. He received more than 1 million popular votes and 22 electoral votes, setting the stage for the most dramatic political and economic showdown since the Civil War.

The Election of 1896

In 1896, both major parties were divided on the silver issue. The political scene hadn't been so disorganized since 1860, and as was the case earlier, there was talk of civil war. This time, it wouldn't be North against South, free states against slave. In 1896, it would be "the people" against "the plutocracy." Class warfare had come to the United States, leading Marxists and other socialists to talk of impending revolution. But under it all was the continuing conflict between Jeffersonians and Hamiltonians. The farmers were, as Jefferson described them, businessmen out to maximize their profits, and so were the railroads and growing industrial forces symbolized by the Republican Party.

The Republicans met in St. Louis in mid-June, with Senators from silver-producing states, led by Senator Henry Teller of Colorado and Richard Pettigrew of South Dakota, threatening a walkout if the convention endorsed the gold standard. Under the leadership of Mark Hanna, the Ohio party boss, the convention was solidly behind gold. "The Republican Party is unreservedly for sound money," and would continue to be until an unlikely international agreement to coin silver was reached. The Republican platform also called for a protective tariff, the independence of Cuba, and the building of a canal in Nicaragua. With this, Teller departed, announcing he and the hundred or so delegates who joined him would support a silverite candidate in the general election. The convention then nominated Governor William McKinley of Ohio for the Presidency.

This placed pressures on the Democrats, who met in Chicago on July 7. Their platform supported bimetallism, which is to say the "free and unlimited coinage of both silver and gold at the present legal ratio of 16 to 1 without awaiting the aid or consent of any other nation." The Democrats also called for greater regulation of big business and the railroads.

The absorption of wealth by the few, the consolidation of our leading railroad systems, and the formation of trusts and pools require a stricter control by the Federal Government of these arteries of commerce. We demand the enlargement of the powers of the Interstate Commerce Commission and such restriction and guarantees in the control of railroads as will protect the people from robbery and oppression.

However, there was nothing about the nationalization of railroads and banks in the platform. It had a vague antitrust plank, and except for the silver pledge was more a reiteration of old programs than a look to the future.

The dominant force at the convention was Illinois Governor John Peter Altgeld, whose candidate was Richard Bland, a silverite and a former Missouri Congressman. As expected, the convention supported silver and the gold Democrats talked about walking out, vowing to form a separate party and field candidates. But Bland did not get the nomination. During the platform debate, William Jennings Bryan, a former Congressman who attended the convention on a press pass, electrified the delegates with what is known as "The Cross of Gold" speech. "You shall not press down upon the brow of labor this crown of thorns, you shall not crucify mankind upon a cross of gold." The convention was swept away. Bryan was nominated and with this, the gold Democrats departed.

Less than two weeks later, the Populists convened in St. Louis, rattled by what had happened. They had expected the two parties to name gold candidates, the silver wings to leave and join them, which would provide them with a major electoral victory. There was talk of nominating Eugene Debs, who refused the bid. When the convention turned to Bryan, many protested. Nonetheless, the Populists nominated Bryan, though to keep their separate identity, they selected a different candidate for Vice President.

Bryan staged the first whistle stop campaign in Presidential history, traveling by train to address crowds throughout much of the nation. Under Hanna's direction, McKinley stayed home, delivering prepared texts to visiting delegations. Behind the scenes, Hanna courted the Black vote, and employers told their workers that if Bryan was elected, the factories would be closed the following day.

McKinley won in a landslide, with 7.1 million popular votes and 271 electoral votes against Bryan's totals of 5.1 million and 155. Bryan captured the South and West, but lost every state north of the Mason-Dixon Line and east of the Mississippi. It was the electoral map of a deeply divided nation. But the nation was fractionalized along other lines as well. Urban workers saw little to gain from inflation and gave the Republicans more votes than ordinarily might have been the case. Blacks were more solidly Republican than ever. There was no great realignment of voters in 1896, but there were signs that to the sectional divisions caused by the Civil War were added other breaches.

John Palmer, running as a gold Democrat, received 132,871 votes, mostly from those who would become Republicans. Joshua Levering, the Prohibitionist candidate, received 131,757, indicating few wanted to waste their votes in this important election. The turnout was 79.3 percent of the electorate, below what it had been when Lincoln was elected in 1860, but high by the standards of the time.

It appeared to some in 1896 that the nation had opted for an urban rather than a rural future, but religion and Civil War memories remained at least as important as silver; 500,000 Union veterans were still alive in 1896.

McKinley would be the last Civil War veteran to be elected President, however, an indication that an age was passing. What the Americans of 1896 could not have known was that the era in which the farmer was central to the business of gathering wealth had started to fade. The signs were to be seen on Wall Street in New York and in the steel mills of Pittsburgh, the oil wells of the Midwest and soon Texas, and in time, on the paved streets of the cities and in the air.

In 1896, the Duryea brothers announced they would manufacture cars at the rate of one per month, which made them the largest American producer. The Appellate Division of New York Court rejected a plan to build a subway due to the costs. Given the depression and unbalanced budget, and the economic thinking of the time, spending had to be kept in check. In its decision, the Court quoted St. Luke: "Which of you, intending to build a tower, sitteth not down first and counteth the cost, whether he have sufficient to finish it." The first motion picture was shown at Koster & Bial's Music Hall in New York. Orville and Wilbur Wright were deeply involved in the development of a vehicle most observers thought would revolutionize travel—the bicycle. They would turn to aviation two years later.

Inventions that appeared in the 1890s—the automobile, the airplane, the motion picture—seemed like curiosities, but in the end, they would alter the fabric of American life more than did the issues of the McKinley-Bryan campaign, and in the process transform the older ways of achieving wealth and create some new ones as well.

CHAPTER *15*

The Arrival
of Big Business

HE railroads that made it possible for businessmen like Gustavus Swift and Adolphus Busch to market their products in regional—if not national—markets brought opportunities, benefits, and problems. The opportunities and benefits included the chance to increase production and realize the profits that come from economies of scale. One of the problems was that others were thinking along the same lines, and so competition became fiercer. In the time of the neighborhood brewery, individuals such as Busch had a captive group of tavern owners. The local butcher of the prerailroad age had few customers, perhaps, but fewer rivals. Now this was changing. Swift was a pioneer, but soon he was joined by Armour, Cudahy, Wilson, and other meat packers. Busch had to face the Milwaukee firms of Pabst and Schlitz as well as others who were expanding their marketing reach. Then, too, by the last years of the nineteenth century, it had become evident that the national rail network was just about completed. Competition was keen, and losses for many lines mounted, as did bankruptcies and reorganizations. In 1894, the nation had 178,000 miles of main track, 41,000 of which were operated by receivers or trustees. Some means had to be found to take advantage of the wider opportunities for merchandising both farm and fabricated goods, meeting the rigors of the new competition, and raising the funds needed for the creation of major corporations. The result was the rise of an industrial America quite different from what either Hamilton or Jefferson might have imagined, with more opportunities to obtain wealth than either could have foreseen.

Pools and Trusts

As might be expected, businesspeople sought means to control the competition that threatened their existence. For a while in the 1870s, railroad pools were popular. Participants in the pools would apportion business and agree to price schedules. Complaints from shippers led to the creation of the ICC in 1887, which forbade pools, leading to their decline. Next it was trusts, in which members of an industry deposited controlling amounts of their shares into an entity and received in exchange trust certificates, the idea being to create a legal monopoly that could control prices and production. The national trusts all were in products from the soil or minerals. The pioneer in the trust concept was Standard Oil, which formed its trust in 1882 and thereby controlled 90 percent of the nation's refining of petroleum, which in this period was used primarily as feedstock to produce kerosene. There followed the Distillers' and Cattle Feeders' Trust, the Sugar Refineries Company, the Lead Trust, the Linseed Oil Trust, the Cotton Oil Trust, and other, smaller ones. The Sherman Antitrust Act of 1890 and actions by the courts put an end to the trust concept.

In order to retain the benefits provided by the trust form, businessmen turned to holding companies. In this form of organization, the parent owned shares in subsidiary companies, sometimes all of them. For example, the Pennsylvania Railroad and other lines were owned by the Pennsylvania Company, and the American Bell Telephone Company owned many operating companies.

The Industrial Corporation

Not only were holding companies, usually simply called corporations, becoming more common, but they were becoming larger as well. From 1881 through 1888, only five corporations capitalized at more than $20 million had been organized in New Jersey, an average of fewer than one per year. From 1889 through 1906, the number ballooned to 124, an average of more than seven a year. These included such well-known firms as American Tin Plate, Federal Steel, International Silver, National Biscuit, American Woolen, Distilling Company of America, National Steel, Republic Iron and Steel, United Shoe Machinery, National Sugar Refining, Allis-Chalmers, Eastman Kodak, American Steel Foundries, and International Harvester. The peak year of 1899 saw the formation of American Car & Foundry, American Chicle, Borden's Condensed Milk, Diamond Match, Electric Boat (the forerunner of General Dynamics), National Carbon, National Distillers, United Fruit, and the restructuring of Standard Oil of New Jersey. The steel industry was swept by a series of mergers, in most cases the acquired company being paid with securities of the acquirer. Economic analyst John Moody wrote of the frantic pace of the mania:

> When one of the smaller "trusts" was being formed, a party of steel men were on their way to Chicago one night after a buying tour. The men had been drinking and were in a convivial mood. Said one, "There's a steel mill at the next station: let's go out and buy it."
> "Agreed!"
> It was past midnight when they reached the station, but they pulled the plant owner out of bed and demanded he sell his plant.
> "My plant is worth two hundred thousand dollars, but it is not for sale," was the reply.
> "Never mind about the price," answered the hilarious purchasers. "We will give you three hundred thousand—five hundred thousand."

This industrial incorporation and consolidation had become the new focus on the business scene. Though in retrospect, it can be seen that the trend brought great efficiencies to the conduct of business, many greeted the new developments with fear for the fate of the traditional businessman. Senator William Lindsay (D-Kentucky) reflected these anxieties when speaking to the members of the American Academy of Political and Social Science in 1900. "We have reached the point at which the individual feels he can no longer compete with his incorporated rival, and where members of old-line partnerships are no longer willing to pledge their personal credit in competition with members of incorporated companies." The financial structure of the industrial corporation was such that its managers had to be concerned with selling securities to the public to raise funds. In contrast, the trusts had no public securities; it was only when trust members wanted to liquidate part or all of their positions that they sold their certificates, which then went into the open market. Sole proprietorships and partnerships relied on individuals, family members, and friends. Those few industrial corporations that did exist prior to the 1890s had difficulties selling securities to individuals for whom railroad, canal, bank, and insurance company bonds were "sound" investment vehicles. Given the small national debt—the interest-bearing debt in 1893 was $847 million—this was not a promising field for investment, not when the railroad debt alone that year came to $5.2 billion.

The debt would grow due to the increased need of American industry for capital. A nation in which labor intensive practices were being supplanted by capital intensive ones made the provision of capital essential. New automatic machinery in the textile industry meant fewer operatives were required and more expensive equipment took their places. In clothing, high-speed cutting machines replaced tailors. Steel-making was one of the most capital intensive industries in the nation.

The investment bankers would have to educate the public on the benefits of investing in the paper of industrial corporations. What this implied was that if corporate America was going to grow, middle class Americans as well as the wealthy would have to be willing to invest in securities issued by investment bankers rather than squirreling away funds in banks and mattresses. They might invest in a home; mortgage-based purchasing at this time was in its infancy. We have no statistics on shareholder and bondholder populations at the turn of the century. There were no shareholder censuses in this period, largely because the techniques were undeveloped and the questions deemed unimportant, since few people owned stocks and bonds. There are some estimates, however. When the economist H. T. Warshaw studied a group of corporations "which might properly be considered representative of the corporate industries of the United States," he concluded that in 1900, there were 4.4 million *shareholdings*, which includes multiple countings. Given the nature of the social and economic scene of the time, it would be reasonable to assume that the large majority of shareholders owned more than one security. On the likely assumption that the average trust portfolios of the time (and most were in trust form) contained 10 different securities, it would mean that one out of every 170 Americans of all ages and both sexes owned common and preferred stock. Of course, whether or not many of these individuals purchased industrial preferred stock cannot be known from what data exists. Anecdotal evidence, however, appears to indicate that they did not do so in any substantial numbers, and that industrial preferred was still purchased by the more sophisticated investors. The business sections of newspapers did not carry the kinds of advertisements of securities offerings that would suggest the market for them was expanding.

In this period, when American investors and speculators were first becoming familiar with industrial securities, bonds in substantial enterprises were the investments of choice for the prudent. Preferred stock was considered rather risky, while common stock was desired primarily by managers and their allies for the ownership privileges it provided. While bank common stocks paid regular dividends, as did some of the railroads and utilities, industrial common paid much less regularly.

One should bear in mind also that at the turn of the century knowledge of the potential gains to be realized from industrial securities was still lacking, and this had an impact on demand. Only a handful of forward-looking financiers, such as the Mellon brothers and later on, J. P. Morgan, as yet fully grasped the promise of industrial concerns. Testifying on this matter before the Industrial Commission in 1900, F. B. Thurber, a New York merchant warned:

> Wall Street has got to educate itself in a variety of industries. It used to study railroading and transportation alone, paying little attention to the methods, details, and statistics of individual industries. In the near future we must inform ourselves in a general way, at least, as to steel billets, barbed wire, freight cars, paper bags, baking powder, electric and air power cabs, passenger and freight elevators, hard-rubber goods, typewriting machines, smelters, cigars, cigarettes, beet-root sugar, pumps, potteries, etc. Our horizon is widening.

To most, these were extremely chancy investments, and the bond underwriting business remained dominated by rails and utilities. Investors (as opposed to speculators), often trustees, were so uncertain regarding the risks involved in industrials that they generally avoided such instruments. Thus, while the supply of preferred industrial stocks was low, the demand was lower still. The result was a high yield on the paper.

The growth of the industrial segment of the economy was affected by business conditions and customer preferences. The generally poor performance of the economy in the first half of the 1890s hindered combination and business formation, but even then, new incorporations were greater than they had been during the 1880s. Mergers, too, were increasingly important. From 1895 to 1904, some 3010 companies were involved in mergers and consolidations, and in the process, the face of the economy was altered. Consider that in 1860, as it appeared civil war was inevitable, the leading American industry in terms of value added was cotton goods, which accounted for $55 million. It was followed by lumber ($54 million), boots and shoes ($49 million), flour and meal ($40 million), and men's clothing ($37 million). The value added by all industries that year was $815 million. By 1910, the top five industries and their respective value added statistics were: machinery ($690 million), lumber ($650 million), printing and publishing ($540 million), iron and steel ($480 million), and malt liquors ($280 million). The total value added had increased to $8.5 billion in that half century. The United States was the world's leading industrial power, producing nearly twice the goods of runner-up Germany. Production of steel, the building block material for the new age, rose from 69,000 long tons in 1870 to 1.2 million in 1880, 4.2 million in 1890, and 10.2 million in 1900. All of the steel companies, along with the others, needed capital to expand, and in the process used the services of investment bankers.

When they did, many of the newly incorporating companies sold both bonds and stocks. The general approach was to issue preferred stocks equal to the amount of the tangible assets and common stock of an equal amount (or more), which was said to represent intangibles, such as good will. The conventional wisdom of the time held that a corporation was worth little more than the net asset value of its entire holdings, and that any part of its price above that was somehow illegitimate. Though today we recognize that intangible assets and future prospects of a company can be quite valuable, and that the price of stock should take these factors into account, to prudent investors of that day, this seemed tantamount to fraud. "Depriving a [corporation] of its stock-watering feature," surmised Senator Lindsay, "is almost the same as depriving a venomous serpent of its fangs." Thus, industrial common shares were considered most suspect from an investment standpoint, not only because of the perceived risk but also because they represented all the "water" in the capitalization.

Preferred stocks were another matter. These bore some resemblance to the perpetual bonds issued in the early nineteenth century. They paid a fixed amount of dividends, and generally speaking, the securities did not contain call provisions. Moreover, most preferred stocks were cumulative, so that past dividends might be paid when and if the company recovered. During the early 1890s, almost all of the industrial preferred issues paid 7 percent dividends at par, at a time when U.S. government bonds were offering less than 3 percent, high-grade railroad bonds less than 4 percent, and New York City mortgages around 5¼ percent.

The consistent 7 percent yield at par may signify the very stable markets of the time, but the fact that the same coupon existed for almost all of the issues regardless of quality indicates this was a convention. Eventually, some preferred sold at premiums, others at discounts. Even so, the returns available from preferred stock were substantially higher than that from bonds issued by the same companies, indicating the perception they were high risk. In all ways—except that they represented ownership rather than debt (only a few of the preferred stocks also had voting rights), and that they were perpetual rather than having a fixed maturity—preferred stocks were to this period what high-yield bonds would be to the 1980s. In at least a couple of cases, trusts converted to the corporate form by calling in their certificates and replacing them with common and preferred shares.

Industrial common stocks remained strictly a speculator's game, since they still paid dividends irregularly or not at all, and in this period dividends were a significant concern. Three-quarters of the industrial companies organized in 1899 and 1900 were not paying dividends on their common shares in 1900, but almost all maintained their preferred dividends. Thus, owners of industrial preferred shares received substantially higher yields than were available from bonds.

The Promoter

In all of this economic change, a new figure appeared on the business scene—the promoter, the person who smells out deals and possibilities, cobbles them together, and then brings the package to investment bankers or investors for financing. Charles Ranlett Flint was one of the best known promoters. Historian N. S. B. Gras described Flint as "an industrial capitalist who became a promoter on the fringes of finance capitalism." John W. "Bet-a-Million" Gates was another of the breed, as was Diamond Jim Brady, but Flint, who was known as "the father of trusts," was more important than either of them.

Born in coastal Maine in 1850, Flint was more than just a businessman. A small, compact man with muttonchop whiskers, he was an excellent swimmer and runner, the owner of the nation's fastest racing yachts, and a motorist who helped found the Automobile Club of America. Flint also flew airplanes at a time when that took nerve. Always on the move, he spent one week in 10 on a ship bound for foreign destinations. "It has been said, perhaps too frequently, that a rolling stone gathers no moss," he wrote. "But I have never heard anyone speak about the fun the rolling stone has a-rolling."

Flint would enter any business that promised a profit. He got his start in international trade, as a commission agent. He dealt in such common items as guano and nitrates, but was better known for supplying munitions to warring nations. At various times, he did so for the governments of Nicaragua, Chile, and Costa Rica, and on occasion sold guns and ships to both sides in a conflict. In 1895, Flint provided vessels for the Japanese to use in their war against China, and a decade later he sold warships to the Russians to use against the Japanese. Later, Flint organized a consortium to sell Wright airplanes to Germany, and he personally instructed the Kaiser on how they might be used in war.

In 1879, while purchasing munitions for the Peruvian government, Flint met Marcellus Hartly, a tycoon who owned a large block of shares in United States Lighting. Flint purchased some of the shares, assumed a managerial role at the company, and attempted to work out an arrangement with the Edison and Westinghouse interests. His plans misfired, and Flint said that this experience convinced him never again to manage a company, but rather to bring together the principals and take a fee for arranging a merger.

All the while, Flint functioned as an advance agent of American industrialism. He wrote and spoke glowingly of the benefits of large-scale enterprise, and defended big business long before the advent of business associations and academic groups. Flint testified before Congressional committees, asserting that mergers improved living standards of workers and made the nation strong. "Viewing the matter from every standpoint, the businessman is benefitted when he operates as a member of a combination instead of as an individualist," he said, while extolling the benefits of lower transportation costs and economies of scale realized by large combinations. "A trade union is a combination of labor, a university a combination of intelligence, and a bank a combination of capital," thought Flint. Why, then, should antitrusters complain about bigness in business?

Flint's first important opportunity to practice what he preached came in 1892, when some rubber manufacturers, seeking an accommodation, approached him and employed his services to organize what became United States Rubber, which was from its beginning the dominant force in its industry. The success of this deal led to others. Flint spent much of his time and energy during 1897–1898 putting together National Starch and American Caramel. This was a prelude for the whirlwind of activity in 1899, when he organized American Woolen, Sloss-Sheffield, United States Bobbin & Shuttle, and a handful of other businesses, including three coal mines and a steamship company. The crowning jewel that year was American Chicle, a union of six firms. When it was observed these had combined assets of $500,000 and he had capitalized Chicle at $9 million, Flint replied that trademarks, good will, and market share, though intangibles, were worth more than factories and rolling stock, a novel idea at the time, but a bedrock notion today.

In 1900, Flint midwifed the creation of International Time Recording, which manufactured and marketed time clocks and was the leader in that small industry. He then organized Computing Scale Co. of America, whose products enabled a clerk in a store to weigh an item and then quickly calculate its cost. In addition, Computing Scale manufactured meat and cheese slicers. None of its businesses did well, and by 1910, Computing Scale's future appeared bleak. Flint hoped to salvage the situation by merging it with International Time Recording in what would appear to be a predecessor of the conglomerates of post World War II America, but quite novel then. Flint spoke of the benefits of "allied consolidations," while also arguing that the two companies were really in the same business, that of measurements.

It was around this time that Flint became interested in a third company involved in measurements, Tabulating Machine, which manufactured and leased census-taking equipment. The company was troubled by competition with a rival and was seeking assistance, which Flint gladly provided. Now he threw the census machine company into the mix, and created an entity he called Computing-Tabulating-Recording. Thus, CTR was a union of a prosperous manufacturer of time clocks, a marginal operation that produced scales and slicers, and an endangered firm that turned out machines called tabulators that had limited use. The company had assets on the books of $17.5 million, of which $16.5 million was represented by the stocks of the three component companies. It was not a particularly promising situation.

Not about to take a managerial role again, Flint persuaded the former president of International Time Recording, Representative George W. Fairchild, to become CTR's chairman, but since Fairchild had to go on a diplomatic mission, much of the managerial work was handled by Frank Kondolf, the former COO at International Time. This was only a stopgap appointment, however. In 1914, Thomas Watson came over from NCR to run CTR, which 10 years later he renamed International Business Machines.

The New Face of Investment Banking: J. P. Morgan

All of this activity placed the investment banker at the center of the new industrial order. There had been investment bankers early in America's national history, but they had little power because there was a lack of substantial numbers of American investors willing and able to purchase stocks and bonds. This changed somewhat prior to and during the Civil War, when Jay Cooke organized his syndicates and sold railroad and government paper. Investment bankers thrived in the post-bellum period, and they came into their own in the 1890s, when J. Pierpont Morgan became the symbol for the "plutocracy" and the "robber barons," whom reformers feared were taking over the country. There is no doubt that business was becoming big, and the power and influence of the Morgan bank was emblematic of this.

There have been four major periods of business consolidation and amalgamation, the most recent taking place in the 1990s. The current vogue, which is global in nature, pales compared with the action of a century ago. There may be more "deals" today, with more money and greater wealth involved, but the mergers and acquisitions at the turn of the twentieth century were played out on a smaller stage and with a gold standard.

Morgan was not only the most influential banker in American history, but the central figure of his era, which would be the 1890s until his death in 1913. He was the son of Junius Spencer Morgan, who was an important conduit for British funds seeking American investments, and American firms requiring capital. In 1856, J. P. entered his father's firm in London, and in 1860 he was dispatched to New York where he organized J. P. Morgan & Company and acted as his father's agent. In 1864, he joined with Charles Dabney to form the partnership of Dabney, Morgan & Co., which rose to some prominence due largely to its London connections. In 1871, Morgan united with prominent Philadelphia banker Anthony Drexel to create Drexel, Morgan & Company, which was known as the "New York end of Drexel."

During the next 15 years, Morgan's attention was focused on railroad reorganizations, working with the Northern Pacific, arranging a truce between the Pennsylvania and the New York Central, and restructuring the Baltimore & Ohio and the Chesapeake & Ohio. By the early 1890s, he had a hand in reviving the defunct Richmond & West Point Terminal Co., which he folded into the Southern Railway Co. Then it was on to the Erie and the Philadelphia & Reading. After the creation of the ICC, Morgan bent his efforts toward achieving more cooperation of and less competition among railroad leaders. He accomplished this through a succession of railroad conferences.

Following the financial panic of 1893, in which many railroads failed, Morgan reorganized the Erie, the Philadelphia & Reading, and in a joint effort with the Deutsche Bank, the Northern Pacific. By the end of the century, through his appointees to the boards of many lines, he was one of the four major figures in American railroading, the others being James J. Hill of the Northern Pacific, E. H. Harriman, and Jay Gould. Morgan had become the very symbol of capitalism triumphant. He was responsible for scores of corporate creations, among them General Electric, International Mercantile Marine, American Telephone & Telegraph, and International Harvester. The 11 Morgan partners between them held 72 directorships in 47 of the nation's largest corporations. Morgan always claimed that the huge enterprises he created would bring order to their industries. The presence of the partners on corporate boards would assure customers who purchased the securities Morgan issued that the bank was on the scene, making certain all went well. Should problems develop, the Morgan representative would step in to make matters right.

Activities such as these ushered in a period in which banks developed close relationships with clients. Indeed, the practice was known as "relationship banking," meaning that the bankers served on boards of directors and were on retainer for their advice on a wide variety of other matters as well as financing. Into the Morgan orbit came First National Bank, Chase National, Banker's Trust, and Guaranty Trust. Several large commercial banks entered the investment banking field. George F. Baker of First National City organized First Securities Company to become a part of Morgan's selling syndicates. Under the leadership of James Stillman, National City Bank became an important underwriter, and in 1911 formalized the arrangement by organizing National City Company as its investment affiliate.

Carnegie and Morgan

What the telecommunications and the Internet are to today's mania, steel, the elemental building block of the emerging industrial civilization, was to the markets of that time. Andrew Carnegie was the Bill Gates of the Gay Nineties. From 1898 to 1900, there were 20 amalgamations in steel, the largest being J. P. Morgan's Federal Steel, which comprised five companies. The book value of the Federal properties came to $56 million. Morgan capitalized the company at $230 million and was able to sell the securities with no trouble. Morgan's name was magic, so there was little doubt the issues would succeed. As a result, a group of "merger millionaires" was created. There would be many more of them. Ever larger enterprises were being formed in steel, and Morgan seemed to believe that in time, competition would be eliminated from this industry.

Others were plowing the same field. National Steel Company was the creation of William and James Moore, who had the reputation for wheeling and dealing. The brothers had already organized Diamond Match, involving themselves in manipulations so complicated and shady that their disclosure had caused the Chicago Stock Exchange to close down for three months. In much the same way, they then organized the National Biscuit Company, which was comprised of three regional companies, to counter competition in the field, set prices, and in general act as Morgan believed such companies should. The Moores then put together American Tin Plate Company—the "Tin Plate Trust," as it was known—which brought together 29 plants controlling 279 mills that produced virtually all the tin plate in the country. American Tin Plate had assets of between $10 and $12 million, but capitalized at $33 million. The brothers rewarded themselves in this instance by taking more than 15 percent of the stock.

This set the stage for National Steel, which brought together under one roof six large plants with 15 blast furnaces, iron mines in Michigan, and nine Great Lakes ships. At the time, it was the nation's third largest steel firm, producing about 12 percent of the industry's output. Close affiliations with American Tin Plate, American Steel Hoop, and another Moore company, American Sheet Steel, enabled National to challenge Carnegie and Federal as an equal.

Andrew Carnegie, who headed the world's largest steel company, had a different view of competition from that held by Morgan. The tale of Carnegie's life was quite familiar to turn of the century Americans, since he was one of the period's industrial success stories, rising from the position of a Scots immigrant bobbin boy to become one of the wealthiest and most powerful business magnates of his era. Parts of Carnegie's story are worth retelling. He became a telegrapher in 1850, at the age of 15, and by sending and receiving messages for businessmen, he learned how they operated. "I am to have $4.00 a week and a good prospect of getting more," he wrote to relatives. "In Scotland, I would have been a poor weaver all my days, but here I can surely do better. If I don't, it will be my own fault, for anyone can get along in this country."

In 1852, Carnegie became personal telegrapher for Thomas Scott, who headed the Pennsylvania Railroad's western division, and in 1859, when Scott became the railroad's vice president, Carnegie took his vacated job. When Scott was named assistant secretary of war, he helped Carnegie obtain the post of superintendent of eastern military and telegraph lines. By then, Carnegie had started to invest. He did so at a fortunate time. Shares were going up due to the Civil War boom, and he made out handsomely. He helped reorganize the Piper & Shiffler Company, which constructed wooden and iron bridges. Carnegie realized that iron bridges would be needed in the war effort, and he took a major position in the company's stock. Piper & Shiffler flourished, and at the end of the war Carnegie reorganized it as the Keystone Bridge Company, taking over management control. This was followed by the acquisition of Kloman & Phipps, a manufacturer of railroad car axles, and in 1864, he formed Cyclops Steel Company, which he merged with his other holdings to create the Union Iron Mills.

At the time, Carnegie did not consider himself a steel or iron magnate, but rather an opportunist in the best sense of the term. Had other possibilities presented themselves, he might have wound up in petroleum, railroads, or some other field. In 1869, he joined with George Pullman to gain a monopoly in sleeping cars. Carnegie became a member of the board of Union Pacific in 1871 and seems to have considered taking an important managerial role there. He even took a whirl at finance, selling some $30 million of American railroad securities to British investors.

In 1872, after visiting Britain to learn more about the steel business and the Bessemer process for creating the metal, he liquidated his holdings and used the proceeds to enter this industry through his new company, Carnegie, McCandless & Company, a partnership, by constructing a plant just south of Pittsburgh. He named it "The J. Edgar Thomson Steel Works," in honor of the president of the Pennsylvania, whose good will he needed. The plant opened at an inopportune time because of the panic of 1873, but Carnegie came out of the experience unscathed. He used his reserve funds to buy out his partners at bargain prices, and when the panic was over, Carnegie held 59 percent of the stock.

In 1880, the price of rails soared to $85 a ton, at a time when Carnegie, McCandless was turning out 10,000 tons a month at a cost of about $36. Within eight months, Thompson returned enough profit to pay for its entire cost, and the steel works showed a net profit of $1.6 million for the year.

The following year, Carnegie restructured and consolidated his holdings, forming Carnegie Brothers & Company, capitalized at $5 million. More plants followed, and Carnegie integrated backward by purchasing coke companies, his own steamers, and even a railroad. His move up the industry ladder was swift and made without the use of the corporate form or investment bankers, both of which he distrusted. Rather, Carnegie employed a series of partnerships and plowed earnings back into the business. Continually seeking improvements, he would abandon a fairly new facility in order to erect yet another one if the latter could apply important economies and efficiencies.

Carnegie searched for hard-working, intelligent, and ambitious young men, who, if they showed promise, would receive rapid promotions. Some would be informed that stock in the company had been set aside for them, to be paid for out of the company's earnings. In effect, these men were given shares as a bonus and were told more would be granted if earnings and dividends remained high and their work continued to improve. Carnegie later said, "Every year should be marked by the promotion of one or more of our young men. We cannot have too many of the right sort interested in the profits." But he rode them hard. When one of his managers told him that his plant had broken all records for making steel that week, Carnegie fired back, "Congratulations! Why not do it every week?" Another telegraphed, "Lucy Furnace No. 8 broke all records today." Carnegie wired back, "What were the other ten furnaces doing?"

In 1887, Carnegie promulgated what was called the "Iron Clad Agreements." Under its terms, the company could repurchase stock given to the partners at book value. If a partner did not turn out well, Carnegie could rid himself of the person in a matter of weeks. This encouraged Carnegie to understate the value of his enterprise and to write off costs as incurred and not over a period of years, as was the practice then and now. Carnegie's operations were always carried at below their true worth, and so his return on capital was greatly exaggerated.

Carnegie also understood the markets. He aggressively cut prices in order to increase market share and then raised them when conditions justified a reversal. He formed and dissolved "communities of interest" in steel whenever it suited his design. "I can make steel cheaper than any of you and undersell you," Carnegie once told the members of one such community just before he terminated it. "The market is mine whenever I want to take it. I see no reason why I should present you all my profits." Carnegie was one of the first to recognize the slowdown in railroad construction. He met this by diverting production to steel girders and sheet steel to meet the needs of the construction industry. Watching this from his perch on Wall Street, J. P. Morgan scorned Carnegie, believing he was a disruptive element on the business scene.

The two titans also were quite different in temperament and interests. While Carnegie relaxed by playing golf at his castle in Scotland, Morgan would retire to his Park Avenue drawing room where, puffing on a fine Havana and sipping brandy, and surrounded by Renaissance art gathered on his collecting expeditions, he played endless games of solitaire. Even in repose, Morgan sought to bring order out of the random deck.

Carnegie had kicked up his heels in 1899, restructuring his holdings in preparation for a foray into the nail, wire, tube, and hoop businesses. Or so it was believed. As usual with Carnegie, it was difficult to fathom his motives. Was he trying to crush all rivals as he had done several times already? Or was this his way of trying to blackmail someone into buying him out? Whatever the reason, Morgan fairly ached to eliminate Carnegie from the scene.

Morgan was present at a meeting on December 12, 1900, when Carnegie Steel president Charles Schwab gave a presentation entitled "The Future of Steel." The room was filled with bankers and industrialists, so it seemed Carnegie was shopping his company around and wanted Morgan to realize that if he wouldn't bid, others were prepared to do so.

With Schwab as his intermediary, Morgan tried to discover what Carnegie was up to. There followed a series of feints and jabs. Schwab finally informed Morgan that Carnegie would sell if the price was right. Carnegie had recapitalized his interests at $320 million, but Morgan realized the price would be higher than that. Carnegie was as famous for squeezing the last nickel from a deal as he was for his daring maneuvers.

Carnegie originally asked for a nice, round $400 million. But then he had second thoughts and upped the price to $492 million, most of it in 5 percent gold mortgage bonds. It was said that Carnegie insisted on those bonds rather than stock because he expected the entire edifice Morgan wanted to create to fail, after which he would take over.

Schwab took the numbers to Morgan, who looked at them for a moment and then said, simply, "I accept this price." A few days later, Morgan and Carnegie met. Morgan extended his hand: "Mr. Carnegie, I want to congratulate you on being the richest man in the world."

Next, with Schwab's help, Morgan set about creating U.S. Steel, the giant he hoped would bring order to the industry. Federal Steel would be part of the new company, as would Morgan-controlled National Tube. The industry's third largest factor, National Steel, came in as well, along with seven other companies. These firms contained what once had been 170 independent companies. In time, there would be additional acquisitions. U.S. Steel seemed like an octopus, taking in everything within its grasp.

The deal required $304 million in bonds, $550 million in common stock, and a like amount in preferred stock, for a total of more than $1.4 billion. Morgan's syndicate took 650,000 shares of the common and a like amount of the preferred for $25 million, at an average price of less than $20 a share for each.

Critics argued that the company was overcapitalized. The Bureau of Corporations later estimated the "real" worth of the properties to have been between $676 and $793 million, which led to charges of stock watering. But investors cared little about this. Morgan's name on the deal convinced them of its soundness. In any case, they were fascinated at the sheer size of the undertaking.

It is not enough merely to observe that $1.4 billion in 1901 was like $100 billion or so today, because simply adjusting for inflation can't indicate the magnitude of this underwriting. Consider that the nation's GNP in 1901 was $20.7 billion, so the U.S. Steel flotation was around 7 percent of GNP. An undertaking of the same relative size today would have to be on the order of a quarter of a trillion dollars.

Even this can't portray what U.S. Steel represented for the Americans of 1901. By itself, Big Steel produced half the steel in the United States. It accounted for one-tenth of America's manufactures and around 5 percent of the assets of all American corporations. One author claimed U.S. Steel owned as much land as Massachusetts, Vermont, and Rhode Island combined, and had a wage bill larger than that of the Armed Forces.

U.S. Steel common debuted at 38, and the preferred at 82. Morgan hired a team of market riggers, led by James Keene, the acknowledged master of the craft, to boost the stock. Keene and his crew succeeded admirably. Within a month the common was at 55 and the preferred at 101, providing Morgan's syndicate with a paper profit of $23 million on top of substantial fees.

As it turned out, U.S. Steel was a corporate dinosaur, too big to develop coordinated policies. Cooperation between the component companies was inadequate, and expected economies were not realized. Earnings were disappointing. The common fell to below 10 in 1904, and the company skipped dividends in 1905 and 1906. By 1913, there was some risk U.S. Steel would go bankrupt, unable to meet interest payments on its bonds. But two years later, as a result of war orders, its mills were operating at 90 percent of capacity, and the price of Bessemer pig went from $14.90 a ton to $19.65. War, not organizational brilliance, saved U.S. Steel and Morgan's reputation. If he ever nursed hopes of foreclosing on the company, Carnegie was disappointed.

Many years later, a Morgan colleague told what may be an apocryphal story of a chance meeting between Morgan and Carnegie on an ocean liner bound for Europe. The two men got to talking and Carnegie chortled at how he had twisted Morgan's arm into paying that outrageous $492 million. Morgan was silent and simply gazed at the ocean. Then Carnegie said, "I made one mistake, Pierpont, when I sold out to you." "What was that?" asked the banker. "I should have asked for $100 million more than I did," came the reply. Morgan stared ahead as though he had waited for this moment to frustrate Carnegie. "Well," he said, "you would have got it if you had."

The Industrial Revolution enriched some people and impoverished others. Those able to capitalize on the new techniques and industries did remarkably well; those who were displaced or could not make the grade suffered. Carnegie had some 30 to 40 partners in 1901, who now were millionaires and eager to live on a grand scale. This was the time for it. It was the age of Newport mansions and townhouses in major cities occupied by the *nouveau riche*. Even so, it does not appear that the distribution of wealth was markedly different in 1900 than it had been in 1860. According to studies conducted by economist Lee Soltow in 1969, the wealthiest 2 percent of the nation's families owned more than one-third of its wealth, and the top 10 percent owned three-quarters of the wealth, in both 1860 and 1900. Such a disparity of wealth has always been a part of the industrial era of American history.

The Carnegie millionaires became legends. Alexander Peacock, who like Carnegie had emigrated from Scotland, was given a job in sales. Within a few years, he was sales manager and partner. Peacock owned 2 percent of Carnegie Steel and with his earnings built a magnificent mansion. William Corey, who started out as a laborer, rose to head Carnegie's cornerstone Homestake plant. He patented a method of hardening steel which by itself would have brought him great wealth. To this was added his share of the Morgan buyout. Seven of the partners set out for Europe and a wild art-buying tour. Carnegie learned of this and lamented:

> These young men were models so long as they knew they had to be—besides they had my example and they were poor. Although making large sums, these went to their credit paying for their interests. Now they see stock gamblers prominent in the company and behind it. They became demoralized. It is too sad for me to see such ruination morally. You will see I cannot speak of it publicly. My influence is best exerted privately upon the others. I am not in the proper position to play critic to my former associates publicly.

But as Carnegie deplored the effects of this great wealth on his partners, some of them were about to reap even greater profits from petroleum than they had from steel.

The Carnegie Millionaires and Spindletop

Many observers of the current business scene have noted that the immensely wealthy entrepreneur-businessmen of the personal computer-Internet period are approximately the same age. Generational wealth is not unusual; it was so during the Industrial Revolution as well, and for those tycoons who dominated the scene in the late nineteenth century. Morgan, Carnegie, and John D. Rockefeller all were born within a four-year period in the mid-1830s, and each began his business career on the eve of the Civil War. In 1860, the 23-year-old Morgan organized J. P. Morgan & Company in New York, and that same year, the 25-year-old Carnegie was elevated by Scott to head the western division of the Pennsylvania Railroad. Rockefeller's career had a somewhat different beginning. Like Carnegie, he came from an undistinguished family and lacked the powerful friends who assisted Morgan. In 1857, at the age of 18, he helped organize the commission house of Clark & Rockefeller in Cleveland, Ohio. The firm did a half million dollars that year, remarkable given that it was a bad time for business.

Also like Carnegie—and unlike Morgan—Rockefeller was uncertain as to what business to pursue. Under different circumstances, he might have become a merchant prince in the Midwest. But just as the Bessemer process changed the course of Carnegie's life, so the discovery of petroleum in Pennsylvania would determine the direction Rockefeller took.

Rockefeller visited the field and liked what he saw: wells busily pumping oil out of the ground as though sucking it from a sponge through a straw. Though he remained in the commission business during the Civil War, Rockefeller also invested in the Excelsior Works, headed by Samuel Edwards. By the end of the war, Excelsior was the largest refinery in Cleveland. With the coming of peace, Rockefeller left the commission field and took charge of his refinery business, now reformed as Rockefeller & Andrews. During the next four years he established new companies, constructed additional facilities in Cleveland, arranged for eastern sales by setting up an office in New York, and even made a foray into international sales. Surveying the industry, Rockefeller concluded that discovery was risky, especially since the price of petroleum gyrated wildly in this period. At first, petroleum was fetching $20 a barrel. Then a rush of oil came to market and the price fell to 10 cents a barrel just two years later, only to rise to $7 in 1868, and then back down to below $4 in 1870. This meant that even successful wells might not repay their costs if the price collapsed. Likewise, retailing kerosene, the major product produced from petroleum, was only marginally profitable, since the retailer was at the mercy of the supplier. Refining was the key to this young industry, thought Rockefeller. The refiner, especially if he was dominant, or better still, a monopolist, could dictate prices to driller and retailer alike.

In 1870, Rockefeller consolidated his interests in Standard Oil of Ohio, which was capitalized at $1 million. The firm owned two refineries, a fleet of oil tank cars, sidings and warehouses in Pennsylvania's oil fields, warehouses in New York, a barrel-making plant, and a forest to supply it with lumber. Then, by cutting prices, Rockefeller proceeded to force out competition in the Cleveland area, driving his opponents into bankruptcy and then buying them out. Or he might offer to purchase a competitor's business at what was generally considered a fair price, and then, only if rejected would he turn the screws.

His base secured, Rockefeller expanded into marketing, acquiring several regional distributing companies. Here too, he would try to purchase operating companies at bargain prices, and when they would not capitulate, he would set up rival firms to force them out of the business. What already had been dubbed "the octopus" wrapped its tentacles around the entire industry, accounting for some 90 percent of refining runs and setting prices. When critics accused Rockefeller of predatory pricing, his defenders replied that under the Rockefeller umbrella, prices were repeatedly being cut.

By 1880, Standard of Ohio was truly the standard for the industry, moreso even than Carnegie was for steel. Two years later, Rockefeller again restructured his holdings, this time to form the Standard Oil Trust, which comprised 14 wholly owned companies, including Standard of Ohio, and 26 partially owned firms, ranging in size from the giant National Transit, capitalized at $30 million, to Germania Mining, with a capitalization of only $30,000. Members of the trust received $70 million in certificates, with Rockefeller and his direct allies owning a majority of them. The structure remained in force for 10 years, being dissolved in 1892 as a result of antitrust actions initiated by the state of Ohio. Rockefeller presided over the distribution. National Transit was the largest of the successor concerns, with the newly structured and renamed Standard Oil of New Jersey, the flagship of the Standard Oil bloc of companies, next in size.

Now the Rockefeller empire came under fire. One source of opposition was a force of domestic critics who attacked the company as the very symbol of rampant, heartless capitalism. A second threat came from overseas. Standard had a strong presence in Europe, and in 1879, European business leaders convened in Bremen to form a united front against the Americans. Oil had been discovered in the Baku area of Russia in 1872, and soon it appeared these wells were more productive than any in the United States. The two Swedish brothers, Ludwig and Robert Nobel of dynamite fame, entered Russia with Nobel Brothers Naphtha Company, and Baron Alphonse de Rothschild organized the Caspian & Black Sea Company, which refined and distributed Russian petroleum. The Shibaieff Company's kerosene competed successfully against Standard's in central Europe. Meanwhile, the Royal Dutch Company and Shell Transport & Trading were intent on dominating the oil of the East Indies.

In 1882, the United States produced 85 percent of the world's petroleum, with Standard accounting for the largest share. Standard's position in 1888 was larger than in 1882, but America's world market share fell to 53 percent. It seemed that although Rockefeller might be able to dominate the American market, he could not hope to do the same in Europe and Asia.

In order to boost his position, Rockefeller added drilling to his operations, and in the mid-1880s, a small but successful well was dug in Lima, Ohio. Others followed, and Rockefeller constructed the Buckeye Pipeline to bring the oil to market. In 1889, Standard purchased the Ohio Oil Company, which held leases to more than 20,000 acres of oil land and had 146 wells already in production. Operations were expanded to West Virginia and Kansas in the 1890s. There was talk of exploring sites in California and Texas, but due to local opposition, Standard would not enter those states. John D. Archbold, a top Standard executive, claimed he was certain there was no oil there, and offered to drink every gallon of crude discovered west of the Mississippi.

Archbold knew better. Some oil had already been found in California, although serious exploration did not begin until the 1890s. At the time, too, there was talk of oil seepages in south Texas, and in 1866, the first Texas oil well was drilled in Nacogdoches County. Even so, from 1886 to 1889, fewer than 4000 barrels were produced in the state. Texas used little kerosene during this period, since the population in 1880 was less than 1.5 million.

What followed was a series of false starts, bungles, lost opportunities, but eventually success. Many parties searched for wealth in southeast Texas. They had strong suspicions that oil was there. There were many players in the field who knew that somewhere there was a pot of gold.

As did several states in this period, Texas, under Attorney General James Hogg, instituted an antitrust case against Standard in 1889. Five years later, Hogg, now governor, pressed ahead with indictments against Rockefeller, Archbold, and other Standard officials. Hogg followed this up by asking New York Governor Roswell Flowers to extradite Rockefeller and his associates to Texas for trial. Flowers refused to do so, but at the time it seemed clear that without a change of heart in Texas, Standard Oil would not be able to operate there.

The citizens of Corsicana, meanwhile, knew little of petroleum and the Rockefellers. Ever since its founding in 1849, Corsicana was a hot, dusty town, just south of Dallas, in a cotton farming area with barely 4000 inhabitants, who were far more concerned with water than petroleum. There was enough water for the cotton fields that then existed, but not if there was to be any expansion. So in 1894, the town fathers organized the Corsicana Water Development Company and began drilling. They did not find the hoped for underground spring. Instead, at 1035 feet, the drillers struck oil.

The Corsicanans were disappointed, and work continued until water was found at 2470 feet. By then, 150 barrels a day of crude were also being collected from the well. Several townspeople organized the Corsicana Oil Development Company, but nothing was done until the arrival of James McClurg Guffey and John Galey in 1895. Oil drillers in Pennsylvania, Guffey and Galey were willing to drill for oil in return for half of what they found. Corsicana Oil Development accepted. Some oil was found, but not enough to justify additional work. Guffey and Gale sold their interest, Corsicana Oil Development was liquidated, and a new company, Southern Oil, capitalized at $100,000, appeared to take its place. Other firms, among them Texas Petroleum, were also organized and drilled for oil. In 1896, the young Corsicana field produced 1450 barrels of crude, and the figure rose to 65,975 in 1897.

By then, the Corsicana companies realized they lacked the managerial skills needed to operate. Capital had to be raised, perhaps a refinery established in town, and the products had to be marketed. All of this was foreign to the cotton farmers, small town bankers, and businessmen of Corsicana, which is why they approached Joseph Cullinan for assistance.

Cullinan had arrived in town in 1897 seeking oil. He seemed friendly, and the people liked him. They might have felt otherwise had they known he was a former Standard Oil man, but he managed to hide this fact. More to the point, Cullinan was backed by New York capital. Standard Oil executives Henry Folger and Calvin Payne had "invested" their own money in him, not Standard's.

Supposedly independent, Cullinan surveyed the field, spoke to suppliers and refinery experts, and returned in 1898 with a proposition. He would contract with the three largest producers—Texas Petroleum, Southern Oil, and Oil City—to purchase 100,000 barrels at 50 cents a barrel over the next two years. At the time, Pennsylvania crude was fetching a dollar a barrel and more, but the Corsicanans accepted, since they felt they had no alternative but to enter the business themselves, which they had no desire to do.

Cullinan signed a contract with Folger and Payne, setting up an entity known as J. S. Cullinan & Company. The firm was capitalized at $100,000, with the Standard partners providing the funding and paying Cullinan a salary of $5000 a year. Now, Cullinan started to construct a pipeline and a refinery. As though in imitation of Rockefeller, he announced that he would process and send 100,000 barrels of Cullinan oil; the other Corsicana outfits would be denied access to the pipeline and refinery.

Soon afterward, J. S. Cullinan took over the other companies. The plan was to start producing, refining, and marketing the kerosene, and when the furor over Standard died down in Texas, merge J. S. Cullinan into Standard Oil. This plan was stymied by events in Beaumont, to which the scene now shifts.

Beaumont lay to the south and east of Corsicana, 21 miles inland from the Gulf of Mexico, on the Neches River. Its major industry was lumber, with rice a close second; more than 60 percent of the state's rice was grown in the swampy land near Beaumont, and the town's citizens planned for the day when they could dredge the river and send their rice and lumber into the Gulf, and from there to other parts of the Southeast. Their dream was to make Beaumont the rice capital of the region.

Some people in Beaumont claimed the swamps were haunted. There was a strange smell like rotten eggs in the place that came from "sour water." The sick would bathe in the waters, and some drank them in the hope that they would be spared diseases or cured of them. These springs became the poor man's spa, but only during the day. At night, the ghosts came out. The more scientifically inclined said it was St. Elmo's fire, a natural phenomenon associated with natural gas, which in turn was associated with oil. The waters, they said, contained oil, which was seeping to the surface.

Old timers knew of Dr. B. T. Kavanaugh, who had drilled for oil in the 1860s but found nothing. He did, however, come upon a "medicinal spring," and on the coast some lumps of what seemed to be wax that had washed up on the shore. When examined, they were found to consist of bitumen and paraffin. Many in Beaumont had heard these stories, but they did not investigate.

Pattillo Higgins, who owned several hundred acres near Beaumont, was interested in starting a brick works. He learned that some in the field had abandoned wood and coal for heat and had converted to oil. Nothing came of the brick venture, but Higgins became interested in oil. He read all he could find on the subject and came to believe there might be oil under Big Hill, near Spindletop Springs on the outskirts of town. In 1892, Higgins purchased an option on land in the area and organized Gladys City Oil, Gas, and Manufacturing, a rather strange name since there was no Gladys City (the Gladys was Gladys Bingham, a childhood friend). The firm was not set up for manufacturing, and at the time there was no indication that gas or oil was under the surface. In any case the company failed, due to bad economic times in the area in 1893.

Two years later, however, Savage & Company, a West Virginia concern, offered to bore new wells in Gladys City property in return for a 10 percent royalty. Higgins agreed, Savage went to work, but did not find anything in the allotted time, and departed the scene. Higgins then gave another option to Texas Mineral Company, which turned out to be Savage under a different guise. More drilling, more failure, and Texas Mineral went off stage. Badly discouraged, Higgins asked Texas state geologist Robert Dumble to look over the situation. Dumble sent an assistant, Robert Kennedy, to Beaumont. Kennedy appraised the situation and informed Higgins there definitely was no oil in Beaumont. Oil was found under rock, he said, and there were no rock formations in the area. A few years earlier, a 1400 foot water well was dug there, he noted, and even this hadn't struck rock. With this, Kennedy left town.

Grasping at straws, Higgins advertised for wildcatters, and in early 1899 Captain Anthony Lucas arrived in Beaumont. Lucas was a true exotic, born in Dalmatia as

Anthony Luchich. He attended the Austrian Naval Academy, graduated, and served as a lieutenant in the Austrian navy, after which he came to America. Liking what he found, he applied for and received citizenship, changed his name to Lucas, gave himself a promotion to captain, married the daughter of a wealthy Georgia physician, and found work as a mining engineer.

Lucas specialized in petroleum discovery and made a reputation for his unconventional ideas. He found some oil in Louisiana in formations not unlike those in Beaumont, and he became convinced that salt domes like those in both Louisiana and Beaumont contained more oil than was to be found in the rocky areas of Pennsylvania and Ohio. He met with Higgins and told him of his ideas. Higgins provided him with an option to drill on the Gladys City property. The captain paid $31,150 to the investors, and in June 1899 went to work with his crew.

Within months Lucas was out of money and had nothing to show for his efforts. He asked the Gladys City people to finance additional drilling, but they would have nothing of this. Now Lucas sought financing elsewhere, and in time went to see Payne and Folger, whose Corsicana refinery was nearing completion and needed additional oil to run at full capacity. Payne visited Beaumont in February 1900, where he and Cullinan inspected Lucas' well. Payne informed Lucas that he had seen oil fields in all parts of the world and knew for certain that no crude would be found under the Spindletop salt domes. Two months later, C. Willard Hayes of the U.S. Geological Survey verified Payne's judgment. He noted that a 3070-foot well had been drilled in a similar geological setting near Galveston at a cost of more than $1 million and no oil had been found. That well was some 40 miles from Spindletop. Hayes advised Lucas and Higgins to cut their losses.

Lucas gave the impression of scrambling around to find someone who would tell him he was right. He found that person in William Phillips, a professor of geology at the University of Texas, who said he would put him in touch with some men who might be of help. And with this, Guffey and Galey reentered the Texas oil scene. The partners learned what had happened at Corsicana after they departed and realized they had given up too soon. Perhaps they would have a second chance in Beaumont. After looking around, they agreed to invest $300,000 in the operation and told Lucas about Al and Curt Hamill, then in Corsicana, the best drilling team in that part of the country. If any oil was in the Spindletop area, they would find it. At the time Guffey and Galey had nowhere near $300,000. What they had, however, was more important: a pipeline to Pittsburgh's Mellon Bank, one of the largest outside of New York and one of the shrewdest investors. The Mellons already had dabbled in several Guffey and Galey ventures and had done well in them. Together they formed the Guffey Petroleum Company, with the Mellons' participation kept secret for the time being so that the Texans would not learn of outside influence in their affairs.

Encouraged, Lucas sold everything he had and used the proceeds to purchase additional leases. He then traveled to Corsicana to meet with the Hamills. Meanwhile, Galey instructed Mrs. Lucas to begin a new well on the south side of Spindletop, a distance from the original site. "Tell that captain of yours to start the first well right here," he said. "And tell him that I know he is going to hit the biggest oil well this side of Baku."

In the meantime, the Hamills accepted the assignment, lined up suppliers of pipe and lumber, and in early October started to drill. In December 1900, at 800 feet, the bit struck a hard formation. Weary and discouraged, the workers took a Christmas break. They returned for work on New Year's Day 1901 and quickly struck gas. Captain Lucas ignited the gas, illuminating the sky. This was taken as a good omen, and the drilling continued. At 1020 feet the bit struck a crevice and was forced off center. Al Hamill wired another brother, Jim, who had remained in Corsicana, for a new fishtail bit, hoping it would drive through the blockage. It was put into place, the drilling resumed, and at 1700 feet the rotary mud started to rise to the surface at a more rapid rate than the Hamills had ever seen. The flow subsided and the workmen prepared to drill once more. Then the ground started to tremble, and the men watched in amazement as mud, water, pipe, rigging—and oil—shot into the sky, a veritable geyser of oil. It was the first one in the Americas. There had been talk of geysers in Russia, but it was believed to be exaggeration. Now, they saw one with their own eyes. More oil came out of Spindletop that first day than most Pennsylvania wells were capable of producing in a year.

The Spindletop discovery marked the beginning of the greatest mineral rush since the gold and silver finds in the West and Alaska, and it was the most important oil discovery since the first ones in Pennsylvania. Wildcatters from all parts of the world rushed to east Texas. Beaumont's population rose from fewer than 9000 in January 1901 to 50,000 two years later. That year, more than 400 companies were organized which sold shares to an eager public at new exchanges organized in Beaumont, Houston, and Galveston. The Houston market alone recorded sales of 7.2 million shares in its first eight months. The scene resembled Washoe during the silver rush, and fortunes were made in securities, provisions, oil field services, transportation, housing, and prostitution. The really big money was not made in the fields, however, but in boardrooms in New York, Pittsburgh, London, and Corsicana.

Surveying the scene, John Galey wondered whether any of the wildcatters really understood what they were about. Didn't they know how Rockefeller had made his millions by ignoring production and concentrating on refining and distribution? Didn't they understand the need for refineries, storage facilities, a railroad or pipeline to the coast, and the like? All of this would cost a great deal of money, and there wasn't enough of it in Texas. Financial needs could only be met in two cities, he thought. First, there was New York, the home of the Rockefellers and Wall Street. The second city was Pittsburgh, Galey's own residence, the site of the Mellon Bank and those millionaires who had made their fortunes in the U.S. Steel flotation. Guffey and Galey meant to tap into this group. Already they had contacted some of the millionaires, among them a relative, James Galey, who had been one of Carnegie's bright young men.

Guffey and Galey also had those contacts with the Mellon Bank. Guffey Petroleum had done well. Now Guffey, together with Andrew, William, and Richard Mellon, organized the J. M. Guffey Petroleum Company, capitalized at $15 million, with 150,000 shares at $100 par value. The new company would purchase all the shares of Guffey Petroleum. In order to raise the money for the purchase price of $1.5 million, 50,000 shares at $30 a share would be sold. The Mellon brothers took 20,000 of these, while a group of wealthy Pittsburgh businessmen, including the steel millionaires, purchased the rest. Of the last 100,000 shares, Guffey was to receive 70,000, while the remainder would rest in the corporate treasury for future use—meaning sale to the Carnegie partners later on, at $66 a share. The former steel men invested blindly, in much the same way they had purchased homes and art. They were most fortunate, for they were to make many times more money in oil than they had in steel.

The Mellon interests and Guffey and Galey next formed the Gulf Refining Company, so named to satisfy Texas pride. This company was capitalized at $750,000. Guffey received a large share and the Mellons were right behind him, while the rest went to the Carnegie partners. Guffey was to be Gulf's president and William Mellon, the family's oil expert, the vice president. In 1902, the Mellons took direct control of Gulf Refining, and in 1906, Gulf and Guffey were united into the Gulf Oil Corporation, capitalized at $15 million.

Marcus Samuel, head of Shell Transport & Trading, was well aware of what was happening in east Texas, and he wanted to be in on the bonanza. He started out by purchasing oil from Guffey, but by 1903 he was prepared to make his own entry into the area with Shell Oil.

Governor Hogg became interested in the region as well. Together with James Swayne, who had been floor leader in the legislature, he formed Hogg-Swayne and purchased mineral rights in the Beaumont area. Cullinan, also eager to have representation there, organized the Texas Fuel Company, capitalized at $50,000, with the intention of buying crude from the producers and refining and marketing it. Eventually, Hogg-Swayne and Texas Fuel came together to form the company which in time would become the Texas Company, later Texaco.

Spindletop was uncapped the same year J. P. Morgan created U.S. Steel. At the time, the steel merger seemed of greater significance. But the appearance of "Big Steel" represented more the culmination of an industrial epoch than a new beginning. Spindletop, however, was a major watershed for what would become the "Age of Energy" in America and the world. Ford, General Motors, Chrysler, and the oil companies that emerged from Spindletop and the breakup of Standard Oil in 1911 were far larger and more consequential a half century later than was U.S. Steel.

So it was that in the waning years of the nineteenth century there arose in America a new industrial elite, the most visible members of which were men like Andrew Carnegie and John D. Rockefeller. The world was about to enter the age of steel and petroleum, and in these fields American businessmen and companies had clear advantages. What this augured for the future remained unknown. But clearly the pursuit of wealth would be simplified by the assets controlled by such men, and the possibilities imparted by such developments were to open a new chapter in the march of capitalism, and new opportunities for those with the intelligence, courage, imagination, and finances required.

American industrial superiority was becoming more evident in the early twentieth century. In 1875, the United States imported $34 million more merchandise than it exported. After this, exports exceeded imports for a century. In 1914, as Europe went to war, the merchandise export surplus came to $436 million. Between these two dates, exports of finished goods rose from $75 million to $725 million. The Europeans were well aware of this situation, and of the industrial might of the United States. Foreigners were still investing in the nation, but the tide was turning. By 1908, more American investment capital went abroad than arrived, even though, on balance, foreign investment in the United States remained greater than American investment overseas. Britain owned some $3.5 billion in American securities, Germany another billion, and France half that amount. Altogether, Europeans owned approximately $6 billion in American stocks and bonds. By 1914, American overseas investments stood at around $2.65 billion. Taking note of America's economic surge that year, a British observer wrote:

> The most serious aspect of the American industrial invasion lies in the fact that these newcomers have acquired control of almost every new industry created during the past fifteen years. . . . What are the chief new features in London life? They are, I take it, the telephone, the portable camera, the phonograph, the electric street car, the automobile, the typewriter, passenger lifts in houses, and the multiplication of machine tools. In every one of these, save the petroleum automobile, the American maker is supreme; in several, he is the monopolist.

The writer was in error. In 1914, Ford Motor Company was the largest in its field.

CHAPTER *16*

The Government-Industrial Complex, 1914–1929

 ROM the founding of the United States there has been a strong relationship between government and business, which involved physical and economic infrastructure, from internal improvements, tariffs, and the creation of the national credit and a banking system in the early years to aid to railroads later on. Theodore Roosevelt and Woodrow Wilson usually are considered "progressives," concerned with curbing any unwarranted powers of big business, but Roosevelt created the Department of Labor and Commerce in 1903, and 10 years later Wilson separated the two functions in order to provide the Secretary of Commerce with broader authority to assist American businesses in marketing their products overseas. During time of war, government purchases enabled businessmen to achieve greater wealth, but after the war, the economic links between government and its suppliers all but vanished.

Such was not the case, however, in World War I. Under President Wilson, there came into being what President Eisenhower would later call the "military-industrial complex." It continued into the 1920s but ended with President Hoover's attempts to put into place the essential elements of what he called "associationalism," a close collaboration between government and business. That Hoover played a major role in the World War I procurement effort is not unimportant, and historians have seen the impact on Franklin D. Roosevelt of his war experience as well. During the "Age of Morgan," wealth came to those who created industrial empires to provide goods to industry and consumers. This continued in the period after 1914, but there now was another path to wealth; working with government to obtain contracts, assistance, and other benefits.

The American Government on the Eve of War

In 1914, the government's role in the economy was still limited primarily to overseeing businesses and in some cases regulating them, as with the ICC, the new Federal Trade Commission, and state and local regulation of utilities. In 1914, there were 401,000 federal employees, of whom 40,000 were in Washington, D.C. The largest government agency was the Post Office. Budget receipts that year came to $683 million and expenditures to $715 million. The greatest sources of income were the excise taxes on liquor and tobacco, followed by the tariff. The income tax, instituted in 1913, produced revenues of $28 million in 1914, almost all of it from the very high earners. Fewer than 360,000 of the 99 million Americans paid any tax at all. The agency to raise the funds for big government was in place, but in 1914 the income tax was perceived by its supporters as a means of redistributing wealth, not raising capital for government projects.

The Federal Reserve Bank was established in 1914, too, so America had its first true central bank since the Second Bank of the United States. It was not seen that way, however. The nation was divided into 12 reserve districts, and it appeared they would act autonomously. There was to be a Federal Reserve Board, with the Secretary of the Treasury as a member. It seemed fairly certain this would be the most influential voice on the Board. All national banks had to join the system, and state banks were permitted to join if they met certain standards. Each of the banks could issue its own currency—Federal Reserve notes—which could be used to purchase government securities in the open market. The "Fed" would be able to purchase commercial paper held by member banks, and in this way head off financial stringencies. At the time this feature was considered most important, moreso than rate setting and open market operations, the latter being barely considered. That the Fed might act as a monetary engine was not recognized when the act establishing it was passed and signed into law, but like the income tax, it would soon become a powerful tool for a larger and stronger government.

World War I: The Neutrality Phase

On June 28, 1914, Austro-Hungarian Archduke Franz Ferdinand was assassinated by a young Serb nationalist. A month later, Austria-Hungary declared war on Serbia, and within a week every major European power except Italy was involved in the conflict. The major foes were the Allies (Great Britain, France, and Russia) and the Central Powers (Germany and Austria-Hungary). What contemporaries called "The Great War" turned out to be Europe's most complete conflagration to that time. When it was over, the German, Russian, Austro-Hungarian, and Ottoman Empires were no more. The United Kingdom and France were the nominal victors, but as a result of the war were reduced in power, prestige, and wealth. The Great War marked the true beginning of the twentieth century and the start of a general state of conflict and preparation for conflict in Europe that, with reprieves during the 1920s, would last until the early 1990s. One of the prescient observers was Lord Grey: "The lights are going out all over Europe," he said when the war began. "They will not go on again in our time."

From the first, Americans took sides in the conflict. Eastern and southern Americans tended to be pro-British. Wall Street and business in general had close ties with London, and were pro-Allies. Americans of German and Irish descent tended to be pro-German, although there were exceptions on both sides. President Woodrow Wilson, a proponent of Jeffersonian ideals who had been the scourge of big business, was himself decidedly pro-Allies. Nevertheless, at the onset of war, he asked Americans to "be neutral in fact as well as in name." The war was one "with which we have nothing to do, whose causes cannot touch us." Later, he would call for neutrality in thought as well as deed, knowing this was impossible. He told his secretary, "England is fighting our fight . . . I will not take any action to embarrass England when she is fighting for her life and the life of the world."

At first, the war had a negative effect on American business. Due to fears of substantial European liquidation of American securities in order to obtain gold, the NYSE closed down, as did every major exchange in the world. Trade ground to a near halt and the belligerents blockaded each other. Germany, which imported 2.6 million bushels of American wheat in July, took none in August. Commerce with Germany, which was $169 million in 1914, fell sharply in mid-year, and by 1916 was only $1 million. Europeans purchased only 21,219 bales of American cotton in August and none in September. A year earlier, cotton imports came to 257,172 bales. Although steel orders were up sharply, the companies found it difficult to make deliveries. By January 1915, the nation's steel mills were working at 50 percent of capacity. U.S. Steel's earnings were down sharply, and there was some question as to whether the company would be able to pay the interest on its bonds. Seth Low, president of the New York Chamber of Commerce, complained, "Europe has placed an embargo on the commerce of the world."

The slump in trade would not last. Europe's leaders had thought it would be a short war, and as it dragged on into 1915, shortages developed—of munitions, clothing, food, and particularly money to pay for supplies. By November, there was rationing of the number of shells the British artillery could fire. A year later, most of the shells fired came from America. Trade with the Allies, which came to $825 million in 1914, rose to $3.2 billion by 1916. Bethlehem Steel entered 1914 with a backlog of $25 million in orders, and reported a $47 million backlog on January 1, 1915. At year's end the figure was $175 million. U.S. Steel rebounded, as did other companies that manufactured war-related materials. More than a third of the company's production went overseas, and most of the rest was used in America for war-related purposes. By 1917, virtually the entire American economy was involved in providing war material to the Allies. During the neutrality period, production of bituminous coal rose from 422 million short tons to 552 million; iron ore from 42 million long tons to 75 million; copper from 575,000 long tons to 943,000; and zinc from 342,000 short tons to 589,000. The export balance of trade during the neutrality period rose from $436 million to $3.6 billion, with sharp increases across the board. Exports of explosives, for example, rose from $6.3 million in 1914 to $803 million in 1917. Shortages developed. Bethlehem Steel discontinued production of steel rails to divert the metal into other uses, and other steel manufacturers did the same. In 1916, Phelps Dodge stopped taking orders for copper wire. Exports to Europe strained the capacity of the shipping industry. Naturally, these shortages resulted in price boosts. Tungsten went from 75 cents a pound to $8.00 during the neutrality, while pig iron rose from $14.70 a ton to $19.65, and other prices followed suit.

Securities prices, which had been at 71 as measured by the Dow Jones Industrial Average when the market closed at the war's onset, stood at 53 at the end of the year. They would not recover to the prewar level until late April 1915, by which time it appeared certain that the war would bring prosperity to America. On the day America entered the war, April 6, 1917, the Dow stood at 95, having doubled in one year. Some of the gains were spectacular. Bethlehem Steel went from a 1915 low of 46½ to a 1916 high of 700, and a long list of stocks doubled and tripled in this span.

As it had been for more than a century, London was the hub of world finance in 1914. Wall Streeters customarily began the day asking about securities prices and interest rates there, and their activities would be influenced by those numbers. By 1917, New York had assumed the leading role. At the time of President Woodrow Wilson's declaration of war, the *Manchester Guardian* editorialized:

> European financiers would be well advised to face the fact that the war has radically transformed the relations between the United States and Europe. . . . The United States . . . by the end of this war will have wiped out most of its debt to foreign investors. It will have a currency of unimpeachable magnitude. The American bankers will have acquired the experience they have hitherto lacked in the international money market and all this strengthened financial fabric will rest upon an economic fabric which the war will have much expanded. It can hardly be doubted that under these circumstances, New York will enter the lists for the financial leadership of the world.

The writer proved prescient. From the position of a net debtor to the extent of more than $3.7 billion when the war began, the United States went to one of a net creditor by $5 billion in 1917. When President Wilson arrived in Versailles in January 1919, the American international investment position showed a balance of $6.4 billion. The gross national product rose from $76.4 billion in 1918 to $84 billion in 1919, and then to $91.5 billion in 1920.

With war came prosperity and wealth of almost unimagined scope for American business. Much of this accrued to American corporations that supplied war materials to the Allies, but since those shipments had to be paid for, the primary beneficiaries were the bankers. After the war, J. P. Morgan partner Thomas Lamont testified before the Senate Special Committee to Investigate the Munitions Industry that "like most of our contemporaries and friends and neighbors, we wanted the Allies to win from the outset of the war." J. P. Morgan, Jr. added, "Certainly we did the right thing [in seeking to underwrite large loans for the Allies]. We would do it again if we had to." Initially, the Wilson administration refused to permit Wall Street banks to finance the Allied effort. In August, a proposed $100 million loan to France, to be underwritten by Morgan, was disallowed. But soon after, Wilson agreed that short-term commercial credits could be permitted, and the Rockefeller-controlled National City Bank advanced $10 million to France and $5 million to Russia in this fashion. The alternative would have been the massive liquidation of American securities that had prompted the stock market closing in July. In late 1914 and early 1915, however, such sales would have disrupted the American markets, which the Wilson administration wanted to avoid. In August 1915, Secretary of the Treasury William Gibbs McAdoo wrote to Wilson that Britain's need for munitions and foodstuffs would boost the economy. "Great prosperity is coming. It is, in large measure, already here. It will be tremendously increased if we can extend reasonable credits to our customers." Secretary of State Robert Lansing added that failure to extend credits or permit loans would result in a decline in trade, which would harm the economy.

Wilson responded favorably to such arguments, and in October permitted Morgan to float a series of bond issues for Britain and France that totaled $500 million. This was the largest flotation to date; it shattered the record of $200 million set by a loan during the Spanish-American War in 1898. The lead banks would be J. P. Morgan, which had a traditional relationship with the British and was the French government's official American bank, and Brown Brothers, originally of Baltimore, which had been conducting international business for close to a century. Morgan organized a $10 million company, American Foreign Securities, to handle the underwritings. Once established, American Foreign sold additional bonds and used the proceeds to lend to foreign governments and companies.

Under the terms of its charter, American Foreign Securities was to "enter into a contract with the French Government whereby the Company will lend to the French Government the sum of $100,000,000, repayable July 31, 1919, and whereby the French Government will pledge with the Company in the United States as collateral security for the payment of the loan, securities having a value of approximately $120,000,000, calculated at quoted prices in existing markets, converted into dollars at prevailing rates of exchange between New York and Paris." The notes would be sold to yield 5¾ percent. The syndicate would receive one-half of 1 percent ($500,000) for services and another 2 percent ($2 million) as a commission. American Foreign sold 100,000 shares of $100 par value stock.

The second underwriting was for a $100 million, three-year secured loan to France. Despite initial reluctance on the part of lenders, the issue was sold out. Other offerings followed. By December 1, almost $1.8 billion in bonds had been placed. During the neutrality years of 1914–1917, the total foreign loans raised on Wall Street came to almost $3 billion.

At first, the underwriting went slowly. German-American influence and the wariness of investors uncertain of the outcome of the war caused institutions to hold back, while the general public, which had responded to Jay Cooke's appeals during the Civil War, was no longer involved with securities. Then, as general prosperity and a stiffening of Allied resistance developed, the sales accelerated.

Ordinarily, such strong demand for goods and services would have resulted in higher bond yields, but that was not the case. The strong market resulted from the veritable flood of investment funds and gold to America, a good deal of which went to purchase American bonds, considered the safest in the world during such difficult times. Not only did British and French investors send their money to Wall Street, but more than $200 million of the gold produced in British mines in south and west Africa each year found its way to America, while $2 billion in American securities were sold by European governments and individuals. In 1915 and 1916, the United States absorbed more than $1 billion in gold. Thus, having taken most of Europe's gold and securities, the American bankers lent the European governments the funds needed to continue the war largely through purchases from American factories and farms.

American Business and the War

America's entry into the war added to the demand for capital, which meant the government also went to the markets. During the conflict, the national debt rose from $1.3 billion to nearly $27 billion. Some of the funds needed by the government to fight the war came from higher taxes, especially the income tax, and from foreign investments. There were four Liberty Loan drives and one Victory Loan. The first drive, which began in May 1917, had a goal of $2 billion, and although the Federal Reserve backed it, in the beginning sales were very slow. When pressure was put on the trust companies, which took $300 million of the offering, sales picked up, and by the time it was over, $3 billion had been raised. A second drive, which was for $3 billion, was aimed at individual investors. Show business personalities like Douglas Fairbanks, Mary Pickford, and Charlie Chaplin urged middle class Americans to purchase bonds to assist the war effort. So they did; $4.6 billion was raised from 10 million subscribers. By the time the drives were over, almost $21 billion had been raised from more than 22 million separate buyers. This "hard sell" of the wartime years had the unanticipated effect of introducing millions of Americans to securities offerings. True, these were government bonds, considered quite safe by the standards of the time, and there is no way of knowing how many of those who purchased them came to view this as an entry into the securities markets of the 1920s. Even so, many Americans had become aware that there were other ways to obtain wealth than those with which they were familiar.

While the investment banking community prospered, its role in raising funds for the government was limited. Most of the loan campaigns were conducted by government agencies, which either sold bonds directly to the public through commercial banks or did so through dealers authorized to market government securities under the terms of the legislation establishing the Federal Reserve System. Since profit margins in this business were quite small, the larger firms tended to ignore it, leaving the business to smaller houses.

This approach undermined the position of the old-line investment banks. Assertive newer ones and once-small operations had the opportunity to expand significantly if they grasped the meaning of the new dispensation and were bold and intelligent in reacting to it. None of this was apparent during the war, but many small and new firms were obtaining business and undergoing experiences that would enable them to play a leadership role in the postwar period. Wrote one student of the scene, "In the money market of the twenties, syndicates of relatively obscure origin and new houses could handle hundred million dollar issues without recourse to the old financial leaders."

The benefits of the economic boom that resulted from the heavy spending trickled down to thousands of small companies, but the major benefits fell to the larger corporations. Workers did not derive much wealth from the war. From 1913 to 1918, wages rose 62 percent, but the cost of living increased by 74 percent in this period, so real wages actually declined. This stable wage level enabled corporations to report high profits, but these did not include writeoffs for capital improvements, depreciation, and special charges. Du Pont, which provided gunpowder and other products for the military, produced 6000 tons of explosives in 1914; by 1918, it was turning them out at the rate of 200,000 tons annually. The company grossed $10.2 million more in 1918 than in 1916, but reported earnings actually declined. During the war, the company's assets rose from $75 million to more than $308 million. This was the pattern throughout war-related industries. U.S. Steel's 1914 assets came to $1.7 billion; in 1918, they were $2.6 billion.

None of this was reflected in the stock market. As noted, on the day of the declaration of war, the Dow Jones Industrial stood at 95. There was little movement until late in the year, when stocks declined because of bad news from the front. On the day the war ended, November 11, 1918, the Dow was at 88. By mid-1921, as a result of a postwar depression, the average had fallen to the low 60s (This situation will be discussed in more detail in Chapter 17).

The War Industries Board

The booming economy during America's neutrality phase prompted leading business-men to organize the Industrial Preparedness Commission, which set to work in early 1915. Purely a business organization, without government participation, led by Hudson Motor Car vice president Howard Coffin, the commission intended to coordinate the conversion of some 20,000 plants to war production. Late in the year, the government gave the commission semiofficial recognition, and in 1916, Congress voted to establish the Council of National Defense, which consisted of cabinet officers, private speculator and Wilson confidant Bernard Baruch, Coffin, Walter Gifford of AT&T, Julius Rosen-wald of Sears-Roebuck, and others. It replaced the IPC. Earlier, Wilson had utilized the antitrust acts vigorously, but from December 7, 1916, when the council first met, to the conclusion of his administration, there were no new prosecutions, and several that had already started were halted. In this and other ways, the President signaled the arrival of a new phase in government-business cooperation.

Secretary of War Newton Baker made several speeches in which he indicated his belief that mobilization was necessary. "War is no longer Samson with his shield and spear and sword and David with his sling," he told one audience. "It is the conflict of the smokestacks now, the combat of the driving wheel and the engine." Baker and Baruch urged Wilson to take action, and in July, two months after the declaration of war, the President authorized the creation of the War Industries Board, which was to have broad but undefined powers. Its chairman was Frank Scott of Warner-Swasey, an important machine tool manufacturer. Baruch headed the raw materials section and was given additional responsibilities when Scott was succeeded by Daniel Willard, president of the B&O Railroad, who proved inept during the first year of America's belligerency. When Willard indicated a desire to step down, Secretary McAdoo urged Wilson to replace him with Baruch, who took over on March 4, 1918. Under Baruch's leadership, the American economy was mobilized as never before or since in a partnership of gov-ernment and business. This pattern would continue after the war ended, and become a major source of wealth for many American companies and their shareholders.

The WIB's tasks were difficult and complicated. Baruch had to mold the economy into a smooth-running, integrated operation. Clearly, such an endeavor would have been impossible without an organizational program and large-scale delegation of responsibilities, which was where the army of businessmen who arrived in Washington in 1917 came in.

Among those serving on WIB organizations were officers of such firms as the South-ern Railway, Westinghouse Electric and Manufacturing, International Harvester, Buck-eye Steel Castings, St. Joseph Lead, Illinois Steel, Continental Can, and many more. The WIB experience was a watershed event for scores of young businessmen. For decades after the war, they communicated regularly and cooperated on deals.

Such major firms as General Motors and Ford had shied away from seeking contracts during the neutrality phase. This changed when America went to war. By mid-1918, Ford not only was meeting all Allied and American military demands for farm tractors, but was also able to fill civilian requirements as well. Without knowing much about airplanes, Ford offered to construct 150,000 annually if the British could send him a model they preferred. Nor did Ford's interest in aviation end with the armistice. In the 1930s, he became a significant manufacturer of passenger planes.

Some businessmen railed against the bureaucracy they encountered and chafed at Baruch's imperious orders and demands. When U.S. Steel CEO Elbert Gary and other industry executives refused to accept some dictates regarding prices, Baruch presented them with an ultimatum: cooperate or have the government take over your plants. As noted, the steel industry did quite well during the war. Even so, animosities remained. "The steel industry also did a superb job of production," Baruch said after the war, "but there is no question that profits, especially of the great integrated companies, were still excessive."

During the war, with some exceptions—as in the steel industry—business accepted federal regulation in return for high profits, and the government came to understand that along with the benefits of bigness came the possibility for excesses. One of these benefits was standardization. Prior to the war, with the exception of the railroads, little had been done to rationalize industry. In farming supplies, there were more than 1700 types of wagon gears, 326 models of plows, and 784 drills and other planting machines. Under WIB guidelines, these numbers declined. By the end of the war, the variety of plows stood at seventy-six, the 232 kinds of buggy wheels had been reduced to four, and the number of different typewriter ribbons shrunk from 150 to four. While wary and fearful that rationalization would result in lost sales, businesses did accept it and recognized its benefits after the war.

The Creation of Radio Corporation of America

The most conspicuous example of government-business collaboration was the creation of Radio Corporation of America. Marconi Wireless, the largest and most successful company in the wireless telegraphy industry, organized American Marconi Wireless in 1899, and soon the technology was in use on American ships. Marconi Wireless owned only 15 percent of its shares, and most of the directors and officers were American. Nonetheless, in Washington it was viewed as a foreign company. It was not a particularly large firm. In 1914, American Marconi had revenues of $760,000.

Two days after the United States declared war in 1917, Wilson ordered the U.S. Navy to take over all wireless operations in the U.S. The British did not protest, believing that after the war, the property would return to its earlier status. The wireless technology proved an important factor during the war, and the company grew substantially, reporting revenues of $1.9 million in 1918. With the end of the war in November came pressures from London for the return of the company to private control. The Navy wanted to continue operation of American Marconi, however, and there were supporters for its position in Congress who held that the government had a monopoly of postal services, and that there was no reason why the same could not be the case with wireless communication. That the telegraph and telephone were in private hands was a fact not raised at the time. Wilson had a different idea, and desired to bring business into the picture. Having worked more or less harmoniously with the private sector during the war, Wilson had shed much of his distrust of business. In this he had the support of J. P. Morgan & Company, which was the dominant factor at such manufacturers of electrical gear as General Electric and Westinghouse, among others.

In early July of 1919, Congress passed a resolution ordering the return to their original owners by March 1, 1920 of all telegraph, telephone, and cable systems seized by the government during the war. With this, Wilson pressed ahead with his plan, his point men in the project being Assistant Secretary of the Navy Franklin D. Roosevelt for the government and Owen D. Young of General Electric, who represented the private interests to be drawn into the company. In the end, the British shareholders agreed to accept $1.5 million for their stake, the only condition being that American Marconi remain independent and not be taken over by any single American company. This was to ensure that the American market would remain open to the British. So it would be. Radio Corporation of America (RCA) received its charter on October 17, 1919, with a majority of the stock owned by General Electric, Westinghouse, AT&T, and United Fruit. Under the terms, RCA was to sell equipment manufactured by its principal owners, with GE to have 60 percent of the market and Westinghouse 40 percent, for which RCA would pay costs plus 20 percent. The Western Electric subsidiary of AT&T would have a monopoly in transmitters. The RCA board was restructured and now comprised four members each from the old American Marconi and GE, three from Westinghouse, two from AT&T, and one from United Fruit. Thus was born a government-sponsored monopoly in wireless, one of the more promising new technologies of the early years of the century. In time, it would become more than that, but even in 1920 it was clear to all concerned that the American government had bestowed the opportunity for great wealth upon the participants.

The Government and Business during the Harding-Coolidge Years

Warren Harding succeeded Wilson as President in 1921. During his campaign, Harding promised "normalcy, not nostrums," and the public took this to mean that he would bring an end to the two decades of reform and war. It also was assumed that Harding would favor business interests. Yet it could not truly be said that the Presidents and Congresses from 1901 through 1920 were antibusiness. Rather, they had been activist, while Harding appeared to favor a more passive approach. In any case, any notion that the association between business and government that had been strengthened during the war would come to an end would prove false. Harding expanded the merchant marine and supported Secretary of the Treasury Andrew Mellon's plan for tax reduction and higher tariffs to protect both industrial and farm interests. He also pressured Elbert Gary to change the twelve-hour work day and seven-day work week at U.S. Steel to an eight-hour day and six-day week. New industries were appearing, and Secretary of Commerce Herbert Hoover brought order to radio transmission and would assist business abroad more vigorously than had any previous cabinet officer.

These policies were continued by President Calvin Coolidge, who took office upon Harding's death in 1923. But there were differences as well. Coolidge was less inclined than Harding to assist American business directly. An instance of this came in discussions regarding aid to the victims after the 1927 Mississippi flood. Coolidge hoped local and state aid would suffice, because the beneficiaries of federal aid would be business interests:

> It almost seems to me as though the protection of the people and the property in the lower Mississippi that need protection has been somewhat lost sight of and it has become a scramble to take care of the railroads and the banks and the individuals that might have invested in levee bonds, and the great lumber concerns that own many thousands of acres in that locality, with wonderful prospects for contractors.

American business expanded into the world during the Harding-Coolidge years, and the world came to Wall Street to finance its economies. By one calculation, American overseas investments rose from $6.9 billion in 1919 to $17.2 billion in 1930, and by another, it went from $3.8 billion in 1919 to $7.5 billion in 1929. Before the war, direct American investment abroad was little more than $1.8 billion. By 1929, it was $7.5 billion, with General Motors alone investing $20 million.

Of equal importance was the matter of foreign trade. Exports rose from $3.8 billion in 1922 to $5.2 billion in 1928, and in the same period, imports grew from $3.1 billion to $4.1 billion. An even more revealing comparison emerges between the 1920s figures and those of the prewar period. In 1913, exports came to $1.8 billion and imports to $913 million. Those who argued that protectionism kept foreign goods out of the United States might have been embarrassed by these statistics.

There were three major players in these developments: the American banks, most of which were in New York; the corporations themselves; and the government, especially the Department of State and the Department of Commerce. In World War I, the enemy had been the Central Powers. In the commercial wars of the 1920s, Americans were pitted against their counterparts in the United Kingdom, France, and other countries. Coolidge was aware of these developments, but he did not plan the strategy or take the lead in the contest for foreign expansion. He did not speak out on the subject. Foreign investment was not a government policy, but a matter for the private sector. All Washington had to do was smile benevolently and offer assistance when it was needed.

The banks were more instrumental than government in expansion abroad. The large New York banks always had an international presence, but before the war they usually played junior partner to the London banks. The war changed this. The largest international debtor in 1914, with net borrowings of $3.7 billion, the United States had become by 1918 the largest creditor, to the extent of the same $3.7 billion, and New York had replaced London as the central capital market. As early as January 1917, the National City Bank's *Monthly Letter* proclaimed, "Americans are able to enter this field [foreign investment] in a new capacity, that of an investor and organizer. The United States has become much the richest country in the world."

The Wilson administration had done what it could to assist American businesses expanding abroad. With the President's blessings, in 1918, Congress passed the Webb-Pomerene Act, which authorized American companies to act together in exporting without being troubled by antitrust considerations. The Edge Act, passed the following year, permitted federally chartered corporations to engage in foreign banking and investment. Harding continued the policies started by Wilson: "We must give cooperation to business; we protect American business at home, and we aid and protect it abroad." Coolidge agreed. "Our government has usually been too remiss, rather than too active in supporting the rights of its citizens abroad," he said in 1924.

Commerce Secretary Hoover was the most visible cabinet member concerned with international trade. Moreover, Hoover received publicity for his efforts to combat foreign cartels whose activities raised commodity prices for American consumers and businesses. There was a British cartel in rubber, a German cartel in potash, a Chilean one in nitrates, while the Brazilians had one in coffee and the Spaniards and Italians one in mercury. Hoover put what pressures he could on businesses in these countries to permit competition, and when this failed, he led the way in the search for new sources of those commodities. In his memoirs, Hoover wrote of some of his successes:

> We urged the Dutch Government that to maintain reasonable prices from their Far Eastern rubber industry was in their long-view interest. They remained out of the combination and proceeded to expand their production. We encouraged American rubber manufacturers to plant rubber in non-British territory, which they did on an extensive scale. This campaign, beginning in the summer of 1925, had by March, 1926, broken the price from the top of $1.21 a pound to 59 cents and by June the price was 40 cents with a corresponding reduction in the prices of tires and other rubber goods. . . . We undertook action against the other combinations by different tactics. Working with the Bureau of Mines, I secured appropriations to drill for geologically suspected potash in Texas and New Mexico. We struck pay dirt and ultimately relieved American consumers from the oppression of the German potash cartel. In the end, we not only destroyed German exports to the United States but exported to the cartels previous markets.

U.S. Government and Business Involvement in Latin America

Some of the U.S. firms had become strong forces in Latin America before the war, and they grew even more during the 1920s. United Fruit was a power in its own right in Central America, and W. R. Grace was a presence on the west coast of South America. Scores of other businesses expanded upon their prewar bases or entered the area. International Telephone & Telegraph was one of the leading players, and its expansion throughout the region offers some indication of how it was done.

Before the war, what was to become ITT had been a small operation in Cuba, Puerto Rico, and the Virgin Islands. Its CEO, Sosthenes Behn, was a native of the region who entered the U.S. Army during the war and left the service intent on expanding throughout the world, creating a global counterpart to American Telephone & Telegraph. In the process, he was aided by National City Bank. To maintain the relationship, Behn opened an office on Broad Street near the National City offices, and by 1923, ITT was considered one of National City's "constellation" of companies.

At the time, Spain's telephone company was in shabby condition—undercapitalized, mismanaged, and operating antiquated equipment. Several European companies, among them Sweden's Ericsson, the Dutch firm Philips, and Germany's Siemens, were interested in obtaining control of Spain's national company. ITT, which was far smaller, not only lacked the resources for such a bid but didn't even manufacture equipment, which the others had been doing for many years. Behn overcame this problem by working out a partnership with International Western Electric, which was AT&T's Brussels-based manufacturing arm. Behn then moved to capture the Spanish telecommunications contract, working closely with the National City branch managers, the Commerce Department's assistant trade commissioner, James Burke, and Ambassador Alexander Moore. The Ambassador assured the government that ITT had his backing, and Burke quashed stories detrimental to the company's interests. With their support, Behn purchased three small Spanish telephone companies.

Behn organized the Compania Telefonia National de España, whose board included prominent and influential Spaniards. Then, with Moore's blessing, he arranged for the purchase of International Western Electric, assisted by the Justice Department's insistence that AT&T sell the company to avoid antitrust problems, whereupon the company's name was changed to International Standard Electric. Along the way, ITT also acquired Thomson-Houston, which had an important presence in the French market. With Spain in hand and now possessing manufacturing facilities, both courtesy of National City and the Commerce Department, Behn set off to invade the Latin American markets.

Mexico was the first country Behn targeted. There were several operating companies there, the largest being Empresa de Telefonos. ITT acquired the firm in 1925, and the following year, through the intercession of the Morgan bank, purchased All American Cables, which operated telegraph lines between the United States and a good deal of Latin America. All American's president, John Merrill, had been at the company since 1884. He knew the leaders of the countries in which his firm operated and was able to introduce Behn to those with whom he wanted to do business.

Within the next two years, ITT acquired a half dozen Latin American telephone companies, virtually all of which had been under British control before the war, and other business was gathered. In Chile, for example, the federal bonds that once were marketed through London were now being floated in New York by a consortium headed by National City, and Chile Telephone became an ITT subsidiary. The United Kingdom once had accounted for more than half the foreign investment in Argentina. Although that country had a long record of anti-American sentiment, Behn was able to obtain control of Compania Telefonica Argentina and United River Plate, two of the country's leading operators.

By the end of the decade, ITT was one of the two most powerful utility companies in Latin America, the other being American and Foreign Power, organized in 1923 by Electric Bond & Share, a General Electric subsidiary. This company started out with electric utility holdings in Panama, Guatemala, and Cuba. With support from American banks and the assistance of the Commerce Department, A&FP purchased properties to the south from their British, German, French, and Canadian owners. By 1929, it operated companies in Ecuador, Columbia, Brazil, Venezuela, Costa Rica, Chile, Mexico, Argentina, and even India and China.

American and Foreign Power and ITT worked in tandem. Behn joined the A&FP board in 1927, and under his aegis there were several joint ITT–A&FP ventures. Led by these two firms, by 1929 American companies had investments of more than $1 billion in foreign utility companies, a fourfold increase over the figure in 1924, with most of it in Latin America, Europe, and Canada.

Government aid extended to other sectors as well. In airlines, America's "chosen instrument" was Juan Trippe's Pan American, started in 1927 to fly a route between

Florida and Cuba. The following year, Trippe purchased control of a small Mexican airline, and in early 1929, together with W. R. Grace, Trippe formed Panagra, which flew the routes to the South American west coast. Coolidge had left the White House by 1930, by which time Pan Am was flying to most Latin American countries and was competing for international business with the UK's Imperial Airways, the Netherlands' KLM, and France's Aeropostale. None of this would have been possible without generous federal assistance, such as the subsidies provided under terms of the Foreign Air Mail Act of 1928, which had Coolidge's endorsement.

Perhaps the most overt example of federal aid to overseas American industry involved the rapidly growing radio industry. During the Harding administration, Secretary of Commerce Hoover held the first of his conferences to structure the industry, and this work continued during the Coolidge administration, as Hoover became a central figure in radio transmission. At first he exercised power through his department and the Federal Trade Commission, but in 1927 Congress passed and Coolidge signed the Radio Act, which established the Federal Radio Commission.

In 1928, the Commerce Department blessed ITT's tender offer for RCA Communications, a subsidiary organized to extend the company's reach overseas, the merger to be handled by a Morgan syndicate under terms that would make RCA the largest shareholder in ITT. This was in response to a British plan to counter ITT's expansion by bringing together British Marconi and Eastern and Associated Cable to form a new entity called Cable & Wireless. Once again, the government, Wall Street, and American corporations had combined to mount an international business effort. Ultimately, the American merger did not take place, due largely to the unrest caused by the stock market crash of October 1929. But absent that, ITT-RCA would have challenged the European companies in what was destined to become one of the most important global industries of the period. Coolidge did not play a direct role in this matter. As usual, the planning and details were left to others.

Wall Street's Pursuit of Wealth Overseas

During the 1920s, American investment and lending expanded in all parts of the world, with the most striking developments occurring in Latin America, where in addition to petroleum and utilities, American companies entered a wide variety of enterprises. While U.S. investments in Europe and Canada doubled in this period, investments in South America almost tripled. Prior to 1914, the United Kingdom had been the leading trading partner there as well as the largest foreign investor. British businessmen controlled railroads in Argentina, copper and nitrate mines in Chile, coffee plantations in Brazil, tin smelting in Bolivia, and telecommunications facilities in all of these countries and others. Behind them were the large London banks, which in addition to financing the companies, made loans to the Latin American countries. By the 1920s, direct British investment in Latin America came to $3.5 billion, which was approximately as much as was invested in the United States, and the figure was growing rapidly.

The war altered this situation. Britain sold many of its investments to pay for the war, and British banks, involved in financing the war, withdrew from their Latin American markets. National City and Morgan had been in the region earlier, but now they enlarged the scope of their operations. More important, these banks and others helped finance American corporate expansion in that part of the world. The State Department, with Harding's and Coolidge's approval, would review underwritings and provide the banks with information and assistance in dealing with governments. The Monroe Doctrine was in place to help Americans against foreign competition. In the past, the U.S. government had intervened to protect American bondholders, and it was understood it would do so in the future.

Few European countries borrowed in the American capital markets before the war. After the war all of them came to Wall Street. So did the Latin American countries and companies. In 1924, Americans held $700 million in Latin American securities. By 1929, that figure had risen to $1.6 billion. Cleona Lewis, one of the most respected authorities in the field, portrayed the situation vividly in her 1937 book, *America's Stake in International Investments*.

> Some 36 houses, most of them American, competed for a city of Budapest loan and 14 for a loan to the city of Belgrade. A Bavarian hamlet, discovered by American agents to be in need of about $125,000, was urged and finally persuaded to borrow $3 million in the American market. In Peru, a group of successful American promoters included one Peruvian, the son of the President of that republic, who was afterwards tried by the courts of his country and convicted of "illegal enrichment." In Cuba the son-in-law of the President was given a well-paid position in the Cuban Branch of an American bank during most of the time the bank was successfully competing against other American banks for the privilege of financing the Cuban government.

The questionable aspects of all this financial activity began to trouble Thomas Lamont, the head of J. P. Morgan & Co., who in 1927 warned against "indiscriminate lending and indiscriminate borrowing."

> I have in mind reports . . . of American bankers and firms competing on almost a violent scale for the purpose of obtaining loans in various foreign money markets overseas. Naturally it is a tempting thing for certain of the European governments to find a hoard of American bankers sitting on their doorsteps offering them money. It is rather demoralizing for municipalities and corporations of the same countries to have money pressed upon them. That sort of competition tends to insecurity and unsound practice.

The government's involvement with the banks and corporations did not go without notice. In 1925 and again in 1927, the Senate Committee on Foreign Relations held hearings to consider resolutions calling upon the State, Commerce, and Treasury departments to desist from "engaging the responsibility of the Government [in] supervising the fulfillment of financial agreements—between citizens of the United States and sovereign foreign governments." A parade of witnesses appeared to criticize these departments' intervention in the matter of lending by American banks to foreign governments. Lewis Gannett, editor of *The Nation* and a constant critic of American economic foreign policy, appeared before the Committee to charge that "irresponsible bureaucrats" were "setting a new precedent in the partnership between the United States Government and the bankers." As evidence, he introduced loan contracts between Bolivia and the Equitable Trust Company, which, he suggested, "turned over the Republic of Bolivia to a group of New York bankers." Government approval of the loan, said Gannett, demonstrated that the American government was prepared to intervene militarily to guarantee the loan.

Others testified along the same lines, asserting that under Harding and Coolidge, the nation was returning to the old "dollar diplomacy" of the Taft era. And as philosopher John Dewey opined: "Government has other business than that of acting as bill collectors in behalf of dubious and highly speculative investments."

Helping Europe and Reaping the Financial Rewards

In 1923, Irving Fisher, the most influential American economist of his time, wrote that Europe resembled an ailing man who couldn't be expected to repay debts, or in the case of Germany, make reparations.

> The sick man after eight years, of course, must first repair his premises; he must acquire new tools for his trade, he must have raw materials. Therefore, for these things we must advance him credit, not altogether for his benefit, but for ours as creditors also, in order that we may put him on his feet and enable him to repay us.

There was only one important source of credit in the world: American bankers. That the United States was bound to utilize its vast new wealth to enter world markets in a major way seemed inevitable. Some of its surplus capital would be used for foreign loans, which would be employed in part to purchase American goods while increasing American influence abroad. Toward the end of the 1920s, many scholars commented on this phenomenon, which in 1917 the *Manchester Guardian* had predicted would happen. Political scientist Max Fisher was one such analyst. "The most striking feature of American foreign trade," he wrote in 1928, "is the fact that our total foreign investments made within the past fourteen years together with our political loans to foreign governments almost exactly correspond to the aggregate excess of exports from the United States over imports into this country during the same period." To Fisher, the lesson was clear enough: America's new role in the world benefited everyone. "In other words, our foreign loans enabled foreign countries to absorb and to pay for our surplus production."

These loans would originate from Wall Street, not Washington, which is to say they would be generated by investment bankers and not by government officials. Secretary of State Charles Evans Hughes made this abundantly clear in 1923 when he said, "It is not the policy of our Government to make loans to other governments, and the needed capital, if it is to be furnished at all, must be supplied by private organizations."

British bankers, once supreme in Latin America, were elbowed aside by their American rivals. There was enough business for all the big banks. J. & W. Seligman dominated the market for Peruvian bonds. Kuhn Loeb had all of the considerable business of the Chilean Mortgage Bank. Hallgarten and Kissel/Kinnecutt were Colombia's bankers, but there was no dominant force for that nation's Agricultural Mortgage Bank. Morgan and National City dominated in Argentina, but Blair & Co. underwrote several issues. Colony Trust and Dillon Read underwrote Buenos Aires province issues; Blyth, Witter took some Buenos Aires city business; and Chase Securities cofinanced one national issue. National City underwrote securities for the state of Minas Geraes in Brazil, and Speyer & Co. was the sole lead underwriter for São Paolo.

The concern with Latin America was part of an emerging pattern. Just as a century earlier British investors with surplus capital proffered loans to Americans, so Wall Street was seeking borrowers. The capital market was awash with American lenders seeking new opportunities. It didn't take long for the Latin American countries' leaders to realize they were welcome on Wall Street. Indeed, it wasn't uncommon for one of them to request, say, a $10 million loan, only to be informed that this was not enough, that he could have $15 million simply for the asking.

Not all American bankers and businessmen were eager to send their capital abroad or underwrite such issues in those early postwar years. European currencies were weak, the French and British economies unsteady, and Germany was shattered. Russia was in the midst of civil war, with the Bolsheviks seeking to spread their revolution to other parts of the continent and world. Circumstances in Germany were complicated and emotionally charged, but there was promise for American bankers seeking opportunities if and when the political situation stabilized. Germany had been devastated during the war, and the victorious French were intent on ensuring that recovery was slow, and never to the point that Germany could again pose a military or industrial threat to its neighbors. The key American bank in Germany was Dillon Read.

In 1928, Ferdinand Eberstadt of Dillon Read would explain to his United States-based associates just how significant the German accomplishments were by going over the roster of firms for which Dillon Read had become the investment banker:

> We have in the iron, coal, and steel industry, the United Steel Works, which is approximately the size of Bethlehem Steel, and second only to the United States Steel Corporation. . . . In the electrical industry we took the Siemens, which recognizes as a rival only the United States General Electric. . . . In the banking field, we selected the Disconto and Deutsche Banks. Now, what do they correspond to in the United States? . . . The Disconto and the Deutsche Banks correspond to the First National and the National City.

Such was the state of the western world at the dawn of what would prove to be an American Imperium.

CHAPTER *17*

The Great Bull Market
of the 1920s

 HE period of the 1920s constituted one of the most prosperous, innovative, and original decades in American history, one during which many
Americans were successful in their pursuit of wealth. The operative slo-
gans of the period were "What will they think of next?" and "New and
improved!" Part of the reason for this prosperity already has been
alluded to: America's new leadership position in the world following World War I.
Another factor was that the lag between invention and widespread realization was being
shortened. The American home and factory were becoming electrified, and economic
savings on a large scale were being realized, leading to increases in productivity that
translated into higher wages and higher standards of living. At the same time, new
industries appeared in which wealth could be realized, such as motion pictures, radio,
automobiles—and organized crime. The statistics are impressive. Production of radio
receivers reached 100,000 in 1921, when 60 out of 1000 households had sets. More than
4.4 million units were produced in 1928, and the average American had more than one
unit. In this time span, the value of electrical appliances produced rose from $83 mil-
lion to $153 million. From 1.4 million automobiles produced in 1921, Detroit surged to
3.7 million in 1928. Electricity usage soared. In 1920, the nation's utility companies
generated 56 billion kilowatt hours, which more than doubled to 117 billion in 1928.
Hundreds of thousands of new companies appeared to produce, sell, and service components and finished goods.

Installment buying became more prevalent, and the combination of greater take-
home pay and time purchasing increased demand for a wide variety of consumer goods,
which in turn meant more jobs and yet higher pay. Access to capital for small businesses
was eased by the banking revolution pioneered by A. P. Giannini. The stock market
soared, and while far fewer Americans were directly involved with securities than ordinarily is believed, many did prosper, and others who were not holders of common shares
enjoyed the afterglow as well. The real estate market also thundered ahead, part of
which was the Florida land boom. And the government assisted in this. Under Presidents Warren Harding and Calvin Coolidge, income taxes were cut four times. In 1920,

15.4 percent of total personal income taxes were paid by people who earned less than $5000. By 1929, it was down to 0.4 percent. In the same period, the percentage of total taxes paid by those who earned more than $100,000 rose from 29.9 percent to 65.2 percent. In his 1928 budget address, given on Dec. 3, Coolidge noted that during the year, 54 percent of federal receipts had been derived from income taxes, up from the 42 percent of 1923.

All of this translated into greater access to the "good" life for more Americans than ever before. The gap between rich and poor had widened at the turn of the century. There was a distinct narrowing of that gap in the 1920s. In Robert and Helen Lynd's *Middletown*, a study of Muncie, Indiana published in 1929, there is a portrait of a middle class individual that illustrates this. Here is the tale of a rather ordinary housewife whose life was startlingly different from those of her mother and grandmother.

> I began to work during the war, when everyone else did; we had to meet payments on our house and everything else was getting so high. The mister objected at first, but now he don't mind. I'd rather keep on working so my boys can play football and basketball and have spending money their father can't give them. We've built our own home, a nice brown and white bungalow, by a building and loan like everyone else does. We have it almost paid off and it's worth about $6000. No, I don't lose out with my neighbors because I work; some of them have jobs and those of them who don't envy us who do. I have felt better since I work than ever before in my life. I get up at five-thirty. My husband takes his dinner and the boys buy theirs uptown and I cook supper. We have an electric washing machine, electric iron, and vacuum sweeper. I don't even have to ask my husband any more because I buy these things with my own money. I bought an icebox last year—a big one that holds 125 pounds; most of the time I don't fill it, but we have our folks visit us from back East and then I do. We own a $1200 Studebaker with a nice California top, semi-enclosed. Last summer we spent our vacation going back to Pennsylvania—taking in Niagara Falls on the way. The two boys want to go to college, and I want them to. I graduated from high school myself, but feel if I can't give my boys a little more all my work would have been useless.

Big business expanded and became even bigger during World War I. While at times Presidents after Wilson would criticize specific business practices, the thought that small enterprises could function efficiently in such industries as steel, automobiles, refining, and meat packing was no longer entertained seriously by students of the subject. Economies of scale were so obvious as to foreclose debate. Even so, small businesses proliferated, and startup enterprises were always a factor in growth and innovation.

Small businesses had to face many problems. While statistics on failures are not reliable for this period, it appears that more than half of the startups failed in the first four years of their existence. The reasons ran from inexperience, competition from stronger units, and, of course, inadequate financing. Entrepreneurship and the drive to own one's own business runs strong and deep in the American character. Financing such enterprises in the late nineteenth century was usually done through recourse to savings or loans and grants from friends and relatives. Loans from banks and other financial intermediaries were not available to such people. Granger banks might lend to farmers, who in the Jeffersonian sense were established businessmen able to collateralize their loans with crops and equipment. Businessmen who had sufficient liquefiable assets might borrow against them, not unlike borrowing from a medieval pawnbroker. As for the rest, they would simply have to defer their dreams.

A. P. Giannini: Financing Small Business

In some immigrant groups it was common for members to pool funds and make loans to those wanting to enter business, a practice that continues to this day. This was the basic idea behind a successful attempt to democratize banking mounted by a man who is as important to opening capital markets to small business as J. P. Morgan was to the larger ones. He was Amadeo Peter Giannini. His guiding concept was that small depositors and borrowers, the kind who were ignored in the late nineteenth century by the large banks, had something to offer one another. Giannini would welcome the small depositors and then pool their deposits to make loans to small businessmen.

Giannini's father, Luigi, was an Italian immigrant who made some money as a gold miner in California. He went home to marry Virginia DeMartini, and then the two settled in San Jose, California in 1869, where they purchased a hotel. Amadeo Peter, better known as A. P., was born the following year. When he was seven years old, his father was murdered and his mother married Lorenzo Scatena, a teamster who soon became a commission agent in the fruit and vegetable business and then entered the wholesale produce business on his own. The family moved to San Francisco, where Giannini attended school until the age of 14, but he worked nights for his stepfather, finding employment there more interesting than school. Giannini prospered and showed acumen in business.

In 1892, Giannini married Clorinda Cuneo, the daughter of a wealthy businessman who died in 1902 after having made a fortune in real estate. He took over management of his deceased father-in-law's properties, which included a minority interest in the Columbus Savings Association, founded and headed by Joseph Fugazi, one of the most prominent men in the community. Giannini succeeded to his father-in-law's position on the board and immediately clashed with Fugazi over policy. Fugazi was willing to accept small deposits, but he refused to make loans to merchants hoping to start or expand their businesses. He lent instead to the community's prosperous businessmen. To fill this gap, Andrea Sbarboro had opened the Italian-American Bank in 1899, which experienced rapid growth. Giannini, who admired Sbarboro's bank, quit Columbus in 1909 to form his own savings institution, which he called the Bank of Italy. That institution started with $20,000 of Giannini money and another $130,000 raised from friends and relatives.

This was a time when American banking was dominated by influential banks in money centers—such as Morgan and later, Jacob Schiff—in New York, and to a lesser extent, banks in Chicago and Philadelphia, whose clients were institutions, corporations, and the very wealthy. These institutions made loans to none but the most creditworthy customers, certainly not to modest, immigrant-run enterprises, and the same approach prevailed among the major California banks, such as Wells Fargo and Crocker National.

From the first, Giannini focused on small depositors and borrowers, intending to open banking to the masses. He advertised for depositors and made certain local business owners knew the Bank of Italy was prepared to offer them its services. On occasion, he would go door-to-door trying to convince residents to open accounts at the Bank of

Italy. His loan policy was strikingly different from other banks. He even made what were called "character loans" to individuals he knew to be honest and hardworking. A year and a half after it opened, the Bank of Italy's loans exceeded its deposits by more than $200,000. By then, the bank had 1620 shareholders, reflecting Giannini's belief that depositors should also be owners.

The turning point for Giannini came with the 1906 San Francisco earthquake and fire. While the larger banks had to close down, Giannini erected a tent on a pier and made loans to distressed businessmen from there. Two days after the earthquake, he took out an advertisement in the *San Francisco Chronicle*: "Bank of Italy Now Opened for Regular Business." With this, the legend of A. P. Giannini emerged. He was barely touched by the financial panic of 1907, since it didn't affect his small-scale borrowers, and now was prepared to undertake bigger ventures. He made loans freely to those wanting to use the money to rebuild their homes, but only half of what was requested, asking the borrowers to raise the other half themselves. Giannini knew that immigrant Italians liked to squirrel away savings outside of banks, which they didn't trust. This would bring the money out of hiding and perhaps into deposits at the Bank of Italy.

Two Canadian banks with branches in San Francisco also came through the financial stringency caused by the earthquake in fine shape. The Canadian Bank of Commerce and the Bank of British Columbia had led the way with branch banking, and this prompted Giannini to visit Canada to study the system. Drawing on the experience of the Canadian banks, he decided to expand into other areas. In 1909, California passed a law authorizing the superintendent of banks to approve branches if they served "the public convenience and advantage." Beginning with San Jose, Giannini started opening branches in other parts of California, all with the same concentration on small depositors and borrowers that had made the San Francisco bank so successful. He also took over failed and failing banks and restored them. This was a boom period for California. As a result of demands in the east for California produce, Los Angeles had become the nation's most productive agricultural area. In addition, an oil boom had begun around Los Angeles. With this, Giannini moved aggressively into the area.

In 1917, Giannini organized a subsidiary, the Liberty Bank, to focus on northern California, with this boosting his total resources to more than $90 million and making the Bank of Italy the first statewide bank in the nation and the fourth largest in California.

Through all of this, Giannini faced solid opposition from the old-line California banks, who came to look upon the Bank of Italy as an octopus, snaring business wherever it went. Through legislation and actions by the regulatory authorities, Giannini was blocked from expanding further. When the McFadden Act was passed in 1927 to extend the branch banking operations for national banks, Giannini joined the system and continued his expansion, the result being a chain of banks that stretched from the Canadian to the Mexican borders, offering loans to small businessmen everywhere in between. *The San Francisco Call* congratulated Giannini for "daring to become the world's first financier to make of banking and investment a huge democratic fraternity." At a time when motion pictures was considered a risky new industry, Giannini was there to lend funds to the heads of the budding studios. When criticized because the collateral was low or nonexistent, Giannini replied, "If a film is offered starring Doug [Fairbanks], Charlie [Chaplin], or Harold [Lloyd], it's as good as cash."

Giannini then turned his attention eastward, opening banks in New York and acquiring others. He made no secret of his ambition to become national in scope, and in time, international as well. These ambitions generated political opposition from Wall Street and Washington, and the rise of regulations to restrict Giannini's expansion of credit access. On Wall Street the Bank of Italy was called a "glorified finance company with the facade of a bank." But Giannini struck back, and in 1928 he acquired the Bank of America (New York), the lineal descendant of the Bank of the United States, though to do so he had to knuckle under to J. P. Morgan, Jr. and face intense opposition from the Federal Reserve Bank of New York.

Giannini had organized a giant holding company, Bancitaly, into which he placed all of his financial interests. In 1928, to make the institution more accessible, he changed the name to Transamerica, an indication of his ambition. In 1930, he acquired the Los Angeles-based Bank of America of California, which already had 21 branches, and this became the name of his activities in southern California. Both operated under the umbrella of the Bank of Italy, which by 1927 had 300 banks in 185 California towns and cities, with capital of $750 million. By then, it was the largest bank west of the Hudson, and the third largest in the country.

Other changes followed. In 1930, the Bank of Italy and the Bank of America of California were folded into the Bank of America National Trust and Savings Association, known simply as Bank of America. Giannini retired as chairman of Bank of America in 1934, but remained as chairman of Transamerica. The Bank of America continued to grow, and in 1945 it became the largest national bank. Critics continued to scoff that the Bank of America was really a glorified finance company. Giannini didn't mind this, since he considered small depositors and borrowers the key to his business.

While other banks suffered during the Great Depression, the Bank of America thrived, with assets rising from $876 million in 1932 to $1.6 billion in 1939. During this period, Giannini had to deal with both the old antagonism to branch banking and opposition from New Dealers, led by Treasury Secretary Henry Morgenthau, who charged he was attempting to create a monopoly. What truly bothered them was Giannini's grasp of the home and farm mortgage markets in California. He did have a large share, but never as much as his critics charged.

By the time of his death in 1949, other banks had followed his example of seeking deposits from ordinary Americans and making loans to small businesses. Giannini's democratization of banking and popularization of small business loans and home mortgages brought to public policy a focus on capital access. It came at a price, however. Often, innovators in finance faced opposition from those whose interests they challenged. Giannini was the first to run the gauntlet in the twentieth century. Others would follow.

The Glamour Industries: Radio, Motion Pictures, and Automobiles

During the 1920s, the American business scene blossomed with new opportunities to make money. Home appliances, plastics, synthetic fibers, and aviation, among others, became areas for growth. But the most important of these new enterprises were radio, motion pictures, and automobiles.

We have seen how, after World War I, American Marconi was transformed into RCA, the theory being that wireless technology provided a convenient and inexpensive alternative to the telegraph, which in time, given additional experimentation, might also provide competition for the telephone. In other words, the wireless was to be used for person-to-person communication. David Sarnoff had other ideas. In 1912, at the age of 21, he had been catapulted to fame when, as an operator at the Marconi office in New York, he relayed news of the sinking of the *Titanic*. An immigrant, Sarnoff arrived in America with his family at the age of nine. In time, he became a manager at American Marconi. In a 1916 memo he wrote, "I have in mind a plan of development which would make radio a household utility in the same sense as the piano or phonograph. The idea is to bring music into the house by wireless." The programs need not be limited to music, he went on, but could include "dramas, news, lectures, sports, and speeches." Which is to say, Sarnoff had grasped the potential of the new medium.

Soon thereafter, Westinghouse and AT&T became interested in Sarnoff's ideas and began experimenting with what would become broadcasting. Both had successes, and each established stations, which they expanded into networks, and these were joined by independent stations wishing to share programming.

In 1926, RCA obtained the AT&T and Westinghouse networks in exchange for shares in the merged entity. The new organization was to be called the American Broadcasting Company, but this designation was soon dropped in favor of National Broadcasting Company (NBC). It was to be 50 percent owned by RCA, with 30 percent going to General Electric and 20 percent to Westinghouse. The AT&T network became the Red Network, and Westinghouse and associates became the Blue. These designations originated from the crayon lines drawn on a map of the United States by RCA's executives.

The networks were quite small in 1926; between them they had 19 stations. They expanded each year, though, mushrooming to 69 by the end of the decade. By then, the networks were RCA's major source of income, with revenues of $22 million and earnings of close to $2 million. In time, Sarnoff negotiated RCA's independence from its owners and took the company into phonographs and records, talent agencies, and a host of related businesses. In 1928, he helped organize Radio-Keith-Orpheum, or RKO, a giant motion picture producer and theater operator. RCA had become the giant of the entertainment business, the class company in a glamorous and profitable new industry, with the largest profits and the greatest promise. What Bill Gates and Microsoft were to the late 1990s, David Sarnoff and RCA were to the early 1930s. It showed in the statistics. From 1921 to 1929, RCA's revenues and earnings shot from $4 million to $182 million and $400,000 to $10.2 million, respectively. It was the shining star of the "Great Bull Market." Then, as radio became more ubiquitous and RCA expanded into new areas of opportunity, earnings advanced smartly, as did the stock, rising from a low of 39 in 1925 to more than 572 in 1929, whereupon it split five for one. RCA common made some people very wealthy, but its impact on American consumers was even greater.

After those first motion pictures appeared at Koster & Bial's music hall, the nation took to films as passionately as they had to radio and automobiles. Even then, American films dominated the world market. By the early 1920s, one-third of the studio's revenues derived from overseas. Film stars became major celebrities; Charlie Chaplin was the most recognizable person on earth.

The film business was divided into three areas: production, distribution, and exhibition. In time these coalesced, and several major concerns resulted, including Loew's, Paramount, RKO, Columbia, Warner Brothers, and a handful of smaller firms. Adolph Zukor of Paramount was one of the pioneers, and he excelled in selling the concept of future profits to bankers and investors. In 1926, he recalled his endeavors in this regard:

> I approached several different bankers and tried to sell them the idea of big profits in the motion picture business. They were very glad and wished me good luck and hoped I would succeed, but they did not see their way to participate in this lucrative business until one day I met Mr. Otto Kahn of Kuhn, Loeb and Company. I thought that on account of his interest in theaters and artists I could refer to the possibilities of the picture business and perhaps he would be interested. I talked to him a bit and he told me he was much interested.

Soon after that, Kahn invited Zukor to lunch to discuss the matter more fully. Jacob Schiff, who headed Kuhn, Loeb, opposed the financing, but others came in. "It was romantic. It had a future," said Zukor. "After a few days they gave me $10,000,000."

By the early 1920s, Zukor, who had begun in films, had moved into the theater business. Marcus Loew, who began in theaters, expanded into films. The public knew little of Zukor and Loew. An increasingly movie-mad nation saw the stars and their pictures, and as far as they were concerned, this was the industry.

In the process of watching films, Americans evolved toward a new ethic. Until then, the American ideal was the industrious individual who got to the top through hard work. The characteristic success story was one like Andrew Carnegie's, who from humble beginnings achieved remarkable affluence. The motion pictures started to change this. Films rarely showed this aspect of life. Rather, they concentrated on consumption, and the audience identified with the heroes and heroines and would try to imitate them. Let Rudolph Valentino lean against a Pierce Arrow and ignite his cigarette with a silver lighter and scores of young men in the balcony, admiring his savoir faire, would make mental notes to go to a department store the next day and purchase a nickel-plated lighter like the one used by the actor.

Likewise, the prevalence of smoking in films encouraged young people to try cigarettes. Tobacco use in this form had grown during World War I, and now it caught on rapidly. In 1919, the per capita consumption of cigarettes in America had been 426; by 1925, it stood at just below 700. Along with radio, motion pictures, and automobiles, cigarettes was a growth industry of the period.

The automobile industry played a very significant role in transforming America in the 1920s. Many Americans believed Henry Ford invented the automobile. Of course, there had been experiments with automobiles close to a century earlier, and autos had appeared on America's dirt roads before the turn of the century. But for all intents and purposes, the automobile age began with Ford.

The first Ford car appeared in 1896, and after driving it around for a while, Ford sold the car to a friend for $200, which in that period was a year's wages for a common working man. Ford built more cars and in 1903 organized the first incarnation of the Ford

Motor Company, which was capitalized at $100,000. Ford himself owned 25.5 percent of the shares. Ford would purchase parts from suppliers, one of which was Dodge Brothers, and cobble the cars together. The model A, with a two-cylinder engine and a six-foot wheelbase, sold for $950. It was followed by the Model B and others. In 1906, the company was reorganized, with Ford owning a majority of the shares. Ford produced his first Model T in 1908, and by 1915, the millionth copy rolled off the assembly line. In 1908, too, General Motors was organized. By then, there were hundreds of automobile companies, if producing a single car qualified one as a manufacturer.

Automobile sales reached 1.4 million in 1921 and rose to 4.5 million by 1929. In the same period, motor vehicle registrations increased from 10.5 million to 26.7 million. By the end of the decade, Ford and GM had been joined by Chrysler, and the automobile age was in full swing.

That automobile production became a big business in which profits were made, myriad jobs created, and unspeakable wealth accumulated is quite obvious. Less well known, perhaps is how the impact of the industry rippled through the economy. The need for roads spurred activity in the cement industry. While not ordinarily considered a growth area, cement shipments rose from 71 million barrels in 1918 to 172 million barrels in 1929. The coming of the automobile also transformed the product mix in petroleum, with gasoline replacing kerosene as the major product. In 1925, petroleum exports came to $421 million. By way of comparison, agricultural equipment and steel plates, major exports before the World War, were $163 million that year. Money was made in products from highway signs to resorts. Also during the twenties, General Motors, soon mimicked by the other manufacturers, began arranging for the purchase of cars on time, opening another new field for business and profit.

Organized Crime: Making Money from Prohibition

Prohibition, a notorious feature of the 1920s, was what Hoover called the "noble experiment." One of the axioms of the pursuit of wealth is that banned products and services that people want will spur illegal activities and make those who provide them wealthy. So it is today with illicit drugs, and so it was during the 1920s with illicit alcohol. A major side effect of Prohibition was the rise of organized crime. Until the 1920s, gangs had been local, but now all of this changed.

"Big Jim" Colosimo was the head of a large Chicago gang, which he ran with the aid of Johnny Torrio, imported from New York to be a bodyguard. The Colosimo interests included bordellos, loan shark operations, and extortion. Persuaded that Prohibition was coming, Torrio urged Colosimo to expand into bootlegging when it arrived. Colosimo was unconvinced. "Stick to women," he said. "That's where the money is. There's no future in bootlegging. Prohibition won't amount to anything." It wasn't the first time a successful businessman failed to understand the changing nature and demands of his market. By the time the Volstead Act passed, Colosimo was little more than a front for Torrio, and both men seemed to know it.

Personally ambitious, Torrio sent for Frankie Yale, a New York gunman prominent in the dealings of that city's Unione Siciliana. For a fee of $10,000, Yale ambushed Colosimo in May 1920 and shot him in the head. Torrio now took over the Colosimo empire in name as well as fact. Although retaining his interests in bordellos, he now turned increasingly to bootlegging. Using methods pioneered by Colosimo in organizing bordellos, Torrio established close relations with major illegal stills as well as bootleggers. Largely through his efforts, Chicago became the leading entry port for Canadian liquor, winning over Cleveland, Detroit, Buffalo, and other Great Lakes ports. The police did little; as long as Torrio kept the bribes coming, they looked the other way. Everyone from the mayor on down was on the Torrio payroll. By 1926, it was estimated that more than three-quarters of the city's police force was involved in one way or another with Prohibition avoidance. Some moonlighted by working as guards on liquor trucks, while still in uniform.

Although interested in all areas of crime, Torrio specialized in the production and distribution of beer, which was more popular in Chicago than hard liquor. He formed an alliance with Joseph Stenson, who, prior to Prohibition, had been one of Chicago's brewing tycoons. Torrio took over five Stenson breweries, had them dismantled and moved to new, secret locations, and soon they were turning out beer for Chicago's thirsty population.

But Torrio was troubled by territorial wars then developing in Chicago and elsewhere. Just as John D. Rockefeller and J. P. Morgan disdained competition, which they felt was wasteful, so Torrio thought cooperation would be best for all involved. In 1921, he brought rival Chicago forces together to divide Cook County into territories. Dion O'Banion, a strange man who loved flowers and had been a choirboy before turning to robbing banks and politics, received the northern part of the city as his domain. O'Banion had a reputation for rewarding friends and punishing enemies. One of his chief lieutenants, Nails Morton, had been thrown from a horse and kicked to death. O'Banion called in his enforcers and gave the word. A few days later, the horse was kidnapped, led to the spot where Morton died, and shot to death.

The West Side went to several gangs. Myles and Klondike O'Donnell and the remnants of the once-powerful Valley Gang received substantial territories there. The "Terrible Gennas"—Sam, Jim, Pete, Angelo, Tony, and Mike—also had a section there, but this was only one of their interests. Recognizing that brewing and speakeasies were controlled by others, they turned their attention to raw alcohol and soon became the Midwest's leading producer of that essential product. Through connections in the East, they were able to ship alcohol to most parts of the country. Within four years, the brothers were worth more than $5 million, and were considered one of the underworld's great success stories.

Torrio reserved much of the West Side for himself, and he also dominated the suburbs. The rapidly growing South Side was his, and this was where Scarface Al Capone made his mark on the city.

Capone was only 24 years old when granted the position of subchief for the South Side. He had come to Chicago a year earlier, Torrio had heard of this New York gunman, who had worked for the Five Points Gang and was a menace on the Brooklyn waterfront. Always on the lookout for talent, Torrio took Capone under his wing in much the same way he once had been mentored by Colosimo. Capone's first important assignment was as bouncer in a bordello. Then he advanced to manager of the Four Deuces, one of Chicago's major bordello-speakeasy-communications centers, and Torrio headquarters. By late 1921, Capone was Torrio's right-hand man and close friend.

Capone concentrated on expanding Torrio's network into neighboring towns. In 1924, he began a campaign to take Cicero, Cook County's biggest city besides Chicago. Torrio struck the first blow by setting up several bordellos and speakeasies. Then Capone moved in, establishing headquarters in the Hawthorne Inn and making contact with local politicians, including Mayor Joseph Klenha. Prior to the municipal election of May 1, 1924, Capone ordered his men to shoot up the town, destroy property, and then inform the citizenry there would be more of the same unless Klenha was reelected. The mayor went on to a resounding victory, and Capone took over in Cicero. Once, when Klenha failed to observe proper respect for Capone, Scarface Al kicked him down the steps of City Hall and then walked over him. He was permitted to rise, but not before apologizing for the slight.

In time, Capone would get rid of O'Banion, who was replaced by Hymie Weiss, who arranged for Torrio to be killed. Miraculously, Torrio survived five shots in various parts of his body. He recovered, paid a $5000 fine on Prohibition charges, served a short sentence, and on his release returned to Italy. Now Capone was in charge of the Torrio holdings.

Then Weiss went after Capone, and Chicago became immersed in gang warfare. Capone sued for peace and Weiss was interested, but he balked when Capone refused to turn over O'Banion's murderers as a token of good will. Whereupon, on October 11, 1926, Capone's men killed Weiss, and Schemer Drucci became lord of the North Side. But not for long; six months later Drucci was killed by a policeman and Bugsie Moran took over. For the next two and a half years, Moran and Capone fought it out on Chicago's streets. More than 350 gunmen gave their lives in this underworld struggle, which culminated in the St. Valentine's Day Massacre of February 14, 1929, when six members of the Moran gang were killed by Capone forces and allies.

The killings shocked the nation and disturbed even the underworld, many of whose most prominent citizens thought the violence had gone too far and had to be stopped. The major racketeers called a meeting in Atlantic City, presided over by New York's Frank Costello. Under the agreement hammered out, Capone was to rule in Chicago, but Moran would have a territory on the North Side. Costello wanted more, however. He demanded and got what amounted to a national solution to the problem of competition. Costello, Frankie Yale, Larry Fay, Dutch Schultz, and Owney Madden would take New York, while Maxie Hoff would control Philadelphia, the Purple Gang would take Detroit, and Cincinnati and St. Louis would be the domain of the Remus Mob. Solly Weissman was to keep control of Kansas City, and other local gang lords would continue in their realms. The division was negotiated with the same degree of professionalism evident in petroleum and steel.

Moran and Capone resolved their differences, but neither trusted the other. Soon after the Atlantic City summit, Capone was taken into custody for carrying concealed weapons, tried, and sentenced to a year in jail. At the time, it was said Capone had arranged the arrest himself, that he wanted to be in a safe place until he saw whether Moran would live up to the Costello agreement.

While in prison, Capone kept in touch with business matters through trusted lieutenants: his brother Ralph, Frank "the Enforcer" Nitti, and Jake "Greasy Thumb" Gusik. Capone was released on March 17, 1930, and returned to his old haunts. By then, the city had a reform administration, however, and he was hounded by police. Federal agents entered the area, too, and Capone learned they were not easily bribed. He traveled for a while and finally settled in Miami. It was there, on October 6, 1931, that he was arrested for income tax evasion. The federal government couldn't prove him guilty of any criminal act other than not paying taxes on his ill-gotten gains. Capone had no desire to go to prison this time, and his lawyers offered the government men a $4 million bribe, which was rejected. Capone received an 11-year sentence. He was released with time off for good behavior in 1939 and died eight years later.

More than any other crime figure, Capone captured the public imagination. Arnold Rothstein, Dutch Schultz, and Legs Diamond had flair, and operated on the larger canvas of New York, but none had Capone's prestige. He was not as innovative as Colosimo or Torrio, and Costello had wider vision and employed more subtle methods, but it was Capone who came to symbolize organized crime. When the movie *Scarface* came out in the early 1930s, no one had to be told who the thinly disguised film was about.

Capone was surprised at the adulation and fear he inspired. "I call myself a businessman," he once said. "I make my money by supplying a popular demand." He complained bitterly against what he considered a conspiracy aimed at his destruction. "I don't interfere with big business," he argued.

> None of the big business guys can ever say I ever took a dollar from them. Why, I done a favor for one of the big newspapers in the country when they was up against it. Broke a strike for them. And what do I get for doing them a favor? Here they've been ever since, clamped on my back. I only want to do business, you understand, with my own class. Why can't they leave me alone? I don't interfere with their racket. They should let my racket be.

As Capone saw it, he was a legitimate businessman who had been done in by individuals who had no appreciation of his activities and were downright unethical. "Why, I tried to get into legitimate business two or three times, but they won't stand for it." Logic was on his side. Capone noted, "If I break a law, my customers are as guilty as I am. When I sell liquor, it's bootlegging. When my patrons serve it on a silver tray on Lake Shore Drive, it's hospitality."

By 1927, the Capone gang was grossing an estimated $60 million a year on beer alone, and by 1929, the figure approximated $100 million. Capone's beer earnings were said to be larger than the profits of Standard Oil of Indiana, Ford, or General Electric. None of this could have happened without Prohibition, which made it possible for a well-managed but relatively small operation of Big Jim Colosimo to be expanded into the giant enterprise of Al Capone. Prohibition marked the beginning of crime on a national scale. Along with motion pictures, radio, automobiles, and professional sports, it was one of the decade's major growth industries.

The Florida Land Boom

In the late nineteenth century, Florida was largely undeveloped, although Standard Oil tycoon Henry Flagler had taken an interest in the state. He demonstrated this by helping to construct a railroad on the east coast, erecting hotels, and promoting tourism — for the wealthy — at such places as St. Augustine, Ormond, and Palm Beach. Flagler had ambitions to expand southward. "If my life and health are spared," he said in 1892, "it seems more probable that I will extend the railroad to Miami within a few years." Work on the extension was begun three years later, and Flagler opened his Royal Palm Hotel in Miami in 1897. By the time Flagler died in 1913, Florida was known as "the state of the future." The citrus industry was developing, as were other businesses. Some middle class tourists had started to vacation there. That year, 69,000 passengers arrived via the Florida East Coast Railroad; in 1900, the number had been 19,000. The Clearing House in Jacksonville, the state's financial center, did $12.7 million in business in 1900. The figure for 1913 was $174 million.

By the time of Flagler's death, another speculator had appeared and was carrying on the missionary work. John Collins, a New Jersey native, had become intrigued with Miami Beach, and in 1896 had invested $1000 in an attempt to grow coconuts there. The venture failed due to storms and poor management, but Collins persisted and next tried avocados. He experimented with bananas and other fruits, but nothing he set his hand to worked out. Soon afterward, John Collins and most of his family returned to New Jersey, leaving behind one of his daughters, Katherine, and her husband, Thomas Pancoast, to continue the work. Pancoast wanted to clear the land, construct a canal and bridge, and make Miami Beach more accessible. The work went poorly, and in 1912 the Pancoasts might have abandoned the effort were it not for the appearance of 38-year-old Carl Fisher, who while speedboating during a vacation in the area, lost his way and happened upon the Pancoast development. Fisher was a wealthy Indianapolis car dealer who had formed the Fisher Automobile Company (not to be confused with Fisher Body Company, organized by the Fisher brothers). He also was one of the founders of Prest-O-Lite Corporation, which was sold to Union Carbide for $9 million, of which Fisher received $5.6 million. He found time to help organize the Indianapolis Motor Speedway, dabble in hot air balloons and motorcycles, and was planning a coast-to-coast highway. One of his avocations was real estate. In return for lending $100,000 to the Lummis brothers, who were Miami Beach realtors, Fisher received 150 acres of land on the southern end of the Beach, and he purchased more, not unlike the way John Jacob Astor had operated a century earlier.

Interested in the Collins-Pancoast operation, Fisher offered to back the bridge with $50,000, with the bridge itself as collateral for the loan. The offer was accepted, and with this, Fisher turned to his real interest, the highway. Work proceeded smoothly, and in 1914, the bridge completed, Fisher advertised homesites for sale. Miami Beach, he said, was "a place to escape from winter." He promised buyers they would have electricity and telephones when they built their homes, with city water and sewers two years later, along with golf courses and fishing facilities. At first, the sales—of what was little more than raw land—went poorly. Undaunted, Fisher, Pancoast, and Collins organized the town of Miami Beach in 1915 and petitioned the state for recognition, which was promptly granted.

Never one to concentrate long on a single project, Fisher returned to his road scheme, which he now called the Lincoln Highway, and made plans for another, this one to be named the Dixie Highway, which would run from Indianapolis to Miami. In October 1915, he traveled through towns along the route, touting what he predicted would be the finest two-lane highway in the nation, which among other things would signal the end of bad feeling left over from the Civil War. Fisher wound up in Miami Beach, interested in building another canal that would provide easier access to Biscayne

Bay and in the process transform Miami Beach into a true island. All of these projects had to be put off when the United States entered World War I.

The war benefitted Florida. Unable to travel to Europe on vacations, some wealthy Americans went to Florida instead. The *nouveau riches*, who would have felt out of place in such resorts as Palm Beach or St. Augustine, went to Miami, and some of them visited Miami Beach. A handful purchased land and planned to build after the war. All the preconditions for a land boom were in place. The railroad was operating as far south as Key West, other infrastructure was being planned and constructed, the Dixie Highway was under way, interest in Florida was growing, and a great deal of money was being made by many Americans during the fighting.

In preparation for what he felt would be a major boom, Fisher began to work on constructing a polo field, in the hope it would attract wealthy sportsmen to Miami Beach, and he planned regattas in Biscayne Bay. These projects indicated that Fisher wanted Miami Beach to become the resort area of choice for his wealthy friends and that he was thinking along the lines set down by Flagler. After a while, however, he changed his mind. His interest in the automobile and faith in its future indicated that perhaps middle class Americans would be a better target. He visualized families driving down the Dixie Highway in their Model Ts, going to Miami Beach for vacations in the sun. In 1912, the year he met Collins, there were 944,000 registered motor vehicles. By 1919, car production was 1.6 million with 7.6 million registrations. Highway construction boomed. In 1914, the states spent $53 million on roads and bridges. By 1925, when 3.7 million cars were produced and total registrations stood at 20 million, highway and bridge construction rose to more than $400 million. State road construction alone was more than 23,000 miles.

Florida's political leaders were well aware of the benefits of tourism to the state, viewing it similarly to the way New York's political establishment had during the Erie Canal period. Governors Sidney Catts, Cary Hardee, and John Martin, who held office from 1917 through 1929, were all highway enthusiasts.

The real estate boom began slowly in 1920, a year in which the economy was in recession, and grew steadily. It was not until 1922 that the great flood of people started to arrive, with the boom phase arriving in 1924–1925. Visitors had come to look the year before and now returned to buy. Land prices inched up at first and then went into high gear. The middle class was well represented, but wealthy Americans came as well, using Miami as a jumping-off spot for trips to Havana, one of the pleasure cities of the western hemisphere. Bimini and Cuba became entrepots for whisky smugglers, who ran an endless convoy from there to Florida's long east coast. While the figures are suspect, there appears to have been more alcohol purchased in Florida than any other state. Tourists and owners of homesites not only imbibed while there, but they would take a supply home where the prices were much higher than in Florida. A case of 24 fifths of Scotch that went for $24 in Bimini and wholesaled for $40 in Miami Beach retailed for between $100 and $120 to tourists, who might sell it to friends back home for $20 for a fifth. Writing of the business in *The Saturday Evening Post*, Kenneth Roberts noted:

> One good result of comparatively cheap whiskey in Miami is the apparently total disappearance of beer-making and other home-brewing activities. There seems to be no market for hops, malt, prunes, raisins, or wash-boilers—which would seem to make Miami an unusually healthy city in which to live.

The state was inundated with outsiders, but most of the activity was concentrated along a 100-mile-long strip of land on the east coast running from Palm Beach to Miami Beach. In this area could be found large rococo mansions designed by architect Addison Mizner and upper middle class suburbs created by George Merrick. Merrick is famous for erecting Coral Gables, a completely planned city on the outskirts of Miami, with country clubs, canals, shopping areas, excellent transportation, and much more.

Leading them all were Miami Beach and Miami. In 1923 alone, Fisher sold $3 million in lots. Sales rose to $8 million the following year and $12 million in 1925. This was when the speculative bug bit many buyers. Those who had arrived and bought lots in 1923 could sell them for five or six times what they paid just two years later. "Why stop at one lot?" asked real estate agents. "Buy several, sell off a few, and the rest would be free." Agents would take binders on a property for as little as 5 percent of the price, with the next payment 25 percent, at which time the deal would be closed. Since business was so brisk, that second payment might take place weeks, even months later, by which time the price of the property could have doubled. This meant that a buyer might purchase a $5000 lot for a down payment of $250, and sell it shortly thereafter for $10,000, realizing a profit of $5000 on a $250 investment. Then the process would be repeated, perhaps several times. It was as though a massive profit-laden chain letter had been set into motion.

The boom was nationwide. Salesmen for Florida real estate appeared in virtually all the states, seeking buyers who willingly assumed high mortgages on unseen land, some planning to build, more intending to speculate. The advertisements were frenetic. One of them read:

> This is a straight-from-the-shoulder message to MY FRIENDS—GET IT AND GET IT QUICK! I had to make a rush trip to New York, and believe me, I am glad to be back in time to get my friends in on the BEST THING YET . . . NOW GET THIS QUICK! When I discovered Lake Stearns I know I had found the best land in Florida. With me is Mr. Walter T. Spaulding, President of the Spaulding Construction Company of New York and Miami, a nationally known constructor. He put his OWN money into this proposition and will handle the construction of all utilities at Lake Stearns.
>
> MR. WALTER DUNHAM, a man of great vision, will direct the selling campaign of this property to the public.
>
> These two associates and I are going to PUT THIS OVER, and YOU are COMING IN ON IT. YOU are coming in with me on the first $150,000 we are going to put in because you KNOW ME and believe in my judgement. I want $5000 out of you for this proposition. NOW DON'T WRITE ME. I WON'T HAVE TIME TO SCRATCH A PEN. I have given you the facts and am offering you a FINAL OPPORTUNITY to get in RIGHT NOW. SEND ME YOUR CHECK and I will put it in the BANK. This is a personal message from me to YOU. You want to make some REAL MONEY now. Get in and come on while the PROPOSITION IS HOT.

The money did flow in. While no clear estimate of the amount of capital can be reconstructed, it was believed at the time that in 1925 alone, some $1 billion from outside sources flowed into Florida projects.

Some of the money came from Wall Street, where speculators sought even bigger killings than could be had from stocks. As a result, the market dipped for a while before recovering and going on to new highs. More money came from small towns and villages, where formerly conservative people withdrew their savings to buy lots in Florida. Money arrived from Europe. The French Riviera and Italy reported poor winter seasons, the result of tourists going to Florida instead. Talk of new Fisher-backed gaming palaces in Miami Beach caused tremors to pass through Monaco, as even Monte Carlo leaders thought their casino might bow before the Miami Beach wave.

How long could it last? "Allow ten years for the Miami Boom," said T.S. Knowland of New York, a leading realtor of the time.

> There are certain lots in Miami which were sold two years ago at $3000. Their present selling price is $25,000. No wonder, then, that the market is brisk with buyers and sellers. The point is, how much higher will these prices go? Nobody knows, for at every turn one is met by the fact that Florida is different from anything of its kind that has gone before. Past booms are a good guide in a general way, but they cannot serve as an exact measure for the present movement.
>
> For one thing, the whole wealth of the United States is interested in Florida. Almost everybody of consequence appears to have a large holding there, and vast sums are being brought from other states for industrial and developmental purposes. The significance of the fact is this: That such names tend to generate deep confidence.

Miami Beach was hectic in the summer of 1926, but not as much as it had been a year earlier. Prices were beginning to level, and the newspapers carried stories about the end of the boom. But the hopeful still arrived—and invested. Then, on the morning of September 18, the skies darkened. A hurricane was on the way. The storm hit after midnight, and floods followed. It was the first major hurricane to hit Florida since 1910, but back then there had been little development to destroy. It was different in 1926, when 392 died, 6281 were injured and treated at hospitals, and tens of millions of dollars in property destruction was reported.

Still, few of the hotels were badly damaged, and within hours of the winds' abatement, reconstruction was begun. The major damage was in the matter of confidence. The hurricane arrived at a time when tourism had already topped out, and it ended what remained of the boom. Fisher ran advertisements in which he asserted that Florida was healthier than ever, and there was some recovery in 1926–1927. A second hurricane in 1928, however, ended the land mania for that generation. And the stock market crash of 1929 put the nail in the coffin.

The Great Bull Market

It was a dazzling period. Anything seemed possible; great wealth was obtainable for any and all. John J. Raskob, who identified himself in *Who's Who* as a "capitalist," certainly thought so. The General Motors executive took time out from helping manage Democrat Al Smith's Presidential campaign to write an article for the *Ladies' Home Journal* entitled "Everyone Ought to be Rich." Raskob wrote that if a person put $15 a month into common stocks, within 20 years, given the rate of increase during the bull market, he would have $80,000. Such an investor could have even more if he got together with like-minded people and formed an investment organization for "the little fellow." The investor would contribute $200 to the pool and a note for $300. In return, he would receive $500 worth of the pool. The purchaser would pay off the note at the rate of $25 monthly. Since stock prices were sure to rise by more than that, Raskob reasoned, the purchaser would receive $500 in stock, free and clear after the note was paid off, for his $200 in cash. And that, he thought, was a conservative estimate.

The impression most people have of the 1920s is of a jazz-obsessed, sports-minded, hard-drinking, materialistic decade. The securities market is central to the portrait. According to conventional wisdom, Wall Street was the biggest game in town, enthralling a generation with dreams of quick wealth and high drama, only to come crashing down in 1929 as the proverbial seven good years gave way to more than seven bad ones. This is little more than a caricature, but the image probably is too strong to be eradicated by contrary evidence.

As usual with exaggerations, there is an underlying element of truth to this view. True enough, in the 1920s more Americans than ever became interested in stocks. Americans purchased Liberty Loan bonds during World War I and so had been initiated to the world of investments.

In the 1920s, however, most prudent investors wouldn't consider industrial stocks. Instead, they bought bonds, especially railroads, and clipped coupons rather than watch the tape. The old money regarded stocks as speculative. If they bought them at all, it was the rails, especially the Pennsylvania. Trustees were forbidden to place capital in industrial stocks, and the few pension funds that existed were in bonds.

This was part of the tradition. Investors recalled the active but small prewar market for stocks, which resembled a lively, wild casino dominated by speculators. In 1901, volume came to 222 million shares, with a turnover of 319 percent, an all-time high. How many shareholders were there at the time? No one bothered to find out, since such matters didn't seem important, but in 1928, statistician John Powers wrote there had been around 500,000 "investors" in 1914. Powers did not say how he arrived at that figure; he did indicate most were speculators.

In 1928, the Treasury reported that millionaires owned less than 7 percent of outstanding common stock. Nick Carraway, Scott Fitzgerald's narrator in *The Great Gatsby*, sold bonds, not stocks, to his wealthy friends. City Company peddled bonds to small investors throughout the country and was the first major operation to realize their potential. In 1929, City Company literature spoke of selling bonds to "persons of limited resources, all of whose capital and income are necessary to insure life's future comforts." The brokerage encouraged such individuals to come in off the street to talk with representatives without charge, "to get the fullest benefit of [his] judgment and vigilance . . . and [be] open in discussing his investment problems as he is in discussing legal problems with his lawyer or his health with a doctor."

Even now, we do not know how many people owned or dabbled in equities or purchased bonds at the time. Approximations vary widely. According to one, put out by the Treasury, there were between 4 and 7 million people "in the market" by 1929, a spread that indicates the unreliability of these figures. Taking the high number, we might conclude that by the end of the decade, one in ten adult Americans owned stock.

Other estimates muddy the waters. In 1929, there were some 20 million shareholders on the books of American corporations, a more reliable figure. But some active speculators held many issues, so double counting doubtless inflated the total. How much? That is unknown. But it makes the Treasury's 4 to 7 million statistic appear more plausible.

One might assume tax returns to be more reliable. Some 9 million individuals declared dividends and interest, but this number isn't very accurate. Of this amount, probably more than half received interest on Liberty Bonds and can't be considered stockholders.

Stockholders aren't necessarily traders. These numbers included avid speculators, but also individuals who held only a few shares and rarely traded, hardly the type that makes for wild markets. The 29 stock exchanges of 1929 reported 1,548,707 active accounts, and of these some 600,000 were margined, the chief means by which speculators played the market. Some of those margin players were wealthy, to be sure, but anecdotal evidence suggests many more were small-timers, the kind of people who today line up to buy lottery tickets.

NYSE volume offers some indication of the extent of speculation. In 1921, with 756 listed issues, volume came to 173 million shares, a turnover ratio of 59 percent. In 1929, when there were 1176 issues, volume was 1.1 billion and the ratio was 119 percent. Numbers like these support the image of hoards of eager speculators throwing the dice at the exchanges. But it still wasn't as wild and frenetic as in 1901.

Of special speculative interest were the investment trusts that became popular in the late 1920s and resembled today's closed-end funds. From 1921 to 1924, new trusts attracted $75 million, and in the 1925–1928 period, $1 billion went into the trusts. Another $2.1 billion came in 1929, when they had $4.5 billion in assets and were being offered at the rate of around one per day. There were some 400 in operation. Most were highly leveraged and were based on the drawing power of famed managers. So they were susceptible to wide swings and engaged in risky investments. Had the bull market lasted, the trusts doubtless would have become even more popular.

Taking all this into consideration, it becomes clear that shareholding in 1929 was broader than what it had been before the great bull market of the 1920s—as was rank speculation.

The weather that summer was unusually hot, and theater owners reported ticket sales were down. Even the advent of "the talkies" couldn't attract movie fans in those days before theater air conditioning. But the brokerages throughout the nation were crammed with speculators and interested observers, who ignored the heat and all else in their pursuit of wealth. *The Saturday Evening Post* printed a poem that illustrated the nature of the mania:

> Oh, hush thee, my babe, granny's bought some more shares
> Daddy's gone out to play with the bulls and the bears,
> Mother's buying on tips, she simply can't lose,
> And baby shall have some expensive new shoes!

This was followed by the stock market crash of 1929. The collapse began on Thursday, October 24. By November 13th, the market capitalization had fallen from $80 billion to $50 billion. In the period from 1921 to 1929, the Dow Jones Industrial Average had risen from a low of 68 to a high of 381. At the bottom in 1933, it stood at 50, essentially where it had been when the century began. Much had been lost on Wall Street and in Florida, and for the next decade and a half the pursuit of wealth was dampened, replaced by the search for survival. Joseph Kennedy, the father of a future President, later wrote: "I am not ashamed to record that in those days I felt and said I would be willing to part with half of what I had if I could be sure of keeping, under law and order, the other half. Then it seemed that I should be able to hold nothing for the protection of my family." Out of such thinking came retrenchment, not adventuresome activity.

CHAPTER 18

The Old and the New
in Post-World War II America

URING the 1930s, the American people experienced the worst and longest-lived depression in the nation's history, which first President Hoover and then President Franklin D. Roosevelt, through the New Deal, attempted to bring to an end. The depression, punctuated by a brief recovery when it appeared the worst was over, only to decline once more, finally ended with the economic stimulation provided by World War II. Following on the years of severe deflation came a period in which inflationary pressures were mitigated by wage and price controls and forbearance on the part of consumers.

In 1938, when it appeared the country would be mired in depression indefinitely, President Roosevelt authorized the establishment of the Temporary National Economic Committee (TNEC), which undertook a thorough study of the American economy. After two years of analysis, the TNEC concluded that a new political and economic structure might have to be created. That the New Deal did not move in this direction can be attributed to the Republican electoral success in 1938 and the coming of war.

While World War II brought full employment and higher paychecks, it did not stir the yearning for risk in investment. Corporate earnings rose, but the profits were used to repay debts and build nest eggs, not for expansion, except for some companies in defense-related industries. So whereas the size of the American economy more than doubled from $91 billion in 1939 to $213 billion in 1945, and corporate profits increased two and a half times over their predepression level, the economy remained largely dependent on government, not private, enterprise. If common stocks were overvalued in 1929 by conventional standards, they were badly undervalued at the close of World War II. Even with such blue chip stalwarts as Firestone and Jones & Laughlin Steel selling for less than four times earnings and Armour less than three times earnings, and paying upward of 8 percent in dividends, the public was unimpressed. Having been burned or frightened by the 1929 Crash, few were interested in the market.

In retrospect, it is easy to see that business people and consumers were overly cautious in the immediate post-World War II period. Some economists predicted a return to depression if and when government purchasing slowed down substantially. Writing in 1943, economist Paul Samuelson recommended vigorous government intervention when the war ended.

> The final conclusion to be drawn from our experience at the end of the last war is inescapable. Were the war to end suddenly within the next six months, were we again planlessly to wind up our war effort in the greatest haste, to demobilize our armed forces, to liquidate price controls, to shift from astronomic deficits to the even larger deficits of the 1930s—there would be ushered in the greatest period of unemployment and industrial dislocation which any economy has ever faced.

Some 10 million servicemen were scheduled for release within months of the end of the war. War-related orders would be canceled. There had been a full-scale recession after World War I; economists like Samuelson had reason to believe it would happen again. Writers like MacKinlay Kantor feared what might happen to those servicemen. In 1944, Gerald L. K. Smith, who had pro-Nazi proclivities, said that he had little hope things would go his way in that year's election, but he foresaw better results for 1948, when he expected to be supported for the Presidency by disgruntled former servicemen.

All the while, the country prospered. During the war, the public had paid down debt and increased savings. In 1938, the last full year before World War II, total individual savings held in accounts came to $500 million. By 1941, when the country entered the war, savings had mushroomed to more than $11 billion. The last full year of war was 1944, and savings stood at more than $35 billion. Savings then fell $7 billion by 1947. What had happened? Americans had done without many products and services during the depression and war. Insofar as a wide variety of goods and services were concerned, catch-up time had arrived. Those servicemen and their families had to be housed, and that meant not only a boom in construction—an area that had been stagnant since the onset of the depression—but also sales of all kinds of household appliances, building materials, and all items that went into houses and apartments, from carpets and lamps to sod and trees. Automobiles had been available during the depression, but sales were poor, and the industry had produced no cars for the civilian market since shortly after the war began. Now there was an explosion of demand that would not be satisfied for years, and this meant large orders for steel, rubber, plastics, and all else needed for car production. A large highway program meant there would be great demand for construction equipment, cement, and related products. Nylon stockings had appeared before the war, but none were produced for the civilian market during the fighting. Now this would change. Meat, sugar, shoes, and other items had been rationed, along with gasoline. That was over. Down the road, into the 1950s, would come motels, fast food restaurants, drive-in movies, and much more.

To add to this, there was a baby boom, as family growth, held back by depression and war, began in earnest. The boom is usually dated from about 1953 to 1963, peaking in the 1957–1959 period, during which more than 4.25 million babies were born in each year. In fact, the babies started coming in larger numbers as early as 1947. In 1940, there were 10.5 million Americans under the age of five. In 1950, the number came to 16.2 million, and in 1960, 20.2 million. This alone meant there would be shortages of all sorts—first in hospitals, then elementary and secondary schools, and teachers. Companies that turned out products and services for babies would prosper, and later there would be others who benefited, from bicycle manufacturers to dentists. The post-World War II baby boom has been likened to a snake swallowing a rat, with the bulge visible as it travels down the length of the snake. In the case of the baby boom, the trip took a generation to be completed, and its effects are still being felt today in the anticipated shortage of retirement homes and problems with Social Security and Medicare.

The Stock Market Slumbers

One might understand the way stock prices reacted to the war once the United States entered the fighting. On December 6, 1941, the day prior to the Japanese attack on Pearl Harbor, the Dow closed at 117. The following Monday, it fell to 115 and continued downward. The war news was bad for a while. By the time of the Battle of the Java Sea in late February 1942—the worst drubbing of the U.S. Navy in the war—the Dow had sunk to 106, and it slipped below 100 on April 11. Then the tide of battle began to change, and on May 26 it was back above 100 once more, and has remained above that mark ever since. By the end of the war, the Dow was at 147, even though the American economy had doubled in size during the war and corporate profits were more than 250 percent above their 1929 levels.

President Roosevelt died before the war ended, bringing Harry Truman to the White House. While today Truman is perceived as having been an effective President, that was not the view during his first year in office. In the international sphere, his handling of Soviet-American relations was criticized by the Henry Wallace wing of the Democratic Party as well as by Republicans. His economic policies were near disastrous. He blundered badly with Congress regarding price controls and with the unions in dealing with the matter of wage increases. The result was a combination of worker unrest and skyrocketing inflation. The Consumer Price Index, which in 1945 had stood at 52.9, was at 72.1 in 1948, the most rapid rise since records had been kept. Even so, there was no depression and unemployment remained low. Workers were paying more for goods and services, but at least they had jobs.

As for the situation on Wall Street, simply stated it was a disaster area. Trading volume for 1948 was 302 million shares, better than the previous year but far below the almost 500 million shares posted in the depression year of 1936, and matters were getting worse. The 1949 volume would be 272 million shares, and that would mark the low point for this statistic. That year, too, a seat on the NYSE changed hands at $35,000, another low.

The most active lists for these years indicate the kind of people buying and selling stocks. All of the top ten volume leaders for 1948 were low-priced stocks, and most of them highly speculative. Commonwealth & Southern was in the process of dissolution, but the final prices hadn't been set, so speculators bought and sold on rumors. Pepsi-Cola was a buyout candidate. Avco was a large military-goods-oriented firm with a good deal of capital and a declining business. Armour had a major loss and seemed to have potential for a turnabout. American Broadcasting was considered a possible acquisition for any company thinking of entering television. International Telephone & Telegraph was a mysterious company, which for years had seemed on the brink of success and had long experience at being a speculative vehicle. The action in all of these stocks was small. American Broadcasting, the volume leader that year, traded 324,000 shares. And who were the people attracted to such stocks? Speculators, the kind who two generations later would purchase lottery tickets. The purchaser of ITT or American Broadcasting hoped to hit it big on a small outlay of money.

There was some interest in the major companies, those whose names were familiar. Their stocks were purchased with an eye toward dividends. Those who bought and held utility stocks were concerned with yields. They reasoned that since bonds had prior claim over common stocks, all things being equal, the latter would have to offer a higher yield to attract attention; the greater the risk, the greater should be the reward. After all, while General Motors was doing well in 1948, what might happen to the company when car sales fell—or another market crash occurred?

By this reasoning, corporate bonds should yield more than government issues, and corporate stocks more than bonds. This concept was popularized by Benjamin Graham and David Dodd in their classic *Security Analysis*, first published in 1934. "The prime purpose of a business corporation is to pay dividends to its owners. A successful company is one that can pay dividends regularly and presumably increase the rate of return as time goes on. It also follows that the price paid for an investment in common stock would be determined chiefly by the amount of the dividend."

Earnings were important, to be sure, but primarily because they were needed to support the dividend. The prime equity investments of the period were AT&T, with its rock-solid $9.00 dividend, and Pennsylvania Railroad, which hadn't skipped a dividend for three quarters of a century. So remained the situation well into the 1950s. In 1950, for example, the yield on the Dow Industrials averaged 6.9 percent, at a time when long-term U.S. governments averaged 2.3 percent and AAA-rated corporates offered 2.7 percent.

There were two kinds of investors in the market in the late 1940s: those seeking high yields and speculators hoping for a killing by purchasing low-priced issues. As for the general public, they shied away from Wall Street, even when signs of a strong economy were in evidence everywhere.

The Housing Boom

We have seen how John Jacob Astor made a fortune in real estate, how real estate interests played an important role in the development of canals and railroads, and how they operated during the Florida land boom. Despite A. P. Giannini's efforts, on the eve of the Great Depression, home ownership was both difficult and costly. In 1890, some 28 percent of owner-occupied homes had mortgages; that figure came to a shade under 40 percent in 1920. At the time, more mortgages were owned by individuals, often relatives or friends, than by banks and other institutions.

Banks were loath to make mortgages—which are long-term loans—when they might have to raise funds to pay depositors. As a result, the bank rates on mortgages were quite high. Government frowned on mortgages, too. Until 1926, nationally chartered commercial banks were not authorized to make mortgages. Savings & Loans were organized in the late nineteenth century for the purpose indicated by their name: to pool funds from depositors who knew that they would be used to make mortgage loans, often to themselves and their friends.

By today's standards, lenders and borrowers went about the process in a haphazard way, with seldom a professional appraisal of the property's worth. This was so in part because both parties usually knew each other, so there was an important element of personal trust involved. In addition, in this period families tended to remain together in the same house for many years, even generations, providing the lender with an even greater sense of security. Finally, almost all mortgages were of short duration, certainly less than 10 years. Interest came due semiannually, and the principal was returned in a single payment at maturity, although the loan might be renewed at that time. More often than not, assuming all went well, the borrower would bring the money to the lender, count out the bills and coins slowly, with a sense of satisfaction, and leave with the canceled mortgage in hand. Just as today, middle class Americans of that era took great pride in owning their homes, though there is a difference. Ownership then meant the mortgage had been repaid, whereas today it infers occupancy and a mortgage. A century ago, the burning of the mortgage was an important rite of passage. Today, comparatively few people reside in a property long enough to own it outright. The passage from then to now transformed America into a land of homeowners, and as property values rose, those homes became an important source of wealth. Americans who wouldn't dream of speculating on margin thought nothing of having a mortgage for 80 percent or so of their homes' value. Financial institutions became more willing to grant such mortgages, and for far longer terms than previously had been the case.

One of the reasons for this change was the appearance of mortgage insurance. While New York State had authorized the operation of private companies offering such insurance in the late nineteenth century and other states followed, the real growth did not appear until the 1920s. In New York, $2 billion worth of insurance was in force by 1928. It was then that a wave of foreclosures began. In late 1931, President Hoover asked for the creation of the Federal Home Loan Bank, which would attempt to bail out S&Ls and banks specializing in home mortgages. With this, the federal government's involvement in the housing industry began. As it happened, it was not enough to halt the slide in real estate. In 1933, which was both the first year of the New Deal and the worst in the history of American housing (only 93,000 housing starts for the entire nation), more than a quarter of a million mortgages were foreclosed. During the famous first hundred days of the New Deal, Congress passed and Roosevelt signed legislation creating the Home Owners' Loan Corporation (HOLC), which would purchase defaulted mortgages from financial institutions and work with the mortgagees to refinance the loans. This continued into 1936 and proved to be one of the most successful New Deal agencies. The HOLC was followed by the Federal Housing Administration (FHA), which took up the slack left by the failures of private insurance companies and became the centerpiece of the New Deal's housing program. Soon, FHA-guaranteed mortgages became the norm, and helped bring about at least a partial revival of the housing industry.

In addition to the FHA, there was what came to be known as the "G.I. Bill of Rights," part of which entailed mortgages guaranteed by the Veterans Administration. Originally, the agency guaranteed the first half of the loan up to $2000, but the limit was amended until the guarantee reached $25,000 or 60 percent of the loan, whichever was less. The GI mortgage was preferable to one guaranteed by the FHA. The veteran did not have to pay a premium, and the loan was guaranteed directly by the government, with no reserve fund as was required for the FHA.

The FHA and VA made home-owning affordable, and the discharge of millions of servicemen at the end of the war, with the need for housing so pressing, provided a broad customer base. In 1944, the last full year of fighting, only 142,000 new units were started. There were only 17,000 foreclosures that year, an indication of just how wealthy the nation had become, and a sign that once the war ended, the housing market would soar.

So it did, with 326,000 new starts in 1945. There were a record one million starts in 1946, and more the following year. Toward the end of the decade, the 2 million mark seemed within hailing distance, and in 1950, close to that amount was posted.

No personality is more closely associated with the building boom than William Levitt, and no one has done more to revolutionize the industry than he. Even now, foreign visitors to New York are taken to Levittowns on Long Island and New Jersey and driven around to see one of the miracles of that period.

In the late 1920s, Brooklyn-based lawyer Abraham Levitt foreclosed some mortgages on Long Island. One lot remained, so Levitt and his sons, William and Alfred, decided to build a house on it. Alfred designed the house and William sold it. In this way, the Levitts drifted into housing as Levitt & Sons. In the late 1920s and early 1930s, the family constructed 600 houses on Long Island, and one development, Strathmore-at-Manhasset, a 200-house community begun in 1934, considered daring for the depression period. It was a success, and in the next seven years, the family erected more than 2000 additional homes, becoming the region's top company.

This was a time when the typical builder was an ambitious carpenter, bricklayer, or plumber who had amassed a little capital and started out building a single house. If successful, he might hope to put up a half dozen a year with the aid of subcontractors. There were some larger operators, especially in apartment houses in cities, but not many in the single-family, detached-house segment of the market.

In 1941, the Levitts won a contract to erect 2350 houses for war workers in Norfolk, Virginia. It was a disaster, obliging William Levitt to seek better and more efficient construction methods. In time, he divided the construction process into different stages, and then trained crews to perform one process each. During World War II, Levitt served in the Seabees, where he engaged in building and was able to refine his ideas regarding construction.

After the war, Levitt wanted to put his experience to use on a massive project geared primarily to providing housing for returning veterans. Levitt recognized that the VA mortgages would enable families formerly restricted to apartments in New York's outer boroughs to move into houses of their own. "The market was there and the government was providing the financing," Levitt later recalled. "How could we lose?"

New York City real estate was too expensive for his plans. So Levitt quietly amassed 7.3 square miles of land in the Island Trees area of Nassau County, not far from the Queens border. Between mid-1947 and late 1951, from a design created by his brother, Alfred, he put up 17,500 homes in two basic models, ranches and Cape Cods. Levitt accomplished this by applying those mass production techniques developed in the automobile industry and in his Norfolk project, and effected economies by making large-scale purchases from the manufacturers. "What it amounted to was a reversal of the Detroit assembly line," said Levitt. "There, the car moved while the workers stayed at their stations. In the case of our houses, it was the workers who moved, doing the same job at different locations. To the best of my knowledge, no one had ever done that before." The original owners agreed. They would refer to their homes as "1948 Cape Cods," as though they were cars rather than houses.

Those early buyers were eager to make purchases. For most of them, it was a first house, which helped the Levitts. Until then, homebuyers might work with the architect and builder, asking for and receiving changes in the basic plan. Each new house, in most instances, was different from all others. Not with the Levitts. In time, there would be some changes in the external appearance of the houses, but inside, all the ranches were the same, as were all Capes.

Levitt had to obtain permission to erect houses without basements, one of his economy moves. Workers were organized into teams, and after the foundation slab was poured and had settled, workers would drop off bundles of precut lumber and other supplies, which would be used to erect the house. Each worker had his own task to perform. One, for instance, did nothing but bolt washing machines to the floors of the houses. These were not "factory-built" houses, however, but on-site construction. The only parts of the house that were manufactured in a factory were the windows. The workers would put up each house in a little more than a week, and then move on to the next one. Writing of the method, a *Time* reporter said:

> Every hundred feet the trucks stopped and dropped off identical bundles of lumber, pipes, bricks, shingles and copper tubing, all as neatly packaged as loaves from a bakery. Near the bundles giant machines with an endless chain of buckets ate into the earth taking just thirteen minutes to dig a narrow four foot trench around a 25 by 32-foot rectangle. Then came more trucks loaded with cement and laid a four-inch foundation for the house in the rectangle. After the machines came the men. On nearby slabs already dry they worked in crews of two and three laying bricks, raising studs, nailing boards, painting, sheathing, shingling. Each crew did its special job and hurried on to the next site. A new one was finished every fifteen minutes.

These "Levitts" were purchased by individuals who often were the first in their families to own their homes. The initial models rented for $65 a month with an option to buy for $6990. Soon, the price was raised to $7990, and after 1949, they could only be bought. For this, the purchasers got a home on what usually was a 60 by 100 foot lot, with two bedrooms, a living room, kitchen, and bathroom—800 square feet of living space. There was an attic that might be expanded into two additional rooms and bath. Most of the Levitts were bought with FHA and GI mortgages, and the veterans who opted for the latter could purchase their homes with no down payment. At the time, critics argued that the houses were shoddy, and they deplored the cookie-cutter approach.

Levittown thrived, however, and a half century later the houses had been so altered by additions, it was difficult to find one that appeared as it first did after World War II. Moreover, 50 years after, the houses were reselling for upward of $170,000. Levitt created wealth for the tens of thousands of Levittowners who bought and sold those houses.

And virtually all of them were white. As did many builders of the period, Levitt placed a covenant in the contract excluding others from sales and resales. In time, this would be declared unconstitutional but even then few Blacks entered the suburban market for decades, and so missed out on one of the major means that generation would have to accumulate wealth.

Levitt went on to produce other Levittowns in New Jersey and Maryland and became the most famous name in home construction. He then ventured into smaller communities. In 1965, the company posted sales of $60 million, double the 1962 figure, and it would rise to $74 million in 1966. In 1968, for the price of $92 million in ITT stock, Levitt & Sons became part of International Telephone & Telegraph. Thus William Levitt completed his own pursuit of wealth by becoming a multimillionaire. He soon lost much of it in other ventures and had to sell his yacht and other luxuries. In 1981, Levitt was charged with taking money from a charitable foundation he established and was forced to repay $5 million. He died a ruined and broken man.

Gene Ferkauf, the Duke of Discounting

Those spanking new houses all had to be furnished. Apartment dwellers would have movers take their furniture to their new homes. If it were a Levitt, the washing machine would be in place, and in time, the houses came equipped with television sets as well. But there was a need for carpeting and other furnishings and appliances. For newly-weds, hand-me-downs and gifts could fill part of the need, but more would be required. Had they assayed the move in the last period of prosperity, the 1920s, they would have shopped in department stores or neighborhood shops. In the 1950s, they went to discount stores and discount department stores. The pioneer in this field was Gene Ferkauf, with his E. J. Korvette stores.

At one time, discounting was prevented by "fair trade" legislation in the states and in the federal Robinson-Patman Act of 1937, which obliged retailers to charge prices fixed by the manufacturers. These acts were passed to prevent large retailers from cutting prices and forcing mom and pop stores to the wall. There were some challenges, but the courts always decided the laws were constitutional.

Ferkauf was born into a middle class Brooklyn, New York family. His father, Harry, owned and managed two luggage stores in Manhattan, and Gene worked in one of them, returning there after service in World War II. In June 1948, Ferkauf opened his first E. J. Korvette store on 46th Street, not far from Fifth Avenue and Rockefeller Center in New York City. He found a way around the law by making his stores membership organizations, not open to the general public. How did one become a member? By accepting a card from a Korvette salesperson posted at the door.

Korvette sold items that included electric razors, TVs, refrigerators, washing machines, and the like at discounts, often as much as a third off the price at department stores.

Other stores followed, and in late 1953 Ferkauf erected his first department store in Carle Place, Long Island, not far from the Roosevelt Field Mall (where Macy's was thinking about putting up a store), and about a half hour from Levittown.

The new Korvette had a barebones appearance, but the customers didn't seem to mind. In addition to bargains on the familiar white goods sold in the earlier Korvettes, there was clothing, linen, and other "soft goods" that hadn't been available there. The

Carle Place store even had a food market, run at a loss, to attract customers. Before this, Korvette had been compared with Masters, Vim, and other discounters that had appeared. Now it was being likened to Klein's, a cut-rate clothing store which had a branch in nearby Hempstead.

Ferkauf prowled the countryside seeking new sites for stores. He found them in New Jersey, Connecticut, and Pennsylvania. Quietly, he closed his small discount stores, and Korvette was soon wholly in the department store business. The business was booming. Revenues rose from $17.8 million in 1954 to $54.8 million in 1956, and topped the $100 million mark in 1958, by which time Korvette had 12 stores. In 1956, *Fortune* noted that Korvette's total sales had gone up an astonishing 2650 percent over what they had been six years earlier. But strains were showing in the higher cost of doing business, and the chain's expenses were skyrocketing. Ferkauf opened new stores at a breakneck pace, and sales rose; they would be over $500 million in 1965. But profits were meager, only $17 million. In 1973, on sales of $606 million, profits were a mere $8 million. In 1977, Korvette reported revenues of $590 million and a loss of $4 million. Sales fell. Losses continued. The company finally closed its stores for the last time in December 1980, after a disappointing holiday season. Nevertheless, Ferkauf and others like him revolutionized retailing, and in the process of boosting their customers' standard of living, they became wealthy.

The Automobile Industry Awakens

The conventional wisdom of post-World War II America held that the two engines that drove prosperity were housing and automobiles. Of course, there were differences between a house and a car when it came to the accumulation of wealth. The purchase of a house, assisted by the tax laws and the government, was an investment as well as a place in which to live. A house purchased at $10,000 would surely be worth more than that when sold several years later, by which time part of the mortgage would have been paid off as well. There were no such government incentives for automobile purchases, and the product would start depreciating the moment it rolled off the lot. Of course, some of the cars would be used to create wealth for their purchasers, but relatively few. Cars offered convenience, access to places otherwise not reachable, and enjoyment at a price the consumer seemed quite willing to pay. Yet automobiles did create wealth, both for the manufacturers and for the workers who built the cars. The United Automobile Workers members were among the highest paid in the labor force. In this period, it was possible for a high school graduate to get a job on the assembly line and within a few years make enough money to purchase a modest house, a car, and more.

When the war ended, there were 22 million cars on America's roads, half of which were more than 10 years old, and most of them well beyond their useful life. "Every week," wrote *Fortune*, "literally thousands of cars will drop dead somewhere in the United States." The figures bore this out. There were 4 million fewer registrations on the day the war ended than on the day it began. No cars for the civilian market had been assembled since 1942, so the arithmetic was compelling. Detroit figured there was a market for 12 to 14 million cars. In no year had more than 4.5 million been produced, and that was in 1929, the last year of the boom decade. In 1941, 3.9 million had been made. In addition, the factories that churned out the cars would now have to be converted back from military production. As a result, there was a tremendous pent-up demand for new cars by Americans who had the money to pay for them, or at least make down payments. So it was widely assumed that every car produced during the next three to six years would be snapped up by eager buyers, and that sales would be strong at least till 1948.

Even so, the depression legacy endured. The industry asked the Society of Automotive Engineers to conduct a poll among potential purchasers. In the autumn of 1945, the society reported that most Americans wanted small, inexpensive, durable, functional models. This is what they got after the war.

Sales for 1945 were fewer than 70,000; that was all that could be produced by the reconverting industry. The next year's sales came to more than 2.1 million, and many more might have been sold had they been produced. Moreover, prices would have risen sharply were they not being controlled by the government. In light of this, many salesmen found ways around the law, still satisfying customers while making themselves reasonably wealthy. For example, they would not sell a new car to anyone who would not turn in a used one. The dealer would pay a very low price for the trade-in and then resell it for a large profit. Thus, each sale of a new car brought a double profit. Another technique was that the dealers would sell the new car at the specified price, but this did not include the extras, such as ashtrays and fog lights. So the customer might pay $875 for the car and another $1000 for an ashtray.

The American automobiles of the immediate postwar period looked like those of the prewar period, and this remained the case until the manufacturers came to understand that customers had changed their minds. Late in the decade, there were new designs and the cars became longer, lower, and sleeker, with more powerful engines and automatic transmissions—and higher prices as well. Profits were high, as were wages, as the automobile industry lived up to its reputation as one of the engines of prosperity.

Cars are useless without roads, of course, and with the acceleration of automobile sales and the growth of suburbia came the demand for more highways. Some had been built during the depression, but none during World War II, when some 80 percent of all war materials were shipped by rails. Recognizing the need for highways, Congress passed the Federal Highway Aid Act of 1944, which was followed by additional legislation after the war. President Eisenhower, who had become an advocate of highway construction when he took a unit of mechanized cavalry across the country after World War I, supported the Interstate Highway Act of 1956, which provided substantial aid to complete a thruway system. The peak year for highway and road construction before 1945 had been 1930, when $1.5 billion had been expended on such projects. This figure was surpassed in 1948, when costs came to $1.6 billion. In 1963, more than $7 billion was spent, and in 1971, more than $10 billion. By the end of the 1970s, it was possible to drive virtually all the way from the Atlantic to the Pacific on first class roads. Thus, as had been the case since the nation's beginning, government was prepared to provide the infrastructure to enable private businesspeople to amass wealth.

The Motelling of America

The opportunities made possible by developments in the automobile industry and highway construction were not lost on major businesses and would-be businesspeople. In the past, the middle class family with a one or two week vacation had few alternatives to a stay at a nearby resort, arrived at by train or bus—if that. Now the automobile could take that family a far greater distance. They could see the country from the highway. But where would they stay? The answer would be motels located near the highway or at the resort.

Business travelers who employed automobiles could also benefit from a different kind of dwelling. At hotels, parking always was difficult, bellboys were everpresent, hands extended, even when they weren't needed. There was the problem of street traffic. Calls to room service were necessary to obtain food or supplies. The prices were often quite high.

There clearly was a demand for inexpensive motels that were easily accessible to cars and at which families and businesspeople could be assured of certain quality standards. These were lacking in 1946. Some businessmen recognized this need and moved to fill it.

Kemmons Wilson was the most important of these people. As did so many others of his generation, Wilson served in World War II. On his discharge he, like William Levitt, recognized the need for housing, so he entered that field, constructing several hundred houses in the Memphis, Tennessee area where he lived. Becoming a millionaire in the process, Wilson looked for other areas to conquer. In the summer of 1951, he took his family on a vacation to Washington, D.C., and was struck by the difficulties of finding a decent place to stay at a reasonable price. The offerings went from overpriced to cheap, from hotels with many amenities to those with almost none. Standards of cleanliness varied. There seemed little sense to the pricing. Wilson saw a gap in the market, a need that he intended to fill. Speaking to his wife about his plans, Wilson confided that he intended to build hundreds of motels across the country.

On his return home, he started to work on the idea. The site chosen for his first motel was a highway that ran between Memphis and Nashville. The motel would have 120 rooms, with a restaurant, gift shop, and swimming pool. The rooms would be air conditioned and have television sets. The price was to be $4 a night for a single and $6 for a double. There would be no charge for children. This was what he had wanted to find on that vacation, and this was what he built, at a cost of $280,000. Searching for a name for the motel, he decided to call it the Holiday Inn, after a famous motion picture of the time.

The Holiday Inn was a success, and within the next two years Wilson built three more of them in the Memphis area. All was going well, but Wilson now had to face two problems: obtaining funds to build other Holiday Inns and finding managers for them. He might be able to oversee motels in his home area, but what about those far from Memphis? This was not a new difficulty for such businesspeople. Even the merchants and bankers in the ancient Near East and medieval Europe had to deal with such concerns, and did so by dispatching relatives to distant places to handle business. Wilson couldn't hope to do this with Holiday Inn, and besides, this would not meet his capital needs.

At the same time, there were thousands of Americans, many World War II veterans, who yearned to have their own businesses. They had access to capital but lacked experience and realized the high failure rates of new businesses. The answer to their problems was already at hand in the form of franchising.

Franchising had been around for decades. Gasoline stations were a form of franchising. The owner built his station with company assistance and was given the exclusive right to market that brand of gasoline and oil in a specified area. The Rexall drug chain,

Western Auto Supplies, and the Ben Franklin stores were all franchise operations. After the war, B.F. Goodrich, Rayco, and other companies entered the field. In 1963, Charles Tandy purchased nine Radio Shack stores and began to expand through franchises. Kemmons Wilson would do the same.

Wilson contacted Wallace Johnson, the vice president of the National Homebuilders' Association, and spoke of his plan. For a $500 fee, a would-be businessperson would be granted the right to own a Holiday Inn in his city. In addition, he would have to pay a user's fee and five cents a night per room. The innkeepers were required to maintain certain standards and agree to permit Wilson's company to have the construction contract. At first, Wilson constructed at the cost of $3000 per room, which he sold to the franchisee at $3500.

Holiday Inn was a huge success. In 1954, eleven were opened, including the first franchised operation. Three years later Wilson had an underwriting of his stock, selling 120,000 shares at $9.75. The stock did well, as did the company. The motels were sought out by travelers, and often were sold out weeks in advance, prompting others to enter the field. Families now went along the highway without reservations, knowing that down the road was a decent motel, many of them, in fact. Marion Isbell, who headed Ramada, one of Holiday Inn's competitors, was once asked how he went about selecting locations. "It's really simple," he replied. "All I do is go into a city and find out where Kemmons Wilson has a good Holiday Inn, and I put a Ramada Inn right next door."

Motels and franchising changed the face of America. Motel receipts in 1939 had been $37 million. By 1958, they came in at $850 million.

The McDonald's Concept

The franchise boom extended into many industries during the 1950s, and has sustained its momentum into the twenty-first century. It has been applied to office supplies, automobile servicing, cleaning services, and office temporaries, among others. The largest and most familiar franchising effort was in restaurants. Indeed, toward the end of the century, this became the path of choice for an increasingly large body of would-be entrepreneurs. The largest area was in take-out food stores, which in time became restaurants.

Middle class American families did not eat out often before World War II, not even during the "roaring" 1920s. That was for the upper class and special occasions. There was the matter of cost to be considered, not to mention taste and tradition. Prior to World War I, a young man would call on a young woman at her home. That would constitute a "date." To a nation just becoming accustomed to dates being movies and a soda, and perhaps a meal in a restaurant, eating out on a more or less regular basis was still a new concept. The practice originated in the suburbs that were springing up all over America. Mothers might go to take-out places and bring home a meal of hamburgers and fries, or fried chicken to feed their children and husbands. From there to taking the family to a restaurant was a stretch, eased, however, by specialty eateries, such as drive-ins, where families were served in their cars by waitresses on roller skates. Then the take-outs became larger, with tables and counters. In time, they came to serve breakfast as well. In the 1980s, more than half of America's meals were consumed in such places. By then, too, builders were experimenting with apartments without complete kitchens, only a microwave and its necessary adjunct, a freezer full of frozen meals, two other developments of the period. In the process, hundreds of thousands of American businesspeople were transformed into holders of great wealth, and the most successful of the companies, McDonald's, was larger in terms of revenues than such old standbys as Colgate-Palmolive, Monsanto, and A&P, a pre-World War II food retailer, and new arrivals like Apple Computer, Federal Express, and Marriott.

Hamburgers were and remain the great American staple. Many "hamburger heavens" dotted the landscape in the 1930s. There even were some chains, such as White Castle, but like the motels of the prewar period, these were often unappetizing and run by management that lacked vision and imagination.

Dick and Maurice (Mac) McDonald, who were brothers, operated a hot dog stand near the Santa Anita Racetrack in California in 1937. When business fell off after the racing season, they decided to erect a larger operation in San Bernadino, selling hamburgers, barbecue, and sandwiches as well as soft drinks and hot dogs. The operation was a success, so much so that the service suffered. Seeking to rectify this situation, they shaved items off the menu, purchased efficient grills, and used paper plates and cups. They stressed speed, cleanliness, and low prices, and it worked very well. The public flocked to the McDonalds. By 1951, they were selling more than a quarter of a million dollars worth of burgers and drinks at that one restaurant. And they were considering franchising as well, the first one being purchased the following year.

Two years later, Ray Kroc, who sold malted milk machines to restaurants, fast food operations, drug stores, and candy stores, delivered a machine to the McDonalds. He knew they were doing a terrific business and wanted to know more about it. After a couple of visits, he asked for and was granted the post of franchise agent.

Kroc recognized that the McDonalds were taking advantage of an America on wheels that had created Holiday Inns and the suburbia typified by Levittown. He would sell franchises to individuals who catered to a family crowd, not only the teenagers who usually frequented the burger joints.

The first of the Kroc franchisees opened in 1955 in Des Plaines, Illinois. By 1957, he had 14 of them up and running. In 1958, the company sold its millionth hamburger and had 100 stores.

Kroc entered negotiations with the McDonald brothers in 1960, and the following year agreed to purchase the company for $2.7 million. By the mid-1990s, McDonald's had become a $10 billion company, expanding rapidly overseas as well as in the United States. Franchisees in the early days had to ante up around $80,000 and agree to accept McDonald's guidance in all matters, while purchasing supplies from companies approved by McDonald's, which paid fees for the privilege. Failure to maintain quality control might mean losing the name and the golden arches that became the company's symbol and a magnet for business.

Frederick Terman and the Arrival of the Military-Industrial-Educational Complex

In the last year of World War II, 1945, national defense accounted for $81.5 billion out of total government expenditures of $95.1 billion. Defense spending declined after the war, bottoming at $13 billion in 1947 (6 percent of GNP) before rising due to the pressures of the Cold War and the Korean conflict. In 1953, government expenditures on procurement came to $76.6 billion, of which $50.4 billion went to the military. An additional $79 million went for space research and technology, all of which added up to 20 percent of GDP. Military spending declined after the Korean War ended, but never again would it fall below $40 billion annually. But procurement was only part of the story. The total spending on national defense, including research, development, consulting, and more, was much higher.

The emergence of the government as the largest single factor in the economy enabled firms that provided it with goods and services to thrive. In 1968, there were 22,000 firms with prime contracts, who, in turn, let out subcontracts to 100,000 other firms. Approximately 76 industries were classified as "defense" by virtue of having more than half their sales in this area. That same year, 5300 cities and towns had at least one defense plant or company under their jurisdictions. They competed with one another for them, not only because they brought jobs and taxes but because of the multiplier effect on the local economy.

Most literate Americans know that in his farewell address, Dwight Eisenhower warned against the influence of the military-industrial complex. In fact, the General was the only post-World War II President to hold the military in check. What is less known is Eisenhower's admonition against the powers of the scientific-educational elite. The solitary inventor has been replaced by "task forces of scientists in laboratories and testing fields," he observed. In the old days universities were "the fountainhead of free ideas and scientific discovery." No more, he said in 1961. "Partly because of the huge costs involved, a government contract becomes virtually a substitute for intellectual curiosity." For this reason, Eisenhower warned that "the prospect of domination of the nation's scholars by federal employment, project allocations, and the power of money is ever present and is gravely to be regarded."

Evidence to support this view was readily accessible. For example, M.I.T. was, by the end of World War II, the largest nonindustrial defense contractor. The Electrical Engineering Department there, headed by Donald Jackson, had strong ties with industry and government agencies, and as one measure of such influence, considered that half a professor's remuneration should be earned outside of the school. Jay Forrester, another M.I.T. professor, led a team that created the nation's missile defense system and at the same time spun off significant research and development in the area of computer design that had civilian applications.

In this period, too, companies that previously had been oriented to the consumer and industrial markets became military suppliers. Raytheon, for example, had practically no military business in 1940. In the post war period, more than 80 percent of its sales were to the military. By 1961, a Boston bank suggested replacing the textile spindle with the Hawk missile to symbolize the local economy. But the symbol might more fittingly have been the Lincoln Laboratory at M.I.T., which was emblematic of the interrelationships between the companies that festooned Route 128 and the campus.

Even more important than the connection between industry and M.I.T. in Massachusetts was the nexus that came into being in California in what became known as Silicon Valley, centered around Stanford University. The key player there was Frederick Terman, an electrical engineering professor and dean of engineering. Most Americans who knew of Karl Compton, Vannevar Bush, and other academic scientists pressed into government service during and after World War II, probably never heard of Terman, a professor whose ambition was to make Stanford the world's premier scientific university. Terman thought the post war years would be crucial for the school. "I believe that we will either consolidate our potential strength, and create a foundation for a position in the west somewhat analogous to Harvard in the east, or we will drop to a level somewhat similar to that of Dartmouth, a well-thought-of institution having about 2 percent as much influence on national life as Harvard."

Terman's proposal was simple enough. Disregard the undergraduates because they didn't pay dividends in grants and prestige. Concentrate on graduate programs, but only in the hot departments. It would be wiser, he contended, to build a few superb departments than to seek excellence across the board. Terman pulled it off. In 1946, Stanford's government contracts came to $127,000. Ten years later they were $4.5 million. After another decade Stanford ranked among the top three universities in government contracts.

Terman also was the mentor of many individuals who would become important in the computer age. In 1955, he convinced William Shockley to establish his company, Shockley Semiconductor, in an industrial park in Palo Alto as a subsidiary of Beckman Instruments. The company did not fare well, and in 1957, eight of its engineers and scientists left Shockley to form Fairchild Semiconductor, the pioneer company in Silicon Valley. Out of Fairchild would emerge dozens of individuals and companies that would lead the way into the electronic age. Fairchild alumnus Charles Spork would become a major factor at National Semiconductor. Jerry Saunders helped found Advanced Micro-Devices. And in 1968, Robert Noyce, Gordon Moore, and Andrew Grove founded Intel.

Intel was destined to become the most important of the new companies spawned by Fairchild. By 1970, it had produced several memory chips, with a capacity of one kilobyte, or 1024 bits of information. At about this time, Intel engineer Ted Hoff developed the concept of placing all of the functions needed in microprocessing on a single chip, hence, the microprocessor, or "computer on a chip." The first of these, the 4004, was considered the cornerstone of the new industry in the early 1970s. Intel's 8080, introduced in 1974, was used to create the first microcomputer. Noyce noted that the chip, which cost $300, possessed more computing power than the ENIAC, the first true computer, was 20 times faster, and cost one 10,000th as much as that giant machine. The ENIAC weighed 30 tons and occupied 1500 square feet. The 8080 set the standard for its time and the path for what was to follow.

Terman also brought industrial parks to Stanford. Alongside the classroom buildings, libraries, and administrative centers are outposts of some of the nation's most innovative corporations. The synergy is complete. Professors double as researchers at these centers, which also employ graduate students in a form of apprenticeship. Terman also is the reason for Silicon Valley's location. Dozens of small, entrepreneurial companies were started and staffed by Stanford people.

Terman made his priorities clear. Education was fine in its place, but there were more important considerations. Commenting on Office of Naval Research contracts, he wrote, "Even though much of the basic research work that these agencies support is carried on in universities, the *primary motive is not to aid education* but rather to accomplish their mission." Fair enough, insofar as the government is concerned. But what is the primary motive of the universities?

This mindset was challenged in 1969 by antiwar demonstrators protesting the involvement of the universities in the Vietnam War. By then, government and industry dominated large segments of the research-oriented universities. "We were churning out defense-oriented graduate students," recalled one M.I.T. professor. "Almost all of our graduate students who didn't go into university teaching wound up in the missile and aircraft industries." As a result of the protests, some of the institutes devoted to defense and industrial purposes were spun off by their parent organizations, and others were reoriented toward different ends. That defense was and is necessary is obvious, but the nexus between the universities and its sponsors came at a price. "Were they training a generation of scientists and engineers so addicted to the wasteful culture of military procurement that they could never flourish in the cost-conscious world of civilian technology?" the professor continued. Even Terman got the message. In 1970, he told the Stanford faculty of his hope that the professors would "cease turning out people in their own image but would rather educate engineers attuned to the needs of non-aerospace, non-defense industries by working on research related to the problems of the world."

By the 1950s, the web that had been constructed between the government, the corporations, and the universities had grown to encompass many of the nation's largest firms and schools, and this continued into the 1960s. In addition, institutes and foundations, the "think tanks," entered the mix. Some of the companies were well known for their concentration on government work—General Dynamics, Raytheon, Rockwell International, Colt, Grumman, TRW, and Lockheed, for example. Others were known to have important military contracts, and these included a host of electronics firms—IBM, Sperry Rand, Texas Instruments, Litton, ITT, and RCA, among others. Companies not ordinarily thought of as military nonetheless received contracts. International Harvester manufactured systems for rocket engines. American Metal Climax turned out precision parts for aerospace applications. Scovill Manufacturing had contracts to provide aircraft parts. Universal Match was also in the missile business.

These firms, and the government itself, hired professors and other researchers. Among the schools involved in the one area of chemical and biological warfare, for example, were UCLA Medical School, Baylor, the University of Texas, Johns Hopkins, the University of Maryland, the University of Minnesota, Yale, and the Illinois Institute of Technology. Cornell's Aeronautical Laboratory was involved, as well as the Stanford Research Institute, which was known in Washington as the "Pentagon of the West." Of course, not every college and university profited from military contracts. According to one count made in 1968, the number that did came to 52, or one out of every 40 schools. Two-thirds of the funds spent on research and development at universities came from the government, and 90 percent of that came from the Department of Defense, the National Aeronautics and Space Administration (NASA), and the Atomic Energy Commission. The government sought schools whose facilities and faculties were suitable, and it worked two ways: where the facilities were not up to par, they would be constructed and equipped, often with large government grants. Researchers hoping to work on government projects would learn where they were being conducted and then try to obtain a teaching position, especially if (along with the faculty appointment) went an association with a nearby institute, such as American Enterprise, Brookings, the Center for Strategic and International Studies, or Hoover. It was not unusual for such professors to earn far more through consulting government agencies than they received for their work on campus. A survey conducted in the mid-1960s indicated that one quarter of the scientists at 12 major universities received portions of their salaries from federal funds, and that at one school, there were 151 professors whose total salaries derived from federal funds. As University of California president Clark Kerr put it, "Intellect has also become an instrument of national purpose, a component part of the 'military-industrial complex.' " To which Air Force Secretary Robert Seamons, Jr., a former MIT professor, added, "We cannot provide the necessary weapons for defense without the help of university research laboratories." John Hanna, president of Michigan State and a former assistant secretary of defense, believed that "Our colleges and universities must be regarded as bastions of our defense, as essential to the preservation of our country and our way of life as supersonic bombers, nuclear-powered submarines, and intercontinental ballistic missiles."

In this way, fighting the Cold War enabled large segments of corporate America and academia to join forces in the pursuit of wealth.

CHAPTER *19*

The Revival
of the Securities Markets

HE average American remained uninterested in securities during the immediate post-war period. While the economy boomed, Wall Street remained somnolent. There was a rally in 1948, when the Dow rose from a low of 165 in March to a high of 190 in November, only to fall back when Harry Truman unexpectedly defeated Thomas Dewey in the Presidential election. In May 1949, the Federal Reserve Board's Index of Industrial Production stood at 179, down 16 points from where it had been on election day. The unemployment rate stood at more than 6 percent; almost twice as many Americans were out of work than a year earlier. Truman's standings in the public opinion polls fell. One survey indicated that more than 40 percent of the public thought a new depression was on the way. Liberal publications warned Truman to avoid the errors that had destroyed Herbert Hoover's presidency. Auto union leader Walter Reuther said, "1929 can happen again in 1949."

A *Time* writer was baffled by the timidity in the markets in early 1949. Rallies would be followed by corrections, and then another rally and another correction.

> Wherever one looked, the U.S. was splitting its breeches. In Texas, cash farm marketings had jumped from $469 million in 1939 to $1974 last year. In mushrooming Houston, millionaires were so common that nobody paid them much attention. In Atlanta, Frank H. Neely, chairman of the district Federal Reserve Bank, took a look at the new industrial South and said: "I think we are more or less permanently at a higher level." And it was a good bet that the Street's baby bull would put on some real meat before the bull-throated roar of the U.S. economy dies down.

Wall Street couldn't decide whether inflation or recession was the more serious threat.

Prices dipped at the NYSE. In early July, the Dow was at 168. Only a year earlier, it had toyed with 200. By then a clear majority of forecasters seemed convinced that recession was on the way. If this were so, then those two engines that hauled the economy, housing and car sales, were bound to suffer. It did not happen. Housing sales continued strong, and autos performed spectacularly, with sales rising from 3.9 million in 1948 to a record 5.1 million in 1949.

Rarely had the experts and investors been so wrong on an industry group. It could be seen in the area of short-selling, which involves borrowing shares and then subsequently selling them, the idea being that they would be repurchased after the price fell and then returned to the lender. Of the 10 most heavily shorted issues in June 1949, four were automakers. Hudson, which sold for 9⅞ on June 14, had earned $5.30 per share the previous year, and in early 1949 had boosted its dividend from an annual rate of $0.70 to $1.00. Thus, the stock that day, based on 1948 results, was selling at a price/earnings ratio of 2 and a yield of 10 percent. Sales rose in 1949, and the company earned $6.30 per share. Not only did Hudson retain its dividend, but the company paid an extra $0.70, which meant that those who had purchased the stock in June had a security that yielded 17 percent based on the price they had paid. Moreover, exactly a year later, the stock sold for 15⅝, and by then the dividend had been boosted to $2.50. So it was across the board for the automobile stocks. All advanced when investors finally realized things simply were not as bad as they had anticipated. Such individuals were viewing the economy through glasses manufactured in 1929. It was very different in 1949, and the key was in consumer demand.

At the time, some of Wall Street's technical analysts had established a "resistance area" at between 163 and 165. Should prices fall below this range, they said, and in the process establish a new low, there would follow a major collapse. This conclusion was not based on empirical evidence, but conventional theory. Still, if enough people believed in it, a decline below 163 might set off a selling wave. On June 10, 1949, the Dow closed at 165, and the following session dipped below 162 on a heavy volume of 1.3 million shares. The average bounded back, however, and by month's end was above 167. There had been no sell-off. The technicians were wrong. Observing this scene, a *New York Herald Tribune* financial writer remarked:

> In effect, the Dow advice of the moment is: We may break through on the downside; if we do then it has been a bear market since mid-1946, even though we told you long after the 1947–48 runup had occurred, that it has turned into a bull market; but now we take that back. On the other hand, while this is significant, don't expect too much of this bearish trend, because it will have then lasted so long it can't last much longer.

The writer went on to warn readers not to make too much of this. "Charts and theories are very valuable when one is looking at what the market has done in the past; their record on what to expect has been a dismal one in the last few years." Such factors as managements, prospects, earnings, and dividends were what really mattered, and historically, stock prices were very low.

Securities analysts took a similar view. Sam Smith of Bache & Co. expected a rebound to the 173 level. Heinz Biel of Laird, Bissell & Meeds thought utility stocks were in a buying range. E. F. Hutton's Lucien Hooper sent clients a list of 225 stocks that were selling at or below their net capital. In common with most of his fellows, Thomas Phelps of Francis I. Du Pont hedged his forecasts, but ended one report by noting that "stock prices are lower than in many years relative to earnings, dividends, assets, and bond prices." That year, the price to earnings ratio on the Dow was 7.6 and the average yield was 7.1 percent, at a time when AAA rated long-term bonds yielded 2.7 percent.

Then began a great bull market that would last for 10 years. The Dow advanced during each of the next 10 weeks. Prices climbed sharply in December, passing the 200 level for the first time since 1946 just before New Year's Day. By then, many of the bears had surrendered. Clearly this was a major move, one that had caught them by surprise.

Investors started to return, or rather (to be precise, since an entire generation had been lost to securities investments), newcomers started to nibble at stocks, concentrating on the old blue chips, while speculators continued to prefer low-priced issues. General Motors in 1949 was the fifth most heavily traded stock. On excellent auto sales, it ended the year at 71⅝, up 12⅞. That year, GM earned $14.64 a share and paid a dividend of $8. Thus, its price/earnings ratio was below 5, its yield more than 11 percent.

The five best-performing stock groups in 1949 were leathers, utility holding companies, papers, soaps, and drugs, the kinds of stocks that paid good dividends and had stable earnings. Radio broadcasting firms didn't do as well as dairy companies; fertilizer stocks outperformed television receiver manufacturers. The market advanced for the year, but clearly the public wanted safety and yield, and was unwilling to take chances in order to have growth.

The Puzzling Case of Television Securities

In 1946, a grand total of 10,000 television sets were manufactured, while 16 million radios were produced. There was not much demand for television receivers that year, since in all parts of the country, there was little in the way of programming. Television was an oddity, not an entertainment and news medium. Two years later, fewer than 1 million sets were produced. But then, as programming developed, sales started to soar. There were 3 million sets sold in 1949, and for 1950, more than 7.5 million, as television became a household utility. Old radio receiver companies produced TV sets and were reinvigorated. Motorola's revenues rose from $23 million in 1946 to $82 million in 1949, while net income went from $620,000 to $5.3 million. A host of other companies, from Admiral to Zenith to GE to RCA, posted similar results.

But as TV boomed, the stocks of the companies that produced receivers languished. All the companies had fine sales and earnings in 1949; some had doubled both over the 1948 figures, and all had increased their dividends. The first quarter of 1950 was even better. Admiral's earnings were triple those of the same period in 1949. Motorola's sales for 1950's first quarter were $35.5 million and profits $3.50 per share. The 1949 figures had been $15.2 million and $1.14, respectively. The stock paid a $1.50 dividend and some Wall Street houses thought earnings for the year would be more than $15.00 a share. Yet the stock sold at 50, twice what it had been a year earlier, but still slightly more than three times anticipated earnings, while yielding 3 percent.

Stock analysts hesitated when it came to recommending such issues. Perhaps they feared so great an upward move could not be sustained much longer. Some considered the possibility of a shakeout in the industry, with several manufacturers squeezed out by the survivors. Brokers urged clients fortunate enough to own shares in one or another of the TV companies to take their profits and seek other investments. The familiar argument for selling was based on dividend yields, which (as noted) was the key to investment in all timid markets. *Business Week* warned investors not to anticipate rapid or sizeable dividend increases from any of the manufacturers. "When you are growing as fast as TV, you have to conserve cash to take care of expansion costs and needs for new working capital. It is doubtful if the industry will be able to pay out in dividends more than a small part of earnings for a long time."

The company CEOs understood this situation and investment philosophy. Hoping to boost the prices of their common shares, they had increased dividends. But the prices of the shares rose rapidly, and so the yields declined. Paradoxically, the manufacturers' stocks became speculative vehicles and were sold by investors as their prices ran up. It was the kind of market in which investors almost feared price advances and were wary of capital gains that came too rapidly. One analyst who had recommended receiver manufacturers in 1947 sent out a sell signal in early 1950. These stocks had been appealing when their yields were more than 10 percent, but now that the yields were down to 3 or 5 percent, they were no longer attractive. Safe utility stocks were available with yields of more than 7 percent, noted one market letter, which recommended a switch from Admiral to Consumers Power.

The same psychology and investment approach penalized young companies in exciting new areas. Such firms hadn't much hope of attracting investors, and there weren't enough speculators in the market to take their shares, so they were faced with unhappy alternatives: they could die, remain small, try to expand on retained earnings, or seek some larger company willing to buy them out. They had no recourse to the new issue market that had all but vanished during the Great Depression. During World War II, the federal government assumed much of the responsibility for financing, and Wall Street remained in the doldrums. The issuance of new corporate securities for public sale was below $700 million in 1942 and 1943, after which it started to rise, reaching $4.1 billion in 1946, when businesses floated bonds to finance reconversion efforts. Little by way of common shares were floated in this period. This was not because companies did not want to sell shares rather than debt. Indeed, selling shares would have been preferred, since it would permit them to husband funds for expansion that otherwise would have been needed to pay interest. But customers for shares simply weren't there in large numbers.

In his college finance textbook of the period, *Investments* (1953), Julius Grodinsky told a generation of students, "The investors in common stocks are the genuine risk bearers in the system of capitalism and free enterprise." And risk was not sought by investors of the time. As late as 1955, Martin Mayer, then a newcomer to Wall Street, wrote that while it might be possible to place such securities with friends and relations, "without such friends a corporation will find that the price for 'venture capital' is high as a gallows."

The Coming of the Computer

The computer was to have an even greater impact on Americans and create still more wealth than did television. While television came into its own in the 1950s, computers were considered esoterica during that decade. The popular image of computers was of massive, powerful mainframes utilized by large corporations and government agencies. This would not change until the 1980s, although long before then shares of computer makers would become features of the securities markets.

According to some experts, the computer was invented either by Charles Babbage in the early nineteenth century, Percy Ludgate in the early twentieth century, or Leonardo Torres y Quevedo soon thereafter. Other scholars trace it to experiments at Bell Laboratories and RCA in the 1920s and 1930s. And a few credit English scientist Alan Turing and his colleagues, who worked on calculating devices during World War II. In addition, John Vincent Atanasoff's claim of origination has a host of supporters.

All of this demonstrates the truism that no single individual can lay claim to having produced any of the truly important inventions, be it the railroad, the car, the airplane, telephone, motion pictures, or whatever.

While it is not possible to ascribe the computer's invention to one person, it can be said with some conviction that the industry began with the work of J. Presper Eckert and John Mauchly. Building on the accomplishments of others and adding their own refinements, they developed the ENIAC computer at the University of Pennsylvania during World War II. After the war, they formed Electronic Control Corp., which in 1947 was renamed Eckert-Mauchly Computer Co., and set about creating the UNIVAC.

The company would have folded for lack of interest were it not for financial help from American Totalizer Co., which operated parimutuel machines. In 1950, American Totalizer sold its interest to Remington Rand just in time for UNIVAC to make its debut in the 1950 census and to predict the results of the 1952 Presidential election.

Remington Rand was soon eclipsed by IBM, then the leader in large calculators. Thomas Watson, Jr. convinced his father to make the switch to computers, and its first product, the 701, made for the military in 1951, was followed by the 702 for the civilian market. The machine was a huge success. By 1956, IBM had 85 percent of the market and was turning out additional machines and developing software for them.

A host of competitors were attracted to this industry. Some were established firms such as Honeywell, General Electric, RCA, NCR, Burroughs, and what had become Sperry Rand. Others, led by Control Data, were new to the industry. But none had IBM's success.

Recognizing these rivals were developing competitive machines, IBM produced a new generation of hardware, known as the 360 series, which was released in 1964, and was another great success. By then, it seemed IBM was destined to lead indefinitely in this rapidly growing industry.

There were ongoing attempts to diminish IBM's dominance of the industry. Some companies were able to survive by concentrating on niches IBM ignored, or attacking in the courts. Cray specialized in "supercomputers," a category IBM didn't think held much promise. Another threat to IBM came from the leasing companies, such as Mohawk, Telex, and Leasco, which purchased IBM machines and then leased them at competitive rates. IBM continued to dominate the market for large computers, which, in the view of most people, were what computers were all about.

Charles Merrill, Keith Funston, and People's Capitalism

While the shares of IBM and other computer makers attracted some attention from investors concerned with growth, center stage on Wall Street was still held by old-line companies that offered high and dependable dividends. This attitude would change as the economy continued its expansion and the market its upward move. Investors who in the late 1940s wanted dividends and then sold their holdings when the yields rose would become accustomed to seeking capital gains, which were much higher than dividend yields. They would start selling their staid stocks and purchasing those of companies in the exciting new areas. This was one of the developments that would transform the marketplace. The other, equally important, was the matter of attracting new investors to Wall Street. This was accomplished by two of the district's best salesmen of the twentieth century, Charles Merrill and Keith Funston.

Charles Merrill, the more important of the two, was not a newcomer to the Street. He was born in 1885, in a small town on the outskirts of Jacksonville, Florida, the son of a doctor who operated a drugstore as a sideline. After graduating elementary school, Merrill was dispatched to Worcester Academy in Massachusetts and then on to Amherst College. He was a poor student, and devoted more time to selling suits to undergraduates and helping run a local boarding house than to his studies.

Before Merrill could flunk out of Amherst, he transferred to Michigan Law School, which he liked even less. He left school for a season of minor league baseball in Mississippi, soon learning he lacked the talent to make it to the big leagues. With nothing better to do, Merrill leaped at an offer by his prospective father-in-law of a post at the Manhattan headquarters of Patchogue-Plymouth Mills.

Everything went badly those first months. Merrill had arrived just in time for the Panic of 1907, which hurt all manner of businesses. Then his engagement was broken and he lost his job. "My two years there," recalled Merrill, "turned out to be the equivalent of a university course in general, and credit, finance, cost accounting and administration in particular."

In 1909, Merrill found a sales position at the commercial paper house of George H. Burr & Co., which asked him to establish a bond trading and sales operation. At last he had found his niche. At the time, the business was restricted. Merrill thought it might be expanded to just about any middle class individual. In a 1911 article in *Leslie's Illustrated Weekly*, he wrote, "Having thousands of customers scattered throughout the United States is infinitely preferable to being dependent upon the fluctuating buying power of a smaller and perhaps on the whole wealthier group of investors in any one section."

Soon after, Burr made its first attempt at underwriting, an offering of $2 million in preferred stock plus 10,000 shares of common for S.S. Kresge, then a smallish chain store. Merrill handled the deal and in the process became entranced with retailing, a field in which he would specialize for the rest of his career.

In 1913, Merrill moved to Eastman Dillon as sales manager, and January of the following year left to create Charles E. Merrill & Co., with his friend Edmund Lynch joining him soon after, whereupon the firm became Merrill Lynch & Co. It was a good team. As one banker there later remarked, "Merrill could imagine the possibilities; Lynch imagined what might go wrong in a malevolent world."

Naturally, Merrill hoped to do a sizeable business in an environment that became increasingly competitive after the outbreak of World War I. Even so, he was more restrained than most, hoping to attract a different kind of clientele than did most of the small houses of the period. He targeted conservative individuals, who at that time were not interested in stocks and bonds, but instead put their savings into bank accounts. Merrill was convinced this was a large, untapped market, and his advertisements of the period were geared to such people. He trained his salesmen carefully, admonishing them to consider themselves teachers and consultants more than hucksters. "I notice a very unfortunate tendency [on the part of our salesmen] to dwell upon the profits a customer is likely to make instead of the merit of an issue as an investment," he wrote in 1916. "We try to be conservative and careful." The salesmen were asked to "bear in mind that in every sale you are either destroying or building good will [for the next sale], which is our most valuable asset."

After stints in the Army during the war, Merrill and Lynch returned to the firm, which in their absence had been run by associates. Now Merrill added underwriting to his brokerage business, specializing in retail stores, perhaps natural considering his interest in sales. He handled underwritings for such firms as Grand Union, Western Auto Supply, J.C. Penney, and National Tea, and in 1926 helped direct Safeway Stores. Even so, Merrill was not a major Wall Street figure during the Great Bull Market, largely because he was far too cautious for the temper of that speculative period. In fact, his retail operation suffered, and Merrill was obliged to do most of his brokerage business through E.A. Pierce & Co., then the nation's largest wire house.

While at that time Merrill entertained no desire to emulate National City Bank's ventures into selling bonds to small investors, he apparently learned much from that operation which he stored away for future use.

By early 1928, Merrill had become convinced stock prices bore no relation to reality. The average P/E ratio for stocks, which had been 9.2 in 1924, had risen to 20 in 1927, an unheard of level. Some spoke of a new era in which such multiples would be the norm, but Merrill was suggesting that his clients lighten their portfolios. "Now is the time to get out of debt," he wrote on March 21, 1928. "We do not urge you sell securities indiscriminately, but we do advise in no uncertain terms that you take advantage of the present high prices and put your own financial house in order."

Shortly after the October 1929 crash, Merrill transferred all of his brokerage clients and employees to E.A. Pierce & Co. and invested $5 million in that house. During the 1930s, Merrill Lynch did a small business in underwriting, and since there were few of these, Merrill spent most of his time with Safeway, also enjoying the good life here and abroad, while Lynch pretty much ran things in New York.

Lynch died in 1938, which meant that Merrill had to put in more time at the office. The following year, E.A. Pierce experienced difficulties, and at the urging of an old associate, Winthrop Smith, Merrill absorbed it and another, smaller house. With this, Merrill Lynch was transformed into Merrill Lynch, Pierce & Cassatt. In 1941, Merrill, now becoming assured the long period of doldrums as a result of World War II was ending, absorbed New Orleans-based brokerage Fenner & Beane, and out of this came Merrill Lynch, Pierce, Fenner & Beane. It was a substantial operation, in fact, one of the nation's largest.

In a letter to his new partners, Merrill set down the principles to which he hewed, and which would be developed more fully during the 1940s. Integrity was crucial, he thought. "Disturbing is the large percentage of potential investors and speculators in securities who are suspicious of the motives and operations of the security business and the people engaged therein."

Merrill suffered a heart attack three years later, and with this, Smith assumed day-to-day leadership. Merrill attended to the needs of a few old clients, but increasingly concentrated on the development of the firm's sales operations and public relations. It was in this area he made his signal contribution, transforming the nature of brokerage and helping to create the first bull market based upon widespread participation. In effect, he had democratized share ownership in America.

In Merrill's view, the most important task facing Wall Street was to gain public confidence, which had been shattered by the Great Crash and Depression. At the time, brokers were deemed mendacious and shifty, certainly not to be trusted. If anything positive were to be accomplished, the public would have to be convinced they were scrupulously honest. So the broker was the key figure in the investment process, a not unusual conclusion, given Merrill's chain store experience. Together with Smith, Merrill developed what soon became known as the "Ten Commandments" at the firm, and eventually outside of it as well. The principal commandment was: "The interests of our customers MUST come first. We in the securities business have a job to do—a job of reestablishing faith in the securities markets as a place for sound investment."

With the exception of the City Company experience, until that time brokers were of two varieties. The first was very much akin to those amiable investment bankers previously discussed, though they usually were not as intelligent and sophisticated, and few were as well-remunerated. They made sales to old college chums, members of clubs they frequented, relatives, and others found in that kind of milieu. Their idea of a large deal might be the purchase of 200 shares of AT&T, while an investment banker's concept of one would be a $50 million underwriting of General Electric bonds. Brokers worked over the phone with clients, hoping to make sales based on developments at a company of which they might know very little. Investment bankers did their business at lunch (the most important hour of the day for them), with chief financial officers who understood their firms very well indeed.

The kind of brokers most customers got to see were out-and-out hustlers. Incompetent or devious brokers switched clients in and out of stocks and bonds in order to earn commissions. The sleazier of them worked out of "bucket shops," making cold telephone calls, hoping to snare the unsuspecting. They had more in common with racetrack touts than brokers. They favored those low-priced stocks, always hoping for a fast double. But there were few of them. Most Americans simply had no interest in stocks. Soon after World War II, Elmo Roper conducted a poll for the NYSE to learn what people thought about that institution. He discovered that most people believed Wall Street was home to some of the nation's slickest, most accomplished crooks, while a substantial segment thought the stock market was a place where cattle were sold.

Merrill's task was to alter both perception and reality. If that could be done, he said, the broad middle class might be persuaded to purchase stocks in the postwar period, just as City Company had done with bonds in the 1920s. This went contrary to current practice. Traditionally, Wall Street discouraged individuals with only a few hundred dollars from investing; they were hardly worth the trouble of consultation, planning, and management.

The investment bankers, who were the dominant force on the Street, were of a like mind. They considered their responsibility to be the provision of advice and information to a select clientele of businessmen, not middle class workers. Indeed, some major investment houses did not engage in a public business. Kuhn, Loeb, one of the most respected forces in the business, not only avoided such operations but took pride in the fact it employed no sales personnel. Dillon Read, one of the Street's most prestigious houses, relinquished its NYSE seat in the early 1930s and saw no need for one in the 1950s. Lazard Freres and Lehman Brothers, likewise, remained aloof from such business. They were lean affairs, proud of the fact that they received large fees for brainpower, and did not have to stoop to dealing with the public.

Merrill considered that novice small investors usually started with little, but in time, if the experience was salutary, might become more substantial investors. In effect, he hoped to do for brokerage what the chain stores had done for retailing: make smaller profits per client but lure many more of them to his operation. "Our business is people and their money," he said in 1946. "We must draw the new capital required for industrial might and growth *not* from among a few large investors but from the savings of thousands of people of moderate incomes. We must bring Wall Street to Main Street— and we must use the efficient, mass-merchandising methods of the chain store to do it."

The NYSE mandated minimum commissions, but there was no maximum, and most brokerage firms extracted what the traffic would bear. Not Merrill Lynch, which not only charged the minimum but campaigned for yet lower rates. Research operations were beefed up, and at a time when brokerages charged for such material, reports were offered free to interested individuals. Other brokerage firms had fee schedules for monthly statements, for holding securities, for clipping coupons on bonds, and for practically any other service rendered. Merrill Lynch waived such charges.

Merrill Lynch was not the first brokerage to advertise, but it carried the art to new heights. In the past, advertisements either were simple statements of availability of services or blatantly sensationalist. Merrill Lynch was interested in educating potential customers. One of its ads, "What Everybody Ought to Know about the Stock and Bond Business," was a long essay, which read more like a textbook than an ad. Merrill Lynch was besieged with requests for reprints, eventually distributing more than a million copies. The firm also published a series of booklets on investing offered free for the asking.

Merrill instituted a rigorous training program, at a time when most brokers had little more than a day or so of orientation and the examination to become a broker was a joke. In this period, trainees with family and other accounts were preferred. Merrill hired bright young men whom, he felt, showed promise, and provided them with leads garnered from his extensive advertising campaigns—another first.

Merrill performed for brokerage what Roy Kroc and Kemmons Wilson would later do for fast food; he made it efficient, trouble-free, and trustworthy. He closed down many of the stodgy offices and opened bright, airy places where customers would feel more comfortable. Merrill Lynch had an elan rare on the Street, and it engendered loyalty, not only to the customer, but the firm as well. In this period, Merrill Lynch brokers were paid salaries, not commissions, and Merrill made certain the public knew this. Brokers at other firms might use the hard sell to increase their income. Not the Merrill Lynch "registered representatives," who were more like investment advisors than sales-people. The Merrill Lynch brokers were compared favorably with the best in any American business. "If you took a group of IBM salesmen and Merrill Lynch brokers and mixed them up, you couldn't tell one from the other," remarked William Schreyer, a future Merrill Lynch CEO who arrived in this period. "Their principles were so similar. When people came to Merrill Lynch in those days, they never thought about going anywhere else."

This approach worked. By 1955, the firm handled 10 percent of the transactions at the NYSE and 18 percent of the odd-lot business. Its gross income came to $45.6 million in 1950. Four years later, it was $73.3 million.

Merrill died on October 6, 1956. That month, there were 18 sessions in which 1 million shares were traded and five in which the 2 million share mark was bested, and the Dow closed at 482 the day before. His legacy was a nation becoming increasingly involved with share ownership. In 1939, there had been fewer than 4 million shareholders. According to the 1952 shareholder census, there were then 6.5 million, and another census conducted in 1962 showed 17 million. By 1966, there were 20 million shareholders. The beginning of what was to be the democratization of wealth had taken place.

(George) Keith Funston became president of the NYSE in 1951, arriving there from the presidency of Trinity College. He was the candidate of Sidney Weinberg of Goldman, Sachs & Company, one of the most powerful men on Wall Street. Handsome, gregarious, intelligent, and well educated, Funston's only shortcoming was that he knew next to nothing about the securities business. No matter. At the time, the real power on Wall Street rested with the investment bankers, men like Weinberg, while Merrill, aged and ill by 1951, served as spokesman for the commission houses, not the industry. The NYSE was only the symbol of American finance, and Funston was well-qualified to become the symbol of the symbol.

There were important similarities between Merrill and Funston. Just as Merrill geared his advertisements and campaigns to middle Americans—he often spoke of "the thirty-three-year-old veteran with a wife and children, a small home and mortgage, and a $5000 a year job"—so Funston glorified what he called "People's Capitalism" and became its most ardent booster. To him, the term signified a free enterprise capitalism in which a large portion of the population owned securities. Through the acquisition of stocks, Americans could become capitalists and share in the growth of the nation. Funston contrasted this with the situation in the early twentieth century, when securities ownership was far more concentrated.

Funston struck a nerve. The early 1950s was a period in which patriotic zeal and fervent anticommunism were raised to new heights. The ultimate goal of the NYSE, said Funston, was public ownership of the means of production, not by the government but through an army of shareholders, "a nation in whose material wealth every citizen has a vested interest through equity ownership." Speaking in New York in mid-1952, Funston asserted, "The way to fight communism is through American prosperity." "We are the epitome of free enterprise," he told a *New Yorker* reporter. "Once that's lost, we're gone." He stated that, "We're trying to broaden the base of stock ownership and thus strengthen the basis of democracy." Or as a NYSE vice president put it, "A regular dividend check is the best answer to communism."

To help this along, the NYSE instituted the Monthly Investment Plan, in which an investor was able to place a small amount of money into accounts in stocks he selected. So, a person might choose to invest $40 a month in IBM and purchase a fractional share of that high-priced stock. It wasn't much, but that investor might feel he had become an owner while at the same time "doing his bit" for the cause of American capitalism. Funston liked this idea, which he viewed as an alternative to the mutual funds that were becoming more popular in this period. Not to be outdone, the American Stock Exchange also sponsored investment clubs, in which like-minded individuals met regularly to discuss stocks, pool their funds, and purchase a portfolio of shares.

Funston's work on the hustings paid off. Under his aegis, the NYSE became an important tourist attraction. In 1951, 144,000 visitors came to the Exchange to view trading and have its workings explained to them by uniformed guides. By 1954, the number of visitors had risen to 271,000.

Mutual Funds

While the efforts of Merrill and Funston helped nudge young Americans of the post-war generation into the markets, they did not suffice for many others. It was one thing to make brokerages more accessible and appeal to patriotism and even self-interest. It was quite another to actually get Americans to take funds from a perfectly safe haven in savings accounts ($51 billion) and savings bonds purchased during the war ($115 billion) and place them in the hands of strangers and in financial vehicles their parents had warned them against.

The introduction of the general public to securities came about gradually, and one of the more important ways was through mutual funds. These funds may have been unfamiliar to the general public, but they were not new. Indeed, sharing risk and placing assets into the hands of professional managers occurred in the Ancient World and during the Middle Ages. The joint stock companies of the Age of Exploration were motivated by forces similar to those driving mutual fund organizations in the postwar period.

In more recent times, a variant of mutual funds, the so-called "closed-end" funds, or "investment trusts," had been features of the last stage the 1920s bull market. Realizing markets were rigged, speculators of that period wanted to participate in the next best thing to a pool run by Jesse Livermore or some other manipulator, which is to say, obtain access to the thinking of a savvy speculator or investment banker. The other reason to purchase such shares was leverage. Unlike today, virtually all of the closed-end funds of the 1920s were highly leveraged; the common shares were preceded by a series of preferred issues and borrowings. The speculator could purchase these shares on as much as 90 percent margin, which is borrowed money, and the fund itself could employ margin in its purchases. So the speculator could pile margin on margin on margin. The equity backing was extremely small. The slightest rise in the market could be multiplied many times over. Ditto declines. During the market decline of 1929–1933, the investment trusts suffered severe losses. One of the most famous of these, Goldman Sachs

Trading Corporation, offered to the public just before the crash, fell from a price adjusted for a stock split of 208 to below 2 before going under completely. By the post-World War II period, closed-end trusts were notably unpopular, most of them selling at discounts to their net asset values.

The mutual funds suffered during the depression. Sales picked up in the mid-1930s, as investors who wanted to participate in the rising stock market but no longer trusted their own judgment went into funds. Some $123 million were placed there in 1936. In 1940, there were some 296,000 accounts in funds that had assets of below $500 million. As a result of aggressive sales tactics, the number of accounts rose to 939,000 by 1950, and the funds had assets of $2.5 billion. Still, the mutuals owned less than 1 percent of all listed NYSE securities, and their impact at that time was more potential than real. But they were beginning to catch on with the public. In 1952, they had $3.2 billion in their accounts, compared with the $6.7 billion worth of shares owned by insurance companies and the $20.8 billion in personal trust accounts.

The mutual funds of the postwar period differed significantly from the closed-end trusts in terms of both organization and clientele. For one thing, the earlier trusts had truly been closed-ended, meaning they were floated like the common shares of companies and traded at what the buyer and seller were prepared to pay. The mutual funds were purchased at net asset value plus commission and redeemed, if desired, at net asset value, an amount available from tables in the financial sections of larger newspapers or by telephone. The mutuals did not employ leverage. Those wanting to buy shares in the trusts did so through their brokers. Mutual funds were sold by sales personnel who received commissions, at that time usually around 8.5 percent of the purchase price. Most of them were sold on contracts. The buyer would commit to purchase, say, $10,000 worth of funds at regular intervals over a period of time. Most of the commission, which would be $850, would be paid from the first $3000 or so. In this way, the salesman received his payment quickly. If the purchaser did not fulfill the commitment, he would have paid a huge commission for shares he did purchase. A small number of funds, called "no loads," sold without commissions. The no loads were not particularly popular because their purchasers had to know about the principals involved and the names and addresses of the no-load companies. In this period, then, it often was said that the funds were not purchased, but rather were sold.

Fund salesmen, most of whom were part-timers and made cold calls, were not as well-trained as the customers' men found at the brokerages. Deception and outright lies were not uncommon when they made their pitches. Many fund companies would give newcomers an indoctrination that lasted no more than a day, making them aware of the few restraints imposed on them by government rules and regulations. Sales force turnover was quite high, but this did not bother the companies, since many salespeople tried to place shares with friends and relatives. When they ran out of them, they would usually quit voluntarily, and be replaced by others with the same set of potential customers. That's how in 1950, Hamilton Management could have 76 salesmen, when the fund had assets of $7 million, and by 1955, 624 salesmen and assets of $31 million.

Even so, the industry remained small by later standards. Not until 1956 would as much as $1 billion in net new money come into the funds, and the $2 billion mark would not be surpassed until 1965. By then, there were 6.7 million accounts, with assets of $35.2 billion in the fewer than 200 mutual funds, and they still owned less than 5 percent of NYSE listed shares.

In 1970, the Investment Company Institute, which represented the mutual fund industry, conducted a survey to determine just who was investing in these vehicles. It learned that the higher the family income, the greater the awareness and participation. Among those whose family income was below $8000, only 17 percent even were aware of the funds and 3 percent owned them, whereas 70 percent of the individuals whose family income exceeded $25,000 knew about the funds and 30 percent owned one or more of them. The same kinds of statistics held in the matter of education: the more years of schooling, the greater the awareness and participation. The most interesting statistic, however, pertained to age. Close to 40 percent of those under the age of 30 knew about mutual funds and 6 percent owned them. For the cohort over the age of 65, 14 percent had an awareness of the funds and 4 percent owned them. It would appear that mutual funds appealed to younger people, and that perhaps this was one of the paths that led them back into investment in securities.

Pension Funds

The idea for a pension plan at General Motors originated with Peter Drucker, who, at the behest of top management, earlier had written *The Concept of the Corporation*, a study of the company. Charles Wilson, GM president, was intrigued and asked Drucker what he thought of profit-sharing programs. When told it wouldn't have much of an impact, Wilson wanted to know whether pensions would be more meaningful. Drucker asked how the funds would be invested. In government bonds? No, replied Wilson, in the stock market, to which Drucker answered, "But that would make the employees, within 25 years, the owners of American business." Wilson's response, which sounded strikingly similar to the ideas being promulgated by Merrill, was that this was "exactly what they should be, and what they must be. For the income distribution in this country surely means that no one else can own American industry unless it be the government." Later on, Drucker would provide such a plan with a name, "Pension Plan Socialism."

Management-provided pension plans hardly represented a new idea. A Bureau of Labor Statistics study had indicated there were several hundred of them in place in 1919, and there were some 2000 of them in place in 1950. Almost all invested funds in corporate and government bonds, a policy considered prudent by a generation wary of anything that smacked of speculation, especially when it came to the investment of so important an entity as a pension plan. Moreover, the "prudent man rule" in many states mandated the purchase of high-quality bonds and, in some cases, preferred stock. This was easing, however, as the older trustees retired. By the late 1940s, some pension funds were nibbling at common shares.

Other factors entered into Wilson's thinking. One of his preoccupations in this period was insuring a decade or so of labor peace, which would enable GM to make and execute long-range plans in such areas as model changes and capital spending. Moreover, he wanted union acceptance of a vast modernization program he had in mind, which workers might oppose as costing them jobs. Wilson believed the alterations brought about in labor thinking by health and pension programs would contribute to the stability he required and the changes he hoped would be made in automobile man-ufacturing. He also thought the pension plan might cement worker loyalty, another matter in which he had a longtime interest.

Wilson was able to bring Walter Reuther around to his way of thinking on most issues, but the union leader balked at the fund owning shares of General Motors. If this were permitted, might not the workers' loyalties be divided? Wilson bowed on this point. The two also agreed on the vital matter of investment guidelines for the independent managers who would control the fund. And as Wilson had predicted, additional pension plans were organized, and these and others were permitted to own common stock.

In the same year of the General Motors pact, several New York life insurance com-panies petitioned for the right to invest up to 2 percent of their assets in common shares, and the state agreed they might do so. Other states followed suit. By 1955, the life insurance companies owned more than $3.6 billion in common stock, while the property and casualty companies, which always had the right to own common shares, held another $5.4 billion. Pension plans now became another source of demand for securities investment. In 1949, they owned a grand total of $500 million of common stock; in 1971, this figure stood at more than $900 billion. The total for all institutions rose from $11 billion to $219 billion in the same period.

In its 1952 census, the NYSE found that only 11 percent of all shares were owned by institutions. In 1976, various pension plans alone owned more than a third of the nation's equity capital. The result was that many Americans who in the 1950s made cer-tain they had no exposure to the stock market now really were in the market—through their pension programs.

The Great Bull Market of the 1960s

Merrill and Funston had one vision of how the American middle class might become wealthy: through the purchase and holding of common stocks. Charles Wilson seemed to think it might be accomplished through pension plans. As it happens, both were right, but the Merrill-Funston version took center stage for most of the time during the 1950s and 1960s.

The institutions and individual investors created a much greater demand for com-mon shares, which had the effect of boosting their prices. This encouraged companies and their bankers to provide new issues, and represented the bedrock for the decade of corporate creation and expansion that followed. Investment bankers now were prepared to take companies public with the lure of attractive stock prices. The statistics tell the story graphically. During no year of the Great Depression and World War II did the value of newly issued common stock come to as much as $400 million. It would rise above $1 billion in 1952, $2 billion in 1955, and $3 billion in 1961.

As the 1950s wore on, investors in new issues were prepared to pay the higher price for earnings and forgo dividends in the hope of capital gains. Just as they once sought high yields, now they became captivated by elevated P/Es. Indeed, some argued the pay-ment of dividends, once considered a sign of business strength, was really a weakness, since the payouts meant the company no longer needed funds for growth, which became the key consideration of the period. Such growth stocks as Texas Instruments, Litton Industries, and Varian Associates offered P/E ratios of more than 50 and paid no

dividends. IBM, too, had a better than 50 P/E, and offered a yield of one-half of 1 percent. By this point, interest in mutual funds had switched from balanced portfolios, usually comprised of bonds and well-known common shares, to growth funds. Never before
had common shares been so popular as they were in the 1960s. In 1970, the NYSE took
the sixth of the shareowner censuses it had conducted since 1952. In this span, the number of shareowners had increased from 6.4 million to 30.8 million. In the former year,
one in sixteen adults owned shares; by 1970, that figure was one in four. America was
well on the way to near-universal shareholding, at least for the middle class, and it
occurred during the greatest bull market since the 1920s.

In the beginning of this long-lived bull market, investors wanted to know the business
of the company, its prospects, earnings, and dividends. Many of the glamour issues of
the period had unusual names, novel products, and cunning promotion, all of which
appealed to inexperienced investors seeking excitement along with profits. This was the
kind of market milieu out of which emerged Xerox, Polaroid, Aerojet General, Itek, Litton Industries, Ampex, and Syntex.

The story of Control Data, which came to market in 1958, is quite typical. The firm
started out by selling 600,000 shares at $1 a share, all of which were taken up by friends
of the founders. At the time, it had no sales or earnings. By 1961, Control Data chalked
up $20 million in sales and earnings of $843,000, or $0.26 per share, and was selling for
more than 100 times earnings.

After a while, however, all that was needed was the name. If it sounded exotic, it must
be good. Especially desirable were stocks ending in "onics," and with certain key words.
An exasperated Jack Dreyfus of Dreyfus & Co. summed it up this way:

> Take a nice little company that's been making shoelaces for 40 years and sells at a
> respectable six times earnings ratio. Change the name from Shoelaces, Inc. to Electron-
> ics and Silicon Furth-Burners. In today's market, the words "electronics" and "silicon" are
> worth 15 times earnings. However, the real play comes from the word "furth-burners,"
> which no one understands. A word no one understands entitles you to double your entire
> score. Therefore, we have six times earnings for the shoelace business and 15 times earn-
> ings for electronics and silicon, or a total of 21 times earnings. Multiply this by two for
> furth-burners and we now have a score of 42 times earnings for the new company.

When the bull market began, interest centered on the old blue chips, after which
attention turned to younger companies that had appeared during and after the war, but
which had not attracted investors. From there, investors sought young, relatively
untested companies whose futures seemed bright. This is to suggest investors started out
by looking to the past, then to the present, and finally to the future—from AT&T and
IBM to Xerox and Polaroid to untested startups, most of which were destined to fail or
be merged out of existence. As the mania gathered steam, Wall Street produced what
should properly be called "junk stocks." Many individual investors wanting to participate in America's industrial boom, sought growth stocks with "a story."

By the early 1960s, the junk stock market had become the focus of speculative attention on the part of individual investors, and at its center was the market for new issues of
unseasoned companies "with stories." It was there one found the highest level of risk and
potential for reward.

Fortunate indeed were young firms in need of funds during this period, even the so-called "concept companies," with nothing more than ideas and small circles of personnel. "Going public" was simple at a time when the appetite for stocks was so great. In January 1961, initial public underwritings were coming to market at the rate of two per day.

At first, few of the older investment banks showed much interest in such firms. They concentrated on obtaining business from the nation's largest and most prestigious companies. Being the banker for the Pennsylvania Railroad was something to crow about; providing such services for Digital Equipment hardly qualified as the same league. So at first, underwritings for young, untested concerns were dominated by young, untested banks.

The Craze for New Issues

Michael Lomasney, Charles Plohn, Donald Marron, and Stephen Fuller led the way in the early years of the craze, and as had been the case during the first wave, the older firms came in only after the market became more familiar with the category. For example, Pocket Book, one of the more familiar companies, was underwritten by White Weld; Restaurant Associates by Shearson Hammill; and Vacuum Electronics by Lehman Brothers. Others utilized the services of second and third-tier houses. Peerless Tube was underwritten by Winslow, Cohu & Stetson and Pneumodynamics by Hemphill, Noyes. These were exceptions. For the most part, the marketeers of junk stocks were very much the new firms, and dealing with them was not unlike operating with the bucket shops of the earlier period.

One of these firms was Charles Plohn & Company. "Two a Week," Charlie Plohn crowed. "I give people the kind of merchandise they want. I sell stock cheap. I bring out risky deals most firms wouldn't touch." The 27-year-old Marron, leader at the firm of Marron, Sloss & Co., spoke openly of his ambition to create a major power in underwriting. Michael Kletz, one of the larger underwriters of small new issues, was more realistic: "All we have is me and 11 girls," he told a reporter proudly. Kletz would later talk of "the other idiot principle." "My clients buy stocks because they know some other idiot will buy it from them at a higher price." So they did, and the game would continue as long as the market did not run out of idiots. Lomasney and most of the others were small-timers who operated on shoestrings and weren't in business for the long haul. Their operations were legitimate enough, but at the same time included dubious practices.

At the height of their power, these new issue bankers had buyers scrambling for shares and scores of small businessmen interested in cashing in on their holdings through initial public offerings. They seemed to have the magic touch; virtually all of their issues rose, sometimes doubling or tripling in a single day. Such usually is the situation at the tail end of manias. The wonder of it all is that the method was so simple.

The purveyor of junk common stock would underwrite, say, 2.1 million shares of XYZ at 5. That price was for the seller. The underwriter would pay the client 4 for 2 million shares, and keep the other 100,000 shares of the stock for himself, at perhaps a penny a share. He would then call a contented potential buyer who had profited from earlier deals to inform him of the new issue. The customer might buy 1000 shares, no more, and would have to promise not to sell until given the word. A morning on the phones and the salespeople would have placed all 2 million shares and have a waiting list.

On the day of the placement, the salesperson would receive calls from the 1000 share client (and some of his acquaintances), along with the others who were not in on the deal, all trying to buy in the aftermarket. In a twinkling, the price would rise to 10—put there by the underwriter—and he would begin to dispose of his 100,000 shares. Along the way, he might start selling some of the shares for his customers as well. But once he was out of the situation, he would let the price rise or fall on its own. Sometimes it went higher, often not, but the underwriter didn't care, since by then he was involved in another deal.

Consider a typical distribution, a Lomasney underwriting of BBM Photocopy, a firm he touted as "the next Xerox." As part of his contract, Lomasney received 20,000 warrants, each to purchase a share of BBM for a penny. He then sold 100,000 shares of the stock at $3, receiving a hefty commission for his effort. Within a short time, the stock was selling for $40, which gave the warrants a value of around $800,000. Thus, Lomasney received a little less than a million dollars for this small deal, while BBM obtained less than one-third that amount. BBM management wasn't complaining, however, since it too owned bundles of what was now a $40 stock.

Moreover, they did not have much choice in the matter. Firms like BBM, which were flimsy operations unable to raise money by other means, had little choice but to pay the required fees and make other concessions. The BBMs of the 1960s needed the buyers controlled by Lomasney. He served a client, the company whose shares were being underwritten and customers who would purchase those shares. He had to maintain an aftermarket so the buyers would have a place to sell. Such has always been the investment banker's function. When the two come together in large numbers, you have the makings of a mania. This was what happened in the 1960s, producing the greatest bull market since the 1920s.

Bewildered by all of this, many small investors sought mutual funds that specialized in this esoterica. There was Shanghai-born Jerry Tsai, who ran Fidelity Capital Fund and became as well-known to that generation of investors as Fidelity Magellan's Peter Lynch would be in the 1980s. When Tsai left Fidelity in 1966 to organize Manhattan Fund, he announced an initial offering of $25 million. From the first, it was clear the issue would be oversubscribed. Tsai wound up with $247 million.

While not as acclaimed as Tsai, Fred Carr became one of the most successful of the managers of "go-go-funds." Born of immigrant parents in the lower-class neighborhood of Watts in Los Angeles, he had worked his way through high school and a few years at the City College of Los Angeles. After service in the Army during the Korean War, Carr worked in real estate sales, construction, and then pumped gas at a service station.

In 1957, Carr talked himself into a job as broker's assistant in the Los Angeles office of Bache & Co., where he learned the rudiments of securities. The market was moving, and so were the young people who arrived at the right time. Soon, Carr was director of research for Ira Haupt & Co., and when that firm collapsed a few years later, he took the same kind of job at Kleiner, Bell & Co., one of the hottest of the new issue houses. Now he was making $100,000 a year, considered very good money in this period. Still, Carr wanted to be his own boss, so he left Kleiner, Bell to take over management of the $21 million California Fund. While working there, he organized Shareholders Management Co., whose only asset was Carr and several other hot shots, later to become known as "The Dirty Dozen" and the "Twelve Angry Men." One of the several mutual funds they organized was Enterprise, which toward the end of the decade became one of the best performing funds in the nation. Carr stocked Enterprise's portfolio with junk stocks at a time when they were all the vogue. He left just prior to the collapse of that market, and of Enterprise itself.

Perhaps only a relative handful achieved great wealth in this period, but the means of acquiring riches in this fashion had been firmly fixed in the national psyche. But then the new preoccupation came to a close in an unusual fashion, to be followed by a still more anomalous period in which new methods had to be developed to obtain wealth, quite different from those that had gone before.

CHAPTER 20

Creating Wealth During the Great Inflation

 n December 2, 1969, several banks, led by Chase Manhattan, raised their discount rates from 6 percent to 6½ percent. At the time, the Dow was at 994, up nine points from the previous session, and the sentiment was that the average might go over 1000 for the first time in history. The mood was euphoric. After seesawing that autumn, the Dow had topped 900 in September, and the next two months saw an impressive explosion to the upside. The discount rate change altered the mood instantly. Prices broke to the downside, collapsing more than 30 points before recovering to close at 983. It wasn't considered a serious sell-off—only two points. But as it turned out, this was the beginning of the end for the great bull market of the 1950s and 1960s. There would be further declines and recoveries. A year later, the index stood below 800 and the mood on the Street was gloomy.

Investors were told that the discount rate move was not the major cause for the decline. Rather, at 15.7 times earnings, stock prices had been extraordinarily high in 1968. Yet they had been higher at other times during the 1960s, having reached more than 21 times earnings in 1961. The real cause was the reason behind that rate increase. As a result of having to finance the Vietnam War and Lyndon Johnson's Great Society programs simultaneously, the virus of inflation had infected the American economy, and things weren't improving. Further discount rate increases clobbered the market. In the summer of 1969, the discount rate was at 8½, before coming down to 8 percent in March of 1970.

There was a recovery in 1970–1971, followed by another sell-off in late 1971, then a rise in 1972, and the Dow closed above the 1000 level for the first time on November 14. It remained there until January 1973.

Then came the second shock. In the early summer of 1973, a barrel of Arabian light crude cost $3.00, and this was paid in depreciated American dollars, the currency used by the Organization of Petroleum Exporting Countries (OPEC). During the Arab-Israeli War in October, because of American aid to Israel, OPEC embargoed petroleum shipments to the United States and raised prices. By January 1974, a barrel of Arabian crude was selling for $11.65, and the United States was tumbling into recession, complicated by a level of inflation not seen (except for a short period after World War II) in the century. In 1962, the consumer price index had inched upward by 2.3 percent. In 1969, it was at 5.4 percent, and then declined to 3.3 percent by 1972. Largely as a result of boosts in the price of petroleum, accompanied by an explosion in the money supply, the CPI rose to 6.2 percent in 1973 and to 11.0 percent in 1974. It fell again, but because of a second petroleum crisis it hit 11.3 percent in 1979 and 13.5 percent in 1980. The inflation, of course, affected the Dow which collapsed from 1067 in January 1973 to 570 in late 1974, the worst slump of the post-World War II period. The Dow rose and fell for the rest of the decade, and in April of 1980 was at 759, about where it had been in late 1963. But during this period the dollar had lost half its purchasing power, and so did the purchasing power of the Dow Industrials. The pursuit of wealth gave way to the struggle for survival. Even so, astute individuals managed to do very well for themselves financially in this period.

The Beginning of Inflation

As every student who has taken a basic course in economics learns, inflation usually is believed to be a general rise in the cost of living, but it can be more accurately described as a decline in the value of money. Since money is worth less, there is a flight to goods and services, especially those for which the supply cannot easily be increased, such as gold, collectibles, real estate, and the like. Then, too, there are basically two kinds of inflation, demand-pull and cost-push. The former appeared in the United States after World War II, when the supply of scarce goods such as automobiles, housing, and previously rationed goods was inadequate to meet the demands of customers, who either bid prices upward, did without, or sought acceptable substitutes, all of which gave providers reason to produce more. When the market demand was met, prices started to decline. Demand-pull inflation is not that difficult to dampen. Cost-push is another matter. This occurs when the costs of inputs that go into making products and services rise. It is seen when wages, the costs of raw materials, financing, meeting government regulations, and the like go up, obliging the provider either to cheapen the product or raise prices. Higher prices prompt workers to demand higher salaries, lenders to ask for higher interest rates, and others to do the same, while consumers respond by seeking substitutes or cutting back on purchases.

Petroleum is one of the essential building blocks of modern civilization. Therefore, sharp price increases and declines send ripples through the economy, causing dislocations and making some people wealthy and impoverishing others. In the face of a sharp rise in consumer and producer prices following OPEC's boost in the price of petroleum, the government might have done nothing. In such a case, consumer income, remaining stable, would not have sufficed to purchase the same quantity of goods that was possible prior to the price increase. Customers purchasing less—decline in demand—would result in a subsequent decline in production, which would mean worker layoffs, and this in turn would lead to further declines. Prices would remain stable, but at the cost of a recession. Another response might be to increase the money supply, providing consumers sufficient funds to make their purchases. There would be no recession, but instead inflation. This was the way the situation ordinarily played itself out. It was different in the 1970s, though. This time, the United States underwent what came to be labeled "stagflation," the combination of inflation and stagnation of a sort that caused higher unemployment.

Consider the case of Switzerland, which was not a petroleum producer. That country experienced a 4 percent increase in prices from 1973 to 1981 by keeping its annual rate of increase in the money supply to 3.4 percent. Switzerland's economy stagnated and unemployment increased, but it was largely among foreign "guest workers," who were sent home. The United States, one of the largest petroleum producers in the world, experienced an annual average increase in prices of 8 percent, caused largely by average annual increases in the money supply of 6½ percent. Unable to raise prices as rapidly as they were obliged to pay higher raw materials costs, manufacturers slashed their work forces. The unemployment rate for 1973 came to 4.9 percent. By 1975, it was up to 8.5 percent, and there were months in 1982 in which the rate went over the 10 percent level.

In general, debtors benefit from inflation, since their higher incomes enable them to repay debts in depreciated dollars. Creditors suffer, since they are on the opposite side of the deal. In other words, a family that purchased a home in 1971 for $50,000 with a $40,000, 6 percent mortgage might have found itself with a home worth $150,000 and, best of all, a 6 percent mortgage at a time when new mortgages were at 16 percent. In such a situation, the lending organization would have dearly loved for the homeowner to repay that mortgage.

This was the kind of economic atmosphere in which those seeking wealth in the seventies and early eighties had to operate. The wonder of it all was that some managed to succeed.

Profiting from the Higher Price of Petroleum

As the price of petroleum rose, several government agencies attempted to fashion a national energy policy, but all undertakings only exacerbated the problems. Spot shortages of gasoline started to appear on the West Coast, and although the price of gasoline did not ratchet upward by much after President Nixon's wage and price freeze ended in the spring of 1974, worried drivers lined up at gasoline stations to top off their tanks. Americans started to abandon their large, gas-guzzling cars in favor of subcompacts, but not the U.S.-made Chevrolet Vega, Ford Pinto, or AMC Gremlin. Rather, they sought the high-mileage cars like the VW Super Beetle, the Datsun 510, and the Toyota Corolla. A favorite of the period was the Honda Civic, featuring the CVCC engine that did not require antipollution devices mandated by the Environmental Protection Agency. When the price of fuel leveled off, however, Americans returned to their large cars and the smaller vehicles became more difficult to market. After the manufacturers had switched their offerings, they had to face the second petroleum crisis, and drivers had to endure those long lines at the gas pump. Out went the larger models, and in came the smaller ones again.

In this period, American manufacturers experimented with electric and steam-driven cars, and even one powered by solar batteries. Several entrepreneurs emerged with imaginative solutions. Those anti-pollution devices were capable of being removed by a skilled mechanic not overly concerned with legal niceties. The new cars required unleaded gasoline, and the nozzles on gas pumps were altered so the leaded gas could not be placed in their tanks. A simple device that sold for no more than $10 could rectify this situation. Several enterprising mechanics in various parts of the country purchased used VW Beetles, refurbished them, and retrofitted them with much larger gas tanks so that the car could hold more than 25 gallons, enough for 500 miles or more between fillups. During one of the shortage periods, one fuel company imported Belgian-refined gasoline, which was not affected by the price ceiling, and sold it for premium prices to grateful customers. Some wealthy Americans purchased their own gasoline stations to assure themselves and their friends a steady supply.

As the higher price of petroleum was passed on to manufacturers, several unlikely ventures appeared. Franklin stoves, hardly used in the postwar period, suddenly became very popular. Many suburban homeowners had them installed and burned wood to keep warm in winter. Sales of insulation soared, as did sales of storm windows. And since natural gas prices did not rise as much as fuel oil, legions of homeowners switched over.

The Golden Opportunity

On April 19, 1933, President Franklin D. Roosevelt took the United States off the gold standard. All Americans who held gold coins (except for those with numismatic value) had a month to turn them in for paper dollars. This done, the price of gold was raised from $20.67 to $35.00. It was widely held that this was an attempt to boost the money supply and thereby stimulate the economy. Those who viewed unemployment and depression as the country's major problems cheered, whereas those who feared the kind of hyperinflation that smashed the German economy in the early 1920s were troubled. Prices did rise 3 percent in 1933–1934, but the overall price increases for the rest of the decade came to less than 1 percent per year.

The stock market already had begun to recover by then, but there was one sector that had its own private bull market during the decline: gold and silver mining stocks. With devaluation, these took off like a shot. Newmont Mining rose 700 percent in this period, and toward the end of the decade had become the highest priced security traded on the NYSE.

Toward the close of World War II, the Allied powers met at Bretton Woods to hammer out the postwar financial system. There, it was agreed that the United States would remain prepared to buy and sell gold to foreign banks at the price of $35 an ounce. In the years that followed, American dollars flooded the world, to the extent that by the late 1960s foreign banks, led by the French, were demanding gold for their dollar holdings. Because of this, President Richard Nixon took the United States off the gold bullion standard in August 1971.

Gold always had been traded, and with this, the activity intensified. Hong Kong and Macao became two of the centers for this trade. Americans still could not own gold, but quite a few did, illegally, keeping their hoards in overseas accounts. In 1972, the price fluctuated between $44 and $70 and the following year saw a rise to $127 on rumors that Americans soon would be permitted to own gold. The news came in late 1974. Starting right after New Year's Day, 1975, Americans would be permitted to own gold for the first time since 1933. Almost immediately, plans to buy and sell gold futures contracts were announced at the Chicago Board of Trade and the New York Mercantile Exchange (American gold traders had been dealing in 400 ounce contracts on the Winnipeg market for several years). Mocatta Metals joined with Drexel Burnham Lambert to form Mocatta Metals Corporation, whose intent was to market gold to interested Americans.

Merrill Lynch formed an alliance with Samuel Montague, a member of the London gold market, to be known as Merrill Montague, which intended to sell the physical metal to Americans. Bache & Company also entered the field, and others followed. The Pacific Coast Coin Exchange, started in 1972, saw business quadruple the following year, and transacted $273 million in business in 1974.

As it happened, this was not a particularly propitious time for making money from buying and holding gold. The first petroleum shock had been absorbed, and for a while inflation abated somewhat. In addition, rumors were floated that the government intended to sell gold from its holdings, and indeed, a few days after legalization, the Treasury announced plans to sell 2 million ounces of gold. The price of gold came close to $200 in 1974, but at times that year it sold for as low as $115. Gold's decline continued into 1975 and 1976, falling to $103 in the latter year, when 25 million ounces were sold by governments and banks.

The rate of inflation for 1976 came to 5.7 percent, and the following year it rose to 6½ percent. As inflationary pressures increased, so did the demand for gold. At the same time, the Union of South Africa mounted a large-scale advertising campaign for its krugerrand gold coins, and other countries indicated their intent to offer gold coins. Gold reached $244 in 1977 and then headed sharply upward.

The price of gold advanced because of inflationary expectations—the belief that the value of the dollar was doomed to continue to decline. In May 1978, the Treasury, attempting both to assure Americans that this was not to be and to ease the balance of trade deficit, started selling gold at regularly scheduled auctions. Some 14 million ounces were sold in this fashion in 1978, but this did nothing to assuage fears. The 1978 high for the metal was $524. The auctions were suspended in November 1979. During the second oil shock, set off by the Iranian Revolution that year, the high reached $850 on January 21, 1980, and gold futures prices went to $960, marks never again seen. By then, interest in gold mining shares and just about everything connected with that metal had replaced concern over stocks as a main topic of conversation on commuter trains throughout America. Not since the Civil War had so much money been made in speculation in gold.

The new importance of gold spun off several ancillary movements, the most unusual one going by the name of "survivalism," based on the notion that we were close to the end of civilization as we knew it and the prudent response was to prepare for an economic and political Armageddon. This was not new. Roger Babson, an economic seer famous for having predicted the stock market crash of 1929, had been a survivalist during the 1930s, convinced there would be a new civil war in America pitting believers in democracy and capitalism against fascists. He recommended the purchase of land in remote areas, guns, supplies of foodstuffs, and other products needed to weather the coming storm. Far more important than stocks and bonds, said Babson, was a supply of gas masks and the knowledge of how to use them. Now, a new crop of survivalists appeared, with similar suggestions. At a time when gold conferences were quite fashionable—individuals would pay several hundred or even thousands of dollars to go to some vacation spot and hear the opinions of the experts—in between the seminars and lectures, attendees might stroll past booths manned by individuals selling a year's supply of dehydrated food, weapons, land deeds in sealed envelopes (so no one else would know the location), as well as gold and silver coins and ingots for use when paper money became worthless. Harry Browne, author of the best-selling *How You Can Profit from the Coming Devaluation*, was a favorite at such conferences and had this advice:

> The investment program can be divided into two main categories. First of all, keep enough purchasing power with you to see you through a few years of no currency and civil disorder—in case that happens. This means silver coins and possibly gold coins. You should make arrangements to store them yourself.
>
> Most families could probably survive for several years on three bags of silver coins, if necessary. If you don't have a safe way of storing more than that, all additional wealth to be kept here should be in the form of gold coins. How much you should have depends upon many individual variables.
>
> Secondly, the rest of your wealth should be stored in a Swiss bank in gold coins (bullion, if you're unaffected by legal restrictions), silver bullion and the recommended currencies.

The purchasers left with a greater sense of security than when they arrived, while all those involved with organizing the conferences and selling those wares profited.

Collectibles

During periods of inflation, when the money supply increases at a rapid pace, investors seek assets whose supply is certain to remain constant—hence, the mania for such collectibles as stamps, coins, artwork, and the like. Of course, there always had been collectors, but now the game was being played not by art lovers, but investors unhappy with the performance of securities and looking for alternative avenues for profit. Christie's, Sotheby's, and other auction houses became the new arenas for speculation. Writing of the auctions, Jim Powell, one of the leading journalists in the field, said:

> In September, the auction season starts with warm-up sales of comparatively inexpensive property. Major American sales take place October through May. You can look for important print sales in November on the East Coast. Americana sales in late January and Impressionist-painting sales in mid-May. Spring and fall are the favorite times for big on-premises sales by the auction houses. The weather is warm, but buyers haven't scattered for their summer vacations. June is cleanup time in the United States, with sales of inexpensive property at most auction houses. But in England it is the month of the major annual sales. Country auctions thrive from June through autumn in most of the United States.

Among the more popular artworks in this period were English and Spanish porcelain, Chinese snuff boxes, American pewter, antique maps, and old master and nineteenth century prints. But almost anything that was considered art found a market among investors eager to buy low and then sell high. For those with little knowledge and time, the investments of choice were autographs, first editions, stamps, and coins. They weren't printing any more commemorative stamps issued in the 1920s or Morgan dollars, both of which, buyers were assured, were "bound to rise in price." Everywhere there seemed a search for the next hot collectible. Those who purchased World War II memorabilia did well for themselves. Not so enterprising individuals were convinced that manual and electric typewriters would make the grade.

Feeding on the mania for collectibles were companies like Franklin Mint, which produced items guaranteed to be in limited editions, such as commemorative plates, coins, and figurines. The aftermarkets for such items were covered in magazines devoted to the subject.

Real Estate

The classic hedge against inflation has been real estate. Higher prices make land, limited in availability, more attractive. The replacement value of homes, factories, stores, malls, and all other structures causes their values to rise as well. For many investors, real estate was far safer and offered better chances for profit than gold, silver, and collectibles. The prices of these depended on supply and demand, and paid no interest or dividends. Houses and factories might be leased, and they had superb tax advantages. A factory could be depreciated. An investment of $1 million in such a facility could be written off in 20 years under the tax code, but in inflationary times its true worth—in terms of resale value—could be many times $1 million, and all the while it would be bringing in rent, which itself would be boosted with each new lease. To those who amassed wealth investing in commercial real estate can be added those fortunate enough to have purchased homes before the "Great Inflation," who held on, and in the process made hundreds of thousands of dollars on their investment. In 1970, the Internal Revenue Service and the Census Bureau estimated there were 575,000 millionaires in the country. The same organizations put the figure for 1990 at more than 1 million. A goodly number of these were individuals who thought themselves middle class whose homes appreciated in value.

The higher prices for homes of all kinds could not escape notice. This phenomenon and the higher mortgage rates of the period made home ownership impossible for many Americans. Still, the prices rose, and this attracted speculators. California played host to some of the greatest speculation in property. It was not unusual for a speculator to purchase an interest in two apartments in a condominium being planned, for $200,000 each, with down payments of $20,000, for a total of $40,000. Then, when the apartments were completed, he might sell one for as much as $400,000 and have the other one free and clear, along with a cash profit of $160,000. Stories like this whetted the financial appetites of thousands of speculators throughout the country.

But sharply fluctuating mortgage rates troubled lenders as well as borrowers. In the 1950s, an S&L might offer a 30-year fixed-rate mortgage (there were only fixed-rate mortgages in this period) at 6 percent, secure in the belief that rates would not diverge much from that level over the life of the mortgage. This was no longer so in the mid-1970s, so the S&Ls sought means to extract higher rates from borrowers.

There was another way to deal with this situation that would provide investors with the means to achieve higher returns with less risk. If the S&Ls could sell investors the mortgages, the debts would be off their books and onto the accounts of the new owners. The vehicle to do this arrived in December 1970 when the first "Ginnie Mae" (named for the Government National Mortgage Association) was put together. This was a bundle of insured mortgages divided into securities that were sold to investors. The payments from homeowners would be passed through to the securities owner, along with his share of any proceeds from mortgages that were paid off. The instrument resembled a bond, but it had no final maturity date. To offset this uncertainty, the Ginnie Maes paid a somewhat higher rate than government bonds.

It took some time for buyers, sellers, and assemblers to become accustomed to the new instrument, but by 1975 some $7.4 billion worth of mortgages were being packaged and sold this way, and the next year's total was $13.5 billion, of which more than half went to large institutions, especially pension funds. In 1976, more than $15 billion in mortgage-backed securities were sold, compared with $30.6 billion in corporate bonds and $33.9 billion in municipal paper. The presence of the Ginnie Mae alternative presented the S&Ls with a means to avoid the risks inherent in offering fixed-rate mortgages, and so eased that market. The creation of variable-rate mortgages and other hybrids also helped, allowing the real estate boom to continue, and in the process enabled speculators who understood the nature and opportunities offered by inflation to prosper.

The Money Market Alternative

Another problem that plagued the S&Ls in this period was something the general public learned about when the industry came under siege: disintermediation. In September 1969, interest rates on short-term Treasury bills stood at a record 8 percent. Savings accounts were paying 4½ percent and the rate could not be raised higher due to Regulation Q, which had been legislated in 1933 to protect the institutions from competition. Depositors, of course, realized that they could withdraw their savings, purchase those T-bills, and increase their returns substantially. Through newspaper articles they learned that this was precisely what the banks and S&Ls were doing. At first few went to the trouble, but as the word got around, more and more people took this route. Thus, they eliminated the intermediary between them and the Treasury, hence *disintermediation.*

The savings institutions tried to get around this by offering bonuses to depositors in the form of irons, radios, TVs, and other incentives to open accounts. In 1972, however, Bruce Bent and Henry Brown received permission to open the Reserve Fund and James Benham created the Capital Preservation Fund, which offered a better alternative. These funds would purchase short-term Treasuries and sell what seemed to be mutual fund shares to the public. These shares were to sell for $1.00 and not vary. But each day, some of the T-bills in the portfolio would mature, and the money received would be used to purchase others. Thus, the interest rate edged higher or lower each day, depending upon the T-bill rates.

The initial organizers of such funds thought they would appeal to institutions seeking places to park their short-term funds, but in time the word got out to small savers, and as interest rates went higher, they too were attracted to the "money market funds." To top things off, the funds later began offering check-writing privileges to share owners, although at stated minimums per check. By 1981, when yield averaged around 16 percent and even went as high as 20 percent, these funds possessed assets of more than $215 billion and accounted for half the total assets of all mutual funds.

The money market funds revolutionized the way Americans saved. At one time, middle class savers had two accounts at their banks: savings and checking. The former paid interest; the latter did not. Now an increasing number withdrew all of their money from banks and placed it in money market mutuals, which while not insured were invested in perfectly safe paper. Even when the money market funds went into less secure instruments, they appeared risk free. On several occasions, when some of the investments went sour, the management companies made up the difference in order to keep the asset value of the shares at $1.00. Banks retaliated by lobbying successfully for the elimination of Regulation Q and for permission to offer certificates of deposit (really short-term debt instruments) at competitive rates, and they were fully insured. Now the saver had the option of purchasing a three-month to five-year note from the bank at a fixed rate or going to the money market funds where rates varied day to day. Did the saver believe rates were headed higher? Then the money market fund was the preferred vehicle. Were they going lower? In such case, a five-year note might be appropriate. American savers, who a few years earlier hadn't given much thought to such matters and had little interest in the securities markets, were now faced with such choices. For a nation interested in accumulating wealth, this was no small matter. There was a time when the financial pages of newspapers attracted only a small readership. Not any more. Now they expanded, and new magazines appeared to satisfy such interests.

Playing the Horses in a New Way

There were some areas in which increases in demand led to increases in supply. Of course, this couldn't be so in rare coins and real estate, but it was possible in thoroughbreds, which experienced a bonanza due to the search for investments that also offered an element of pleasure and took advantage of the tax laws. Typically, thoroughbred owners had derived most of their earnings and enjoyment from racing itself. Always a blue blood sport, the ownership of horses was not for those in need of money. In the 1970s and 1980s, a curious change came over the thoroughbred sport and business. Earlier horsemen and women bred horses in order to race them. Now races were held to determine which stallions and mares had the best breeding potential. And this contributed to the willingness to ignore the fan-base.

In 1973, there were 149 thoroughbred breeding farms in New York alone. By 1990, there were 535. Only 214 foals were born there in 1973. By 1990, the figure was close to 2000. At the height of the mania, New York Racing Association President Gerard McKeon said breeding was the reason the state valued racing. "Racing in New York used to be a great source of revenue, but now we're insignificant, only about $180 million in a budget of $29 billion. So the way for government to look at racing now isn't so much as a source of tax revenue, but as the source of 600 breeding farms in the state and 40,000 jobs."

Due to a boom in breeding fees, the large stables prospered. At a time when the tracks were suffering and the country was experiencing a negative balance of trade, horse sales brought fresh funds from abroad and enriched breeders.

This occurred in tandem with the appearance of new players in the sport and business. The greatest generators of wealth in the world during this decade were the Japanese and the Arabs. Electronics and petroleum bred a generation of multimillionaires anxious to work—and play—among the aristocrats, and in sports this meant thoroughbreds. The way to enter the field was to build stables, which entailed purchasing fine horses capable of proving themselves at the tracks. Just as professional baseball requires the minor leagues to provide players for the majors, so thoroughbred racing demanded the breeding of stallions and mares. The supply of outstanding horses could not keep up with the demand, and prices soared.

So the locus of the sport shifted in the 1970s. Track revenues were eclipsed by stud fees and yearling sales. In 1972, Secretariat, who would win the Triple Crown the following year, was syndicated as a two-year-old for $6.08 million. The shares went for $190,000 apiece. Ten yearlings sired by Secretariat, offered at the Keeneland auctions, brought $2.61 million, and three more were sold at Saratoga for $1 million. There was a single million-dollar sale in 1978, and by 1983, 28 of them. Within two more years, a yearling was sold for $13.1 million.

According to track journalist Steven Crist, in the seventies and early eighties horses that won the Kentucky Derby were almost automatically worth $4 million. Derby winners put to stud had been sold or syndicated for at least 10 times the amount of the Derby purse. Seattle Slew, the 1977 Triple Crown winner, earned $214,700 in the Derby, and was syndicated for $12 million in 1978. Affirmed earned $901,000 in his 1978 Triple Crown year. But that paled in comparison to breeding and yearling payments. The owners created a syndicate for Affirmed, dividing it into 36 shares at $400,000 each. Thus, the owner valued Affirmed's breeding potential at $14.4 million.

Production increased throughout the 1970s and continued into the early 1980s. By then, the progeny of highly successful and visible horses whose earlier yearlings did well still fetched high prices. This made such stallions as Seattle Slew, Northern Dancer, and Nijinsky all the more valuable, along with their colts. In 1980, the July sales at Keeneland fetched around $60 million. In 1984, the figure rose to almost $180 million.

How could this continue in the face of declining track attendance? In order to combat this falloff in interest, the industry opted to offer richer races. It was felt there was an insufficient number of big ones like the Triple Crown. Then too, without victories, thoroughbreds could not prove their mettle and justify those high prices. Under their distressed circumstances, however, the tracks could not afford to stage many more truly big stakes races. It was a paradoxical situation. A thriving business (breeding) stood in danger of being strangled due to dwindling public interest in racing.

Faced with this situation, several of the large breeders decided to organize their own races, which they called the Breeders' Cup. The idea was first broached to John Galbreath by John Gaines in 1982. Two of the sport's leading and most respected figures, they united in proposing a series of races to be sponsored by breeders rather than track promoters. Out of this came a plan to stage seven races on the same day in autumn with purses of $13 million. To be inaugurated in 1984, the action would rotate annually among the leading tracks. Funding would come from each owner paying an amount equal to his stallions' stud fees, which would qualify his progeny to compete in the races, plus a small one-time fee for each newborn foal. Gaines was to be president of Breeders' Cup Ltd., reporting to a 23-member board, which was to be comprised of the nation's leading breeders. Gaines announced the program in April 1982 at the Kentucky Derby Festival Luncheon. He told guests the seven races would include all age, gender, and distance divisions, and would be televised worldwide.

As with all such major events, corporate sponsors were lined up. Included in the initial group were familiar advertisers such as Anheuser-Busch and Joseph Seagram. There also were such status names as DeBeer's Consolidated Mines.

This recognition of breeding as a source of wealth came as the market started to become glutted with horses. One of the basic axioms of economics is that an increase in demand results in higher prices, which in turn brings additional product to market, and that prompts a decline in prices. This is precisely what happened with thoroughbreds in the second half of the 1980s. The supply of yearlings increased, the demand for them did not, and so prices fell.

Other factors beside increased production adversely affected the business. One was a change in the tax laws regarding thoroughbreds. Until tax reform, the IRS had viewed the horse's cost, operating expenses, and profits received from sales as business expenses and profits and losses. Under the provisions of accelerated cost recovery, the owner could depreciate the purchase price and subtract it from his taxes during a three- to five-year period. After this initial interval, the owner could subtract expenses as they occurred, and a shrewd accountant could save the owner large sums by arranging these in the most beneficial fashion. Moreover, profits from sales were counted as long-term capital gains. Thus, the sport of kings also represented a tax haven for the affluent. Under the terms of the Tax Reform Act of 1986, the government closed many loopholes that favored the wealthy. In the case of thoroughbreds, it took away most of the tax advantages of horse ownership. With the end of these benefits came sharp declines in the prices of horses.

To this was added the slump in petroleum and the collapse of the Tokyo Stock Exchange, prompting multimillionaires in the Middle East and Japan to cut back. The peak for thoroughbred prices came in 1984–1985, when the best yearlings fetched $500,000. By the end of the decade, prices had fallen by more than half. At the Saratoga auctions, second only to Keeneland, 200 top yearlings fetched an average of around $250,000 each. By 1986, the price dropped to less than $187,000. The autumn sales at Keeneland brought average prices of $28,381.

The result was predictable. In 1986, 51,000 yearlings had been registered with the Jockey Club. That number fell to 28,000 in 1989, some of which could be attributed to the slack in foreign demand. In 1983, foreigners accounted for 65 percent of sales at Keeneland. Their share fell to 63 percent in 1984, and then to slightly over half that in 1985. The opportunity for wealth through speculation in horses had lasted nearly two decades, but like all booms based on assets that can be replicated, this one came to an end with a glut on the market and the demise of several major players in the field, including the fabled Calumet Farms.

The End of the Great Deflation and the Coming of the New Era

The Ford and then the Carter administration tried mightily to contain inflation through the use of fiscal policy and deregulation, but the problems continued into the summer of 1979. The old bugaboo of stagflation haunted the Carter people, along with the political frustrations that attended the Iran hostage crisis and the increase in petroleum prices from slightly below $15 a barrel to slightly less than $40. The nation's drivers were once more plagued by shortages. On the first summer weekend, half the nation's filling stations were closed.

Paul Volcker, who became Chairman of the Federal Reserve Board on August 6, was prepared to use more drastic methods. On October 4th, the Commerce Department announced that the Producer Price Index had risen by an annualized rate of 17 percent in September, the largest increase in five years. The following day, the Labor Department disclosed that unemployment had declined slightly to 5.8 percent. Taken together, these figures seemed to indicate inflation would rise that autumn.

At a press conference on Saturday, October 6, Volcker declared a full 1 percent increase in the discount rate to a record 12 percent. There would be stiff new reserve requirements on some bank accounts, which would discourage banks from making loans, and there would be new credit controls. Even more important, Volcker announced that the money supply would increase at a slow, steady rate. Interest rates would be permitted to fluctuate. Economically literate people who listened to this knew what it meant. Volcker intended for interest rates to rise sharply, to levels where they would choke off economic activity and smash inflation and inflationary expectations. In this way, the Fed became the central player in the anti-inflation war.

As anticipated, both stocks and bonds fell the next session, going from 898 to 884, and within a month the average was below 800. But then it recovered and started to rise, passing the 900 level in mid-February 1980. By December, the Dow was once again flirting with 1000. However, interest rates had risen sharply, and the bond market was savaged. From the time of the Volcker announcement to December of 1980—little more than a year—bonds had fallen from 77 to 61. Not since 1932 had that market been so critically injured.

Even so, inflation was abating. In 1979, the Consumer Price Index had risen by 13.3 percent. The figure for 1980 was 12.5 percent, and for 1981, 8.9 percent. It would decline to 3.8 percent in 1982 and remain at that level for three more years until dropping to 1.1 percent in 1986. Early in the decade, most Wall Street pundits thought the decline was temporary, and indeed, bond prices actually fell for a while. By mid-decade, however, the ranks of those who expected renewed inflation dwindled, though the widening of the budget deficit was cause for fears of higher prices. These did not materialize.

The reason, of course, was the Volcker medicine. In 1979, the average Federal Funds rate, the rate at which banks borrowed from one another, came to 11.2 percent. It would go to 13.4 percent in 1980 and 16.1 percent in 1981, peaking at a shade below 20 percent in June. The consequence was a short, brutal recession in 1980, followed by a recovery, after which there was another recession that lasted through the early years of the Reagan administration. For the first time since the 1930s, the nation experienced double-digit unemployment.

Then in August 1982, the Fed cut the discount rate, and the mood began to change; the Dow started to rise. Investors noted that corporate earnings were good, and the prices of stocks low historically, so they started to buy. Months later, analysts concluded that the bear market had ended, but they weren't certain a bull market had begun. As it turned out, it was the beginning of a bull market that would continue, with some minor interruptions and one major correction in 1987, throughout the 1990s.

CHAPTER *21*

The Democratization
of Wealth

 ISTORY does not repeat itself, of course, but there were striking similarities between the intellectual environment in America in the late 1970s and early 1980s and the immediate post-World War II period. At both times, there was confusion, demoralization, and despair, which was reflected in the securities markets. In 1979, as in 1948, few appreciated the opportunities that lay ahead, opportunities that would enable more Americans to attain far greater wealth than the preceding generation. Stock prices were even lower in 1979 than in 1948. The P/E ratio for the Dow-Jones Industrials in 1948 averaged 7.8. In 1979, it was 6.8.

The major difference was that in the post-World War II period, the fear of depression remained strong. In the late 1970s, the problem was inflation. Virtually all goods and services rose in price during the 1970s—except those of common stocks and bonds. It was catch-up time.

There was another important element caused by the inflation. Shares of a host of major companies, especially the conglomerates fashioned in the 1960s and petroleum companies, were selling for prices far below their breakup values. An understanding of this situation, combined with the new interest in mutual funds and pension plans, would contribute to making hundreds of thousands of Americans into millionaires and spark a bout of takeovers that stunned and frightened business elites, and concluded in a crescendo that seemed to mark the end of the bull market. It wasn't. Instead, technology-driven companies took center stage, and the bull market continued, or to be more precise, metamorphosed into something quite different.

Due to disparities in value, those undervalued companies became the targets of raiders. Those who opposed their actions called them predators who sought to become wealthy by trimming payrolls and throwing thousands of workers out onto the pavement. The raiders countered that incompetent management was the reason shares were selling below the breakup value of these firms and that they were unlocking values for the owners, i.e., the shareholders. Moreover, those managers had permitted the firms to become bloated and inefficient, and to compete successfully, trimming was needed. In the process, the raiders helped boost the prices of the targeted companies, and their shareholders—including those mutual and pension funds—saw their values rise as well. The old managements did not do too badly for themselves. Often they would depart with "golden handshakes" and "golden parachutes,"—generous bonuses and contracts that fetched them many millions of dollars. The investment banks that arranged such deals and acted as consultants also reaped large rewards. The 25-year-old banker with a $2 million contract and a $5 million bonus actually did exist, and Wall Street produced a large number of young millionaires before the hostile takeover frenzy ended in the late 1980s.

At the beginning of the 1990s, the Cold War ended with what amounted to a Western victory, and the Japanese challenge that had so worried American business and political leaders during the 1980s fizzled. Now globalization became the operational term, and a new wave of mergers and acquisitions that dwarfed those of the early 1990s appeared, bringing fortunes to new players.

New methods of and interest in investments and savings, combined with a roaring bull market, created a class of wealthy Americans with expectations far beyond those of any previous generation. In effect, by the end of the century, the nation had experienced a democratization of wealth exceeding that of any other civilization. Technology, which had powered the economy since the end of World War II, accelerated, and huge fortunes were made in computers, telecommunications, and related fields. Toward the end of the decade, it appeared the "American century" predicted by Henry Luce 50 years earlier was about to dawn. It wouldn't be the twentieth century, however, but the twenty-first.

The New Industries: Personal Computers

While attention in computers was riveted on the rivalries between IBM and its American and Japanese competitors, others were experimenting with "desktop" computers. A group of these people organized Micro Instrumentation Telemetry in 1968, and in early 1975 produced and sold the Altair to hobbyists. Soon afterward, Osborne and Kaypro achieved success with their "transportable" computers. Both bowed to newcomer Apple, organized by Steve Wozniak and Steve Jobs. The Apple II and later the Macintosh, not the Kaypro, were to be the popular version of computers designed to appeal to consumers, not companies. In the summer of 1981, Jobs, who quickly became a symbol for the new desktop computers, attempted to explain why he thought they had become popular.

> The whole concept of it was this: for the same capital equipment cost as a passenger train, you can now buy 1000 Volkswagens. Think of the large computers as the passenger train and the Apple personal computer as the Volkswagen. The Volkswagen isn't as fast or as comfortable as the passenger train. But the VW owners can go where they want, when they want, and with whom they want. The VW owners have personal control of the machine.
>
> In the '60s and early '70s it wasn't economically feasible to have the interaction of one person with one computer. Computers were very costly and complicated; 50 people had

to share one computer. Back then, you could have the passenger train but not the Volkswagen. But with the advent of microelectronic technology, parts got smaller and denser. Machines got faster. Power requirements went down. Finally, electronic intelligence was affordable. We finally had the chance to invent the personal computer.

By the late 1990s, desktops costing less than $3000 had as much power as the million-dollar mainframes of the early 1980s.

IBM introduced its own desktop, the PC, in 1981, and immediately became the industry leader, setting the standard for other companies that followed with their "clones." IBM's willingness to share its technology and its encouragement of others, especially independent software companies, was a major move that helped determine the future of the computer. By permitting these companies to purchase its components rather than making them seek permission to use its patents, IBM made it possible for many rivals to enter the field. This approach may have resulted in a diminution of IBM's power, but the strategy led to the establishment of hundreds of new companies and transformed the industry. Clone manufacturers proliferated: Packard Bell, Columbia, Corona, Dell, and many others. In time, Japanese, Korean, and British personal computers came to market as well.

Apple remained aloof, refusing to cooperate or license its technologies. As a result, two standards arose in the young industry, but the IBM approach ensured its victory. Others continued to attempt to win niches. Texas Instruments, Commodore, and Radio Shack made their bids and failed. Compaq, organized in 1983, did much better by producing a superior version of the IBM PC, and assumed the lead in some areas of technology. Still, by mid-decade it appeared IBM and Apple would become the GM and Ford of personal computers, while IBM continued its domination in the category of mainframes. Even in those early years it was becoming apparent that the computer field had been reinvented, and that in time, the small machines would achieve the status of a household utility.

Several significant developments scrambled the computer business, to the point that it is no longer a single industry but rather a web of related enterprises, with additional ones added regularly. For example, relationships have evolved among computers, telecommunications, electronics, entertainment, and education. Computers are being used as television sets, telephones, FAX machines, learning devices, and even disc players, as well as information retrieval systems and the entry to the Internet and the World Wide Web. All these developments spawned new companies and generated enormous wealth. The computer industry appears capable of doing for the twenty-first century what railroads did in the nineteenth century and automobiles in the early twentieth century.

Companies that once were major players, like Control Data and Honeywell, became minor forces or left the industry, their places taken by newcomers. Sperry Rand united with Burroughs to become Unisys. RCA ceased to exist. Apple rose and declined. IBM lost its dominant position. And although the Japanese challenge proved less ominous than it once seemed, the Japanese still held a strong position in the area of laptops, which transmuted into notebooks. Software dislodged mainframes and even desktops as the driving force in the industry, with Microsoft, founded in 1977 by Bill Gates, hailed as the IBM of the future. In this area American companies enjoyed a clear lead, with more sales than the rest of the world combined. As the workstation concept displaced some desktops, Sun Microsystems became a powerhouse. The arrival of the Internet shook up the industry. Netscape came from nowhere to become an important force. All of this occurred in less than a decade. Bill Gates of Microsoft, Marc Andreessen of Netscape, Java's Kim Polese, Jerry Yang of Yahoo!, and scores of others helped remake not only the telecommunications scene, but Wall Street as well.

As recently as the early 1950s, software was viewed as an adjunct to hardware in the personal computer area. Each company had its own operating system; there was no industry standard. At the time, this seemed as unimportant as the fact that once each typewriter brand took a different kind of ribbon. The same was true for applications software, such as word processing. As for utility software used to perform support tasks for the operating system, this was an unknown category. There were games created to be played on computers, but in this period the division between desktops and computers used for games was fairly distinct. IBM and Apple were for the office and home, while Atari and Nintendo were for kids and play.

The first operating system that seemed capable of becoming the PC archetype was CP/M. Microsoft purchased DOS operating software for the bargain price of $75,000 and improved it. When IBM decided to use DOS, it quickly became the PC standard. The IBM-Microsoft contract permitted Microsoft to sell DOS to other suppliers, when IBM could have insisted upon some better financial arrangement. On several occasions, IBM might have controlled Microsoft, which would have died without IBM's early patronage. Even as late as 1986, Bill Gates was willing to sell IBM a major interest in his company. In the early years, Lotus and Borland, two important software companies, would have gone nowhere without IBM's patronage. They, too, would have sold themselves to IBM at low prices. When IBM finally did purchase Lotus, the price was exorbitant.

In the area of applications software, the first word processing systems were quite simple, in part because the early machines lacked the capacity for anything more complex. As the machines became more powerful, new systems appeared. In the mid-1980s, Wordstar seemed capable of becoming an industry standard, only to be displaced by WordPerfect, created by a privately owned Utah-based company. Then Microsoft developed Word, and soon challenged WordPerfect and other systems.

Next to word processing in importance was the spreadsheet, which revolutionized business planning. The first significant spreadsheet was VisiCalc, superseded by Lotus 1-2-3. In 1984, Lotus, which had become the leader in this sector, released Symphony, an attempt to present users with an advanced integrated program, but it proved technically too difficult. Similar problems plagued Ashton-Tate, another major software house, and its dBase III. Microsoft entered the field, and Corel, which purchased WordPerfect, came out with WordPerfect Suite.

Applications programs appeared weekly. Companies rose, advanced, merged, or declined before their marks could be made in any way considered permanent. It was an industry so young and yeasty that predictions about the future were not feasible.

The New Industries: Health Care Transformed

Defined broadly, health care became one of the nation's largest industries in the 1980s. In part, this was due to the introduction of Medicare and Medicaid, followed by sharp increases in costs. Another factor was the enormous expenditures required to develop new drugs and new techniques. Moreover, payment by third parties enabled medical personnel and hospitals to pass on costs to insurance companies.

If you consider health care to include medical care of all kinds, dental services, medical insurance, nursing homes, social services, and many other related areas, approximately 15 percent of GDP was being devoted to the treatment of illnesses, and regardless of political efforts to hold down costs, the figure appeared bound to rise as the population aged.

Health care services and the drug companies emerged as two of the fastest growing industries in the nation. Demography alone dictated this. And by 2010, half the population will be over the age of 40, while the 85 and older cohort is growing at 3 percent a year. Paradoxically, the vigor and imagination of the drug industry will result in an even longer-lived population, which will intensify the demand for more health services.

However, this is an industry that constantly surprises even insiders. New drugs, more stress on preventive medicine, and better diagnostic care could result in a healthier older population in need of different kinds of services than those now offered.

In the late 1960s, such companies as Hospital Corporation of America, Beverly Enterprises, and Humana, among many others, gobbled up poorly performing hospitals or obtained contracts to manage them. By the mid-1980s, close to a third of the nation's hospitals were investor-owned proprietaries, which boasted of economies of scale and even the advent of brand consciousness. It is no coincidence that HCA was cofounded by Jack Massey, one of whose earlier endeavors had been Kentucky Fried Chicken. The need to effect economies continued as a driving force in the hospital industry into the 1990s. It also affected delivery of services, with Health Maintenance Organizations growing in popularity. Should the federal government institute a medical care program in addition to Medicare and Medicaid, it doubtless will reverberate throughout the industry and effect major changes, as well as enriching a new group of entrepreneurs.

Pharmaceuticals has enjoyed the same kind of growth and profit patterns as health care. The modern drug industry can be traced to the arrival in the 1940s of antibiotics, led by penicillin, streptomycin, neomycin, and the tetracyclines. Then followed tranquilizers, such as Librium, and amphetamines such as Dexadrine. New products arrived in a rush. Jonas Salk and Albert Sabin produced vaccines for poliomyelitis. Syntex developed the birth control pill, and with it leapfrogged dozens of other companies to become a major player in the industry. By this point, the industry leaders included such firms as Merck, Lilly, Pfizer, and Upjohn.

The creation of a new drug can result in almost startling modifications in treatment and billions of dollars in sales for the companies that control the patents. In the process, scientists become superstars. James Black, for example, joined Imperial Chemical Industries in 1958. In the early 1960s, he developed beta-blockers, which have since been perfected. Propranolol, released as Inderal, used to treat a host of cardiovascular, kidney, and psychological problems, helped win Black the Nobel Prize in 1988. It also provided huge profits for ICI. Black left ICI for what then was Smith, Kline & French, where he developed Tagamet, one of the most popular drugs for ulcer treatment, and whose sales topped a billion dollars a year.

One of the advances that perhaps holds the greatest potential came in the late 1970s with the development of biotechnology, sometimes known as genetic engineering. Based on discoveries about the nature of DNA, for which John Watson and Francis Crick won the Nobel prize in 1962, biotechnology has given new direction to the pursuit of wealth in this field, energizing established companies and prompting the organization of many new ones.

Biotech also has stirred philosophical debate, since it skirts on the edge of the creation of life itself. In this sense it has blurred the distinction between biology and medicine. For example, in 1973, scientists Herbert Boyer and Stanley Cohen successfully implanted a frog's DNA into a common colon microbe. And several companies devoted research time and dollars to artificial life forms that might be used to control oil spills.

The Supreme Court ruled in 1980 that companies had the right to control new life forms. But activists concerned about the moral aspects of the problem stood fast in opposition. When Myriad Genetics announced it had discovered a gene linked to breast cancer, the company was hailed for its breakthrough. But when Myriad tried to patent the gene, it encountered vocal opposition.

Even so, the Court's ruling prompted the formation of scores of ventures. By the mid-1980s, there were several hundred firms in the DNA business, most known only within the industry but with some $1.5 billion of invested capital.

The rising costs of research, the need to plug away at multimillion-dollar projects with no idea of when or where they will end, and the knowledge that competitors might develop a drug that would render all of that effort worthless, takes a toll. Funding has consistently been a major problem in biotechnology. As early as 1971, Ronald Cape formed Cetus Co., which was involved in genetic manipulation. Like most of the other biotech firms, Cetus raised funds for its pure research from private sources and then sold stock to the public. Then, when research proved promising, it entered into relationships with other, larger, better-funded companies. Cetus joined with W.R. Grace in 1984 to form a jointly owned company called Agracetus, the objective of which was to conduct research into producing genetically engineered rice, wheat, soybeans, and corn that would be able to resist infestation and disease.

Nor was this kind of arrangement uncommon. Cetus formed relationships with several companies. Other biotech firms obtained financing from venture capitalists such as Kleiner, Perkins, Caulfield & Byers. But promise often proved difficult to translate into financial viability. In 1985, Cetus developed a drug known as Interleukin-2, which failed to win approval from the FDA, and with this setback the company faded.

Some of the biotechs became well-known to the general public only to undergo the same fate as Cetus. Genentech emerged as an industry leader when it succeeded in synthesizing insulin and a growth hormone called Protropin. It was one of many companies involved in the development of Interferon, a promising antiviral protein that offered promise in fighting cancers. But financial constraints were chronic at Genentech. By 1986, the company had raised more than $75 million in two equity offerings and $106 million from three limited partnerships designed to fund investigations into specific products. Even so, like most biotech firms, Genentech was obliged to seek a financial backer and in 1990 sold a 60 percent interest to Switzerland-based Roche Holdings for $2.1 billion.

Biogen, too, experimented with Interferon, and in 1980 announced it had produced a genetically restructured bacteria to manufacture the drug. In order to raise funds, realize profits, and hedge its research in the face of challenges from other biotechs, Biogen entered into relationships with Schering Plough, SmithKline Beecham, and Merck.

In such a competitive and costly environment, many biotechs simply sold themselves and disappeared. Genex, Cetus, Centocor, Integrated Genetics, Genetics Systems, and Hybritech were taken over by larger companies.

Amgen, founded in 1980, is one of the more successful biotechs. It developed two high profile products: Epogen, a protein that stimulates the production of red blood cells, and Neupogen, a natural protein that sets off white cell anti-infective activity. Like others, Amgen took the partnership route, allying with both Johnson & Johnson and Hoffman La Roche.

This experience has become a hallmark of biotech, which is described as an all-or-nothing industry. Xoma, a promising Silicon Valley-based biotech, appeared to have the lead in creating methods for treating toxic shock syndrome and was well funded by Dillon Read. But its treatments came late to the market and it was beaten by other companies. One false step, and Xoma was on the ropes.

The Rebirth of Equities

Traditionally, bull markets end with an explosion and begin so slowly that the origins often are in dispute and cannot be accurately pinpointed. It was different for the bull market that ended in 1969 and the one that began in 1982. The 1969 bull market ended with a whimper, when interest rates started to rise; the 1982 bull market began when the rate fell.

On July 30, 1982 the Fed cut the discount rate from 11½ percent to 11 percent. Later, this came to be seen as a signal that the long period of tightening was coming to a close, but at the time, investors and their advisors remained wary. Stocks responded with a rally, as did bonds. Paul Greenwald, vice president of the Austin National Bank, agreed this was a good sign, but he said, "We don't believe this is the beginning of a major bull market." On August 2, on a volume of 53 million shares, not considered particularly active in those days, stocks advanced more than 13 points to close at 822, but fell the next two days until it stood at 803. It kept falling, closing on Friday, August 13, at 777, having lost 45 points in eight sessions. Then came reports that money market mutual fund assets rose more than $3.5 billion the previous week, a sign the public expected higher interest rates. There now was a record $216 billion in such funds, and although this was an indicator of bearishness, it also represented a huge amount of money that might be poured into stocks should sentiment change.

On Friday, August 13, the Fed cut the discount rate again, this time to 10½ percent. This signal could not be misunderstood. Several banks responded by lowering their prime rates to 14½ percent. That same day, a new tax package aimed to raise close to $100 billion to cut the budget deficit cleared the House-Senate conference, and this was considered bullish. In the face of all of that good news, stocks rallied and gained 12 points that day. Volume was higher the following Monday, and the index rose another 4 points. On Tuesday, August 17, the market exploded with a 40-point advance. By the end of the month, the Dow was over the 900 level, and most on the Street believed that new highs were ahead. However, many of the bulls had doubts the rally would take prices above the 1000 level permanently. Stocks did plateau in September, but action picked up in October, setting a new record in closing at 1036 on October 22. By then, all doubts had disappeared. Everything was in place—low stock prices, falling interest rates, an administration whose popularity was growing, and cash in the money market mutual funds. Individual Retirement Accounts and Keogh Plans were in place to enable small investors and the self-employed to put money into the market on a tax-deferred basis.

The bull market of the 1980s had begun, and aside from a few pauses, continued into the 1990s. More Americans than ever became investors, if not directly, then through mutual funds, of which there were more than 7000 by the late 1990s in a bewildering variety of families, constructs, and types. From 1991 to 1998 corporate profits doubled, while the Dow rose by 250 percent. Not all stocks were affected positively. IBM experienced a disastrous run, although by 1994 it reported higher profits and its stock advanced smartly. Not so for Bethlehem Steel, however, whose earnings never returned to their levels of the 1950s. Its stock price reflected this, staying at less than half of what it had been then. Even so, the mania of the 1990s swept up scores of Internet-related companies, some of which didn't even have earnings or much in the way of revenues, but they skyrocketed nonetheless.

No wealth-creating, long-term bull market can continue without the emergence of some new concepts to replace those that have outworn their welcomes. While this bull market began with a revival after a long financial drought, during which stock prices caught up with realities, it could not survive for long without new techniques and products. The 1980s saw the carving up of conglomerates and a plethora of drastically undervalued companies, especially those in petroleum, circumstances that helped spark what came to be known as the hostile takeover movement.

Metromedia Shows the Way

In 1984, Wall Street was shaken by a deal that seemed to confound traditions and the conventional sense of values, but it wound up unlocking wealth for both buyers and sellers. John Kluge, a little-known businessman, had created a diverse conglomerate, Metromedia, which owned television and radio stations, outdoor advertising, and such enterprises as the Ice Capades and the Harlem Globetrotters. He had purchased depreciation rights to $100 million worth of New York subway cars and buses, invested $300 million in the young mobile telephone industry, and then spent $400 million in a stock buyback program. All of this required heavy borrowing. Metromedia had $550 million outstanding in long-term debt. Kluge owned 26 percent of the stock, which was going nowhere. How much was the company worth? It was difficult to say, but the market indicated the value was around $30 a share. Kluge thought it was worth more than that, and so did Leon Black, a banker at Drexel Burnham Lambert, known primarily for its original issuance of low-rated bonds for mid-sized companies, familiarly known as "junk," and the ability of banker Michael Milken to place these bonds with his customers.

Black intended to offer Metromedia shareholders $30 in cash and bonds with a face value of $22.50, but with an actual value of around $10 for each share tendered. Soon afterward, threatened by shareholder lawsuits, Black added half of a warrant to purchase another bond, plus a 19 cent per share dividend, which brought the package's value to around $41 per share. The repurchase program went well, transforming Metromedia into a debt-laden concern and boosting Kluge's stake to 75½ percent of the common.

Black borrowed the money needed for the exchange from a consortium of banks. The next step was to arrange for permanent financing. This took the form of a complex offering composed of $960 million in zero coupon bonds, offered in six batches maturing from 1988 to 1993; $335 million in variable rate debentures; $225 million of 15⅝ percent debentures due in 1999; and $400 million in variable rate debentures offered at a discount.

Prudent Wall Streeters predicted Metromedia would default on interest payments. Then in May 1985, Kluge sold Metromedia's TV stations to Rupert Murdock for $2 billion plus $650 million in debt. Other sales followed, so that by early 1987 Kluge had raised close to $6 billion through asset sales, some of which was used to pay off debt. Kluge now ranked as one of the nation's wealthiest individuals, and Drexel Burnham had emerged as the greatest creator of wealth in the nation.

The Metromedia deal was a vivid demonstration of just how undervalued some of the nation's companies had become. Such had been the case at other times in American history, but little was done then about the situation to realize wealth. Now it was different. From 1984 through 1990, so called "leveraged buyouts" would account for $216 billion in financing, with the peak coming in 1989 at $54 billion. In this period, the debts of nonfinancial corporations rose close to 12 percent annually, compared to 8.3 percent for the period from 1950 through 1980. In the process great wealth was created as stocks advanced in anticipation of a leveraged buyout in which the shareholders would be offered premium prices for their shares.

Leveraged buyouts were only a part of the picture. During the 1980s, more than a third of the Fortune 500 were acquired, merged, or taken private, at a rate faster even than the leveraged buyouts. These techniques were employed in deals worth more than $1.5 trillion, for which the bankers and others involved received some $60 billion in fees. During the 1980s, the Dow quadrupled, in part due to these deals. According to one estimate, stockholder gains from such operations came to more than $650 billion. In the 1920s, speculators had wondered which stock would be taken in hand by which wheeler-dealer. In the 1960s, the question was, "Which company will be the target of which conglomerateur?" In the 1980s, shareholders were on the prowl for undervalued companies that might be raided and then carved into pieces and disposed of, as had been Metromedia.

Beatrice at the Carverie

The whittling down of Beatrice is a classic case of realizing value from a bloated company. Originally a food company focusing on dairy products, it became a conglomerate in the 1960s through the acquisition of more than 100 related businesses, such as LaChoy (Chinese foods), Tropicana (juices), Dannon (yogurt), Hotel Bar (butter) and Coca-Cola Bottlers, along with unrelated ones like Samsonite (luggage), Avis (car rentals), Stiffel (lamps), Culligan (water purification), and the biggest one, Esmark, which included parts of Swift & Co., once the nation's largest meat packer, which owned Playtex (women's undergarments), Vigaro (fertilizers), Pro-Tek (toothbrushes), Max Factor (cosmetics), Peter Pan (peanut butter), and much more. By 1985, Beatrice was another one of those companies with many different operations that easily could be detached and sold, and whose stock did not reflect its true market value.

The leverage buyout firm of Kohlberg Kravis Roberts (KKR) recognized this and mounted a hostile takeover, acquiring Beatrice for $6.2 billion in 1986. Then KKR sold Avis ($250 million), Coca-Cola Bottlers ($1 billion), Max Factor ($1.3 billion), and many more companies, which more than repaid the purchase price, leaving Beatrice a viable food company. The total profits came to $1.7 billion, with CEO Donald Kelley alone making over $400 million on his initial investment of $5 million.

The Oil Well on the NYSE Floor

The dramatic increase in the price of oil contributed to several familiar actions that take place whenever the price of any commodity rises: customers try to find substitutes, cut back on consumption, and seek new sources. During the 1970s, the consuming world learned to conserve oil, when possible switched to alternatives, and found new supplies in such places as the North Sea, the Gulf of Mexico, and Alaska. Indeed, the search for new sources was so successful that the power of OPEC was blunted and prices started downward.

As a result of the falling oil prices, the earnings of companies in the business declined. Exxon, which earned $5.7 billion in 1980, reported $4.1 billion in 1982, and similar results were posted by other companies in the industry. Seeking better opportunities outside of petroleum, some of the companies diversified, more often than not unsuccessfully. Because of the developing oil glut and various diversification failures, the prices of oil stocks declined to the point where the companies were worth more dead than alive. In the summer of 1981, Getty, which had assets of $250 a share, was selling at $72. Marathon, with $210 a share in assets, sold for $68. Cities Service had $130 a share in reserves and went for $56. In time, all would become the targets of hostile takeovers. What of the giants? Standard Oil of Indiana had a market valuation of $15.2 billion; its oil reserves alone were worth $30.3 billion at then current prices. Nor was this a short-lived phenomenon. Two years later, the engineering firm of John Herold estimated that the shares of the major petroleum firms were selling for around 40 percent of their net asset values. Why seek oil in the North Sea or elsewhere at a cost of $12 to $15 a barrel, when oil companies could be purchased for less than half that amount per barrel? Why indeed, thought potential raiders.

The takeover movement did not begin with the raiders, but with friendly tender offers. Shell purchased Belridge Oil in 1979 for $3.6 billion, and the following year DuPont acquired Conoco for $7.4 billion in cash and stocks, and there were others. This situation changed with the appearance on the takeover scene of T. Boone Pickens, who more than anyone came to symbolize the movement.

Pickens, the CEO of Mesa Petroleum, was no stranger to the takeover scene. In 1959, his Petroleum Exploration Inc. purchased Altair Oil & Gas. Five years later, he sold his first stock issue, changed the name of his firm to Mesa Petroleum, and then attempted to acquire Hugoton Production. His offer was turned down, and Hugoton opted for a merger with Reserve Oil & Gas. Pickens then went after Southland Royalty, which led to another rejection. Undeterred, he succeeded in a bid for Pubco Petroleum.

All of this was preparatory to Pickens' bid for Cities Service, which began in 1981. At the time, the stock was selling in the low 30s and Pickens thought it worth at least $90 a share. He lined up some partners, intending to bid $45 for 20 percent of the stock, but the news leaked and Cities Service retaliated by putting out a tender for Mesa. There was much parrying, but in the end Cities Service found a "white knight" in Gulf Oil, whose tender of $63 was accepted. The Pickens group sold their shares into the tender, and emerged with a profit of around $45 million before deductions for costs. In the process, the raiders learned that win or lose they could realize large profits from such dealings. As it happened, the Gulf deal did not eventuate, and when this became evident, Cities Service stock fell from the high 40s to 32. By then, however, the Pickens group had realized its profits and Pickens himself moved on to other ventures.

Pickens and his colleagues attempted to raid Supron Energy, General American Oil, and Superior Petroleum, failing every time but earning more than $60 million. They then set out for another big fish: Gulf Oil itself, then a $29 billion concern. Pickens started accumulating shares in August 1983. By early October, he had 2.7 million shares, much of this acquired with borrowed money using the stock to collateralize the loans. Needing more capital, Pickens went to see Michael Milken, who offered to raise $1.7 billion for him. Backed by Drexel Burnham and with 13.5 million Gulf shares already in hand, Pickens trumped a rival offer from Atlantic Richfield. The purchases continued. Matters came to a climax on March 5, 1984, when Gulf shares stood at 69½. Atlantic Richfield hit $72 a share. KKR talked about an $87.50 offer in the form of cash and debt. Chevron also entered the contest, and in the end won with a bid of $80 a share in cash, which came to $13 billion. During the contest, the value of Gulf shares rose by $6.5 billion.

There was more to come. According to one estimate, during the 1980s more than $100 billion went to owners of petroleum companies through mergers, takeovers, and recapitalizations. Pickens' forays at Cities Service, General American, and Gulf had accounted for $9 billion of that amount. Pickens and his associates did well for themselves, but the major legatees, as a group, were the shareholders. Participants in pension funds and owners of shares of mutual funds who read about the raids and tried to puzzle out their meanings, or even condemned them, nevertheless benefitted hugely from the takeover movement.

Other raids followed, on Phillips and Unocal, most prominently. More raiders appeared, and the movement spread to additional industries. The bull market of the 1980s did not rest upon takeovers, though. Economic growth was real, as was the end of the great inflation of the 1970s. But just as the conglomerate movement of the 1950s and 1960s helped fuel the bull market of those decades, so takeovers provided the spice for investors in the 1980s, enriching them greatly and creating the megamillionaires whose activities were analyzed on front pages as well as in the business sections. Pickens later boasted:

> My name became synonymous with the corporate takeover. There had never been any-
> thing like it in the annals of Wall Street. It made me a controversial figure in corporate
> America, and clearly changed my life. One oil company director told me not long after-
> wards, "We spend more time talking about Boone Pickens at our board meetings than
> anything else."

The hostile takeover movement came to a crashing end with revelations of insider trading and related chicanery, and a successful prosecution of Michael Milken, who along with Pickens had become a symbol of the movement. The takeovers slowed down toward the end of the decade, but the activity did not end. Rather, it metamorphosed into a different kind of mergermania. By the late 1990s, mergers were being done at a trillion dollar a year clip. While all industries were affected, the activity seemed concentrated in financial services, defense, telecommunications, the Internet, and electric utilities.

Three factors impelled the mergers: public policy, technology, and globalization. During the Reagan administration anti-trust came close to being a dead issue, and while there was some activity during the Clinton years, such regulation was not as high a priority as it had been earlier. Legislation in the field of electric utilities caused companies once committed only to providing gas and electric services to move into a wide variety of new areas, and even to overseas expansion. The end of the Cold War militated in favor of mergers among defense companies. The Internet and computer software industries saw many small, imaginative firms that lacked capital gobbled up by larger companies that had capital but needed new ideas and new blood. In telecommunications, the drive for universal service became a mantra, while in banking the desire to reach out to new customers and become a "financial supermarket" was a prime consideration.

While all of this had profound implications for the national and even international economies, it was good news for those seeking profits on Wall Street. Let there be a rumor of a takeover, friendly or otherwise, and the stocks of the companies involved would spring up or down, more likely that of the acquired rising, while the stock of the acquirer declined. By the 1990s, the merger movement became a worldwide phenomenon, and statisticians started presenting figures on takeovers in Europe, Asia, and Latin America as well as North America. For the recession years of 1990 and 1991, total mergers and acquisitions came to 11,342 and 15,984 respectively. They peaked at 23,418 in 1997, when the volume was $1.6 trillion. All of which was reflected in the Dow. In 1987, at the bottom of a major correction that October, the Dow was below 2000. In the summer of 1999, the index was above 10,000. Trillions of dollars of profits had been made, and by a wider cast of investors than ever before.

The Changing Face of Savings

Beginning in the 1970s and continuing into the 1990s, the ways the nation's middle class saved underwent great changes. Just as the appearance of money market mutual funds and before that, credit cards, transformed the everyday financial operations for tens of millions of Americans, so the appearance of new means of saving in the early 1980s altered retirement and related savings, enabling the middle class to accumulate wealth in new ways. As it happened, these changes coincided with the arrival of the new bull market, a fortunate development for those interested in accumulating wealth through the ownership of stock.

In 1962, Congress passed and President Kennedy signed into law legislation creating Simplified Employee Retirement Pensions, more familiarly known as Keogh Plans, after their sponsor, New York Congressman Eugene Keogh. When the law was first put into effect, self-employed individuals were permitted to place a tax-deferred $2500 annually into a retirement account. Over the years, the amount has been boosted, and from the first, employers taking advantage of the Keoghs had to make them available to their employees and contribute to their Keoghs as well. The Keoghs were followed in 1981 by the Individual Retirement Accounts (IRAs), which permitted salaried individuals to invest $2000 tax-free in retirement accounts. Then in 1997, the IRAs were joined by Roth IRAs, in which the employee does not take advantage of the tax deferral but can withdraw the funds for retirement tax-free. Many companies also offered 401(k) plans, in which employee contributions were matched by employers and placed in a retirement fund. By the early 1980s, in all three, the bulk of the investment was in equities, just in time to benefit from the bull market. At first, most funds were placed in S&Ls and commercial banks; in 1981 they consisted of more than 63 percent of all accounts, and mutual funds were less than 10 percent. Three years later, as the bull market progressed and participants became more knowledgeable, the percentage in savings accounts fell to 53 percent, while those in mutual funds increased to 13 percent. The complexity of the investment scene and the lack of familiarity on the part of IRA and Keogh investors with the markets, prompted a large number of them to invest in mutual funds. At the time, retirement accounts represented more than 35 percent of total mutual fund industry assets, having risen steadily through the bull market. By 1992, more than three quarters of a trillion dollars were invested in IRA and Keogh accounts alone, and mutual funds were the preferred vehicle for a large majority of participants in the plans. Investments in the funds passed the $1 trillion level in 1995, $2.8 trillion when other retirement plans were added.

During the 1980s, investing became more complex than ever, with a wide variety of new instruments created by imaginative investment bankers. The computerization of Wall Street made the gathering and use of information easier and quicker. However, all of this made it more difficult for individual investors to compete against the professional money managers who worked at their jobs full-time and had more information and technology at their disposal than most people could hope to amass and use. While the deregulation of Wall Street cut commission rates drastically, and in time it was possible to make trades over the Internet, small investors started to feel inadequate to trade or even invest with any degree of confidence. The result was the growth of mutual funds.

In 1970, there were 361 mutual funds, and early in the decade their numbers and the number of accounts declined. The funds had $55 billion in assets in 1971, and by 1974, when money market mutuals started to become popular, $34 billion, of which $1.7 billion was in money market accounts. The entire industry started to recover in the late 1970s, and the money market funds led the way. In 1981, there was $77 billion in stock and bond mutuals, and $182 billion in the money market mutuals. But this would soon change. While money market mutuals remained popular, the other funds started to recover with the coming of the bull market. By 1984, there were 820 stock and bond mutuals, with assets of $137 billion.

By then, too, families of funds, which permitted cost-free switches, had made their appearances. In the future there would be funds that invested in only one industry, overseas funds, single-country funds, single-region funds, and funds that were geared to special populations, such as parents wanting to amass money for their children's educations. Small capitalization, large capitalization, social responsibility, and real estate funds made their appearances. Funds that mimicked the Standard & Poor's 500 were very popular. For those seeking long-term tax-deferred savings there were annuity funds. There was an equally large variety of bond funds. One might purchase taxable and tax-free bonds, the latter issued by states. High yield bond funds, funds that invested only in federal government obligations, those that went overseas, and more were created. Owners of a mutual fund put out by such large organizations as Fidelity, Vanguard, T. Rowe Price, AIM, Colonial, Kemper, and Franklin could switch in and out of funds depending on which way they thought markets were heading. Or they could go out of the markets and into the money market funds taxable or tax-free, as their circumstances demanded. By 1996 there were more mutual funds than listed NYSE stocks. That year, too, as a result of the great bull market, Americans had more money in securities than the value of their residential real estate.

In this period the nation read, saw, and heard news stories about the large disparity of wealth in the country. The rich were getting richer, the poor poorer. One commentator asserted that the top 5 percent of the population owned 90 percent of the wealth. How this could be known is difficult to say, since no government agency, including the Bureau of the Census and the Internal Revenue Service, collects such data. Information on the money income of families is available from the Census Bureau. In terms of the percentage of total income earned in aggregations of 5 percent, the highest received 17.3 percent of total income in 1950, the number fell to a low of 15.3 percent in 1980, and then was up to 17.4 percent according to the 1990 census, virtually unmoved in 40 years. The lowest 5 percent received 4.5 percent of total income in 1950, which rose to a high of 5.4 percent in 1970, and declined to 4.6 percent in 1990, again, almost unchanged in the 40-year span. Adjusting for taxes, however, the 1990 percentage for the highest 5 percent came to 36.8 percent, and the lowest 5 percent to 7.3 percent. One has to take into account that over time, a newcomer to the ratings tends to move up. Holders of their first full-time jobs do not receive large incomes, but these improve as they age and become more experienced, and then decline upon retirement. According to the 1990 census, householders between the ages of 15 and 24 had a mean income of $21,484; those between the ages of 45 and 54 had $50,003, after which it declined to $24,586 for those over the age of 65. It seemed evident that there was no way other than with anecdotal evidence to document income disparities, but the figures for securities ownership, both directly and indirectly through 401(k) plans, indicate that one of the most striking features of the 1980s and 1990s has been the democratization of wealth.

Another way to judge the democratization of wealth in the United States toward the end of the second millennium would be to look at the global scene. While global mergers and acquisitions proceeded apace, poverty persisted. Toward the end of the century, the United Nations estimated that the global GDP came to $30 trillion, though, of course, such figures are quite incomplete. The UN also estimated that some 1.3 billion people lived in poverty, using an income level of one dollar a day as the cutoff point. Most of these people resided in Southeast Asia, East Asia, and Sub-Saharan Africa. While North America, Western Europe, and parts of Eastern Europe and Latin America are becoming wealthier, that is not the situation in much of the rest of the world. The share of income of the poorest 20 percent of the population, according to these admittedly flawed statistics, was 1.4 percent in 1991, down from 2.3 percent in 1960. Perhaps over time, the democratization of wealth will spread more evenly than is now the case. What is more certain is that the pursuit of wealth, evident at the dawn of human history, will continue.

The new atmosphere for investing brought about changes in the creation and diffusion of information. Not only did newspapers expand their coverage, but they devoted more and more space to mutual funds. The larger funds published magazines, and investment-oriented publications proliferated, as did television shows devoted to reporting on market happenings. Internet sites dealing with investing and mutual funds were available to all who had access to computers equipped with the technology.

For speculators interested in the Internet market but not able or willing to devote the time and effort to day trading—and with little confidence in their abilities to play the game as the rules seemed to require—mutual funds appeared to provide professional expertise. ProFund Ultra OTC and Potomac OTC had highly leveraged portfolios, attractive to risk-takers. Internet Fund, Grand Prix, and Berkshire Capital Growth & Value were well-known for their major wagers on handfuls of preferred Internet issues. By the winter of 1999, new mutuals were appearing at a startling rate, and their performances both amazed and startled industry veterans, some of them doubling in value within a month of issuance.

As the century drew to a close, the future of the Internet seemed assured, but the wealth-creating potential of the major companies in the field was questionable. During earlier manias—canals, railroads, automobiles, radio, and television—dozens of firms appeared, only to disappear when the shakeout took place. Radio set manufacturers like Fada, Atwater Kent, and Crosley are remembered today only by old timers and hobbyists, while RCA, Admiral, Motorola, and General Electric went on to become major forces. What will be the fates of Netscape and other well-known players in the field in the late 1990s?

The Internet companies, founded by the same kind of bright young people who had pioneered in so many other technology-based companies and industries in the twentieth century, were bound to have major winners and losers. As always, selecting the winners was a problem for investors seeking to make the kind of killing that came to those who recognized the value inherent in RCA, Boeing, Pan American, and others in the 1920s and IBM, Control Data, Digital Equipment, Apple, and the like in the various stages of the computer age. During previous booms, investors sought knowledgeable brokers able to obtain stock for them in initial public offerings, and of course those brokers made fortunes for themselves as well. There was a difference in the late 1990s, related to the computer. By then, interested speculators would sit at their consoles and trade stocks on a regular basis. Known as "day traders," they provided much of the volatility that this market featured, and led observers to conclude it was all a "bubble," bound to be burst. It was not at all unusual for an Internet favorite like Cisco or Amazon to rise or fall close to 100 points a session, only to reverse course the following day.

That the pursuit of wealth is more complicated today than it was a century ago is a given. Small businesses now grow more rapidly than do the giants, but despite the many stories published in the business press regarding wealthy entrepreneurs being cast forth in the high technology spheres, the quest for wealth for many more Americans is centered on securities and the values of their homes. The would-be capitalist at the turn of the new millennium would be better advised to open a franchised fast food, auto repair, leasing operation, or some similar business. This is to suggest that the pursuit of wealth continues and will not abate, but today it is within the purview of what used to be considered the "masses," and not merely the "fortunate."

Epilogue

Traditionally, books end with a conclusion. This is not fitting in a work dealing with such a wide-ranging topic as the pursuit of wealth, which has no beginning or end. This is to say, the search for wealth has not concluded. Indeed, one of this book's themes is that it has been a hallmark of civilization for as long as we can trace it, and has been present since the beginning of civilization. It has remained much the same as when it appeared originally in the ancient Middle East, but has been adapted over the centuries and millennia to meet changing conditions, circumstances, and opportunities. The Mesopotamian trader, transported to the Chicago grain pits of the late twentieth century, might be amazed by the technology, speed of operations, and other aspects of the business, but in a short period of time he would be able to adjust and function. One can almost hear him say, "This arbitrage you are so taken with. We were doing it 5000 years ago." Risk arbitrage might seem exotic, as would many of the contracts traded on commodities markets, but these too could be adjusted to with relative ease. A futures contract for petroleum would not be alien, but the technology by which it was traded certainly would be. The trader would not be surprised by the fact that the buyer was ensconced in London and the seller in Singapore, since he, too, conducted business over a wide ranging area.

All of which is to suggest that the pursuit of wealth may well be part of human nature, with the forms changing according to circumstances. So it has been in the past. So it will be in the future.

Index

About the Author

Robert Sobel, Ph.D. (1931–1999), was a noted financial historian, Senior Fellow at the Milken Institute, and the Lawrence Stessin Distinguished Professor Emeritus of Business History at Hofstra University. Dr. Sobel has authored many noteworthy books, including *Dangerous Dreamers: The Financial Innovators from Charles Merrill to Michael Milken, Coolidge: An American Enigma,* and *When Giants Stumble: Classic Business Blunders and How to Avoid Them.* He wrote a popular column on financial history for *Barron's,* and his articles and reviews appeared in numerous publications, including *The New York Times, The Wall Street Journal, The Washington Post, The Philadelphia Inquirer,* and *The Institutional Investor.*